Shining Humanity

*To dear Anne
on the same path
of peace and reconciliation*

Li Chen

Stanford 2015

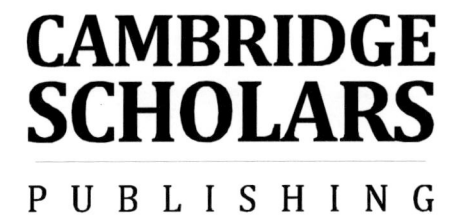

Shining Humanity:
Life Stories of Women in Bosnia and Herzegovina

By

Zilka Spahić Šiljak

CAMBRIDGE
SCHOLARS
P U B L I S H I N G

Shining Humanity: Life Stories of Women in Bosnia and Herzegovina
By Zilka Spahić Šiljak

This book first published 2014

Cambridge Scholars Publishing

12 Back Chapman Street, Newcastle upon Tyne, NE6 2XX, UK

British Library Cataloguing in Publication Data
A catalogue record for this book is available from the British Library

Copyright © 2014 by Zilka Spahić Šiljak

Cover page image designed by Sanja Vrzic

All rights for this book reserved. No part of this book may be reproduced, stored in a retrieval system, or transmitted, in any form or by any means, electronic, mechanical, photocopying, recording or otherwise, without the prior permission of the copyright owner.

ISBN (10): 1-4438-6023-9, ISBN (13): 978-1-4438-6023-9

I dedicate this book to all women peacebuilders of Bosnia and Herzegovina.

> You were born with potential.
> You were born with goodness and trust.
> You were born with ideals and dreams.
> You were born with greatness.
> You were born with wings.
> You are not meant for crawling, so don't.
> You have wings.
> Learn to use them and fly.
>
> (Rumi)

TABLE OF CONTENTS

List of Photos ix

Acknowledgements xi

Introduction xiii

Story One 3
Justice for Survivors of Violence
Sabiha Husić

Story Two 39
I Brought Neighbor to Neighbor
Danka Zelić

Story Three 71
Identity of a Woman in Black
Jadranka Miličević

Story Four 107
Designing Civil Activism
Lidija Živanović

Story Five 141
Diversity Is a Fortune I Never Intend to Give Up
Nada Golubović

Story Six 177
Peace Rests upon the Needs of Ordinary People
Stanojka Cana Tešić

Story Seven 213
Woman of Trust
Besima Borić

Story Eight 247
Civic Education: A Safe Platform for Communication and Understanding
Rahela Džidić

Story Nine 283
Peacebuilding Is My Life Calling
Amra Pandžo

Story Ten 317
The Power of Voice
Radmila Žigić

Story Eleven 349
Undivided Care in a Divided City
Jasminka Rebac

Bibliography 382

Index 392

LIST OF PHOTOS

Fig. 1-1 6
Fig. 1-2 10
Fig. 1-3 21
Fig. 1-4 30
Fig. 1-5 Courtesy of Pravo Ljudski Film Festival,
  Photo by Vanja Cerimagic 33
Fig. 2-1 44
Fig. 2-2 47
Fig. 2-3 52
Fig. 2-4 59
Fig. 2-5 61
Fig. 2-6 66
Fig. 3-1 76
Fig. 3-2 81
Fig. 3-3 83
Fig. 3-4 91
Fig. 3-5 98
Fig. 4-1 114
Fig. 4-2 118
Fig. 4-3 122
Fig. 4-4 128
Fig. 4-5 130
Fig. 5-1 152
Fig. 5-2 157
Fig. 5-3 160
Fig. 5-4 166
Fig. 5-5 170
Fig. 6-1 180
Fig. 6-2 187

List of Photos

Fig. 6-3 196
Fig. 6-4 204
Fig. 6-5 206
Fig. 7-1 219
Fig. 7-2 222
Fig. 7-3 225
Fig. 7-4 230
Fig. 7-5 242
Fig. 8-1 253
Fig. 8-2 255
Fig. 8-3 261
Fig. 8-4 271
Fig. 8-5 275
Fig. 9-1 286
Fig. 9-2 294
Fig. 9-3 298
Fig. 9-4 305
Fig. 9-5 307
Fig. 10-1 326
Fig. 10-2 331
Fig. 10-3 333
Fig. 10-4 336
Fig. 10-5 340
Fig. 11-1 356
Fig. 11-2 362
Fig. 11-3 364
Fig. 11-4 368
Fig. 11-5 372
Fig. 11-6 377

Acknowledgements

Working on this book, I was given the opportunity to hear some extraordinary stories told by Bosnian women about their paths to peace, their humanity reaching out to other human beings, about their successes and disappointments, their obstacles and the ways they overcame them, their moral dilemmas and choices. I have learnt a lot from their continuous peace adventures and I believe that these life stories will serve as a stimulus for younger generations who seek the motivation and inspiration to act with perseverance and believe that change is possible if one is brave enough to take this step.

Women peacebuilders in this book were brave, but they also had a vision of how to re-establish relationships between friends and neighbors in a divided and impoverished post-war society as well as to establish new ones for the sake of peace and reconciliation. They have enticed many people to walk on the paths of peace as their intents were to bring smiles and relief back to the faces of returnees—women and children who had experienced various forms of violence during and after the war. They wanted to enable women's and young people's political and economic empowerment and to find systematic solutions to gender equality issues through laws, policies and mechanisms in state institutions.

Thanks to the whole-hearted help of the UN Women Project Office in Sarajevo who supported the project "Women, Peacebuilding and Reconciliation in BiH," I was able to document eleven life stories and give my contribution to the history of women which, I hope, will be somewhat richer through this book.

My research was carried out in cooperation with my associates Aida Spahić, Elmaja Bavčić, Sedžida Hadžić, and Natalija Petrič, who helped me with interviews and, in part, with the preliminary analyses of a number of transcripts; I thank them with all my heart. My colleague Aida Spahić carried the heaviest burden as she worked with me until the very end of the project, translating certain parts of the transcripts into English as well as parts of the book into Bosnian. I owe special gratitude to Julianne Funk who advised me about the contents, narration and some sources and technically harmonized the references and quotes.

During my stay at Harvard University, I worked on the English version of the book; thanks to my colleagues from the Women's Studies in Religion Program: Ann Braude, Judith Casselberry, Christine Bloomer, Lory Pearson, Gemma Betros, Hauwa Ibrahim, Amanda Izzo, Lihi Ben Shitrit, Jacquelin Williamson, Sarah Bracke, and Hsiao-wen Cheng—who gave very useful proposals for improving my manuscript to make it more acceptable to the wider public.

I will also use this opportunity to thank my reviewers, Ambassador Swanee Hunt from Harvard's Kennedy School, Professor Elisabeth Porter from the University of South Australia and Cynthia Cockburn from the University of Warwick in UK. I also want to thank Imrana Kapetanović who has taken outstanding photographs for the cover of every story.

I owe a special thanks to Cambridge Scholar Publishing, UK, for agreeing to publish the English edition of the book and who complied with the majority of my requests regarding the book's technical arrangements.

As always, special thanks go to my family for having patience, understanding and love, for believing that my work was purposeful and that I should persevere, as it is important to record the testimonies of a time.

Finally, I want to thank all the women peacebuilders in this book for entrusting me with their stories and letting me interpret and present them to the world.

INTRODUCTION

People are like stained-glass windows. They sparkle and shine when the sun is out, but when the darkness sets in, their true beauty is revealed only if there is a light from within. (Elisabeth Kübler-Ross)

There is a candle in your heart, ready to be kindled. There is a void in your soul, ready to be filled; you feel it, don't you? (Rumi)

Genuine humanity resides in the heart and shows its power and beauty when darkness and fear govern life. Courageous people do not allow the light of humanity to be extinguished. They remind us on the importance and sacred nature of human life. Some women in Bosnia and Herzegovina (BiH) have preserved this light in the face of enormous destruction and the hopelessness of war. They did not vacillate, hoping that the good would prevail, therefore permitting the hidden and forgotten light in other people to shine again. These women dared to imagine a life beyond the imposed boundaries of violence and fear. They accepted the challenge to embark into the unknown; their 'moral imagination' was strong enough to encompass the complexity of circumstances and provide space for new opportunities.[1] They knew that when one comes to the edge "one of two things will happen—there will be something solid to stand on, or one will be taught how to fly."[2]

The life stories of these women disclose the power of humanity fueled by faith in kindness, love and God. Humanity (ljudskost) is a

---

[1] John Paul Lederach, 2005, *The Moral Imagination: The Art and Soul of Building Peace*, Oxford: Oxford University Press, ix.
[2] Barbara J. Winter quoted in Kathe Schaaf, Kay Lindahl, Kathleen S. Hurty, Reverend Guo Cheen, 2011, *Women, Spirituality, and Transformative Leadership: Where Grace Meets Power*, Woodstock, VT: Skylight Paths Publishing, 11.

conceptual term in much research[3] where respondents reflect the light of their humanity, but they also heal, connect, and humanize others. Women in Bosnia and Herzegovina did the same, believing that all people reflect humanity, and they made decisions at critical moments to protect their neighbors, friends, and fellow citizens. Their *weltanschauung*[4] was to make life easier, at least for the moment; in this same manner George Eliot describes the purpose of life: "What do we live for, if it is not to make life less difficult for each other?"[5] They tried to give a voice to the voiceless, to help those in need, to promote women's human rights, to foster dialogue, and above all to provide a "safe space"[6] for telling stories and healing traumas. These women inspired many to join them on their journey toward peace, even though they are neglected by the media and in the political, national, and religious discourse. Their stories should be told to remind us of what we have forgotten in our life journeys—journeys of becoming human beings.

Stories are important in our lives, and they can be compelling and powerful motivations for action. They can mobilize our emotions and hearts for the first time, but they can also move us to do heroic work. Everybody has a story, but some of us are better narrators than others. Some peacebuilders in this book were not comfortable revealing their stories without being asked specific questions: "You do not have a question, yet you want me to tell you my life story?" When I answered yes, they usually said something like: Oh dear, I do not know what to tell you (Ah, šta ću ti ja draga

---

[3] The notion of *insaniyyat* or *munashayat* is used in the research of Yasmin Saikia in Bangladesh where survivors used it to interpret the need to humanize other human beings. (Yasmin Saikia, 2011, *Women, War and the Making of Bangladesh: Remembering 1971*, Durham: Duke University Press, 24.)
[4] Philosophy or view of life.
[5] George Eliot, 1907, *Middlemarch, A Study of Provincial Life*, Edinburgh: William Blackwood and Sons, 467.
[6] Ristin Thomassen, 2006, *To Make Room for Changes, Peace Strategies from Women Organisations in Bosnia and Herzegovina* Johanneshov, Sweden: The Kvina till Kvinna Foundation, http://www.peacewomen.org/assets/file/Resources/ NGO/kvinna_tomakeroomforchanges_2006.pdf (accessed September 3, 2011).

pričati).[7] And then they would go on with accounts that took over fifty pages to set down in print.

As Marshall Gantz explains, personal stories are important because they tell us about "journeys of learning to be a full human being and faithful person."[8] These journeys require strength, dedication, curiosity, passion, strategies to find solutions when facing difficulties, and making right choices. "We can inspire others and share our own wisdom. Because stories allow us to express our values not as abstract principles, but as lived experience, they have the power to move others."[9] I hope these Bosnian women's stories will move readers to find the right direction in their own personal journeys, enabling them to make decisions that stir the light of humanity, which is often silenced or suppressed by the hardships of life.

Why this Book?

Living in the BiH post-war reality for the last two decades, I feel personally and academically motivated to tell a different story of BiH—a story of humaneness, heroism, compassion, friendship, respect, peace, and reconciliation. The prevailing public media discourse regarding BiH consists of coverage of past crimes and current prosecutions. Both of these problems need to be addressed, but people face other challenges as well, thus the residents of BiH need encouragement to re-build their lives. Media portrayals of everyday Bosnian life focusing on corruption, ethnic tensions, and ethno-nationalistic rhetoric are depressing, and they obscure all the positive developments in peacebuilding and coexistence in the

---

[7] Svenka Savić had a similar experience with her research on women's stories in Serbia and titled her book *Životne priče žena. Ah šta ću ti ja jadna pričati* 2008), Novi Sad: Futura Publikacije i Ženske Studije i Istraživanja.
[8] Marshall Gantz, 2009, "Why Stories Matter," *Sojournes: Faith in Action for Social Justice*, www.sojo.net/magazine/2009/03/why-stories-matter (accessed September 3, 2013).
[9] Ibid.

region. With the stories told here, perhaps a broader audience both within BiH and throughout the world will learn that community life as well as faith in a peaceful future and *suživot*[10] remain in this region, though they are not recognized as important news alongside other narratives. The book may be a useful tool for university teachers and students, especially in the fields of peace studies, history, anthropology, ethnography, sociology, political science, and gender and religious studies. The purpose of the book is also to: help peacebuilding initiatives in BiH and worldwide; to promote the peace and political leadership of women; teach a new generation how to nurture and preserve humanity, compassion, and respect for others, but also how to protect others; to offer women's narratives as a tool in peace education and the empowerment of women locally and internationally; to demonstrate that human beings can overcome all barriers based on identity, because such action was initiated by women from all ethnic and religious backgrounds in a divided BiH; and, finally, to remind us how a person's inner voice can empower him/her to bring change even during the hardships of war.

This book sheds light on the heroines of BiH who have been working on peace and reconciliation issues for the last eighteen years. Initially I wanted to achieve four things: 1) to understand how moral imagination mobilized women to become peacebuilders, 2) to discover through life stories the particular dynamics, values, and norms of the society of Bosnia and Herzegovina in that specific period, and 3) to show what was the role of religion in peacebuilding, 4) to make visible and available the light of the humanity within these Bosnian women peacebuilders to new generations. Among the specific reasons motivating me to launch this research were the following:

---

[10] Julianne Funk, 2013, "Women and the Spirit of Suživot in Postwar Bosnia-Herzegovina," in Nadija Furlan Štante and Marijana Hacet (eds.), *Spirituality of Balkan Women. Breaking boundaries: The Voices of Women of ex-Yugoslavia*. Koper, Slovenia: Univerzitetna Založba Annales.

First, women's stories and achievements have not been recorded, and as one Bosnian woman explains elsewhere: "discontinuous memory and ignoring women who performed heroic acts in the historical past keep women in the position of having permanently to fight the same battles."[11] I do not want women from BiH to be forgotten. I want to offer their full stories; the hopes and challenges and moral choices they made teach us that we can accomplish so much, as long as we have faith and vision. The women interviewed for this book have not had time for keeping records, because more important tasks, such as the building of relationships, restoring dignity, and providing support to others comes before visibility. When asked if they will chronicle their many successes, they usually reply that they have work to do and there will be time to tell their stories later, that one day, perhaps when they retire, they will write a book or their memoirs. Of course, written records are crucial because they are the best guarantee for preserving information and memories; as Virginia Woolf noted: "Nothing has really happened until it has been recorded."[12]

So far, very little has been written about the work of these women. I found some reports and a few studies about local women's organizations.[13] The only individual testimonies of

---

[11] Zilka Spahić-Šiljak, 2012, *Contesting Female, Feminist, and Muslim Identities: Post-socialist Contexts of Bosnia and Herzegovina and Kosovo*, Sarajevo: Center for Interdisciplinary Postgraduate Studies of the University of Sarajevo, 234.
[12] Quoted in: Nigel Nicolson, 2000, *Virginia Woolf*, New York: Penguin, 2.
[13] Cynthia Cockburn, 1998, *The Space Between Us: Negotiating Gender and National Identities in Conflict*, London: Zed Books; Cynthia Cockburn, 2013, "Against the Odds: Sustaining Feminist Momentum in Post-war Bosnia-Herzegovina", *Women's Studies International Forum* 37 (March–April), 26–35; Swanee Hunt, 2011, *Worlds Apart. Bosnian Lessons for Global Security*, Durham: Duke University Press; Elissa Helms, 2003, "Women as Agents of Ethnic Reconciliation? Women's NGOs and International Intervention in Postwar Bosnia-Herzegovina", *Women's Studies International Forum* 26.1, 15-33; Paula M. Pickering, 2007, *Peacebuilding in the Balkans: A View from the Ground Floor*, Ithaca NY: Cornell University Press; Ghislaine Glasson Deschaumes and Svetlana Slapšak, 2003, "Žene Balkana za mir. Aktivistkinje prelaze granice" *ProFemina*; Dubravka Zarkov, 2002, "Feminism and the Disintegration of Yugoslavia: On the

Bosnian women who resisted the war and its ethnic divisions can be found in the work: *This Was Not Our War* by Swanee Hunt.[14] Other individual testimonies of both women and men were collected by Svetlana Broz in her book: *Good People in an Evil Time*, but it focuses more on civic courage during the war.[15] I wanted to go further to provide life stories of women who have been working on peacebuilding without a break, not only during and immediately after the war but also today, and who have become respected peacebuilders in their communities. This book is not only about their resistance and courage, but also their peace journeys.

Many criticize the women's NGOs in BiH for being apolitical and distant from feminism. In the first years after the war, as Elissa Helms noticed in her research, women were preoccupied with humanitarian activities and reconciliation efforts and did not declare their feminist identities and political sentiments,[16] but it was also probably the case that the majority of women in BiH knew nothing about feminism. Over time, however, women in this book accepted the idea of identifying themselves as feminists. Most of them had worked long and hard to empower women in politics and public life, and "their feminist identities first emerged through education that was directly connected to activism."[17] However, since these

---

Politics of Gender and Identity", *Social Development Issues* 24.3; Nejra Nuna Čengić, 2013, "Noise, Silence, Voice. Life Stories of Two Female Peace Activists in BiH," in Renata Jambrešić Kirin and Sandra Prlenda (eds.), *Women Narrating their Lives and Actions*, Zagreb: Institute for Ethnology and Folklore and the Center for Women's Studies 70; Zilka Spahić-Šiljak, 2013, "Do It and Name It: Feminist Theology and Peacebuilding in Bosnia and Herzegovina", *Journal for Feminist Studies in Religion* 29.2, 178-186.
[14] Swanee Hunt, 2004, *This Was Not Our War: Bosnian Women Reclaiming the Peace*, Durham: Duke University Press.
[15] Svetlana Broz, 2005, *Good People in an Evil Time: Portraits of Complicity and Resistance in the Bosnian War*, translated by Ellen Bursac, New York: Other Press.
[16] Elissa Helms, 2013, *Innocence and Victimhood, Gender, Nation, and Women's Activism in Postwar Bosnia-Herzegovina*. Madison, WI: University of Wisconsin Press, 158-192.
[17] Spahić-Šiljak, 2012, 220.

individuals have been completely dependent on foreign donors who generally do not support organizations with clearly stated feminist agendas, and who also require these organizations to secure a certain percentage of their funding from the state as part of structure of the grant support, women did not wish to emphasize the feminist nature of their organizations. These women also needed continued access to others of their gender in the patriarchal BiH society, in which feminism was thought of like a contagious disease.[18]

Second, women are the ones who work on peace issues at the grassroots level, while men handle the negotiations related to such matters at higher decision-making levels. Although women tend to be the key players and peace workers in their local communities, as Elisabeth Porter[19] notes and Ambassador Swanee Hunt confirms in her research,[20] they still do not have the power to bring their perspectives to the decision-making table,[21] and they remain marginal in public life.[22] However, as Svetlana Slapšak points out, due to their marginal position in society and politics, women were always more ready to communicate, reconcile, and help and create networks of support.[23] Men are mostly involved in peace activism at the higher levels of power, where they are visible, recognized, and awarded for their work. The relation to power positions in peacebuilding is similar to their power relations in other fields. Many women stood for peace and re-building relationships, but were also determined to share power and responsibility for

---

[18] Ibid.
[19] Elisabeth J. Porter, 2007, *Peacebuilding: Women in International Perspective*, London: Routledge, 3.
[20] Hunt 2004.
[21] Swanee Hunt, 2011, *Worlds Apart: Bosnian Lessons for Global Security*, Durham, Duke University Press.
[22] Dona Pankhurst, 2009, *Gendered Peace: Women's Struggles for Post-war Justice and Reconciliation*, New York, Routledge, 26.
[23] Svetlana Slapšak, 2001, "The Use of Women and the Role of Women in the Yugoslav War," in Inger Skjelsbaek and Dan Smith (eds.), *Gender, Peace, and Conflict*, Thousand Oaks, CA: Sage, 181.

decisions that affected the lives of both women and men. All social issues are women's issues, as they say.

Third is the fact that narrating and listening to the stories of women is a political act.[24] Women's stories are important for the creation of women's history and the disclosure of the social, political, and cultural dynamic in BiH and the Balkans, both in socialist and post-socialist contexts. Their stories go beyond personal narratives and help to situate women in society. These women made important choices, and as Kathleen Barry claims, "making choices moves the individual from receiving reality to acting upon it and thus translating received reality into her life."[25] Therefore, it is important to write women's biographies in order that their work be remembered—not only their domestic work, but also the courage, creativity, and unheralded heroism that was part of their work outside the home.

Fourth, the accounts of these women's humanity can awaken younger generations who live today in BiH in ethnically homogenized communities. These young people should be exposed to peace narratives and learn that their next-door neighbor might be actively working on peace issues. The work of these women can serve as a model and inspiration for young people to do something by which new generations will remember them and that will provide meaning to their lives.

Fifth, women have the capacity to build peace and reconciliation by creating webs of relationships and networks, establishing very strong and at times unexpected links. This is exactly what women in

---

[24] Cynthia Enloe, 1990, *Bananas, Beaches and Bases: Making Feminist Sense of International Politics,* Berkeley: University of California Press; Yasmin Saikia, 2007, "Overcoming the Silent Archive in Bangladesh: Women Bearing Witnesses to Violence in the 1971 'Liberation' War," in Lawrence Skidmore (ed.), *Women and the Contested State. Religion Violence and Agency in South and Southeast Asia,* Notre Dame: University of Notre Dame Press, 68.

[25] Kathleen Barry, 1992, "Toward a Theory of Women's Biography," in Teresa Iles (ed.), *All Sides of the Subject: Women and Biography,* New York, Teachers College Press, Columbia University, 34.

BiH did for the sake of their families and communities. They were determined to leave peace as their legacy to future generations because they believe that each generation should leave a pledge for the future, with peace being the greatest wealth and pledge.

Women's peace efforts in BiH have been supported by many international donors, including UN Women (formerly UNIFEM), which in the last twelve years, using the UNSCR 1325 resolution on women, peace, and security as an additional tool in the existing human rights legal framework, has been present there to help women pursue gender equality, justice, and peace.

Selection of Peacebuilders

The research for this book included the life stories of eleven women, leaders, and peacebuilders who come from varying ethnic backgrounds, both religious and non-religious. The group is made up of women who declare Bosniac, Croatian, Serbian and Jewish identity. Most of them declare their religious identities, while some say they are agnostics. They have been active over the last two decades in peace and reconciliation efforts in BiH. It was not easy to single out those women who were finally selected from among the dozens of activists who have been working on the peace and reconciliation process in BiH, but I managed by setting a number of very important criteria with my research assistants.[26]

First, recognition by the community—The "Baseline Study of Women and Peacebuilding in BiH,"[27] conducted in fifteen cities of BiH,[28] consisted of field and web surveys that helped identify women in local communities who were acknowledged as prominent in the peacebuilding effort. Such acknowledgment, however, was

---

[26] Research assistants: Aida Spahić, Elmaja Bavčić, Sedžida Hadžić and Natalija Petrič.
[27] Spahić-Šiljak, Aida Spahić and Elmaja Bavčić, 2012, "Baseline Study on Women and Peacebuilding in BiH," Sarajevo: TPO Foundation Sarajevo, www.tpo.ba.
[28] Ibid.

not the only criterion for selection, but it was useful in locating possible candidates for interviews. Second, I also looked into the scope of the work for which local communities recognized these women, including a broad spectrum of activities such as conflict resolution, education, humanitarian aid, protection from violence, psycho-social work and therapy, peace research, and human rights activism in the widest sense. Only one woman in this book is not mentioned by name in the Baseline Study, but I have included her because of her extraordinary accomplishments in the city of Mostar (Story 11) that were recognized also by many civil society activists. Third, the ethnic and secular, or non-religious, activities of the women were also considered. My thesis is that women of all backgrounds were involved in peace work, and that it was their essential humanity that was the key to their overcoming considerations of identity and division. The fourth criterion was geographical distribution. Although some women from Sarajevo received more coverage in the Baseline Study than did selected women from other cities, my assistants and I did not want to interview only women from the capital of BiH. Our goal was to include women from other, smaller communities who had to cope with more challenges in their peacebuilding work than women in urban centers. The fifth criterion was about leadership traits. All women in this book possess some of the personality characteristics necessary for community leadership that will be discussed later. It was important to choose those who acted as leaders in their communities.

The selected women live in six cities/towns/villages of BiH: Sarajevo (Rahela Džidić, Jadranka Miličević, Besima Borić, Amra Pandžo); Banja Luka (Nada Golubović and Lidija Živanović); Zenica (Sabiha Husić); Bosansko Grahovo (Danka Zelić); Bijeljina (Radmila Žigić); Bratunac (Stanojka Tešić); and Mostar (Jasna Rebac). Most are active in women's organizations and carry a high profile as women's human rights activists.

Religion as an Argument in Peacebuilding

Although the Balkans region faced the de-secularization[29] of public life in the late eighties, women's peace activism in the post-socialist and post-war BiH context was not initially motivated by religion, and religion was not a conversation starter in the first civic initiatives.[30] Peace actions of these women in BiH were driven by "care ethics and feminist ethics of justice and compassion," by the still-existing socialist ethics of unity and equality, and by the universal human rights norms integrated into the legal system of BiH through the Catalog of International and European Human Rights norms and standards.[31]

Most of the peacebuilders in this book are religious, but they acted as agnostics, particularly at the beginning of their work. Religion came into play later, but only as one of many equally important and relevant arguments in their peace work. Some peacebuilders used religion in psycho-social therapy, while others used the religious ethics of care, solidarity, and compassion to initiate dialogue across the entity borders within BiH.[32] Some used religion to protect women from violence.

There are many reasons for excluding religious arguments in the peace work of secular nongovernmental organizations in the years after the war: the politicization of religion, the involvement of religious authorities in blessing war criminals, the silence of religious authorities about crimes, and the close collaboration of

---

[29] Peter Berger (ed.), 1999, The *Desecularization of the World, Resurgent Religion and World Politics*, Grand Rapids: Eerdmans.
[30] Ina Merdjanova and Patrice Brodeur, 2009, *Religion as a Conversation Starter: Interreligious Dialogue for Peacebuilding in the Balkans*, New York: Continuum, 108-124.
[31] The catalogue of human rights norms and standards is a part of the legal system of BiH, which consists of basic international and European conventions, declarations, and protocols.
[32] BiH was internally divided according to the Dayton Peace Agreement in 1995, with half of the territory established as the Federation of BiH, populated mostly by Bosniacs and Croats, while the other half, Republika Srpska, has primary ethnic Serbs as residents.

ethno-national political parties with religious communities and churches in pursing their common agendas.[33] Many citizens who declare religious identity (more than 90 percent) did not want to bring religion into the conversation on peace because of the marriage between politicians and religious authorities.[34] Religious authorities were preoccupied with re-establishing control over their destroyed and impoverished congregations and with getting their nationalized property back from the state after the war.[35] Religious communities were not prepared for working on peace issues and did not have enough human resources to undertake peacebuilding activities. Religious leaders "are generally locked into positions taken with regard to the perspectives and issues in conflict. They are under tremendous pressure to maintain a position of strength vis-à-vis their adversaries and their own constituencies."[36] Finally, foreign donors sought partners among secular civil and human rights organizations and not among faith-based organizations and religious communities. After 2000, the scenario changed, and faith-based organizations began to receive foreign funding for peace activities, primarily through the offices of the Interreligious Council of BiH.[37]

---

[33] Neven Andjelic, 2003, *Bosnia and Herzegovina, the End of a Legacy*, London: Frank Cass; Michael A. Sells, 1996, *The Bridge Betrayed: Religion and Genocide in Bosnia*, Berkeley: University of California Press; Paul Mojzes, 2011, *Balkan Genocides: Holocaust and Ethnic Cleansing in the Twentieth Century*, Lanham, MD: Rowman and Littlefield.
[34] Dino Abazović, 2006, *Za naciju i Boga*, Sarajevo: Magistrat Sarajevo; Alen Kristić, 2009, *Religija i moć*, Sarajevo: Rabic.
[35] Ivan Cvitković, 2012, Ivan Cvitković, 2012, *Sociološki pogledi na naciju i religiju* Vol. II, Sarajevo: Center for Empirical Research on Religion in BiH.
[36] John Paul Lederach, 1997, *Building Peace: Sustainable Reconciliation in Divided Societies*, Washington, D.C.: U.S. Institute of Peace, 40.
[37] See Merdjanova and Brodeur 2009.

Methodology

I have employed the biographical method in working on this book because it has provided a useful structure with which to interview individuals who have lived through traumatic life experiences, such as war and genocide,[38] and to understand the significance these people give to the stories they tell,[39] or to describe the turning-point moments that cause individuals to change themselves and their world.[40] These moments or epiphanies often come during crises that "alter the fundamental meaning and structures in a person's life."[41] In the case of our women peacebuilders in BiH, these epiphanies resulted in positive effects and changed not only their lives, but also the lives of those they reached out to.

Some scholars use the life story technique both as method and as final product.[42] Some refer to this as the biographical method with the life story as the key instrument. From life stories we can learn how women create and interpret the life conditions and events they are narrating. In this way it is possible to see, as Theresa Iles says, "the fabric of life which often slips through the net of quantitative research."[43] We can also learn how these women create meaning and interpret parts of their lives within the social contexts in which

---

[38] Amia Lieblich, Rivka Tuval-Mashiach, and Tamar Zilber, 1998, *Narrative Research: Reading, Analysis and Interpretation*. Thousand Oaks: Sage; Gabriele Rosenthal, 1993, "Reconstruction of Life Stories: Principles of Selection in Generating Stories for Narrative Biographical Interviews," in Ruthellen Josselson and Amia Leiblich (eds.), *The Narrative Study of Lives*, Vol. 1, Thousand Oaks, CA: Sage, 59-91.
[39] Max van Manen, 1997, "Phenomenological Pedagogy and the Question of Meaning," in Donald Vandenberg (ed.), *Phenomenology and Educational Discourse,* Durban: Heinemann Higher and Further Education, 41-65.
[40] Norman Denzin, 1989, *Interpretive Biography*, Thousand Oaks, CA: Sage.
[41] Ibid., 70.
[42] Svenka Savić, 20011, *Vojvođanke (1917/1931): životne priče*, Novi Sad: Futura Publikacije i Ženske studije i istraživanja.
[43] Theresa Iles (ed.), 1992, *All Sides of the Subject: Women and Biography*, New York: Teachers College Press, Columbia University, 94.

they live.[44] In addition, we note what they do not say, or name—some of it unspeakable.[45] Some women spoke about war, crimes, and expulsion, and even named the perpetrators, while others spoke more generally.

Biographical research enables us to "search for women's subjectivity, where the subject becomes known to us through her actions and her history."[46] Bosnian women peacebuilders were driven by an ethics of care and compassion and a deep faith in humanity, but they did not want their existence to be limited to their private lives. Most of them make strong references to their families as an important foundation and inspiration for their work and feminism, but some skip that part of their life and consciously narrate their stories beyond their personal lives, emphasizing only their actions and accomplishments in the public sphere.

This work is based on biographical thematic analysis[47] with microanalysis of the text, but to write a monograph with compelling stories and make visible each of the eleven women peace heroines described here, I decided to pick up several themes from each of the analyzed interviews and create a story that does not follow the chronology of the storytelling, but rather highlights the peacebuilding activities of these women.

The entire process of analysis, writing, and checking details and interpretations was a combination of the insider's view of the narrator and the researcher's analytical skills. In this dialectic it was crucial to check meanings and interpretations with these women, who fortunately were there to authorize the final story shape.[48] It

---

[44] Julia Chaitin, 2002, "How do I ask them about the war? Collecting and Understanding the Stories of Soldiers and Victims of War," *Social Science Research Network Electronic Library.*
[45] Čengić 2013, 74-75.
[46] Barry 1992, 33.
[47] Rosenthal 1993, 60-61.
[48] Every woman signed the consent form for the final version of her story, which had been sent to her via email. The forms were also signed by the author of the book and the research assistant, Aida Spahić. All consent forms signed by the women were transmitted electronically and hardcopy to the author.

was also important to decide together what to keep in the story, because some of the women still live under political pressure and one would not want to jeopardize their safety. I also learned that our understanding of someone's story, even if we personally do the interview and analyze the transcript, is limited by our own views of certain phenomena and events. Clarifications are thus crucial to avoid misinterpretations.

Theoretical Framework

The theoretical framework of this book rests on the concepts of care ethics and feminist ethics of compassion and justice, as well as peacebuilding theories and the scholarship on feminist leadership. Care ethics scholars[49] portray women as key leaders in their local communities and as active advocates for peace. However, they go beyond gender stereotypes in describing both women and men as caring persons, while claiming that women are not inherently peaceful and can in fact have the same warmongering tendencies as men. Still, much research indicates that women are more involved in peacebuilding than men, particularly in their local communities.[50] Elise Boulding explains this by saying that women's traditional social roles allow them to be less bound by conventional definitions of security and military necessity, and that they also have access to people in local communities to create networks and opportunities for acquiring new skills.[51] Fiona Robinson[52] underlines the idea that caring qualities are not

---

[49] Carol Gilligan, 1983, *In a Different Voice: Psychological Theory and Women's Development*, Cambridge MA: Harvard University Press; Nel Noddings, 2002, *Starting At Home: Caring and Social Policy*, Berkeley: University of California Press; Fiona Robinson, 2011, *The Ethics of Care. A Feminist Approach to Human Security*, Philadelphia: Temple University Press.
[50] Porter 2007, 3.
[51] Elise Boulding, 2000, *Cultures of Peace: The Hidden Side of History*, New York: Syracuse University Press, 71.
[52] Robinson, 2011, 32-33.

exclusively female, and together with Nel Noddings,[53] claims that a more substantial reduction of the overwhelming poverty in the world could be achieved if care-oriented ethics came into play instead of traditional justice-oriented approaches. Motherhood is also closely linked with peacebuilding, but as Sara Ruddick[54] warns, proper linkage is possible only when maternal thinking is a part of a "rationality of care," meaning that a woman is attentive to the needs of others and behaves in a protective and supportive manner. Both women and men can employ maternal thinking in the public realm, and if they do so, they will not risk the nurture of their children at the expense of the victory of their nation.

The scholarship devoted to feminist ethics of care and justice[55] pays more attention to care and justice as mutually interdependent and important elements for peace and security: "Part of the linkage between feminism and peace is about breaking down the logic of domination,"[56] Elisabeth Porter explains, adding that the politics of compassion is the third important element in delivering peace on both an individual and a societal level, and it consists of attentiveness to suffering, active listening, and quick responding.[57] In trying to overcome the existing dichotomies between proponents of justice and compassion, she points out: "It is not care alone that enables compassionate responsibility, but a merging of the compassionate drive with a search for justice, equality, and rights that is more likely to address people's needs."[58]

The women identified as peace-seeking heroines in this book have embodied the concept of compassion as an important part of the ethics of care and justice that they practice, and some of them

---

[53] Noddings 2002.
[54] Ruddick 1992, 46.
[55] Porter 2007; Martha C. Nussbaum, 2000, *Sex and Social Justice,* Oxford: Oxford University Press. Pankhurst 2009; Uma Narayan, 1995, "Colonialism and its Others: Considerations on Rights and Care Discourses", *Hypatia* 10.2, 133-40.
[56] Porter 2007, 56.
[57] Ibid., 103-104.
[58] Ibid., 117.

have even essentialized Bosnian women as special human beings able to surmount the highest barriers for the sake of their families and communities. They use what what Gayatri Spivak calls "strategic essentialisms"[59], and Elissa Helms in her study with Bosnian women reveals that the alignment with motherhood and other affirmative characteristics of women and men was strategic, what she recognized as strategic use of affirmative essentialism.[60] Most of them, however, believe that women are not inherently peaceful, but that their socially constructed roles have made them more oriented toward peace. Only when women have the same amount of power as men, will we know if they are genuinely better peacebuilders.

In contrast to the "great man" theory and its emphasis on charismatic individuals with inborn traits of leadership, some scholars have elaborated both a feminine and a feminist style of leadership. Bernice Lott notices that femininity as a quality is more attributed to nature and to socially constructed gender roles, while feminist leadership styles are about equal opportunities for all. They place a specific emphasis on those who are vulnerable and disadvantaged, but the approach is also about empowerment, change, and peace.[61] Other scholars have tried to offer a more comprehensive definition of feminist leadership as "transformational in nature, seeking to empower and enhance the effectiveness of one's team members while striving to improve the lives and conditions of all."[62] Many authors emphasize the

---

[59] Spivak, Gayatri Chakravorty, 1993, *Outside in the Teaching Machine*. New York: Routledge.
[60] Elissa Helms, 2013, *Innocence and Victimhood, Gender, Nation, and Women's Activism in Postwar Bosnia-Herzegovina*. Madison, WI: University of Wisconsin Press, 9.
[61] Bernice Lott, 2007, "Discourses on Women, Feminism and Leadership" in Jean Lau Chin, Bernice Lott, Joy Rice and Janis Sanchez-Hucles (eds.), *Women and Leadership: Transforming Visions and Diverse Voices*. Hoboken, NJ: Wiley-Blackwell, 25-28.
[62] Natalie Porter and Jessica Henderson Daniel, 2007, "Developing Transformational Leaders", in Jean Lau Chin, Bernice Lott, Joy Rice and Janis

collaborative style,[63] empowerment, coalition building,[64] and an egalitarian approach.[65] Feminist collaboration is also said to be inclusive and not ethnocentric, not focusing on one race (white), ethnicity, and region. It is reflective and depends on context, enabling women of different social, political, and cultural backgrounds to develop their own style of leadership that can change according to their particular society. Finally, feminist leadership perspectives also support the premise of shared knowledge.[66]

Another approach to women's leadership combines feminine and feminist approaches through the concept of IDEA-based leadership traits.[67] Mary Lou Décosterd uses feminine characteristics for the four key leadership traits, describing women as being as capable as men in combining the left and right sides of the brain to embrace the whole picture with vision, intuition, empowerment, and focus to finish tasks. Bosnian peacebuilders showed both traits, feminine and feminist, but some emphasized the more feminine side of women's leadership and did not necessarily include values of

---

Sanchez-Hucles (eds.), *Women and Leadership: Transforming Visions and Diverse Voices.* Hoboken, NJ: Wiley-Blackwell, 249.
[63] Carol J Singely and Susan Elizabeth Sweeny, 1998, "In League with Each Other. The Theory and Practice of Feminist Collaboration", in Elizabeth G. Peck and JoAnna Stephens Mink (eds.), *Common Ground. Feminist Collaboration in the Academy*, Albany: State University of New York Press; Judith Worell and Norine G. Johnson (eds.), 1997, *Shaping the Future of Feminist Psychology: Education, Research and Practice*, Washington D.C.: American Psychological Association.
[64] C. Cryss Brunner (ed.), 1999, *Sacred Dreams Women and the Superintendency,* Albany: State University of New York Press.
[65] Joyce K. Fletcher, 2001, *Disappearing Acts: Gender, Power, and Relational Practice at Work*, Cambridge, MA: The MIT Press.
[54] Mary Lou Décosterd, 2013, *How Women are Transforming Leadership. Four Key Traits Powering Success*, Santa Barbara: Praeger.
[67] Ibid. There are four IDEA-based leadership traits: Intuition is about looking at life with vision and embracing the whole picture instead of just a piece of it; directive force refers to an innovative spirit that can get the task done while focusing on the outcome; empowerment means giving authority to make others more confident; assimilation is about bringing people together in constructive ways as well as transforming situations in the sense of solving conflicts.

feminism in their program goals. It is important to underline that most of these women "became leaders 'accidentally' through contributions ... [and they] may be more likely to see themselves as influencers, collaborators, or contributors," but not necessarily leaders.[68] None of them spoke directly about their leadership. However, they were recognized by their communities as peace leaders, and what they did and still do demonstrates some of IDEA-based leadership traits.

Peacebuilding scholarship[69] not only defines the concept of peacebuilding but also offers models and methods to achieve the fulfillment of peace ideas.[70] Johan Galtung[71] coined the notion "peacebuilding" as constituting a positive peace and he says: "Just as a coin has two sides, one side alone being only one aspect of the coin, not the complete coin, peace also has two sides: *absence of personal violence*, and *absence of structural violence*. We shall refer to them as *negative peace* and *positive peace* respectively." Additionally, "A positive notion of peace also includes the increase

---

[68] Karen L. Suyemoto and Mary B. Ballou, 2007, "Conducted Monotones to Coacted Harmonies: A Feminist (Re)conceptualization of Leadership Addressing Race, Class, and Gender", in Jean Lau Chin, Bernice Lott, Joy Rice and Janis Sanchez-Hucles (eds.), *Women and Leadership: Transforming Visions and Diverse Voices*. Hoboken, NJ: Wiley-Blackwell, 41.

[69] Lederach 1997; Lisa Schirch, 2008, "Strategic Peacebuilding: State of the Field", *Peace Prints: South Asian Journal of Peacebuilding* 1.1 (Spring); Johan Galtung, 1976, "Three Approaches to Peace: Peacekeeping, Peacemaking and Peacebuilding" in *Peace, War and Defense: Essays in Peace Research*, Vol. II, Johan Galtung (ed.), Copenhagen: Christian Ejlers; Louise Diamond and John MacDonald, 1996, *Multi-track Diplomacy: A Systems Approach to Peace*, 3rd ed. West Harford CT: Kumarian Press.

[70] Louise Diamond and John McDonald coined the term "multi-track diplomacy" and they developed nine diplomacy tracks based on the first two tracks: track 1. government activities, track 2. NGO activities proposed by Joseph Montville 1985. Nine diplomacy tracks are: 1. Work with governments, 2. Professional conflict resolution, 3. Support of business, 4. Private citizens, 5. Research and education, 6. Activism, 7. Religiously motivated peacebuilding, 8. Finance and providing funding for peacebuilding, 9. Public opinion.

[71] Galtung 1976.

in social justice and the creation of a culture of peace among people within and across societies."[72]

Later the UN system accepted the term peacebuilding and it became widely used in other institutions, academia, and the NGO sector. Lisa Shirch has added to this the idea that peacebuilding is accepted by many as an "umbrella term" or "meta term" including a wide range of activities. It is "a process of building relationships and institutions that support the peaceful transformation of conflict."[73] One of the peace heroines in this book, Amra Pandžo, describes peacebuilding as anything that can bring justice, prevent violence, and affirm women's human rights, as well as accept identity differences.[74]

All of the women peace heroines in this book particularly emphasized their role in the creation and nurturing of relationships crucial for peace work. One of Lederach's most fundamental claims for peace scholarship is that "relationship is the basis of both the conflict and its long-term solution."[75] These women were tireless in re-building broken relationships and in creating new ones with voiceless, powerless, and marginalized groups of citizens. They recognized that relationships are crucial not only on the personal level, but also when peacebuilding activities need to move on to other levels—societal, institutional, and global. They had what Lederach calls "moral imagination", which is a basic element for peacebuilding. Jonathan Jones, referring to previous sociological and philosophical writings, defines the moral imagination as "an intuitive ability to perceive ethical truths and abiding law in the

---

[72] "A positive notion of peace also includes the increase in social justice and the creation of a culture of peace among people within and across societies." ("Peace, Peacebuilding, Peacemaking", 2012, in *Berghof Glossary on Conflict Transformation. 20 notions for theory and practice*, Berlin: Berghof Foundation, 59.)
[73] Shirch 2008.
[74] Tanja Topić, Aleksandar Živanović and Aleksandar Žolja, 2008, *Mirovni aktivizam u Bosni i Hercegovini*, Banja Luka: Helsinki Citizens' Assembly., 31.
[75] Lederach, 1997, 26.

midst of chaotic experience ... a uniquely human ability to conceive of fellow humanity as moral beings and as persons, not as objects whose value rests in utility or usefulness."[76] Lederach also believes that moral imagination allows people to rise above the vortex of violence. For him it is:

> the capacity to imagine ourselves in a web of relationships that includes our enemies; the ability to sustain a paradoxical curiosity that embraces complexity without reliance on dualistic polarity; the fundamental belief in and pursuit of the creative act; and the acceptance of the inherent risk of stepping into the mystery of the unknown that lies beyond the far too familiar landscape of violence.[77]

During the war, moral imagination brought some of these women to moral dilemmas when deciding to go against their own communities to protect someone's life. As David Hampton argues: "Living in conflict zones requires individuals to make moral choices on regular bases ... Part of that involves serious evaluation and criticism of one's own community and traditions, perhaps even of one's own family's tradition."[78] In confronting their own communities, these women employed different strategies to protect others' lives and dignity; some of them reported that during the war one could easily be killed if issues like war crimes were raised. Some women have openly criticized war and ethno-national politics, while others avoided direct confrontation in order to protect themselves and their loved ones because human life can have little meaning in the midst of war. Instead, they decided to do what could be done in those circumstances. But all of them were determined to connect people despite the divisions and to help them

---

[76] Jonathan Jones, 2009, "Defining 'Moral Imagination'", in the blog 'Postmodern Conservative,' *First Things* (July 1), http://www.firstthings.com/blogs/postmodern conservative/2009/07/01/defining-moral-imagination/ (accessed November 7, 2013).
[77] Lederach 2005, 5.
[78] David Hampton. 2012, "The Fog of Religious Conflict," *Harvard Divinity Bulletin 41,* Cambridge: Harvard University Press, 56.

rebuild their lives and good interpersonal relations after the war, believing wholeheartedly in their decisions and efforts to leave a legacy of peace for future generations.

Ordinary Women with Extraordinary Life Journeys

The eleven women who dared to show the light of humanity in a time of disgrace and evil are not saints. They are, as most of them would say, ordinary women who had the courage to stand against injustice, oppression, ethno-national divisions, and exclusion. Their stories do not portray an idealized image of women or of perfect peace activists; rather, they tell the tales of ordinary women—with all their advantages and disadvantages, successes and failures—who bore witness to horror but chose to live in hope.

Their lives, like the lives of other engaged persons, are subject to assessment and criticism in terms of what they have done or failed to do, particularly in times of great political pressure when every act might not have been consistent with the peace path they opted for. It can be difficult to understand the personal dilemmas and situations in that shape specific choices but the social and political contexts greatly influence the decisions and strategies of each woman individually and as a leader in her community. One should have in mind that the topics of dialogue and reconciliation in BiH are still not generally accepted while public dialogue and culture of peace are not encouraged. Promoting such concepts is therefore difficult.

Peacebuilders in this book are not perfect women, they are as entitled to mistakes and fear like anyone else, but what makes them stand out is the strength to stand tall and do things to make life better for other people. When it comes from the soul, as Rumi explains, "you feel a river moving in you, a joy." Their deep belief that the light of humanity exists in every person and just needs encouragement gave them the strength to continue on their peace paths. They knew that when a spark of humanity appears in the eye of one person, it is possible to see the whole universe sparkle. They have done it countless number of times and that makes their stories special and important.

I hope that in their stories the readers will recognize the capability of ordinary people to drive change and achieve results in circumstances in which people must dare to imagine lives beyond the imposed social, ethnic, political, and/or gender frames. These women dared imagine a different world, one without fear and imposed divisions and this makes their stories worth hearing.

Organization of the Book

This book is divided into eleven chapters in the style of a traditional Asian circle fan covered with rich and colorful life stories. Each story can be read as the first or the last chapter, but due to the physical constraints of publishing, one of the chapters opens and another closes the book. When deciding on the order of the stories, I happened to see one day in Boston the "Old Japan" store with its big circle fan and got the idea to shape the book similarly as a peacebuilding fan. I did not want the book to impose a hierarchy on the stories, because every woman has done a remarkable job in her local community and more broadly in BiH. All of these women are unique despite the similar traits that we find in their narratives and argumentation. Thus, the symbolism of the Asian traditional fan with the top in the center as the beginning of life and the petals as life paths, which spread in different directions searching for goodness and happiness, appeared to be the appropriate solution to the story order. Readers, however, can start from any story in the volume and proceed through it on their own.

The top of the Bosnian peacebuilding fan might be viewed as the seed of humanity these women nurtured and kept alive. The petals can symbolize their moral imagination that reached beyond ethnic borders and gender boundaries. Depending on how much of their moral imaginations remain hidden, the petals of the stories could spread far beyond this book. And I hope they will.

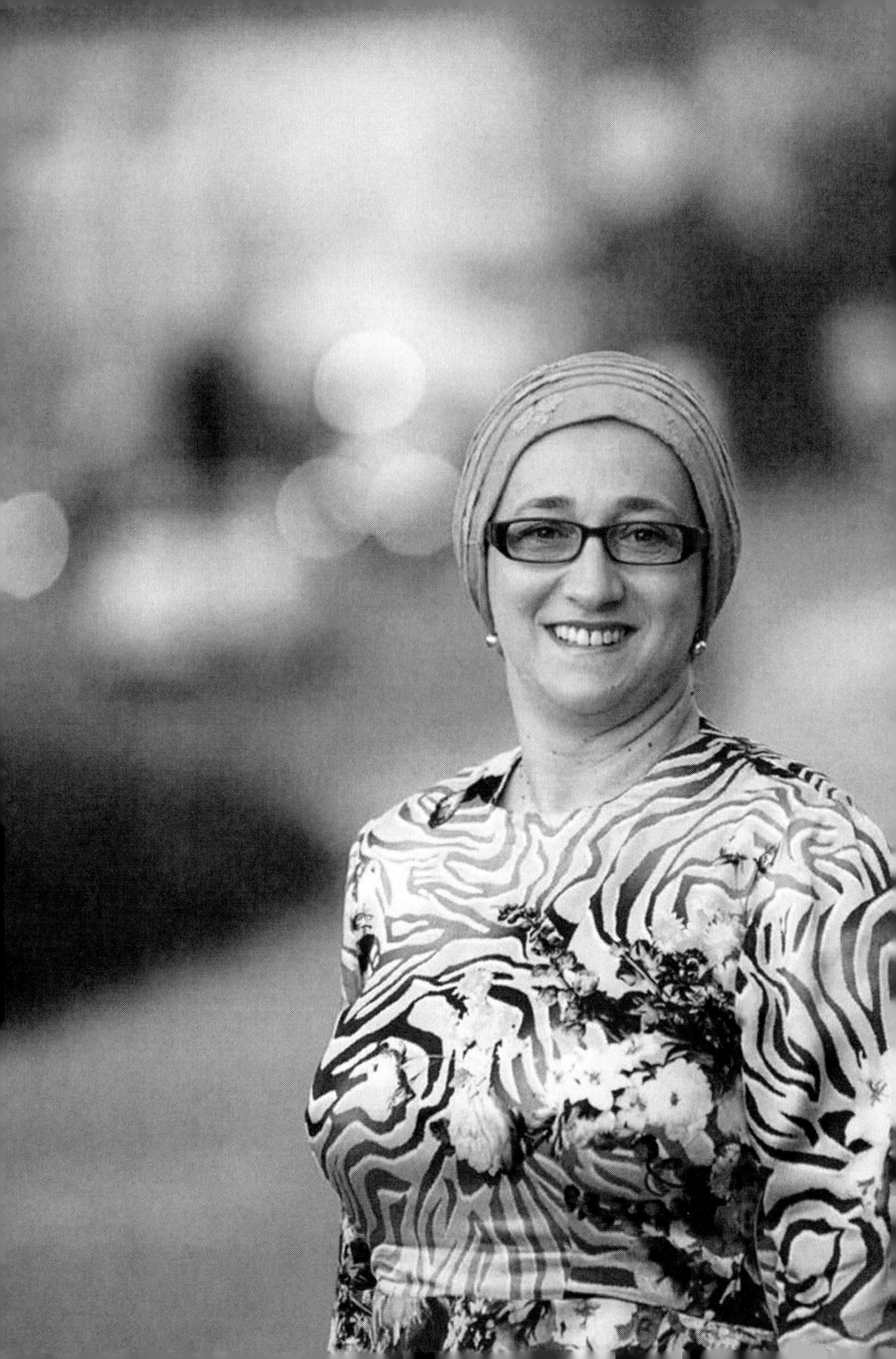

STORY ONE

JUSTICE FOR SURVIVORS OF VIOLENCE

SABIHA HUSIĆ

Biography

Sabiha Husić was born in 1971 in Vitez (central Bosnia), the third child in a traditional Bosniac Muslim family. Her middle-class family was well off during those years. Her father worked in a local state company but also ran a private business that enabled his family to have a better life, including educational opportunities for the children.

Sabiha graduated from primary school in Vitez and then moved to Sarajevo to attend the Muslim religious high school Gazi Husrev-bey Madrasa. She went on to graduate from the faculty of Islamic Studies at the University of Sarajevo. During the war, Sabiha and her family were expelled by the military HVO (Croatian Defense Council) to the city of Zenica where they became refugees who had to cope with the many challenges found in their new social setting. In an effort to assist other refugees there, Sabiha soon started working at a local NGO helping wartime rape survivors and women who suffered from domestic violence.

Her work was very hard but also fulfilling, inspiring her to learn more and more in order to help these women and herself. She attended courses and seminars to study counseling, particularly counseling for survivors of wartime sexual violence and trauma. One of the programs she attended helped prepare her to use psychodynamic therapy with survivors. Sabiha also attended a one-year specialized course teaching non-violent communication and conflict resolution skills through various cultural approaches. In order to improve her managerial skills, she completed a Master's degree in State Management and Humanitarian Affairs at the University of Sarajevo. Today, with her husband Aladin, daughter Nedžma and son Afan, she lives in Zenica—her adopted home.

Introduction

Sabiha is among the youngest peacebuilders featured in this book but has, nevertheless, the longest track-record as an activist. She began her work in the first female-run NGO in BiH, Medica Zenica, established in 1993 by German feminists who came to Bosnia-Herzegovina to help women and children survivors of the war.

As a refugee in Zenica, Sabiha's particular situation resulted in her having to be responsible not only for herself but for the other members of the family as well. Equipped with a strong work ethic resulting from her family background and with a firm faith in God, she trusted that whatever problems arose, there would always be a way to solve them. Thus, she began her human rights activism in refugee camps in Zenica and later moved to Medica Zenica. Motivated by a desire for self-empowerment, she was enabled to help and serve others, and she constantly invested in her own education in order to better assist women and children in need.

Sabiha was my colleague at the University of Sarajevo. When the war started, we met in Zenica as refugees and worked for a while together in Medica Zenica. In my recent interview with her, she narrated numerous stories about her "interrupted youth" and the devastating challenges of the war, in which she became responsible for things she may not have been ready for. Her primary concern was her family, to keep them together. When the results of the

Baseline Study on Women and Peacebuilding in BiH[1] came out, I informed her that her name appeared at the top of the list both in the field and web survey. She was happy, but like all her fellow peacebuilders, she commented that there were so many other women who deserved to be on that list, and that she had only been doing what she believed in.

The first interview brought back to her many sad memories. From time to time, she tried to control her emotions by changing her body posture and lowering her gaze. This was especially apparent when she mentioned the expulsion of her family by the HVO, as well as when she recalled memories of rape crimes during the war and the struggle to provide justice for survivors of these crimes. Sabiha's biggest achievements are related to her work with the wartime rape survivors. She brought them comfort and hope while advocating for societal recognition of rape as a crime against humanity. This was followed by her struggle to obtain legal rights for women victims of wartime rape and for survivors of domestic violence in the complex domestic legal system.

Protection of the Survivors of Violence

> I believe that each individual can make positive changes, no matter how slowly and quietly it seems to be going. If we, the ordinary people, don't discuss the societal changes that need to be made, we cannot expect someone else, who perhaps should have noticed it long ago, to do something about it.

Sabiha did not expect someone else to resolve her problems when she became a refugee in Zenica. She took her destiny into her own hands and dedicated herself to fighting for human rights, protection, justice, and equality. She wanted to help people become responsible citizens and self-advocates. As a refugee, she

---

[1] Zilka Spahić-Šiljak, Elmaja Bavčić and Aida Spahić, 2012, *Baseline Study on Women and Peacebuilding in BiH*, Sarajevo: TPO Foundation Sarajevo, www.tpo.ba.

experienced expulsion and persecution just for belonging to a particular ethnic and religious group. Her treatment was exacerbated due to her perseverance in coming to the aid of women who reported rape and torture in the camps. She was aware that legal protection and recognition of rape as a war crime was an important first step in building systematic and sustainable security for these women. Together with colleagues also working for Medica Zenica—Marijana, Mirha, Nurka, and Aida—she tirelessly initiated dialogue with institutions, both international and national, to stop stigmatizing the rape of women and rather help women regain their dignity and re-integrate themselves into their families and societies.

Fig. 1-1

These years of persistent work and advocacy were successful. The biggest victory of Medica Zenica, and medica mondiale from Germany[2] was the recognition of rape as a weapon of war both at

---

[2] medica mondiale (http://www.medicamondiale.org) has its headquarter in Germany while local Medica organizations in several countries, including BiH operate as independent organizations.

the International Criminal Tribunal for Former Yugoslavia (ICTY)[3] and the Court of BiH.[4] For the first time in the history of international law, rape was recognized as a crime against humanity when, in 2001, the ICTY issued the first verdict confirming rape as just such a crime: "The acts were part of a systematic and widespread campaign. The acts included elements of enslavement."[5]

The next step was to provide legal status for these women in BiH. However, the BiH legal system is overly complex because of its two entities: the Republika Srpska and the Federation of BiH (FBiH), itself further divided into ten cantons, and then into separate districts, such as the Brčko District. Such a legal structure was a challenge; Sabiha had first to work within the legal structure of Zenica-Doboj Canton[6] in FBiH and then within networks in other cantons and entities.

Sabiha persevered, trying to convince state institutions to grant these women the legal status of civilian victims of war. She said

---

[3] According to the website of the ICTY, "[i]n a number of landmark judgments, the Tribunal advanced the development of international justice in the realm of gender crimes by enabling the prosecution of sexual violence as a war crime, a crime against humanity and genocide" (http://www.icty.org/sid/10314).

[4] Rape and other forms of sexual violence are legally foreseen in the BiH Criminal Code (Art. 171: Genocide, Art. 172: Crimes against Humanity; Arts. 173-175: War Crimes), as in international law, as potentially amounting to war crimes or crimes against humanity or even genocide, provided sufficient contextual evidence.

[5] The first criminals were prosecuted and convicted in The Hague, including the Serbian commander Kunarac and his soldiers from Foča in eastern BiH. This case was the first one that made rape a part of the language of international criminal law ("How Rape Became a Crime against Humanity," http://clg.portalxm.com/library/keytext.cfm?keytext_id=74).

[6] According to the Dayton Constitution, the Entity Federation of Bosnia and Herzegovina consists of ten cantons, one of which is Zenica-Doboj Canton in central Bosnia. It includes twelve municipalities of which Zenica is the biggest with 96,027 inhabitants (Muslims 44.85%, Serbs 18.48%, Croats 16.54%, Yugoslavs 15.32%, others 4.07%) according to the prewar 1991 census. For more details see: "Ethnic Composition of Bosnia-Herzegovina's Population, by Municipalities and Settlements, 1991 Census," Sarajevo: Bureau of Statistics for Bosnia and Herzegovina, Bulletin 234.

that Medica Zenica initiated the process and launched the first roundtable in Zenica right after the war. However, the entire process was not finished until 2006 when an amendment to the FBiH Law on Social Protection, Protection of Civilian Victims of War and Families with Children[7] granted protection to raped women as civilian victims of the war,[8] which according to Sabiha, is the first law to do so in the world. Obtaining the status of war victim was important for acquiring financial support, but Sabiha argues that there are still many obstacles to the implementation of the law in terms of procedures and sufficient funding.

Major work remained, such as providing psycho-social and financial support for women who testify in court. The mainstream approach in the prosecution of rape crimes did not take into account the re-traumatization experienced during trials and the support needed because of this. For Sabiha and her colleagues, it was very important to protect and accompany these women during the court hearings. If they had enough courage to go to court to try to attain justice on behalf of the many survivors of wartime rape and other kinds of sexual violence, they should not be left alone to suffer in silence or be forced to pay unaffordable expenses:

> From the beginning, Medica Zenica used that approach toward all victims, especially toward the survivors of wartime rape. During the trial in The Hague it stressed the importance of having a sensitive and thoughtful approach, so as not to summon a woman as just another witness who would be testifying, but to prepare her psychologically and logistically.

---

[7] Adopted in 1999, amended in 2004, 2006, and 2009 (*The Right to Social Protection in Bosnia and Herzegovina: Concerns on Adequacy and Equality*, 2012, Sarajevo: OSCE Mission to Bosnia and Herzegovina).
[8] Guide for Civilian Victims of War: How to Enjoy the Right to Protection As a Civilian Victim of War in the Federation of Bosnia and Herzegovina, 2007, Sarajevo: International Commission on Missing Persons, Missing Persons Institute of Bosnia and Herzegovina, Centre for Free Access to Information.

Another very important step was to establish a network of support for the witnesses of wartime rape and sexual abuse crimes. A necessarily gender-sensitive attitude was missing in the ICTY and BiH Court prosecutions. Only the female-run NGOs insisted on a gender-sensitive approach to enable better conditions for these women who cried for protection: "Somehow it was important to me that the representatives of state institutions and relevant ministries finally understood what kind of pain this is ... what it really means for a woman to testify." Using education, training, and discussion, Sabiha promoted for these women a program of understanding and partnership with Medica Zenica. For Sabiha, partnering with state institutions in these matters is compatible with the feminist autonomy of Medica Zenica, although some consider this union problematic.[9] She was aware that those in power sometimes manipulated women, even abused them by their insensitive attitudes. But she understood that there is power in numbers, so she created a support network to connect all relevant institutions. This network is itself a "platform" for constructive change, a "relational space" where creative processes and solutions are generated.[10] Today, police officers, judges, prosecutors, social workers, and psychologists make up a team of professionals in the "network of support to victims/witnesses in war crimes cases, sexual violence, and other kinds of criminal offenses": "All we wanted was the fulfillment of justice, equity ... to not neglect those who are the most important, those who suffered the most, those who experienced it in their bodies and their souls."

---

[9] Cynthia Cockburn, 2013, "Against the Odds: Sustaining Feminist Momentum in Post-war Bosnia-Herzegovina," *Women's Studies International Forum* 37 (March–April), 26–35.

[10] John Paul Lederach, 2005, *The Moral Imagination: The Art and Soul of Building Peace*, Oxford: Oxford University Press, 85.

Fig. 1-2

Sabiha believes there will be no justice until each victim is adequately protected and provided for. Consequently, she is engaged in expanding institutional support networks for witnesses, based on the model developed in Zenica-Doboj Canton, to other cantons and also to Republika Srpska, where Medica Zenica collaborates with the NGO Udružene Žene (United Women) from Banja Luka and Izvor in Prijedor. Additionally, the goal is to establish an institutional network at the state level according to these models and to integrate this approach for the protection of victims in BiH.

Since Medica Zenica has worked not only on the protection of wartime rape survivors, but also of survivors of domestic/family violence, Sabiha's next goal has been to include these victims in the Law on Basic Social Protection in Zenica-Doboj Canton:

It is the first law in our Canton to specify exactly who the victims of domestic violence are, and further it includes victims of violence in the community ... Among other measures, it specifically regulates the provisions and rights available to victims, such as shelters.

Sabiha first had to work within the legal structure of the Zenica-Doboj Canton to define survivors of domestic violence as those with social rights, on the basis of models and legal solutions existing in FBiH.[11] Medica Zenica became a partner in these matters with the municipality, the Zenica-Doboj Canton (ZDK), the Central Bosnia Canton, the BiH Federation and certain state ministries; this has included modest but important financial support. Based on their Protocol of Cooperation, signed in 2010, symbolic amount of is assigned to support Medica Zenica's shelter, but Sabiha sees this is an important step in the recognition of the NGO as a credible organization. One of its important achievements was designing the first domestic violence database, which served further as a model for other municipalities of FBiH[12] and was applied by the Gender Center of the Federation of BiH.

In its first years, Medica Zenica was, as Cynthia Cockburn describes it, "on the cusp between [the] women's voluntary sector and the feminist movement."[13] It took them more than fifteen years of persistent work, advocacy, and lobbying to be seen as a reputable organization by state institutions and people in the community. Today, when domestic violence occurs or when state institutions do not show the appropriate amount of resolve, people just say: "We

---

[11] The 11th session of the Assembly of Zenica-Doboj Canton, held on September 7, 2011, adopted the Law on Amendments to the Law on Social Protection, Protection of Civilian Victims of War, and Protection of Families with Children, that regulates these issues in Zenica-Doboj Canton.

[12] Sabiha emphasizes that the established referral mechanism of the Municipality of Zenica serves as a model for other FBiH municipalities, and it is also applied by the Gender Centre of the Federation BiH.

[13] Cynthia Cockburn, 1998, *The Space between Us: Negotiating Gender and National Identities in Conflict*, London: Zed Books, 189.

will report it to Medica Zenica." This means Medica Zenica is not only an organization that provides professional psycho-social support, but also a respected and valued voice of community consciousness. It also means that Sabiha and her colleagues have done a lot for the community, such that people identify Medica Zenica as a powerful voice protecting their rights. At the time this story was being finalized, Medica Zenica was celebrating its twentieth anniversary with an international conference as the main event, "Working toward Dignity: Twenty Years of Fighting Conflict-related Sexualized Violence," and the conference gathered together theoreticians and activists from many countries.[14]

Over the last two decades Medica Zenica has served as a "safe place"[15] for female victims of war and violence. It has also increased the city of Zenica's quality as a place where Sabiha could build a new life with her family. She had never thought she would be expelled from the city she was born in, but she was able to establish a new home in Zenica and, moreover, be a beacon of humanity, courage, and reconciliation in her community.

---

[14] The Conference was organized in Zenica by Medica Zenica and Medica Mondiale from Germany on October 23rd and 24th, 2013. Conference participants included representatives of governmental institutions from all levels in BiH, survivors of war rape, BiH nongovernmental organization and representatives of international organizations with offices in BiH, as well as guests from the United States, Germany, Switzerland, Ruanda, Afghanistan, Liberia, Spain, Jordan, Croatia, Serbia, Kosovo, Hungary, and other countries. One of its important conclusions was that the model of Medica Zenica, developed over the years, could be applicable in other parts of BiH, as well as in other countries. It stressed the importance of establishing responsible partnerships with state institutions and creating an environment in which survivors of wartime rape and other forms of trauma can feel safe, supported, protected, and can achieve their rights with dignity.
[15] Ristin Thomasson, 2006, *To Make Room for Changes, Report by Kvina till Kvinna*, http://www.peacewomen.org/assets/file/Resources/NGO/kvinna_tomake roomforchanges_2006.pdf (accessed September 3, 2011).

Displaced Identities

Sabiha established a new home in Zenica, demonstrating courage and faith during the hardest moments of her life. Despite displacement, she persisted and did not lose hope. When she spoke about that experience, she raised her head proudly and sat more upright as if to confirm her determination. Although she was scared, wondering how she would survive in a new place and provide for her family, she was confident she would find a way. She has never allowed herself to be defeated by hatred and revenge, but has searched for opportunities to help other refugees who arrived in Zenica from eastern and western Bosnia, where the first exodus of Bosnian Muslims occurred.

Sabiha commented that she found it unfathomable to lose one's country overnight. In her case, she lost a home in which everyone had been living peacefully, and she had a happy childhood where her Catholic and Orthodox Christian neighbors lived in peace side by side. All of them had been Yugoslavs, Tito's pioneers (those who followed Tito), celebrating brotherhood, unity, and equality. Sabiha's traditional Muslim family was, according to her memories, a family that did not fully observe their religion but was still attached to it. She recalls anti-fascism celebrations where citizens from all ethnic backgrounds came together because they remembered that "Kozara, Sutjeska, Neretva [well-known battles against the Nazis in BiH] were symbols of suffering for all of us." Like most children in Yugoslavia, Sabiha was also a "Tito's pioneer," wearing a red scarf and a white cap with a star, and passing on the baton of the Relay of Youth for Tito on his birthday. At the same time, she was a believer who attended *mekteb* (Islamic instruction for children) at the mosque and recited her prayers. She enjoyed both, and it was not problematic to nurture one's religious identity unless one sought an appointment to high-level decision-making positions or challenged the communist ideology with alternative intellectual and political ideas. Ordinary people had freedom of religion to a certain extent because religion was considered private matter.

In 1992, Sabiha learned about these out-of-reach political and decision-making realms when politicians and militarists changed the lives of millions in the region, displacing them not only from their cities and homes, but also depriving them of their common Yugoslav identity. Citizens were forced into ethnic boxes and their identity was equated only with their ethnicity. Paralyzed by fear and hatred, many began to practice exclusivist politics toward others, their pre-war neighbors.

When the war started, Sabiha was in the city of Pljevlja, Montenegro, doing an internship required for students of the faculty of Islamic Studies in Sarajevo. She was to spend the month that coincided with Ramadan (the fasting period) somewhere in BiH other than Sarajevo, or abroad with the Bosniac/Muslim diaspora. This was one of the rare occasions that involved women traveling with men, preparing for and observing rituals (muqabala, mevlud, tevhid),[16] singing spiritual songs together, and interacting with other young people. Ramadan was a good opportunity for these young theologians to engage in religious service, experience the richness of the spiritual and cultural life of Bosniac Muslims, and also to develop friendships.

Sabiha could not imagine that Ramadan in 1992 would be her last as a Yugoslav citizen. She left for Montenegro with an ID from one country, and a month later that country as she knew it no longer existed. She could not cross the new borders established between

---

[16] *Mukabela* (Arabic, *muqabala*) means "encountering." In the Bosnian Muslim religious tradition it refers to daily encounters with the Qur'an. Every afternoon during Ramadan, a portion of the Qur'an is recited. Imams, intern theologians, and some congregants sit together and recite, while the rest of the congregation follows along with the Qur'an in hand. This way, the entire Qur'an is recited during Ramadan, called *hatma*. *Mevlud* (Arabic, *mawlid*) is the birthday of Prophet Muhammad, celebrated with specific poetry and songs in mosques, tekkes, private houses, and today also in the media. *Tevhid* (Arabic, *tawheed*), or oneness of God refers to repeating God's names, accompanied with other Qur'anic verses during certain rituals, such as funerals, memorials, or petitions.

former Yugoslav republics: "The war surrounded us ... we were in shock, we could not believe what was happening to us." Life was interrupted, friendships broken, neighbors terrified and divided. Everything was upside down. She reported that it was not safe for Muslims in Montenegro: many refugees from eastern Bosnia came, searching for security and protection, but when they saw people suffering for having Muslim names, they moved on. Sabiha saw her friend and host, a prominent public figure in Pljevlja, imprisoned and tortured by Serbs in Montenegro. Sabiha decided to leave with the other refugees.

The normally short trip of several hours by bus from Pljevlja to Sarajevo became a twenty-three day trip. She and the other refugees travelled to Macedonia, where they got new identity papers, then to Bulgaria, and from there to Hungary and on to Croatia. She later learned that what she experienced was called human smuggling and is today forbidden by international law. When she arrived in Zagreb, she discovered she would be able to take "the road of salvation," so named because everybody who needed to travel despite the dangers of war managed via this "road" to reach their desired destinations. Her parents back in Vitez were without news of her, but her father asked for information from every bus and taxi driver who traveled to Split in Croatia, in hopes that she would one day appear. And finally she did. From Zagreb via Split she arrived in Vitez, where her family and neighbors as well as Catholics and Orthodox Christians celebrated her return all together: "I felt that they were truly happy about my return."

Sabiha had heard stories about the war and what was going on in Vitez, but she could not imagine that, after the exodus she experienced in Montenegro, her neighbors would expel her from her home. She also could not understand why some local people were not friendly toward refugees who started coming to central Bosnia in 1992. Some of her neighbors, both Muslims and Catholics, did not have sympathy for the refugees' suffering, commenting: "Why didn't they defend themselves?" and "Couldn't they take better care of their clothing?" She recognized that these refugees had probably traveled many days and nights through the mountains after expulsion, but upon arriving in her city, they were not greeted with understanding and empathy.

The peace in Vitez did not last long. The Croatian Defense Council (HVO) occupied some cities in central BiH where Croats were in the majority (Vitez, Busovača, Novi Travnik), and on the morning of April 16, 1993, soldiers came to her house. She remembered that her father was about to leave for work: "Thank God he had not left yet, for he would have been killed." The army started shelling the Muslim houses in her neighborhood, and then she heard soldiers enter the grocery shop fronting her house. Her family was hiding in the house when the soldiers found them and asked them to come out and immediately thereafter to leave Vitez. During these moments, Sabiha had concerns about her wardrobe, concerns that she now recognizes as absurd:

> Probably because of the comments I had heard [about refugees] … it was important to me to look good. I cannot explain it to myself. Shells were coming from all sides, everybody was lying on the floor, and I had the need to look good, to take my leather jacket and perfume … I never thought I was going to be killed.

They left their house intact and headed toward Zenica, where the majority of Bosniacs/Muslims lived and to which thousands of refugees were fleeing from eastern and western BiH. The journey was exhausting, especially for elderly people and children. They had to walk entire days through the mountains, before finally reaching Zenica. Even after they obtained refugee status, they still hoped to go home in a couple of days. They were in denial about the war.

In Zenica, Sabiha's father was injured, and since her brothers had already gone off to join the army,[17] the young girl with the leather jacket and wearing perfume was now in charge of her family. It was a rude awakening, to realize that she was responsible for their care.[18] Her first job was in the Islamic Community with refugees who had settled in the Ivan Goran Kovačić School in Zenica. Although she had no experience in counseling and the psycho-social effects of trauma, she approached these people with a sympathetic attitude. They were hungry for conversation, smiles, and a space to tell their stories: "We were sitting together, talking, studying, helping ... figuring out to handle the essentials of life, such as how to make coffee and cake out of lentils."

One day, I met Sabiha in Zenica and asked her to join me at Medica Zenica to work with the wartime rape survivors. She began working with us there in 1993 and stayed at Medica Zenica for nineteen years. From a frightened refugee girl, expelled from her home, she became the successful manager of Medica Zenica and a respected human rights activist. When she first met rape survivors, she knew she would stay with them as long as they needed help. It was this second moment of awakening during the war that truly changed the course of her life. Norman Denzin explains such moments as epiphanies in one's life during periods of crisis.[19] After finding a new home for herself in Zenica, Sabiha in turn made Medica Zenica a home for many women and children who had suffered torture and violence. She brought peace to her family and to the community and demonstrated how to nurture people's various ethnic and religious identities. While their identity had become crucial for many people, the efforts of Medica Zenica allowed women to transcend their differences for the sake of their own well-

---

[17] One brother went to Nova Bila where he was captured by the HVO and expelled from Nova Bila with his family. He then joined the BiH Army, but was later captured by the Bosnian Serb Army.
[18] Norman Denzin, 1989, *Interpretive Biography*, Thousand Oaks, CA: Sage.
[19] Ibid., 70.

being. Particularly important to Medica Zenica's work was providing space for religious practices, and for the use of these spaces as a healing tool.

The Healing Function of Religion

> Medica grants the absolute right, opportunity, and democracy, whatever you want to call it, for a woman to choose what helps her most, what she wants, without imposing anything on her ... I think that in this regard Medica Zenica is unique in the world.

Sabiha is proud of Medica Zenica's work and achievements, and she glorifies its openness and freedom. Women in Medica Zenica can choose the treatment that works best for them. If it involves religion, they will get such support, but Sabiha underlines that Medica Zenica is not a religious or faith-based organization; it is secular and open to women of all ethnic and religious identities, as well as to women who are non-religious. This policy drew her in from the beginning, for she recognized it as a sign that in the middle of the war's madness, multicultural life still existed. The resistance to ethnic divisions also attracted researchers such as Cynthia Cockburn, who found that women of different ethnic identities could work together in the midst of the war and that their "anti-nationalism and trans-nationalism [was] a factor grounding and characterizing their feminism."[20]

The war was a hard time for everybody and especially for the rape survivors, who were searching for spiritual support to bring hope back into their lives. This support would allow them to re-establish both their human and professional capacities, which were critical in facing the challenges to their families and communities. As an observant Muslim woman wearing *hijab*, and as an educated theologian, Sabiha used religion in the healing process for these women survivors as well as for other refugees who did not know

---

[20] Cockburn 2013, 30.

how to re-build their lives as displaced persons in the new social and political context.

At Medica Zenica, both Sabiha and I had the welcome opportunity to work with well-known human rights activists and feminists like Monika Hauser from Germany, a woman who also recognized the importance of religion during wartime and offered us the chance to join the Medica Zenica team. We remembered that at the time, we did not know what feminism was:

> My colleagues and I were deeply enmeshed in the pain, suffering, and trauma that these women brought to us. Their words were our words, and our deeply intimate, shared pain fueled our desire to hasten the healing process. Out of these shared moments of suffering, feminist theology was born.[21]

Sabiha and I attempted to provide answers to questions like: why did God let these women be raped and tortured? How can I believe in God? Should these women continue their pregnancies? Is it sinful to abort? Should they treat the child as a Muslim or not? How can they bear the shame and stigma of living in the patriarchal Bosnian society? We thus practiced feminist theology without being aware of it. The Islamic Community was not ready to deal with these issues, and the only good thing they had done regarding this was to issue the decree (*fatwa*) that "raped women should be considered our heroines,"[22] an important step, but only a symbolic one. These women needed a safe space to tell their stories, to receive advice and spiritual guidance, but the male leadership in the Islamic Community refused to discuss such issues. One of our professors at the Faculty of Islamic Studies, Enes Karić, criticized the Islamic Community at that time because it had not provided anything for these women, not even a small room where they could

---

[21] Zilka Spahić-Šiljak, 2013, "Do It and Name It: Feminist Theology and Peacebuilding in Bosnia and Herzegovina," *Journal for Feminist Studies in Religion* 29, no. 2, 178-186.
[22] Cockburn 1998, 180.

talk with someone.[23] For Sabiha and for me, the work we did with these women consisted of *ad hoc* theology while struggling to meet their immediate needs. Later, through our studies, we learned to put language to what was happening. However contextualized interpretations of Islam answered the women's immediate needs and were crucial for healing; they helped many women cope with their traumas and the social stigma attached to those traumas. Additionally, it helped them eventually become generators of change themselves.

Several times during our interview, Sabiha emphasized the relevance and importance of religion in the process of healing from such traumatic events:

> In a holistic, multidisciplinary approach, religion is recognized as a strong source of healing. Trauma destroys the relationship with oneself [and] the relationship with others, but the third pillar of Islam, which remains the strongest, is a faith in the universe, the relationship with God. This is something that helps people rebuild the other broken pillars.

Sabiha's creative potential in contextualizing the interpretation of Islam provided rape survivors a foundation for reconciling many of their inner conflicts as well as conflicts within their family and society. For example, the ritual of naming a child, which symbolizes connecting a child with God, was used as a way to re-connect families. The simple "rite of passage" ritual[24] became powerful in its contextualized and adjusted form. Whereas, in the

---

[23] Enes Karić, 1992, "Intervju: Mi smo sebi gori od četnika (Interview: We are ourselves worse than Četniks)," *BH Dani*, no. 3, quoted in Zilka Spahić-Šiljak, 2010, "Images of Women in Bosnia and Herzegovina, and Neighboring Countries, 1992-1995," in Faegheh Shirazi (ed.), *Muslim Women in War and Crisis: From Reality to Representation*, Austin: University of Texas Press, 223.
[24] W. Victor Turner, 1969, *The Ritual Process: Structure and Anti-structure*, Harmondsworth UK: Penguin.

Islamic tradition, men normally conduct the naming ritual,[25] Sabiha and I usually did so in this context. Having this ritual led by women was quite a new and refreshing approach and was accepted by all those coming to Medica Zenica.

Fig. 1-3

Sabiha spoke about the children who were conceived through rape. Often the mother's family did not want to hear about these children and would have no contact with them. When they visited their daughters at Medica Zenica, they absolutely rejected these children. But as Sabiha has emphasized, Medica Zenica's first priority was to strengthen the mother and validate her feelings.

---

[25] The naming ritual (Arabic, *aqiqa*) is a religious and cultural event. It begins with a recitation from the Qur'an, then recitation of blessings on the Prophet Muhammad (*salavat*), and then the key part when *ezan* is recited into the right and *ikamet* into the left ear of the baby. Then one says the name of the baby three times. "And then the child is passed from arm to arm of all present, to feel this, God's gift, this human being who will belong to this community." The ritual ends with a prayer (Arabic, *du'a*) during which all present turn their palms to the sky, following the person leading the ritual, and say Amen at the end.

After a woman suffered wartime rape, she would decide on her own what she wanted to do, whether she would keep the child or not. With the help of the naming ritual, Medica Zenica staff would soften families' emotions, and they would then begin to see the child as innocent, not sinful or guilty, but a deserving part of the community. Sabiha commented:

> When we organize the ceremony of naming a child and invite the family, we see a completely different picture. Emotions rise and those who yesterday were against the baby and could not see this baby as their grandchild, would suddenly change their opinion.

Sabiha became the godmother of some of these children and has been involved in their lives from their enrollment in primary school all the way through their enrollment in university. And today, those babies are successful students.

The naming ritual (in Arabic, 'aqiqa) is both a religious and a cultural event. It starts with reciting verses from the Qur'an, singing some blessings for the Prophet Muhammad, and then, crucially, reciting or singing the call to prayer (adhan) in the baby's right ear and the second call to prayer (iqama) in the left ear. After that, the baby is called by its name three times. "The child is [then] passed from one person to another, so that this new human being, who belongs to this community, can be accepted as a gift from God." The ritual is concluded with a special prayer of supplication (Arabic: du'a) where everybody turns their palms to the sky, following the leader of the ritual, and closing with an Amen (which means "so be it").

Sabiha noted that the naming ritual has one more special dimension; it not only brings together mother and child with the mother's family, but as she said, "It also brought us closer at Medica Zenica; no matter what our religious affiliations, we all looked forward to a naming day." The cooks at Medica Zenica, Nusreta and Meliha, prepared special meals and cakes, while Milenka organized a special present for the baby on behalf of

Medica Zenica. All the employees joined in the ritual. They would celebrate and give gifts to the newborn and the mother. In that atmosphere, the mother felt she received another chance at life with her child. Many of these women used that chance to accomplish incredible achievements in furthering their education and serving the community. Sabiha estimates that this kind of therapeutic work in Medica Zenica has transformed many of these women's lives and cites religion as very important in the process. She believes that if this mechanism were preserved, the following processes would be facilitated and become much easier for these women.

Power to Reconcile and Power to Divide

The role of religion was not only important in healing trauma wounds, but also in reconciling people after the war. Medica Zenica recognized the potential of religion from the beginning and continuously looked for opportunities to use that potential in peacebuilding and reconciliation with women of Catholic, Orthodox Christian, and Muslim religious affiliations. "If we speak of religion as a source that helps us in our daily lives and if we see what we have in common, what it is that brings us closer together, then religion can be very important in the process of reconciliation and forgiveness." The Medica Zenica team often spoke to groups of women about forgiveness, focusing specifically on whom these women needed to forgive and for what transgression. Sabiha explained that women often used to say: "I ask God to forgive me if I have sinned, and I too can forgive, in my own name, but others can chose to forgive or not to forgive." She concluded that every religion calls for forgiveness not in order to forget or condone the crime committed, but purely for the benefit of the person forgiving because it is so helpful in improving their quality of life.

For Sabiha, religion is helpful in bringing people together, but she notes that most people in BiH do not know much about their own religion, not to mention *other* religions. When she mentioned her school days in Vitez, she said that she knew about big religious feasts and brought cakes to celebrate, but she did not know much about her neighbor's faith. Her knowledge was superficial, and she did not have time to pay much attention to religion. And besides, at that time, such a practice would have been against the Marxist-oriented, atheistic teaching of the state.

Sabiha's was motivated to join the European Project for Interreligious Learning (EPIL), initiated by two Swiss women in 2001, and to learn more about other religions and how they might bring women together. Through this program, women of monotheistic religious traditions traveled together twice a year to spend a week in different countries in Europe and in Lebanon to learn from one another. During the third EPIL module, Sabiha realized how little knowledge people in BiH had about each other. She expressed with surprise: "We thought that we knew each other in BiH, and then two participants admitted that this was first time they had entered a church." This realization highlighted the fact that people were so divided it never even occurred to them to visit sites important to other religious denominations.

The EPIL program was also helpful for Sabiha in enriching her theological knowledge:

> I thought I knew so many things, but when I visited Beirut, entered the church, and heard the prayer in Arabic, I whispered to Teny [a Christian colleague], "I feel like I am in a mosque." ... I was moved, it was the same feeling of satisfaction, although the service was in an Orthodox Church in Beirut.

EPIL taught Sabiha a powerful lesson about how religion can successfully bring people together if they are willing to hear the message that God is one. Although prayers may be different, they all lead to God. Those not ready to hear this message tend to cling to their own religion without attempting to understand others.

The power of religion to bring people together and reconcile conflicts is evident. However, like other peacebuilders in this book,

Sabiha has experienced the power of religion to both divide and connect, to ravage and heal.[26] One of the ways religion divides BiH society is through religious instruction in public schools, introduced during the middle of the war. Over 95 percent of students now attend religion classes,[27] and while one would expect students to be oriented toward peace between religions, the younger generation seems more close-minded and militant than their parents. The parents fear assimilation and feel safer in homogenized communities; therefore they choose this confessional religious instruction for their children in order to create a more tight-knit and exclusive group.[28] For Sabiha, as a parent and a professional, the introduction of religious instruction during the war was problematic. Religion was greatly misused during the war and might be why it has not generally served to bring peace and reconciliation in this context. Sabina also brought up an important point about the structure and methodology of instruction:

> I think somehow what we studied in churches and mosques ... was simply transferred to schools ... and it actually divided children and taught them that the other is not welcome or acceptable. I would prefer religious instruction that was objective and neutral, in order to bring children together, to learn about Islam *and* Christianity ... What's happening now is segregation; [it is] especially [problematic] for minorities in areas where you have majority ethnic groups ... the minority child is excluded, labeled, and marked.

Today, Sabiha lives in Zenica, where Bosniacs/Muslims are the majority, but she realizes that the minorities will experience exclusion, especially in the classroom, where they will be

---

[26] R. Scott Appleby, 2000, *The Ambivalence of the Sacred: Religion, Violence, and Reconciliation*, Lanham, MD: Rowman and Littlefield.
[27] *Podijeljene škole u BiH*, 2009, Sarajevo: UNICEF (http://www.skolegijum.ba/static/pdf/4ebbccdd4d97a.pdf, accessed April 15, 2013).
[28] Ibid.

segregated during religious classes. She suspects that this might produce tension and identity crises for the children themselves. Comprehensive religious education that brings children together to learn about all religions is something Sabiha wants for her own children. She has argued that it would teach children more about their neighbors and would reduce their misinterpretation of other religions. Today, many misuse and hide behind their religions for fear of losing power. She pointed out the phenomenon of "two schools under one roof,"[29] established in the cantons in FBiH where Croat/Catholic and Bosniac/Muslim children go to the same school but do not participate in any activities together. Here, children do not communicate at all. Some of Sabiha's relatives attend these ethnically divided schools in Vitez because they do not have a choice:

> It is terrible, they don't even have lunch together … on top of the fact that they get different religious instruction … how can we say that we are preparing our youth for a better future … if we have fear and don't get to know the people we fear … It creates great division. We need to be able to work together and study together.

Sabiha is completely aware of the power of religion to both reconcile and divide, that it depends on the way religion is taught, interpreted, and lived as well as whether it serves daily political goals and is nurtured for nationalism and ethno-politics.[30] She considers that its role should be to "facilitate life and make it easier." She believes that religion is meant to help people, not imprison them. Religious communities were not involved in

---

[29] Saša Madacki and Mia Karamehić (eds.), 2012, *Dvije škole pod jednim krovom* (Two Schools under One Roof), Sarajevo: Center for Human Rights, University of Sarajevo and the Alumni Association of the Center for Interdisciplinary Postgraduate Studies (http://www.shl.ba/index.php?option=com_content&view=article&id=71:studija-o-segregaciji-u-obrazovanju-pod-nazovom-qdvije-kole-pod-jednim-krovom, accessed April 15, 2013).
[30] Asim Mujkić, 2008, *We, the Citizens of Ethnopolis*, Sarajevo: Center for Human Rights, University of Sarajevo.

peacebuilding after the war, as Sabiha confirmed, although today the situation is a little bit better. There are some imams and priests who collaborate with Medica Zenica, for example, but their efforts are mostly individual efforts, not institutionally structured programs orientated toward peacebuilding. Sabiha was, however, reluctant to generalize, claiming that she does not have enough information to speak about other religious communities. She knows that in the Islamic community, women are still excluded from decision-making positions and do not have opportunities to contribute more to peacebuilding; she is hopeful that with time this will change.

Empowering Women with(out) Religion

Whatever other people think ... I cannot separate religion from my personal and daily life.

Sabiha is one of the rare Muslim women engaged in public life who bears her civic and religious identities in a harmonious and complementary dynamic that empowers her to be a responsible believer and citizen. Although she never emphasizes her religious identity in conversation, it is visible in her fashionable, colorful *hijab*. As a *hijabi* feminist who rejects a monolithic feminist identification,[31] she perceives Islam as an empowering and comforting religion that makes her life more productive, purposeful, and happy. She wants her Muslim feminist activism to be acknowledged as legitimate feminist work among others, and not be told what feminism is.

Additionally, she observes the basic pillars of Islam, but follows her own interpretations on many issues, listening to her inner voice for justice, freedom, and equality:

I live my faith in everything I do in my life. For me, that is what faith is. We facilitate our lives through faith, not make them harder.

---

[31] Cockburn 2013, 30.

> No matter how the other *'ulama* [scholars] see it, with all due respect to them, I gave myself the right, as I give it to myself today, not to separate religion from myself as an individual and from my everyday life.

That attitude comes out of her resistance to the predominant patriarchal understanding of religion in BiH that discriminates against women and withholds women's basic rights. Although her own family encouraged and supported her education, she noticed throughout her education (and work) that many women did not have these same rights and opportunities in their families. They were especially oppressed in religious communities. Her family was not happy when she chose to go to the religious high school in Sarajevo, because during the socialist period, diplomas from religious schools were not recognized. They worried about her future because of the stereotype that most children attending religious schools had been rejected by other schools or came from low-income, rural families. In Sabiha's case, however, it was quite the opposite. Her family could afford her education in other schools and she was always one of the best students. Even her homeroom teacher in high school tried to convince her to give up religious studies for physics and mathematics. But Sabiha had her dream and was motivated to learn more about Islam:

> I was interested in gaining more knowledge and religious understanding. I was interested in the status of women in religion, how religion was often used to oppress women. In a traditional context, men readily interpret Islam in the way *they* find appropriate, particularly for different behaviors and attitudes toward women, speaking in the name of Islam.

However, she realized during the war that her parents were right; with the diploma of Islamic Studies she could not get a job unless she was willing to accept rules she did not believe in or take a position that was beneath her educational background and skills.

She felt pressure from both the Islamic Community, which did not have and still does not have any plan for the employment of female theologians, and the larger community, which was not ready to accept a *hijabi* woman in the public sphere.

Her first such experience was with the Arab humanitarian organizations that came to BiH during the war, stating that they were there to help people, not to use religion to impose rules and colonize local brothers and sisters. In her job interview, they expressed displeasure with her *hijab*, asking her to change the way she wears it, and insisted on their own rules about the style in which a *hijab* is worn—basically they asked her to accept another interpretation of Islam. This was hard for her to process; she disagreed but also needed a job in order to support her family, including her sick father and two absent brothers. "God what should I do?" she anxiously requested, and then her inner voice reminded her: "It's war. I did not die. They did not kill me ... I would rather die hungry, but remain my own person ... I do not want someone to change me against my will." She refused the job, and looking back, she is proud of her decision, which has helped her to support others in maintaining their own identities and choices. Freedom of choice, especially in religious matters, is crucial for Sabiha, because she believes God cannot be worshiped out of fear, but only out of love and freedom. She learned this from the Qur'an (2, 256) a long time ago. Freedom of choice motivated her to challenge the post-war, ethno-nationally homogenized communities in Zenica-Doboj Canton.

In struggling to provide freedom and protection for women, she expected the same freedom and protection for herself. But as a *hijab*-wearing Muslim woman, she faced obstacles from Muslims and non-Muslims alike. She gave some examples from her field work: "People have a bias when they see a woman with a *hijab*: they automatically place her in a certain box and they begin judging her without any real communication, contact, or dialogue." Sabiha was determined to have freedom and to be respected for her identity.

> Unfortunately, there were some difficult moments. If I weren't the way I am I wouldn't have been able to handle it … but I heard some people, including some women, say: "Who is this one with a *hijab*, why is she lecturing us and playing smart; she doesn't belong here. Why would a woman with a *hijab* be in the NGO sector?"

Fig. 1-4

Sabiha did not let this discourage her, however, but allowed it to motivate her, because she believes that the best way to change these perceptions was for people to get to know her and to have a chance to dispose of their prejudices about religion. She has followed this practice in municipality meetings in which she had to negotiate with the majority Croats/Catholics, who rarely had had contact with a woman in *hijab*. Her decision to take the first step, to knock on the doors of these communities, helped soften their attitudes and eventually allied them to Medica Zenica: "Through communication and contact with the people, you actually help them admit that they do not want to take this exclusionary approach."

Her battles to overcome the tensions related to her Muslim identity in the community were empowering for her personal and professional life. The women she has worked with, particularly those in rural areas, have also experienced discrimination, especially in obtaining equal rights with men. Male children once had priority in education and in some remote villages this is still, unfortunately, the case. Furthermore, women in rural areas do not inherit family property; instead it is given to their male siblings.[32] Sabiha was aware of these cases before the war and remains unhappy that women are still subordinated in their families and communities:

> In terms of acquiring material goods, from the question of whom to build a house for [to] the question of whom to buy a car for, the man always comes first. In terms of inheritance ... it was common for a female child or sister to renounce her inheritance in favor of her brother, without asking herself what she would do tomorrow if, God forbid, some unforeseen situation occurred, or if she were divorced, and so on. Where would she go and what would she do.

In retrospect, giving such power to men has nourished violent relationships. When a woman gets married she is less privileged and often suffers because she is economically dependent. "He puts food on your table. There is always someone else putting food on your table," Sabiha explained, raising her voice passionately, knowing well the extent of these women's subordination. She is aware that male siblings forget their sisters, who by God's rules and worldly laws, also have a right to property; but brothers have

---

[32] Zilka Spahić-Šiljak, 2010, *Women, Religion, and Politics. The Impact of Religious Interpretations of Judaism, Christianity, and Islam on the Status of Women in Public Life and Politics*, Sarajevo: IMIC, Center for Interdisciplinary Postgraduate Studies and the TPO Foundation, 216-24.

renounced this. This practice therefore disadvantages women without any justification, argument, or obligation for men to help.

Sabiha associated this type of relationship with the traditional cultural approach to gender roles as well as with patriarchal religious interpretations. Little is known about why such an approach has been adopted and passed down from generation to generation, without referencing the relevant religious sources. When sacred texts are used, it is typically done incorrectly, or the words may be taken out of context or removed from the logic of the core religious message.[33] Sabiha is aware of the misreading of the Qur'an both by ordinary people who do not have a basic knowledge of it, and by imams and scholars who are not gender sensitive, but perpetuate interpretations from the past that do not correspond to the contemporary context. "Being gender sensitive means being able to give up some privileges. Many find it difficult, because they are taught to have privileges," says Sabiha. The privileged position given to men in religious communities has preserved a tradition that rejects the positive teachings of the Prophet Muhammad toward women. This selective tradition is the most successful tool used by male imams and scholars to keep their positions of power and maintain women's silence and invisibility.

Sabiha, however, is anything but a silent woman. She knows the power of her voice and she uses it against the subordination of women in order to promote their rights. She is against interpretations of religion that intimidate believers, such as "'don't do that, it will make you a poor believer,' 'do not do that, God will punish you,' and so on. For me, religion is not that, it cannot be that, but people often use it for their own interests." Her understanding of Islam as well as the way she lives her life are in compliance with her role as a human rights activist. She does not

---

[33] Amina Wadud, 1999, *Qur'an and Woman: Rereading the Sacred Text from a Woman's Perspective*, Oxford: Oxford University Press, 3.

find a tension between the two. They inform each other and help her to be a better believer and citizen.

Fig. 1-5 Courtesy of Pravo Ljudski Film Festival, Photo by Vanja Cerimagic

It is important to note that Sabiha works in a secular NGO run by women and uses her authority to advocate for the enforcement of secular laws such as the Gender Equality Law (2003), the Law on Domestic Violence (2005), and many other legal documents and policies relevant to women's rights. She views living in a secular country as the best framework because it provides freedom for all, believers and non-believers alike. She does not want to help only Muslim women, but all women in BiH. Setting an example as an observant believer and a human rights activist, she wants to teach Muslim women that it is possible to be both. She finds it important to dare to imagine a better world where everything is possible if fears and prejudices are removed. This is not easy, she says, but it is worthwhile and fulfilling. As a true leader, she is able to see beyond the norms of her context and culture.[34]

The Work Must Go On!

Sabiha has had moments when she felt tired and thought she was abandoned and betrayed by people in her local community. There were moments when it seemed she faced too many obstacles in her work. At these times, she says she seeks answers for why she was unable to help a certain individual. But she cannot turn away from the problem:

> At times, I thought this was not my only obligation and duty. And then I reminded myself that if we as individuals give up, there will not be any help at the moment when people need it, so then I go back to work again.

She has not allowed anybody or anything to defeat or discourage her. A deep sense of responsibility has motivated her to keep going. Helping those in need she sees as her duty. She mentioned at the beginning of the interview that she is still investing in her own education, having attended continuing education courses and master's programs to improve her skills and thus provide better services.

There are several reasons why she remains strong and confident in her work. First, she is consistently thinking on behalf of women in need who are not equipped to successfully advocate for themselves. She seeks people with expertise and experience to support them, to teach, encourage, and help them reach out to the police, courts, prosecutors, social workers, donors, and even to their own families. In her work with domestic violence and rape, Sabiha knows that because these women typically have low self-esteem they need much support to exit the cycle of violence. The smiles

---

[34] Mary Lou Décosterd, 2013, *How Women Are Transforming Leadership: Four Key Traits Powering Success*, Santa Barbara, CA: Praeger, 27.

and relief women show when this happens are a continuing motivation to Sabiha. She sees God's presence in these women and believes the best way to serve God is to serve people in need.

The second important driving force is Sabiha's wish to transcend the divisions in BiH that claim people of different ethnicities cannot live together. She believes people are in general more similar than they are different, and that they just need to communicate their similarities: "Maybe some people find it easier to say we are different and don't need to invest in ourselves, but I rather look for our similarities ... Questioning my [own] position allows me to grow psychologically, and helps strengthen my virtues." For Sabiha, although her displacement to Zenica has had many disadvantages, it has allowed her to build a new life for her family and for many other women who have needed her support. Displacement can provide space for new relationships and identities that need not follow the often artificial divisions of BiH society.

The third motivation is the economic and political empowerment of women, especially in rural areas where they are socially excluded and less privileged than women in urban areas. Therefore, she speaks often about the UN Security Council Resolution 1325 on women, peace, and security, the ideals of which were already present in BiH before the UN resolution was enacted, in 2000. Women's organizations work to promote peace, often by empowering women economically and politically to provide for their families and gain decision-making positions. Sabiha and her team work closely with many NGOs in BiH to increase women's political participation. They organize street demonstrations, educational opportunities, and advocacy events to help women step forward and take the lead.

For Sabiha, as long as there is a need, she will continue. It is through her journey that she wins other women and men to her side—to the path of equality, peace, openness, and acceptance, despite the many imposed divisions in BiH.

Conclusion

Young Sabiha began her path of peace work early and has become the most well-known female peacebuilder in BiH. After an incredible journey at the start of the war and beginning a refugee's life as the head of her family, she found her peacebuilding vocation at Medica Zenica. She never accepted the change that took place from her previously "normal" life alongside her Catholic and Orthodox Christian neighbors to the new life harshly marked by ethnic divisions, and she has worked persistently against the changes. Sabiha has been involved with Medica Zenica, the first feminist NGO in BiH, for the full extent of its work, which most notably has included supporting survivors of rape—empowering them, helping them re-establish relations with their families and community, and advocating for their legal rights. As a Muslim believer, she sees faith as a crucial part in building peace, from healing wounds to reconciling people. She has been doing this persistently, showing that one can simultaneously be a faithful believer and a responsible citizen sensitive to the problems of other people. Interpreting and contextualizing verses from the Qur'an in her work has provided guidance for many of the women she has helped.

Sabiha has also played a key role in raising gender sensitivity in BiH, especially at decision-making levels, via networks of actors and institutions involved in women's issues. It is important for her to ensure justice and protection for each person who survived violence and other traumatic experiences. Thus, she has concentrated her efforts on establishing cooperative networks between governmental institutions and nongovernmental organizations dealing with these issues. Her efforts and commitment together with those of her colleagues have made Medica Zenica a recognizable and respectable public voice.

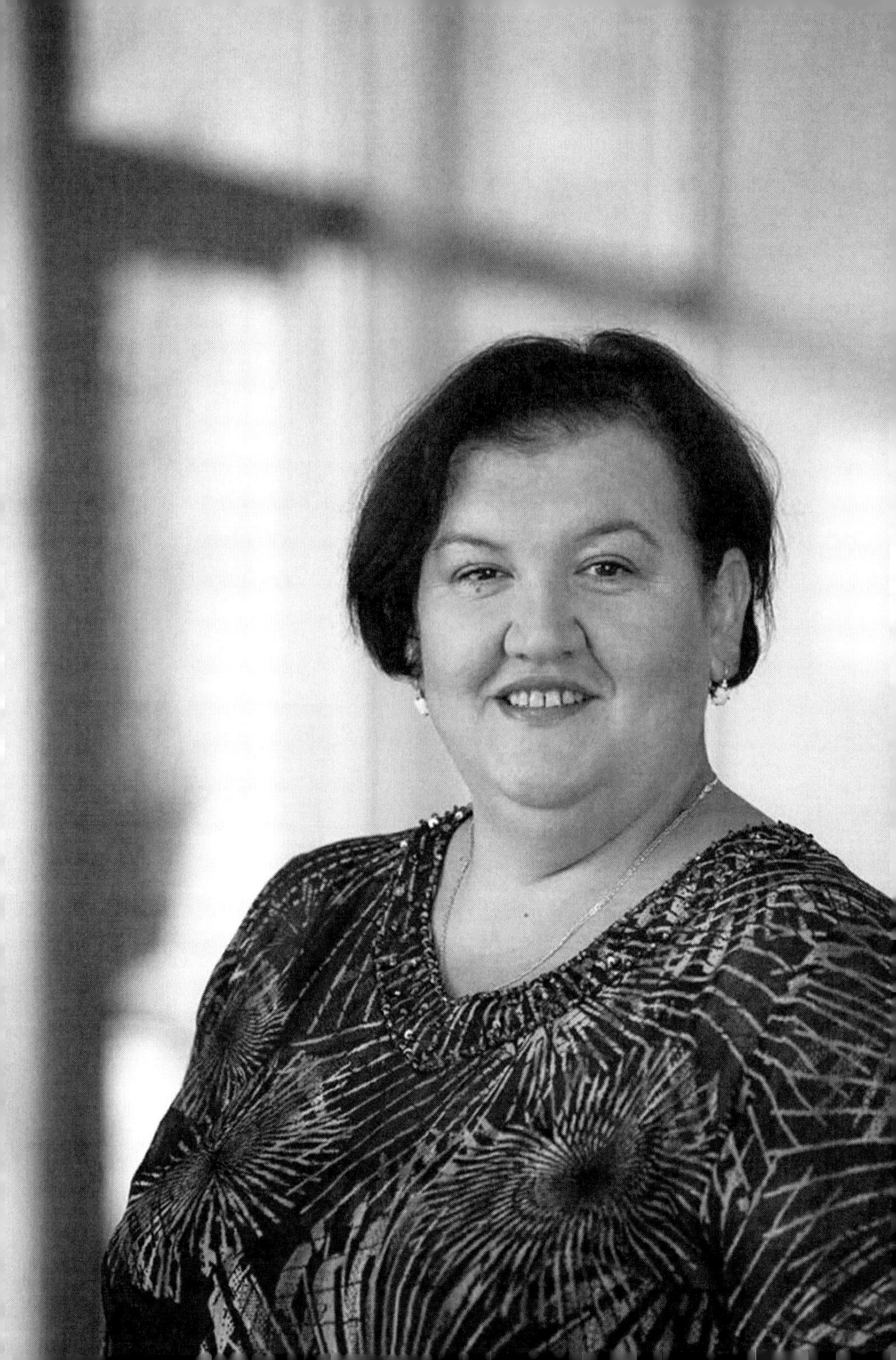

STORYTWO

I BROUGHT NEIGHBOR TO NEIGHBOR

DANKA ZELIĆ

Biography

Danka was born in 1973 in Livno, in southwestern Bosnia and Herzegovina. As the youngest of six siblings she was quite pampered, and in addition to her parents, her older sisters Stjepanka and Mirjana had the most significant influence on her upbringing. Her father was her great supporter and role model, as well as authority, whose word was respected and obeyed, but her mother's care, love, and merit-based principles shaped Danka's peace work. She was brought up as a practicing Catholic and this was very important to her identity and activity. When the war began in 1992, she moved briefly to Split, where she studied at the Faculty of Law, and then to Zagreb and later Germany.

Soon thereafter, however, in 1993, she returned to Livno, continued her education at the Police Academy in Zagreb, and in 1996 got a job in Bosansko Grahovo. This is where she met her husband Miroslav, also with the police, who supported her efforts to assist returnees. Poverty, hopelessness, and the government's lack of understanding of the needs of the returnees prompted Danka to try to provide additional help. Together with her associates, she registered a new organization called Women Citizens Association Grahovo in 2000 for this purpose. She actively worked on reconciliation issues to bring people together in order to overcome their fear and hatred and to provide humanitarian assistance, particularly for the returnees in rural areas. "Toward the person," regardless of nationality, was Danka's guiding principle in peace work, inspiring her to visit people in remote villages, to see how they lived, and to discover how she could help them. Her neighbors became a reflection of her humanity and taking care of them prevailed over all other matters and tasks. In 2002, she quit her job in the police force and dedicated herself to the work for the Women Citizens Association.

During this time, she obtained a degree in agronomy in order to professionally address the needs of the returnees who were starting or rebuilding farms. She focused her attention specifically on the empowerment of women and their active participation in public and political life, and on dialogue among the divided people of BiH. Today, she lives and works in Livno and Bosansko Grahovo. She says she is always on the road, and it can be rightfully said that she is forging a road of kindness, understanding, and peace.

Introduction

> The notion of peace work to me represents a big bubble filled with many smaller bubbles. ... All the smaller bubbles consist of people who deserve the care of others. That, for me, is peace work.

Danka's definition of peacebuilding as care for others is crucial to her work. She is the youngest peacebuilder in the group of eleven women to be interviewed about their lives in BiH. Despite her youth, she has become known as a selfless guardian of returnees. She brings with her fifteen years of rich peace work experience in southwestern BiH. Instead of keeping her stable, salaried, permanent appointment in a police force, which filled a very important role during the post-war period, she decided to explore the unknown by helping returnees who were Serb/Orthodox Christians. Her work has restored their dignity and faith in goodness and justice.

I have known Danka for a long time, and we have worked together on various women's human rights initiatives. She has chosen to work in a very remote and isolated area of BiH called Bosanko Grahovo, an undeveloped region with an aging population. It is hard to imagine living and working in this area for a long period of time; most human rights activists visit it only briefly and cannot imagine staying longer. It is often referred to as a land forgotten by everyone. Danka has remained there and with great optimism she has built peace there.

When I called to ask Danka if I could interview her, she paused for a while and then asked: "Why?" I explained that people in her local community believe that she is a peacebuilder and someone who has done much work in that region on reconciliation. Hearing that, she was excited and confirmed the interview. Her husband was also thrilled that people recognized her work and could not wait until she came home to tell him the details of the interview. She had already been working there for years without documenting what she had accomplished, and she knew that the next generation would need to learn from her and her fellow female peacebuilders' work in BiH.

After she had finished the narrative part of the interview, she asked: "Is this enough? Is that what you expected me to say? I do not know what else to say." She was more comfortable with guided questions, although it was up to her to decide what she wanted to share. Danka struggles like many other women in BiH to change the imposed suppression of women's voices that dates from the time of their family upbringing, and today she is aware that women do much more than what is advertised. I was impressed by the passionate solidarity and care that she exhibited, qualities that shaped her character and made her sensitive to the needs of others. Her mission is simple but full of impact: bringing neighbors together.

My Neighbors are a Mirror of My Humanity

> Peacebuilding for me means that I reconciled two neighbors who will continue living together and supporting each other, and their children will use the same bus to go to school. Peacebuilding means that for me.

Danka's story is embedded with the message of bringing one person into dialogue with another person and about the reconciliation of neighbors divided under the threat of violence, expelled from their homes, and needing help and support for coexistence and survival in impoverished post-war BiH. Her ethics of care[1] is reflected in her determination to help returnees, despite the resistance of the local authorities. She started by visiting villages of returnees. With sadness in her eyes, she talked about those days. She was traveling around Bosansko Grahovo city looking for returnee Serbs who needed help. People were suspicious at the beginning, but then, as Danka narrates, her kind words and honest approach would open their hearts and the doors of their homes: "You sit down with people, and it takes time, and then they make coffee and start to talk, ... and they will accept your help, and they start crying. The smallest thing is helpful to them. 'Would you be able to bring some medicine?' they would ask." Danka's answer was yes. She started with small things—bringing medicine, driving them to hospitals, helping to get new ID documents, food, and clothes—but she ended up re-building their houses. Her work with returnees in Bosansko Grahovo arose out of

---

[1] Carol Gilligan, 1983, *In a Different Voice: Psychological Theory and Women's Development*, Cambridge, MA: Harvard University Press; Nel Noddings, 2002, *Starting at Home: Caring and Social Policy*, Berkeley, CA: University of California Press; Kathleen Barry, 1992, "Toward a Theory of Women's Biography," in Theresa Iles (ed.), *All Sides of the Subjects: Women and Biography*, New York: Teachers' College Press, Columbia University; Sara Ruddick, 1989, *From Maternal Thinking: Toward a Politics of Peace,* Boston, MA: Beacon Press; Fiona Robinson, 2011, *The Ethics of Care: A Feminist Approach to Human Security*, Philadelphia, PA: Temple University Press.

her desire to help those who had lost everything, and despite their suffering, she wanted them to return to their town, where they were still not welcome.

In 1997, when the first Serb refugees applied to return to their pre-war homes in locations where they used to be a majority,[2] most of them were elderly women and men. They wanted to find out what was left of their homes and whether they could re-build their lives there. Danka could not remain silent as Croatian authorities continued to prevent certain people from returning. "You know what you're up against ... when a poor man desperately needs help, and you know that the institution will not help him and [yet] that poor man keeps coming back, but there is no help, because we know how it [the system] is structured." She could not sit back and watch these people be rejected and excluded just because they belonged to a different ethnic group. The pain, illness, and loss the Serb refugees experienced here during the war moved her to act. Elisabeth Porter points out: "A compassionate person attends to the sufferer's interests, through listening, heeding, and judging perceptively in order to discern how best to respond."[3] So Danka did the same, watching people who came back to their hearths, who came back carrying their belongings in plastic bags, the same way they had left. She was moved that most people were elderly. "They did not have anything and were frightened. They were so afraid to approach us, to ask for any information. It took them a year to ask how they could get papers."

---

[2] According to the census of 1991, Serbs were the majority (94.9%), then Croats (2.8%), Others (2.2%), and Muslims (0.1%).
[3] Elisabeth J. Porter, 2007, *Peacebuilding Women in International Perspective*, London: Routledge, 103.

Fig. 2-1

Post-war Bosansko Grahovo was, according to Danka, "completely destroyed, devastated ... only the Police station and bakery were functioning and there were only one hundred or two hundred citizens." Many would refer to Bosansko Grahovo at that time as a spectral city that was not only physically destroyed, but also completely devastated, without its vital life functions and infrastructure—like a ghost city. Nobody, including her family, could understand why Danka would return to a war zone to work with refugees and displaced persons instead of staying in Germany, pursuing her education and living in safety. But Danka could not stand to watch her people suffer. She could not stand to watch from outside her country.

The turning point in her life[4] was experiencing the suffering of her fellow Yugoslavs when they revealed their stories of exodus;

---

[4] Norman Denzin, 1989, *Interpretive Biography*, Thousand Oaks, CA: Sage, 70.

this made her return to Livno. She started working for an amateur radio center to connect families in BiH with the outside world. At that time in 1993, phone lines did not work and the only way to communicate was by radio. Danka's peacebuilding started in the middle of the war. The best she could do at the time was to enable communication between families and friends who were stuck in various parts of BiH that were controlled by different armies and ethnically homogenized governments.

She also pursued her studies in the Police Academy in Zagreb during this time. In 1996, she graduated and got her first appointment in Bosansko Grahovo. "The very thought of me in Bosansko Grahovo was a shock for my mom. She thought I would go there for a couple of months, I would understand that this was not for me, and then I would return. ... However, she was wrong, God rest her soul." Her family worried about her in Bosansko Grahovo's difficult political and economic conditions after the war; they thought the situation there would not be conducive to a new female police officer's success. Unsatisfied with the life expected by her family in safe and secure Germany, Danka missed the spirit and the soul of BiH, as reflected in her interaction with people: "There is [in Germany] no communion as we had it in my city, there are no friends. ... Before [the war] it was nice to know that I could visit somebody in her or his home, sit with my friends Marina and Ilija." Building relationships in Germany was hard for Danka due to some of the social norms and requirements. While in BiH, she could simply knock on a friend's or neighbor's door or call to say: "I am coming over for coffee." She drew attention to local practices of neighborliness (komšiluk)[5] that survived the war and

---

[5] Tone Bringa, 1995, *Being Muslim the Bosnian Way: Identity and Community in a Central Bosnian Village*, New Haven, CT: Princeton University Press, Princeton, NJ; Paula M. Pickering, 2007, *Peacebuilding in the Balkans: A View from the Ground Floor*, Ithaca, NY: Cornell University Press.

are important channels for peace.[6] Danka did, however, emphasize some positive aspects of life in Germany, like successful businesses and organizations, the rule of law, and just treatment by others, attributes she tried to bring into her community. As a young person she recognized the values of both societies and wanted to upgrade her life in Yugoslavia by incorporating some positive achievements from the west, without abandoning the activity of nurturing relationships.

Her family's idea of solidarity was conditioned by self-protection and security, while Danka's perspective on solidarity was to help those in immediate need, no matter whether they lived in a dangerous place or belonged to a different ethnic group. Her vision and capacity for re-building lives and imagining a better society for the powerless returnees in Bosansko Grahovo motivated Danka in her work. As Lederach explains about such peacebuilding work,

> Perhaps the greatest mystery of peace … is rooted in the courage of people and communities to be and live vulnerably in the face of fear and threat, and ultimately to find therein that human security is not tied primarily to the quantity or size of weapons, the height or thickness of the wall that separates them, nor to the power of imposition.[7]

Danka's determination and deep faith that she could make a difference helped slightly to change her parents' perspective and soften their protective attitudes. She would come home saying that everything was fine, that people were normal but needed help. She would tell them that the people were in such a bad situation with nothing to eat, sleeping under blankets and plastic sheets. "That changed their minds. They started making packages with personal

---

[6] Julianne Funk, forthcoming, "Women and the Spirit of Suživot in Postwar Bosnia-Herzegovina," in Nadija Furlan Štante and Marjana Harcet (eds.), *Spirituality of Balkan Women,* Koper, Slovenia: *Annales.*
[7] John Paul Lederach, 2005, *The Moral Imagination: The Art and Soul of Building Peace,* Oxford: Oxford University Press, 63.

items and clothing. They brought stuff from Germany for me to distribute throughout Grahovo. I managed to lure them over to my side somehow."

Her family still expected her to return to a less challenging place such as Livno where Catholic Croats are the majority or to Germany where she could easily become a citizen. However, she had made her choice to be with these people and stand for their rights and dignity. She also had support from a colleague in the police force, the officer who later became her husband. Signaling her intention to stay in Bosansko Grahovo, her family finally accepted her decision. In the beginning, her husband also worried about her, knowing that she might be in jeopardy from the local Croatian authorities who did not like her supporting the returnee Serb population: "At first, he kind of tried to restrain me, saying, "Dana, that's not necessary, don't be so loud about it, don't do this, don't do that", but very soon he realized that we have to work honestly, that we must help." He always stood by her, but he was afraid of revenge.

Fig. 2-2

Danka said that right after the war the government imposed a sort of "socio-political rule" to "discipline citizens," which more or less forbade them to communicate with the returnees, to give them any information, or even to greet them:

> We had to keep quiet. However, I could not keep quiet. ... I can't say that it's safe for them to go to a village ... if I know that there are mines in that village. I can't tell the group that came from Banja Luka or from somewhere in Serbia, who suffered the long hours on the bus ... it's safe for you to go there. The very thought that something might happen to them, I don't know, my conscience would bother me for as long as I live, and I would not be able to live with it.

Danka refused "discipline," she was guided by her heart and acted according to her conscience to protect people. While her husband rationalized their decisions, estimating the consequences of their activities, Danka's vision and persistence were stronger, overcoming the threats and difficulties. She is a leader who listens to her intuition. Giten Dyhan notes that "to see life from the perspective of intuition is to have vision ... [it] is like looking at life from the summit of the mountain, whereas seeing life only from the perspective of intellect is like looking at life from the foot of the mountain."[8]

Danka's welcoming words to returnees were accompanied with basic household goods, important especially to women who perceived her efforts also as a message re-initiating relationship. Various donors helped her provide for the basic needs of returnees and very often she delivered the goods personally: "For each woman I brought bedding and blankets, as a symbol of welcome."

Being outspoken about returnees' struggles did bring Danka problems with her superiors in the police force, especially when she

---

[8] Swami Dyhan Giten, 2012, "On Intuition and Healing," excerpt from "The Silent Whisperings of the Heart—An Introduction to Giten's Approach to Life," www.selfgrowth.com/articles/GITEN2.html (accessed September 2, 2013).

accompanied returnees to their village. "I was constantly interrogated in meetings [with the police] where they always asked me: 'why you?' They sent me on some assignment, to be as far away from it all as possible." In addition, a part of the community considered her to be a traitor: "They labeled me as 'that woman who is against us' but it did not bother me. There were more people who knew my true self, who know what I did for these people. I do not regret it and I would do it again." She was pressured to stop what she was doing, and some local authorities even tried to make her an outcast, but she was convinced that she was doing the right thing.

Danka could not remain silent and openly said, in front of her community, that her people had committed crimes and that her ethnic group's leadership was to blame for the fact that many people had nothing after the war. This was her moral choice, to speak up, and it was difficult because she had to criticize her own community, which was in power at that time.[9] Her moral imagination[10] empowered her to risk stepping outside the imposed "ethnic box" of her community. It took great courage to stand up and say:

> People did not burn their own houses. ... I openly said that the Croatian army did that. I don't care if that sounds fair [or not], but I said it: my people did that. I don't know if anyone was ever held accountable for that, or [if they] will ever be held accountable, but many lives were lost, many have experienced trauma, a complete population was forced out of that area.

It took incredible courage for Danka to go against the local authorities whose aim of ethnic cleansing and of homogenized communities was undermined by the returnees' arrival in Bosansko Grahovo, with Danka's support. Her inner sense of justice, duty,

---

[9] David Hampton, 2012, "The Fog of Religious Conflict," *Harvard Divinity Bulletin* 41, 56.
[10] Lederach 2005, 62.

honesty, and compassion[11] was stronger than any threats, but she also relied on her husband and his authority in the city as part of the police force. Many others were afraid to reflect upon their own actions and were more inclined to "look at the speck of dust in the other's eye" (Matthew 7:3).

In many situations, Danka put others before herself and her family. She exposed herself to danger and criticism from the community and was at risk of being expelled from her community. However, she had a deep sense of moral conviction. She could not accept her neighbors' ostracism when they had lived together before the war: "I was confused as to why our community did not make any progress. ... Why? Because somebody divided us into Serbs and Croats?" Danka remembered her neighborhood in Livno, where she knew and was friends with her Muslim and Orthodox Christian neighbors, visited them in their homes, and was familiar with their customs. After the war, she would not accept the imposed ethnic divisions and life in isolation. She decided that her first step was to visit her neighbor returnees, to help them rebuild their lives and settle down into their homes, and to bring neighbors together again.

Genuine Feminism in the Power of Care and Compassion

> In my opinion, women are much more involved in peace work; they do it in a much more efficient and better way. [This is] probably due to their persistence and endurance. What I discovered through my work is that many men give up at the first hurdle; they say that it is impossible to solve a problem; they give up easily. They perceive it all superficially. However, women are persistent and we want to convince other people ... that someone's life is at stake.

---

[11] Porter, 2007; Dona Pankhurst, 2009, *Gendered Peace: Women's Struggles for Post-war Justice and Reconciliation*, London: Routledge; Uma Narayan, 1995, "Colonialism and Its Others: Considerations on Rights and Care Discourses," *Hypatia*, 10, no. 2, 133-40.

In describing her own experience of peacebuilding, Danka gives most of the credit to women, saying that they have demonstrated more patience and persistence in finishing peace work than men, who initiate something but do not have enough patience to complete it. This is exactly one of the characteristics of the IDEA-based leadership concept: directive force,[12] focused on outcomes. In her marriage and family, Danka was courageous and perseverant. She says that although she learned this from her mother, her father also helped instill in her a great work ethic. Her father was a *gastarbeiter* (guest worker) in Germany, which was a common occupation in that region at that time. He would come home once or twice a year with money for the family, which meant they had to earn the rest for the family budget. Thus, a strong work ethic was encouraged in her family:

> I remember when my father used to come home for Christmas and he'd say to my mom—he called her Fila although her name was Ilinka—he'd ask her, "Fila ... how much did you and the children earn?" And we lived off of that—oh, I don't know how—agriculture and from selling handmade goods, but it was not even close to what my father could earn in Germany.

Danka's father was the authority in their home, but her mother was closer to the children. Danka said that her mother was always there for her children: caring for them, nurturing and supporting them with love and compassion. Her father loved them but was seen as a distant authority that should be obeyed. Although she described her mother as a tender and fragile person, Danka thinks that she inherited her rebellious nature from her mother: "My mother was born into a wealthy *bey* (aristocratic) family, and got married without her parents' consent to my father who was from a working-class family." She thinks that they were raised not to pay

---

[12] Mary Lou Décosterd, 2013, *How Women Are Transforming Leadership: Four Key Traits Powering Success*, Santa Barbara, CA: Praeger, 47.

attention to wealth and material values: "Love is important; it is essential to respect each other, and everything else will come to you in one way or another." Danka believes that we should evaluate people by their merits and not by their family backgrounds, and she pointed out that "this kind of morality should come first and that it doesn't really matter *how much*, but *with whom* you'll share things and be happy." She applied these lessons not only in her family, for example, deciding to help her sister-in-law with her five children after her brother's death, but also in her community. Such maternal care is, as Sara Ruddick points out, part of a "rationality of care"[13] that goes beyond family. Danka's close neighbor was also a person in need and as long as there was need, she felt she should keep working.

Fig. 2-3

---

[13] Ruddick 1989, 46.

Danka's sense of compassion came from the moral obligation she felt to stand for the justice and dignity of people outside her Croatian ethnic group.[14] She perceived the women she worked with as great human beings who had endured the worst of situations. With her great faith in women she glorified them and their contributions, both in their families, and in their community-building efforts. Danka wishes not to essentialize these caring qualities as exclusively "feminine,"[15] but her experience showed her that women's courage was greater than men's and that women were the ones who initiated and completed peace work.

Nevertheless, most of the women in rural areas were completely subordinated to their husbands. Danka has always tried to address the woman first when she would come into a household. A woman welcomes her, makes some coffee, talks to her, but when decisions need to be made, she becomes silent. Danka recalled that "when I said 'you need to come to a seminar, [or] to go on a trip,' [or] 'I want to donate some cattle to you, but first you have to attend training,' that's when the men piped up. And then either the husband said something, or the woman's father-in-law, or her father. The woman's answer was repeatedly: 'whatever they say, let's do whatever they say.'" Danka was unwilling to accept women's subordination; therefore she encouraged these women to become self-conscious and independent. Today, she estimates that women are more ready to travel, to learn, and to join in decision-making in the family.

Working with these women, Danka discovered how special they were, always ready to do more even if they received no recognition for their efforts:

> Very few women can bear that burden, that sadness, that pain, that anguish, in the way our women bear it, and in spite of all this

---

[14] Martha Nussbaum, 1999, *Sex and Social Justice,* Oxford: Oxford University Press, 6.
[15] Robinson 2011, 120.

trouble, she is smiling and cheerful, she talks to you again, she complains to you and in five minutes she is laughing with you, singing, and she is ready to make miracles happen if you just give her a little push.

When she speaks about *our* women, she means women of all ethnic and religious backgrounds in BiH whom she has met on her peace journey. Danka spoke about these women's uniqueness, saying that they are incomparable to others. "The family comes first, the power to rise, to advance, to make something, not to be at the bottom, to help your neighbors, to come running, to give, and, I don't know, to fight. It's not like this everywhere. It is specific for us Bosnians."

Danka glorifies Bosnian women who use what Elissa Helms recognized as strategic use of affirmative essentialism,[16] and who persevered through pain, sacrificing themselves for their families and being the rock for these families during the war. These women also helped their husbands, who came back from the frontlines, to heal both their psychological traumas as well as their physical wounds. They rarely took time to express their own needs and feelings. And before Danka came to their villages, nobody had ever asked them what support they needed. In this context, the man was the center of everything and his needs and wishes were prioritized. Danka described how men would have tantrums like young children during these hard times: "the woman feels pity for him … but she keeps struggling … she has strength and energy to keep on going, to rebuild everything, to bring up her children on the right path, and the man is behind, somehow he does not come up to her knees." With sadness in her voice, she tried to find an explanation for men's lack of help: "During their struggle to survive, there was the male ego, which means it was hard [for them] to go to the Red Cross or

---

[16] Elissa Helms, 2013, *Innocence and Victimhood, Gender, Nation, and Women's Activism in Postwar Bosnia-Herzegovina.* Madison, WI: University of Wisconsin Press, 9.

Merhamet [the Muslim charity organization], it was hard for men to ask for help." This unequal contribution to family care continued after the men returned from war: "It was on men as heads of families to make decisions concerning their return, but they only made the decision! Everything else was on women: packing, finding transportation ... changing the children's schools."

Danka tried to explain to me the phenomenon of men's disempowerment after the war: they claimed they had fought, were defeated, could not find a job, and were without financial means. This life led them to alcohol, drugs, and gambling. Many of them were diagnosed with post-traumatic stress disorder and have not been able to heal. To compensate for the lack of support from men, women took the initiative to seek help and find solutions. She recalled how they would have to knock on the door of some donors ten times to get a cow or something else they needed. Danka jokingly said that these women have a "gene" that makes them rise to the occasion and care for their families. Danka assisted in these efforts, encouraging them to keep providing for their families, to keep rebuilding their homes and relationships with neighbors, and to make their voices heard. It shows that Danka possesses another important leadership trait, one explained by Mary Lou Décosterd: "a feminist leadership perspective supports the premise of shared knowledge."[17]

Although Danka was raised in a culture that discouraged women to speak for themselves, instead telling them to follow their husbands and be wise (read manipulative) if they wanted to achieve something or get ahead,[18] over time, she understood the importance of women having a voice, of highlighting their achievements and promoting them in public. The gender hierarchy taught them from

---

[17] Décosterd 2013, 118.
[18] Zilka Spahić-Šiljak, 2010, *Women, Religion, and Politics: The Impact of Religious Interpretations of Judaism, Christianity, and Islam on the Status of Women in Public Life and Politics*, Sarajevo: IMIC, Center for Interdisciplinary Postgraduate Studies and the TPO Foundation Sarajevo, 191.

youth that "the silence of a man is better than the talk of a woman." Danka heard these messages, but decided that these rules no longer applied: "Men and women are equal, and I would give advantage to women over men. ... I know they are more responsible, and they specifically resolve problems in a way to find the most peaceful solution."

Discovering one's voice was a process for many women and Danka tried to teach them that once they developed their voices, they should not remain silent. Each voice is important and, as Lederach says, each can have an influence on decision-making processes.[19] In addition, women should demand that men support their mothers, sisters, and wives and honor them for their accomplishments. Danka observed that: "men don't honor anyone" and are egocentric. She said that men

> consider us less important, in general, for the society, the community. They think that women only belong in the house, to take care of the household and the children, but all decisions, all the power, all they see as important, all of that is their God-given right, something only for them to discuss, to work on, and to manage. But this is changing.

In addition, she notes that women's work is not recognized and is considered less relevant in the predominant patriarchal culture and that women do more work than talk. Danka's experience shows that men are constantly seeking acknowledgment and make a point of flaunting it afterward. This type of praise bothers Danka, and she comments: "I've noticed that ... they love to flaunt it [their achievements] and talk about it for years. ... [T]hey know how to frame the praise they receive and they know how to present it where it needs to be presented." When women do something, Danka notices they tend to keep quiet about it; it is assumed that this is something they should do and then move on. Women move

---

[19] Lederach 2005, 56.

on, looking for new problems to solve, while a man might solve a tiny problem and somehow gain the community's respect for it. As for women: "there is no fanfare, and it is kind of understood that this is how it should be, that this was passed on to women from generation to generation."

Danka wanted this to change, and she encouraged women to talk about their achievements. She shares information about their successes, but she admits that it is hard to change the culture and perception of socially acceptable behaviors. In her attempts to make changes, she mentions the UNSCR 1325 on women, peace, and security, which has been in force in BiH for many years, but still without significant results. Together with her colleague Emira Hodžić from the organization Li-Woman, she was involved in the promotion of the resolution and says: "We should engage more people for this cause and work with a broader audience." For her it means systematic changes in state institutions and better cooperation with state mechanisms for gender equality, as well as with non-governmental organizations on changing cultural norms and assigned gender roles.

As an empowered and engaged feminist, Danka is upset with men's feelings of entitlement based on their sex. Danka said that this can no longer be tolerated. However, even her mother has reprimanded her rebellion from traditional views on gender hierarchy. She used to tell Danka: "You will not go very far with this kind of attitude; a man should be respected." Danka, however, has accomplished much with her feminism. While aware of the negative connotation feminism has in our social context,[20] she happily encourages personalized discussions of feminism. She has not hesitated to declare her feminist identity in public, but many other women do not: "That [feminism] can be seen through all of my work. However ... many women do this but they don't flaunt

---

[20] Zilka Spahić-Šiljak, 2012, *Contesting Female, Feminist, and Muslim Identities: Post-socialist Contexts of Bosnia and Herzegovina and Kosovo*, Sarajevo: Center for Interdisciplinary Postgraduate Studies, 138-47.

that identity in public. ... Essentially, I think that this job, what I do, what I fight for, this is genuine feminism."

Danka believes her fight for justice, equal opportunities, and serving those in need are righteous causes that are required in order to follow both God's laws and human laws. Her feminist identity is not in tension with her religious identity because she, like many other BiH women, has her own vision of feminism—promoting women's power to listen, to help, to bring people together, to communicate and reconcile themselves. She sums it up by saying: "our work is to bring neighbors back together again, in peace."

Danka is a tireless protector of women in a patriarchal, conservative society. She sadly admitted that she still has to remind women of their rights as human beings; they sometimes forget, especially when under pressure. She thinks this could be due to fear of their existence or of stepping outside socially acceptable roles. For example, Danka invested great effort in convincing people to accept a divorced woman: Petra, a local woman, got married but then divorced her abusive husband. His family expelled her from the house, so she went to live in the hen coop: "The entire community was silent about it; they did not have the will [to help]. Everybody judged her, saying that she deserved it because she left her husband, a man who was a troublemaker and meanwhile had passed away." Danka intervened in her case and in many other cases to provide shelter and basic needs, and above all to advocate for this woman in the community—so that she could be accepted and not judged. She reminded the community that none of us knows when we might experience similar exclusion and abandonment.

Fig. 2-4

Peace is about Communication and Relationships

There is no household or village in Bosansko Grahovo in which I have not been. ... I came to know these people and became one with them.

A small place like Bosansko Grahovo had many problems, and after a while Danka understood that she had neither the capacity nor the ability to solve these problems alone. One person needs a house built, another person needs the water installations set up, a third person needs his pension organized. Then there is the person who needs to be taken to a doctor, and the fellow who needs to have surgery, and the one who must sort out his identification documents. Of all these requests, Danka says: "You simply weave the entire network around you in order to make it as easy for them as possible." Danka emphasized the importance of good and continuous communication and re-building relationships among people in order to channel peace. Her vision, "imagin[ing] the canvas of mutual relationships ... as an ever-evolving web,"[21] led her to invest all her time in communicating with people. Her vision reminded me of the Bosnian Franciscan ethic of being among and living with people. That was the best way to open people's wounded and frightened hearts during the war.

Danka started alone to help returnees, as many individuals did, but when she understood she could not meet all the needs, she gathered around her women with similar worldviews. In 1999, there were thirty activists who had the goal of helping returnees and improving their living conditions, which is quite a big number for this small community. Other peacebuilders in small communities had problems in gathering that many women, which was the number of people who were required to register a non-governmental organization (NGO). Thus, in 2000 they started the Association of Citizens of Bosansko Grahovo in order to provide more systematic changes. Her collaborative and relational style of leading this group demonstrates what feminist leadership theory describes as common skills and competency exhibited by women in leadership.[22] She exhibited pride and excitement when speaking of her dedicated colleagues.[23] These women were: "Pioneers in all of these activities, they would go above and beyond in their work. For example, they would boldly visit the mayor and without restraint tell him everything on their minds."

---

[21] Lederach 2005, 35.
[22] Jean Lau Chin, Bernice Lott, Joy Rice, and Janis Sanchez-Hucles (eds.), 2007, *Women and Leadership: Transforming Visions and Diverse Voices*, Hoboken, NJ: Wiley-Blackwell, 6.
[23] With excitement, she listed them by name: Olivera Radlović, Dragica Galić, Milka Čeko, Milena Sarić, Rajana Blagojević, and Ljubinka Marić.

Fig. 2-5

These women were genuine, bold, undeterred human rights activists in their fight for justice and support for returnees. Like them, Danka did not allow any man to use her work as a justification for his failure to deal with refugee return. One reason she decided to pursue a degree in agronomy was to be respected and have legitimacy when discussing issues of farming or reconstruction. She commented that she did it in defiance of the men in municipal offices who wanted to sway her based on political connections and privileges. She supported returnees who remained in their homes and the criteria were clear:

> We visited every village and checked whether there was smoke coming from the chimney—which means a person returned home—whether there was a chicken [in front of the house]—which means a person definitely returned home. ... Then you check out how they live, how many children they have. ... You enter the

house and you know whether they have lived there for a month or for a year. That is the way we made our decisions.

Danka, however, explained that they did not have strict plans and schedules, because they had so many immediate needs to be met. They solved so many things on the fly, but one specific case required her quick reaction and courage: a woman returnee about to give birth could not get to Livno (65 kilometers away), where there was a regional hospital, because they were snowed in. The woman's husband came to Danka for help. Danka heard that the road to Knin in Croatia was clear, but there was no certainty that this Serbian woman would be allowed to enter Croatia. After the dissolution of Yugoslavia, this region (Kninska krajina) had expelled its majority Serb population during the war. Danka took a risk by bringing the woman into Croatia, hoping that they would accept her:

> I sat in the car with them and we had to entrust our lives into God's hands. She had documents for the border control. ... We did not say that she was going to deliver a baby, but that we were visiting Knin city. They took care of her. And yes, these are situations where it is necessary [to react]. I think every normal human being would do the same, would take the risk.

Danka took all these risks in helping returnees, but she soon realized that she also needed to know more about NGO management for furthering this work. In terms of her own empowerment in this area, she is particularly thankful to her colleagues from the organization Li-Woman in Livno and two leaders, Emira Hodžić and Jasminka Borković, who helped her and taught her, and who are also recognized peacebuilders in their community. Together they have been building networks and empowering women in public life: "They were like our older sister leaders; they taught us how to work ... they showed us the right path." Other important support came from the organization Viktorija in Livno, and its leader Ruža Rimac: "She was like a mother to us; we could go to her for help at midnight if needed." Danka also mentioned La Strada from Mostar, Udružene žene of Banja Luka, and other civil society organizations that contributed to peace with the support of American, European, and Asian organizations. In 2004, for example, the efforts of Danka and her colleagues contributed to the election of the first woman mayor in Drvar through their campaign, "Let's vote for change, man and woman shoulder to shoulder," organized within a larger project entitled "They should be heard and seen." Anka Dodig-Papak was elected and served two mandates as mayor. Later, she became Minister of the Economy in the Canton 10.

Danka remembered the arduous first meetings between the Croats and Serb returnees in Bosansko Grahovo, which they left without any agreement. But she did not give up. "With persistence you can probably change everything, and I brought people around the table to talk without offense, without quarrels and hard words." But this was not enough for Danka, who wanted to move these relationships to another level: "I wanted them to get to know each other." With the support of donors, sixty women and men of Croat/Catholic and Serb/Orthodox Christian origin had the opportunity to participate in their first interreligious journey. Prior to the journey, they visited *both* churches for mass and liturgy services.

> Together we traveled to Međugorje, where the apparitions of Mother Mary took place [and] to Montenegro to the monastery Ostrog. ... We spent two or three days there and at other meetings and lectures. People started to relax, to think differently. ... This was the turning point, when they started to go out together, to appear together in cafes.

She believes that the perception of their Women's Association was changed from that time forward, because it was not only Danka, a Croatian director, but also women of different identities who became members and felt part of it all. Together these women worked on different projects such as re-building the hospital and dental clinic, finding jobs, and providing education for everyone in special schools that offered courses as requested by each ethnic/religious group (language, literature, history, religious education) in order to nurture their ethnic identities.

Danka understands her work as a mission entrusted to her: "Almighty God knows that. He created us in His image and assigned duties to us; it should be like that." She is aware that her duty is difficult, but she accepts it and bears it with pride and in good faith. She repeatedly emphasized the power of communication and connection: "Sometimes it is not necessary to bring them [returnees] anything, but instead to have a talk with them." This is something she would like to do more of in her future work.

Spirituality and Religion in Peacebuilding

I'm not the kind of a believer who goes around saying "I'm a believer, I'm a believer. I go to church, I pray the rosary." Faith should be preached, but faith should also be demonstrated through actions. We should act as the Bible and the holy books teach us. Faith should be more work and less talking and boasting about being a believer.

Danka mentioned her Catholic roots as an important part of her identity and her life, but she never imposed her religious views on others through her peace work. She has wanted her religious ethics to be reflected in her work and not in her words. This became particularly important and relevant in BiH after 1990, when religion re-emerged with a vengeance as the primary marker of competing ethnic identities among Bosnian Muslims, Catholics, and Orthodox Christians.[24] Religions have come to embody new political platforms, whereas many believers prefer to reflect a religion's

---

[24] Adrian Hastings, 2003, *The Construction of Nationhood—Ethnicity, Religion, Nationalism,* translated by Miroslav Jančić, Sarajevo-Rijeka: Buybook-Adamić, 126.

spirit and teachings as they work in their community. In Danka's case, she was simply brought up believing that one has to help a person in trouble: "That is your obligation as given by God, you've got to help them, and I think that if tomorrow I find myself in such a position, other people would help me." Danka's strong sense of duty to help those in need comes out of her religious upbringing and her understanding that faith must be reflected in deeds. She admitted that she could not fix all the returnee problems, but she could listen and share what she had. She believes that she will keep helping until the day she dies: "No matter the cost, I'll help. One day, it will be repaid. I don't know what our future has in store for us, but I believe that God sees all and that God is watching. He'll repay us in some way, and even if He doesn't … it's normal to do something like that."

Danka's childhood in Livno was marked by the multicultural life of Muslims, Catholics, and Orthodox Christians living together. When she was trying to find an explanation for her peace activism and her motivation to become so engaged in this work, she says that she came to know, respect, and love both what was hers and what was derived from the tradition of others. "It was just ingrained in me from an early age. … I really don't see another reason for why I am the way I am and why I do what I do. I don't have any other motive aside from helping a person in trouble."

Many, however, who were raised in this city and lived together, were either afraid to initiate something or simply preferred to concentrate on their own well-being. Danka was different because she was touched by people's stories and could not watch their suffering and pain without feeling a duty to act as a human being and as a believer. When she started helping Serb refugees and visiting their ruined homes, she did not require any (religious or other) conditions for giving this support, nor did she emphasize that she was helping them out of religious convictions and duty. When she saw the suffering of those people, she was not paying attention to their religion. She saw it as one human being approaching another human being, and later after they had established some sense of relationship and trust, she brought religion into the discussion when she saw that it might help in reconciling Croats/Catholics and Serbs/Orthodox Christians.

Today she acknowledges that helping and bringing people together was genuine peace activism, which required forgiveness. "It was very difficult to convince these people that they were not to blame for being in this position. And even if they were to blame, it is part of human nature to forgive, and that we must get over this and show the meaning of 'turning the other cheek.'" She believes that forgiveness is essential to building peace, inherent in human nature, and taught by Jesus Christ. As Hannah Arendt says: "Forgiving is the only reaction which does not merely react but acts anew and unexpectedly, unconditioned by the act which provoked it and therefore freeing from its consequences both the one who forgives and the one who is forgiven."[25]

Fig. 2-6

---

[25] Hannah Arendt, 1958, *The Human Condition*, Chicago, IL: University of Chicago Press, 241.

Like most women in BiH, Danka considers her religion an important part of her identity, but thinks that it should not be intrusive or misused as an argument to divide people. Religion can bring people together, but only after paving the path of good communication and understanding; then religion can come to support dialogue and reconciliation. As such she does not consider religious instruction in BiH public schools a good solution. She believes that this will further divide people who are already ethnically homogenized, people who do not have any experience of coexistence as she, for instance, had in pre-war Livno. Danka would rather see children taught cultural studies of religion in school while religious instructions itself should be provided by churches and faith communities. As such, she is a good example of a believer who was raised in socialist Yugoslavia but managed to maintain her religious identity as a source not only of ethics, but also for religious rituals and prayers.

Healing the Self for Service

Danka acts out of a deep humanity as well as from her religious convictions. When she is exhausted, she re-energizes herself by reading inspiring stories, undertaking spiritual pilgrimages, praying, and above all, valuing the needs of others over her own needs. "There are downsides [to this work] ... when you are emotionally exhausted ... when you hear terrible stories, or when somebody's house would be rejected at a tendering procedure. ... You also fall apart with that person, but it is for a short time and the shot [incentive to move on] comes from somewhere." Danka mentioned five ways that she heals herself, how she gathers new energy to continue and endure the many hardships she faces in her peace work.

First, she values being alone at times when she can contemplate both her successes and failures. She says that focusing on the positive cases helps stir the fire of her humanity that can burn out under everyday pressures. She is encouraged by some of her accomplishments and is not defeated by temporary powerlessness.

Second, she is inspired by other people's humanity, for example, through books that encourage her to persevere. She retreats for some days and reads good stories about overcoming life's big challenges. This motivates her to go back to work.

Third is what she describes as "fighting fire with fire." At times, she would feel so helpless that she would stay home, complaining about her aches and pains; she remembers being under a blanket thinking that the pain in her wrist was unbearable. Her family would tease her, unhelpfully, about not taking care of herself while helping others: "Are you done with your missions, is this the end?" While she was in this mood, people with much bigger problems would stop by her house to ask for help, and that would energize her and motivate her to get out of the house. "I would say to myself, 'Danka how can you be so selfish, sitting at home, crying over yourself … and this guy has a sick child; how can you continue with this?' … and there is something that moves you to go on."

The fourth way of rebuilding her strength is to visit religious sites and pray. She had always wanted to visit the Mother Mary sanctuary in Lourdes, France, so she did. "I spent six days there and it helped me a lot … being in that silence, peace, and prayer." She traveled there with her friend and cousin and they asked Mother Mary for assistance with the problems they faced. Danka believes that Mary helped her. The visit provided some kind of spiritual healing for her, and she found it useful for her mental and physical well-being.

Fifth is the power of friendship, which helps her to overcome psychological hardships. She talks to her close friend Josipa, a gentle soul who is like a fourth sister. Their friendship helps her heal through deep empathy, love, a spirit of kindness, and mutual understanding: "It is a blessing to spend a few days with her … but I usually have only couple of hours. It is only conversation and relaxation through chatting."

Conclusion

Danka is an outstanding young peacebuilder in perhaps the most forsaken region of BiH today. She operates on a very simple "policy" of treating the other as herself. If someone is in need, she does all she can to help. From her privileged role in the police to her later participation in the NGO network of women peacebuilders, she has actively opposed the taboo to shun or block Serbs returning to her majority Croat municipality. Instead, she has been a channel of assistance and has focused on relating to those "others," and building bridges between the now-divided ethnic communities. She is a feminist who embraces the feminine qualities of care and compassion as strengths women can bring to a psychologically and materially needy post-war situation. While Danka's Catholic faith is a very important part of both her identity and her underlying motivation, she does not bring it into her relationships until they are already strong and can maintain the challenge of such dialogue and reconciliation. She is sensitive to the role of religion in maintaining the conflict between ethnic communities. Danka is tireless in her work, putting others above herself always. While this takes its toll on her body, mind, and spirit, she heals herself through prayer, contemplation, friendship, and the inspiring stories of the success of others in the face of difficulties. As an inspiration to many, she has brought other women along with her in the continuation of peace work in this generally forgotten corner of BiH.

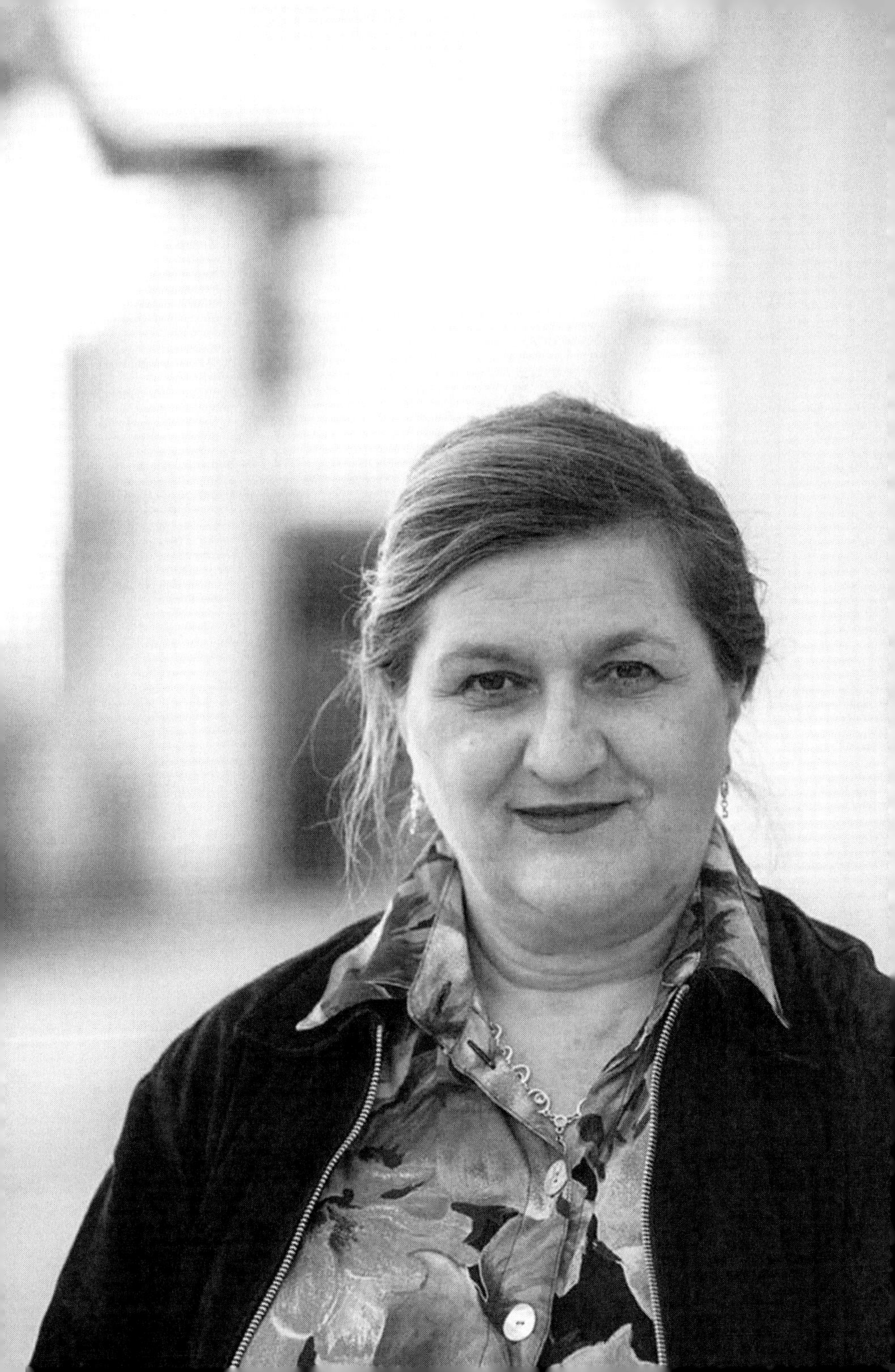

STORY THREE

IDENTITY OF A WOMAN IN BLACK

JADRANKA MILIČEVIĆ

Biography

Jadranka Miličević was born in Sarajevo in 1957 into an Orthodox family that espoused the socialist principles of the Yugoslavia of that period. She graduated from the Law College in Sarajevo in 1982 and worked in the State Accounting Office there from 1978 to 1992. After her marriage to Goran, she lived in the suburbs of Sarajevo, in Briješće, where she and her husband built a home for themselves and their two sons, Igor and Peđa.

Jadranka was raised in a multicultural environment and had friends of different ethnic, religious, and non-religious identities, many of whom were part of an ethnically mixed marriage. They all lived peacefully with their neighbors in Sarajevo and found it difficult to believe that war in their region would ever be possible. War came, however, and soon thereafter, Jadranka left Sarajevo with her mother, her two sons, and her friend and neighbor Duška and her children. Jadranka's husband and her father stayed in Sarajevo, where her brother lived in the nearby settlement of Visoko. In 1992, Jadranka went to Belgrade, hoping to find work there and to organize her own and her children's life in the best possible way, while not renouncing her Bosnian identity. Soon she got involved with a group of women activists in Belgrade, the Women in Black, who were protesting the atrocities that were occurring in Yugoslavia. Jadranka was an active member of this women's movement for the entire war period. The women worked with female victims of rape, and with refugees and deserters, they organized packages to be sent to Sarajevo, they visited refugee camps, all the while facing harsh pressure from the ruling political elites who proclaimed them traitors. During this whole period, Jadranka lived in constant uncertainty regarding her status, for she was neither a refugee nor a citizen of Serbia. After the war, she decided not to return to her pre-war job but rather continued in her activist role. By 1997, she had become one of the founders of the Žene ženama organization (Women to Women), where she worked until 2005. She also established the CURE Foundation Sarajevo, in 2005, and for the last couple of years she has been working for CARE International while continuing to be present "on the street" as an activist for CURE Sarajevo. Jadranka personifies the term activist and feels at home in this role. Today, she works in Sarajevo and lives there with her two sons.

Introduction

> I might be one of the lucky women doing what I love both professionally and privately—supporting and assisting not only women and youth, but also all those who need help. That might be the best definition of my peace work.

Jadranka Miličević is a woman recognized for her peace activism and her advocacy for women's human rights. She is committed to working with people at the ground level and building support networks that focus especially on the rights of women and ethnic minorities.

Although she spoke little of her pre-war life, it was her family and its civic values that determined her anti-war engagement in an environment that proclaimed it treasonable to speak against the regime in Serbia. Many people left Sarajevo during the war, but Jadranka's departure to Belgrade did not denote separation from Sarajevo and its destiny under the siege, which her husband, father, and other family members continued to endure. Instead of moving to some small place in Serbia to take care of her two sons, she left for Belgrade, the center of events, where her anti-war campaign and peace activism started.

I have admired Jadranka for years as we worked together on numerous peace initiatives, but it was the citizens of BiH who also recognized her engagement.[1] When I suggested a life story interview, she readily accepted, aware of the importance of media and academic promotion of women's achievements, achievements that are rarely recorded. My colleague Aida and I visited her at the CURE Foundation[2] and asked her to share her life story. It was chilly in the room of the Human Rights House that the foundation was occupying at the time. She started her story by saying: "Well, my biography is not so rich, I don't have much to say." However, the narrative soon encompassed one event after another, quickly making us forget about the cold; the only thing that reminded us of the harsh winter was the pattern of snowflakes on the windows. Jadranka's story revealed her desire to confront the hatred, darkness, division, and killing in the region by assisting the refugees and displaced persons who were victims of the terrible events that had ensnared them, and help them find their way through the whirlpool of war and tribulations that affected everyone in the area.

Searching for My Identity

I was always saying that I do not belong to this or that ethnic group, but the identity that I felt proud of was the identity of a Woman in Black. It was always important to me.

---

[1] Zilka Spahić-Šiljak, Aida Spahić, and Elmaja Bavčić, 2012, *Baseline Study: Women and Peacebuilding in BH*, Sarajevo: TPO Foundation Sarajevo, www.tpo.ba.
[2] Jadranka launched the CURE Foundation Sarajevo in 2005 and points out that the word *cura* (*cure* is plural) for girl/young or unmarried woman in Bosnian/Croatian/Serbian languages communicates authenticity and freedom. More at: www.fondacijacure.org.

In the beginning of the 1990s, one's ethnic and religious identity became the destiny of people in the Balkans. Individuals who failed to define themselves within the traditional identities were deemed wrong, problematic, and traitorous. A person's "identity" had meant nothing to Jadranka before the war, and now she searched for a setting or a society wide enough to accept those who were in solidarity with the suppressed, with the people who had no rights, regardless of their identity or origin.

Her search had started during the war, when everything collapsed and became divided according to an ethno-national trinity. People found themselves in highly unusual circumstances that were sometimes very turbulent and dangerous. Jadranka confessed that she had discovered her real self in peace activism, although it never even occurred to her that she was doing anything illegal. She recalled with a smile the moment when she asked herself how she had come to be a part of this world, and her friend, a psychologist from the Women in Black organization, Lepa Mladenović, told her that she had something deep inside of her, just waiting for the right moment and proper environment to come to the surface.

The war triggered this change, as did Jadranka's discovery of herself.[3] Jadranka remembers those times when humanity and inhumanity, good and evil, came to the surface. There was not much humanity, however, because of people's ignorance, fear, and weakness, but Jadranka took action to help those in trouble, and in the process saved her own humanity. She stressed that one of the strongest motivations for her actions was the feeling of guilt she had for leaving Sarajevo, so she decided to get involved in the Belgrade Circle and the group called Living in Sarajevo:[4]

---

[3] Norman Denzin, 1989, *Interpretive Biography*, Thousand Oaks, CA: Sage, 70.
[4] The Belgrade Circle and Women in Black established an informal group called Living in Sarajevo.

I came to Belgrade and the general perception was that I joined my own flock—which I hadn't. I had nowhere else to go, so I came to Belgrade. My motive was to let everyone know that I disagreed with the politics of the country and city I lived in and I wanted to work on uniting people.

When she arrived to Belgrade in 1992 with her mother and sons, she was able to live off her savings for some time, fortunate to be able to stay in the apartment of some relatives. After a few months, however, she realized she would have to find work. She refused help from her relatives, because they tried to convince her that something else was going on in Sarajevo, something other than the aggression, siege, and killing of innocents. "You bring your mom and two kids to visit and they start getting all smart, [like] they know better than any of us what is going on in Sarajevo." The same thing happened with her husband's mother, who lived in South Serbia and was not able to comprehend why her sons had stayed in Sarajevo: "She was bothered that her sons would give their lives for *balijas*[5] when they didn't have to."

Jadranka could not tolerate the nationalist rhetoric and this one-sided view of the war in BiH, and she was not willing to tolerate the pressure she felt from all sides to be in solidarity with her own ethnic group. She resisted it all, while also understanding that the people in Serbia were, as she claims, under the influence of media propaganda, believing they were right and therefore failing to react against the war:

> If the TV propagates one thing, and your friends and the environment you live in confirm that it's true, you must, after a year and a half, start believing it. One had to have the alternative information to be aware of what was actually going on. On the other hand, you can't but wonder how it is possible to keep people in informational isolation that way.

---

[5] *Balija* is a pejorative term for Bosniacs/Bosnian Muslims.

Fig. 3-1

To avoid becoming exhausted by constantly trying to persuade those with differing views to change their mind about the war in BiH, Jadranka found support and peace within the circle of her friends, who opposed the war and the regime in Serbia. She met Staša Zajović from Women in Black,[6] a newly founded organization that acted as an informal support group and as women peacebuilders. Jadranka recalls the beginnings: "They did not have any place to meet, they had nothing. Fifteen girls in a café bar with just enough money for two cups of tea and one coffee." There was, however, an SOS line at the Youth House, a single tiny room where they could gather and start to work toward supporting victims of violence. After her conversation with her friend, she knew she would work with them, because as she says, "It was important that we all had the same opinion about the responsibility of Serbia and the Milošević regime and we were unified in assisting and

---

[6] Staša Zajović, 1996, *Žene za mir* (Women for Peace), Belgrade: Women in Black.

supporting others, regardless of whether they were Serbs, Croats, Bosniacs, gay or of any other sexual orientation. We were united in that."

The circle of friends was an important psychological and moral support for Jadranka, because with them, as she said, she was able to laugh, cry, quarrel, make peace, and work together on everything, being always aware that she had a shoulder to lean on. She needed this stability while away from the part of her family that was surviving the difficult times under the siege in Sarajevo. Along with Lepa Mlađenović and Staša Zajović, there was Neda Božinović, an AFŽ[7] doyenne in the former Yugoslavia,[8] and her friend Rada Žarković, who had escaped from Mostar. In this circle, Jadranka started creating one of her most important identities, a Woman in Black. Affiliation to something that went beyond ethno-nationality empowered Jadranka to help other people. Women in Black became Jadranka's home and a stronghold in which she discovered herself and the fact that other identities can be more important than ethnic ones:

> Women in Black was my family. They were the circle of friends who were truly important, because everyone creates his or her family as they like. We don't have to have a family in which people are in the same bloodline. That is not a guaranty of safety and love. We should create a family in which we feel good and with whom we have the best communication and which will support us.

Women in Black supported Jadranka, and she started working for the SOS line. She had to attend training in order to be able to help victims of violence. That's when she was faced with wartime rapes and the difficult destinies of women who reported such cases. She remembered the day she went with Lepa and Stanislava, a medical doctor, to visit a young woman who was seven months

---

[7] AFŽ—Women's Anti-Fascist Front.
[8] Gordana Stojaković et al., 2002, *Neda, jedna biografija*, Novi Sad: Futura publikacije.

pregnant and refused to communicate with anyone. While they were with her, Jadranka said to Lepa in Bosnian slang: "Come on girl." The specifically Bosnian "come on, girl" made the young women turn her head and ask Jadranka where she was from. When Jadranka said she was from Sarajevo, the woman started talking for the first time. She told them the story of how she was a Serb from Sarajevo and that she was raped and did not know what to do with her life. Jadranka underlines that in working with victims of violence it was important to gain their trust, and then to be there for them, to fully close the circle of recovery. That is what happened in this case. First, Jadranka supported the woman so she could start living with her child, helped by the Autonomous Women's Center. The poor young woman, however, could not go through with this arrangement psychologically, so the Women's Center found a family to adopt the child. Later, when she went back to Sarajevo, Jadranka continued to help this woman face family challenges and to get her apartment back as well as to obtain a small pension for her subsistence.

Jadranka mentioned seven other cases of raped women whom she cared for at this time and the memories of whom she keeps even today, memories from a time of extraordinary circumstances. After some months, however, she realized she was no longer able to provide such help, so she focused her activities on working with refugees and handling administrative affairs for the Women in Black, who before that time, did not have their own working premises. The group rented its first apartment, eventually to be its office, in the center Belgrade in 1993, and they started gathering there and profiling the political engagement of their organization and their support for refugees.

Against the Government, Not against the People

Though I cannot change anything, at least I will not keep quiet because that usually means you agree or you don't care.

In the beginning of the 1990s, the war propaganda was so strong that little could have been done to affect it. People were intimidated and were served only one-sided information. Women in Black tried to symbolically express resistance to the war and the politics of the Republic of Serbia in three ways: "by the black color as a symbol of grief for all victims and a warning against the war, by their silence, as no words could be found to express the tragedy, and by their bodies that screamed against the violence."[9] It was important to show that by standing together quietly in a public place and by clothing their bodies in black to symbolize grief, crimes could not be committed in their names. Jadranka and her friends went to the main Belgrade square every week and stood in quiet protest against the war:

> Every Wednesday, never missing a single one, we were on the street. Even when they hit us, spat on us, when it was raining and when the sun was shining. Even when there were only three of us, we waited for the others to show up because our canvas [protest sign] was too large and we couldn't hold it in the wind. For me, it was important to be visible and to clearly distance myself from the official politics of the place where I lived.

Standing on the streets of Belgrade with visible black banners containing messages of their anti-war campaign was the clear political orientation of Women in Black. Daša Duhaček emphasizes that the women publicly demanded that the government assume responsibility for events in Serbia,[10] which meant the women faced insults, harassment, detention, and interrogation at the police station. But they were not discouraged and therefore became a

---

[9] Women in Black, Belgrade, http://www.zeneucrnom.org/index.php?option=com_content&task= view&id=20&Itemid=15 (accessed August 4, 2013).
[10] Daša Duhaček, 2011, "Engendering Political Responsibility: Transitional Justice in Serbia," in Ola Listhaug, Sabina Ramet, and Dragana Dulić (eds.), *Civic and Uncivic Values: Serbia in the Post-Milošević Era*, Budapest: CEU Press, 258.

symbol of resistance not only against the wars in the Balkans, but against war anywhere.

Along with their public protest and anti-war campaign, Jadranka and her colleagues decided to assist the refugees coming to Serbia from BiH and Croatia:

> All that time we stood on the street against Milošević, the regime, and the war, and we were the bad Serbian women, bad women, "Alija's and Tuđman's whores," this and that, and then we went and supported refugees—Serbs in refugee camps, those who had lost everything.

Refugees from Croatia started arriving in huge numbers, particularly after the military operation *Oluja*[11] during which the Serbian population was driven out of Knin (in eastern Croatia). People used to ask her why she stood on the street against the Serbian regime and then went to refugee camps where the refugees had hung portraits of the war criminals, Karadžić and Mladić, on their walls. Jadranka used to respond: "The poor people know of nothing else, nobody asked them anything, they were just put in trucks and sent to Serbia." Listening to their stories, Jadranka became aware that these people were uninformed, badly manipulated by the regime that gave them false promises. The only thing they really wanted was to go back to their homes and families.[12]

---

[11] Oluja—the Storm.
[12] Jana Bland Mintoff (ed.), 1996, *Nobody Can Imagine Our Longing: Refugees and Immigrants in the Mediterranian*, Austin, TX: Association of Women of the Mediterranian Region, Plain View Press.

Fig. 3-2

Refugees in Serbia lived a difficult life in inadequate camps organized in former halls of culture[13] or other facilities. More than fifty people would be crammed into a single room, with a single toilet outside. Babies and the elderly shared the same space, a space that lacked even minimum hygienic conditions. Jadranka told us how she and her colleagues cooperated with other peace activists and with Women in Black from Germany, the United States, and Switzerland to provide humanitarian assistance at the four refugee camps.[14] They also helped Bosniac refugees and the wounded who had found refuge in the Bajrakli Mosque in Belgrade. They had an

---

[13] *Kulturni domovi* or cultural halls were a common feature of communist Yugoslavia. All municipalities would have one of these communal centers for meetings and political and cultural activities.
[14] The four refugee camps that Jadranka and her colleagues visited regularly were: Mikulja in Smederevska Palanka, Kovilovo on the road to Zrenjanin, Mala Krsna on the road Požarevac, and Olga Dedijer Paediatrics Hospital in Belgrade.

arrangement with the mufti there, Jusufspahić, to bring aid and assist people in getting the necessary travel documents.

Talking about her peace engagement, Jadranka said that although Women in Black was recognized as a feminist and peace organization, the peace work was the most important segment: "That's why I can't say that we dealt mainly with women's human rights when we also took grandmas and grandpas to the doctor, taught children, took people shopping—all that is true peace activism. The point was to heal the wounds, the most burning ones, and to help them." For Jadranka, the work of peacebuilding meant direct contact with people who needed help, because such work took place during the moments that Marshall Gantz describes as a "cognitive odyssey," when one reaches the fullness of humanity.[15]

Each week they visited the four camps, both at times when they had no projects underway and when the projects they were working on allowed for a more systematic organization of support. People needed help, but they also needed conversation and the feeling that someone cared for them. That is why they did not give up even when there were no ongoing projects, even when the authorities prohibited them from entering the camps, or when they were spat at and criticized: "When you have a goal, you accept all criticism and even spitting. But I think there is someone watching what we do. I am not saying God, or people, but there is someone caring, someone who will make our work recognized in the end."

In time, Women in Black members were forbidden to work with refugees because of their political statements and their anti-war campaign:

> Sometime in 1994, we were prohibited from entering into any refugee camp. [This directive came] from the Ministry for Human Rights and Refugees of the Republic of Serbia. Women in Black

---

[15] Marshall Gantz, 2009, "Why Stories Matter," *Sojournes: Faith in Action for Social Justice*, www.sojo.net/magazine/2009/03/why-stories-matter (accessed September 3, 2013).

could no longer go in. And the camp directors called us and told us, "you just keep coming, but don't talk about it to the media too much."

On the one hand, the authorities wanted to devalue the humanitarian work of the "traitors" who openly opposed the official policies of the Serbian government, but on the other hand, the actual needs of the refugees had to be met: medicine, food, and hygienic products, regardless of where any particular refugee's political sympathies lay. In agreement with the camp directors, Women in Black continued to provide medicine and other products, but kept this help less visible to the media.

Fig. 3-3

The prohibition of work in refugee camps was not the only problem that Women in Black had with the regime in Serbia. Women in Black were taken to the police station on several occasions and questioned. Jadranka experienced this for the first time in November 1993, when she was summoned to the Ministry of Interior for questioning. The alleged reason was her status, as she was not formally registered as a refugee and did not have Serbian identification documents. She proudly said in the interview that during her stay in Belgrade she kept using her old Yugoslav ID and driver's license with her Sarajevo address: "It was my form of spite and my resistance."

The second time she was taken to the police was in February 1994, but this time the policemen came to her door in Zemun. Jadranka's friend, the attorney Nikola Barović, member of the Belgrade Circle and a friend of Women in Black, told her that she need not respond. She did not want the police to arrest her, however, in the presence of her children and neighbors. On the second occasion, she was questioned about her husband and the reasons he remained in Sarajevo and about why she was in Zemun when she had a rented apartment in downtown Belgrade. Women in Black always tried to deceive the authorities, as much as they could, so they had registered the Belgrade apartment in Jadranka's name, explaining that she was a refugee needing a place to stay, and that she cared for her mother in Zemun. Evidently, the police were well informed and they told her that they knew all about Women in Black, that the organization was against Serbia, that the women were traitors.

> You just realize that the police keep a file on you, they keep an eye on what you do and say. I got scared for a moment; I didn't know how to get out of all that. I had no passport, I forgot mine in Sarajevo and they could have caused problems because of that fact.

Jadranka spoke about various types of pressures exercised on her colleagues as well, particularly Staša Zajović, the leader of the organization. When she was in Spain in 1994, the authorities threw all of her things out of her apartment onto the street: "It was a horror, but we knew who was doing it—the Serbian regime." In this way, as Svetlana Slapšak explains, "the image of women as traitors to the nation was strongly grounded in the nationalist propaganda during the war, and Serbia retained this even after democratic change."[16]

What helped Jadranka and other peacebuilders in the Women in Black organization was the huge informal network of supporters who for various reasons might not be able to stand in protest with them on the square, but who nevertheless helped them financially, politically, legally, and psychologically. "We had a network of supporters and not a single one of us kept more than a hundred German marks at a time, unless we had to pay for something." Jadranka remembers that they had their people in all segments of society, some of them in high-ranking positions. The support of friends was particularly important during the war because they could keep their documentation at the homes of these supporters, exchange money, borrow funds for some activities, and acquire accommodations and many other important things while under police surveillance.

Jadranka underlines that she did everything honorably and in the interest of BiH and all of its citizens, and because of that she used any and all opportunities to tell the world about BiH, but also to enable the flow of information into and out of BiH through the friendly networks of people whose hearts were with them, but who could not publicly show it. Such networks throughout the Balkans helped her later when she organized the first border crossings.

Crossing Ethno-national Boundaries

> We have responsibility only for ourselves. We ourselves set the boundaries and we may not allow someone else to do it.

---

[16] Svetlana Slapšak, 2002, "Identities Under Threat on Eastern Borders," in Gabrielle Griffin and Rosi Braidotti (eds.), *Thinking Differently: A Reader in European Women Studies*, London: Zed Books, 51.

As the war progressed, Women in Black tended to renew the broken relationships with the women from BiH and Croatia, Macedonia and Kosovo and to build new ones. Contacts were established in various ways, both individually and through conferences and seminars as well as at donor meetings in European countries.

Cooperation with colleagues from Croatia was slower in the beginning due to, as Jadranka explained, wartime events and attitudes toward the war. However, there was good will on both sides for the women to meet and jointly act in building peace. Jadranka recalled that already in 1993 and 1994, there were women's conferences on anti-war activism in Subotica and Novi Sad hosting women from Croatia, Slovenia, Macedonia, Montenegro, and other European countries. However, there were other peacebuilders in Serbia and Croatia who gave statements about breaking all links with each other's countries due to the war. This fact motivated Americans to gather women from the two countries in Pula, Croatia, to try to settle the grudges:

> So we went to Pula for a conference. The Americans wanted to moderate the talks of the then so-called Serbs and Croats, even though women with other names and identities were present as well. But this is how they announced the feminist gathering, to see where the problem lay. Women in Black communicated with everyone at such conferences. The problems were statements by certain individuals.

From Jadranka's story, it seems that the point was to bring the two groups of women together. They then entered into a dialogue that lasted until three o'clock in the morning, deciding finally to continue working together. The Americans commented that their attempt at conflict resolution failed because the women managed to resolve everything by themselves!

In August 1995, the International Conference of Women in Black took place in Subotica, Serbia. At that time there was a great

Croat offensive in Bosanska Krajina causing thousands of refugees to flee to Serbia. Strategically, the conference was organized on the Serbian border with Hungary in the Totovo village, Trešnjevac, where not only women from Serbia and Croatia had assembled nearby, but also activists from Italy and Germany, Denmark, Spain, Sweden, Great Britain, Switzerland, Macedonia, Montenegro, and Kosovo. The village was famous among feminists, Jadranka recalls, as a sort of spiritual republic, because in 1991 women from this village forbade their husbands to join the army or the reserves: "For more than two months, the Serbian and Yugoslav army occupied the village, which had a majority of Hungarians (85 percent) and a minority of Serbs (15 percent), but none of the villagers ever joined any army."

Coming to Trešnjevac was, however, not easy for Croats and other Europeans. Sanja Cesar, Roza Roje, Maja Barić, Sanda Malbaša, and others called Jadranka from the border to inform her that they had been denied entry by the Serbian authorities at the Horgoš crossing, and that they would try to come to Subotica and Trešnjevac via another crossing. However, the Serbian authorities also blocked their entry at the second crossing. Jadranka and her colleagues Nataša Milenković, Lepa Mlađenović, and Savka Todorovska from Macedonia, and some other women decided to travel to Hungary to hold the meeting there with the Croats and Italians. The Italians, who were also denied entry to Serbia, had travelled by bus carrying humanitarian aid for a nursing home in Bečej, Serbia. When Jadranka and her colleagues reached Hungary, they held a workshop with the Italians and Croats, and on their return took with them the bags that the Italians had brought.

At the Serbian border, the police arrested Jadranka and questioned her. A few hours later she found out that her colleague, Lepa, was also being held by police and had been questioned for hours. Jadranka held to the story that she was a refugee from BiH smuggling goods from Hungary to make her living in Belgrade:

They held me for six-and-a-half hours and that's when I realized that they had the power to make me disappear. A policeman came and told me to empty the contents of my bag. I did so and they started questioning me about what I do. I told them I smuggle products, but then a man showed me a document with my signature requesting permission to stand on the square in Subotica. I was cool and responded that the paper proved nothing, I am still a refugee and I smuggle things for a living. Then he asked me: "how will they manage standing there without you today?" I said, "maybe they won't have to; maybe you'll release me in time."

It was clear they knew everything; they knew the Italians had tried to cross the border at four border crossings and found such perseverance suspicious, so they looked for money. Jadranka explained that there was no money, and the goods in the bus were prepared for the nursing home and the hospital in Bečej. The police then asked how it was possible for her and her colleagues to cooperate with Croats after the military operation in Oluja. After hours of questioning, they were released, but they had to pay customs duties on the goods that Lepa carried in the bag. They paid the duties in order to move on as soon as possible, and they arrived in the Totovo village at ten at night, where the other women waited for them.

Tired from the questioning at the border, they met Staša, who was in a panic: "'Did they take the money?' I played the fool and asked her, 'what money?' I had planned ahead and hidden the money we needed to cover the costs of the conference, so the police didn't find it." Such resourcefulness in difficult situations helped Jadranka survive and meet difficult challenges, and she was able to look ahead and predict possible obstacles while still focusing on finishing the task.[17]

---

[17] Mary Lou Décosterd, 2013, *How Women Are Transforming Leadership: Four Key Traits Powering Success*, Santa Barbara, CA: Praeger, 47.

Thanks to the cooperation with the women from Hungary and Italy, who exchanged information with them, Jadranka and her associates managed to react in time to all events going on in the region. In July 1995, when the Srebrenica genocide took place, friends from Budapest helped them, so that already that same year they were able to visit the nearby city of Tuzla, where the survivors had fled:

> We sent a letter of support that was forwarded to Nada Mladina in Tuzla after May 25, 1995, and the Kapija events, then to Medica Zenica and other organizations. We wrote also after Srebrenica fell on July 11, 1995. We visited Tuzla on October 22, 1995. People already knew who we were and what we did. That is why I say that I am proud of the identity of a Woman in Black. It is important and people recognize me by it.

Jadranka and the Women in Black not only wrote letters and stood on squares protesting the war. After the events of 1999 and the NATO intervention in Kosovo and Serbia, they launched the initiative "Women Activists Cross Borders." They gathered some fifty women from all places in the former Yugoslavia, including women from Srebrenica who had previously sworn never to set foot in Serbia, to travel together by bus throughout the region. Jadranka managed to gain the trust of these women, and they followed her on the journey across the Balkan countries that until recently had been part of a single state. Her colleague Žarana Papić, one of the initiators of the crossing borders project, described the caravan in the following manner: "We are not here by chance. ... First, we are all different. Second, we are all against nationalism and we are not nationalists. Third, we have the will and capability to overcome these borders and come to an agreement."[18] They recorded the journey and made a film of their trip as a testimony to the strength

---

[18] Ghislaine Glasson Deschaumes and Svetlana Slapšak, 2003, "Žene Balkana za mir: Aktivistkinje prelaze granice" (Balkan Women for Peace: Activists Crossing Borders), *ProFemina* 31-32, 126.

of Balkan women to overcome the newly established boundaries in the face of the atrocious war crimes committed within them. It was their way to face this new life. "If I believe in peace and reconciliation and if I live this belief," Jadranka firmly stated, "then it must bear fruit and it is my obligation to support it."

Communicating with common people is important for peacebuilding, as Jadranka noted, because these people have maintained contact and found ways to work together and help each other. "We know that people separated in different cities and by borders [still] communicated amongst themselves, and they continued to do so after the war. That was peacebuilding." For Jadranka, communication was of the utmost importance, particularly with people from Sarajevo, and therefore she used every one of her contacts to obtain information and she visited Sarajevo at every opportunity.

Back to Sarajevo

> I was in Belgrade, but my soul was in Sarajevo. I just waited for the right opportunity to go back to where I belonged.

Jadranka had left Sarajevo to protect her children from the war, but she refused to give up on her city, family, and friends back home. She insisted on communicating with Sarajevo, finding various channels to send letters and packages and to show solidarity by using her voice against the regime in Serbia. She registered to go to Sarajevo on the very first occasion possible, hoping that soon she would be able to return along with her children to the rest of her family. The Serbian Civic Council of BiH organized its first meeting in June 1994, deciding to invite a group of people from Serbia to visit Sarajevo in order to send the message to the world about life under the siege:

> A team of seven people from the informal group Living in Sarajevo was getting ready to enter Sarajevo upon the invitation of the

Serbian Civic Council of BiH. Women in Black nominated me to go. The group included Vesna Pešić, Miladin Životić, Nebojša Popov, Lula Mikijelj, Aleksandar Čotrić, and Ljubomir Berberović. And thus we commenced our journey to Sarajevo.

Fig. 3-4

Jadranka described the thrill of preparing packages for her family and friends; after two years she was about to enter her city again. The group first traveled to Zagreb, and the BiH Embassy there organized a formal reception for them as an official delegation of peace activists from Serbia. Then, with the support of the UNHCR, they entered Sarajevo: "We landed in Sarajevo and I remember even today the amazing image of a witch on a broom and a sign saying: 'Maybe Airport,' Sarajevo. A UN armored vehicle took us into the city."

Although she could not wait to see her husband, her father, and her friends, the protocol required them first to visit the offices of the Presidency of BiH, where the president of the Republic of BiH, Alija Izetbegović and other presidency members welcomed them. For Jadranka, it was important to obtain a new BiH passport while there, because she had left Sarajevo without one, and did not want to take out a Serbian passport:

> I was given a BiH passport and I felt safer. It was all finished in the 48 hours we spent there. The passport meant that I could be bolder; I could travel as a citizen of a country, not fearing border crossings.

After the reception, she met with her family and friends. She recalled with sadness how everyone had an exhausted, but dignified look. They were very happy to see her after two years, and they kept thanking her for the letters and packages. Her friend Jasna Diklić, an actress in the Sarajevo War Theater, said: "Well, Jadranka, I get it, you sent packages. But how in the world did it occur to you to send us hair color and cosmetics?" Those were the moments when she understood how small gestures meant the world to the people under siege in Sarajevo. For an actress performing in plays all through the war, such a thing as hair dye was important. It was a very heartfelt defense of human dignity in the dehumanizing conditions of the siege. From 1993, Women in Black had regularly sent packages and letters through journalists and other contacts: "There wasn't a single journalist in the International Press Center Belgrade who wouldn't let us know about a trip to Sarajevo so we could send letters, money, food, and medicine. We had a system and everyone knew who sent how much and to whom the package should be delivered."

The second time Jadranka entered Sarajevo was in 1995, with Lepa and a big group of peacebuilders. They traveled over Mt. Igman and through the famous Tunnel of Hope. She described how claustrophobic it was to walk through the narrow tunnel in knee-high water:

We had just entered the tunnel and I could hear Lepa's voice: "it's OK, darling, just calm down and breathe." I thought someone had been sick, but when we came to the end I saw Filip Vujošević from the Helsinki Parliament of Montenegro. A huge man with a beard, he had been scared when he entered the tunnel and could not move. Lepa took his hand and walked with him.

Jadranka managed to get from the end of the tunnel, near the airport, into the city and meet her husband and her father, even though it was difficult at that time to find any transport from Butmir (suburbs of Sarajevo) to the city center. But she managed, met with her family, and then returned through the tunnel to Belgrade with the group.

Finally, in May 1996, she decided to return to Sarajevo with her children. The war had ended months before, but it was still unsafe to move around, so she waited for her contacts to let her know if she could travel. Unfortunately, the situation was not safe and the agreed-upon transport arrangement was cancelled. Jadranka sadly called her husband to let him know that they were not coming. However, just then she received a call from her friend, Bojan Aleksov, the well-known historian who founded the organization Conscientious Objection and was also a member of Women in Black:

> I was crying and told him: "can you imagine, I had to cancel the trip?!" And he said, "don't be silly, come over to Banovo Brdo and off we'll go." We started off in the morning and arrived at the famous [neighborhood of] Vraca above Sarajevo where Goran and his brother were waiting for us. I think ours was the first car with Belgrade plates to enter Sarajevo. Bojan took a picture in front of Morića Han [a restaurant in the oldest part of town, Baščaršija] to show his parents.

Jadranka left her younger son with her husband and returned with Bojan to Belgrade to wait for her older son to finish his school year. Finally they were all united in Sarajevo in June 1996.

Naturally, before her return, she lobbied and advocated for financial support from many international organizations, traveling to Italy, Switzerland, and Germany where she met some women from BiH whom she later worked with on promoting women's human rights and feminism.[19]

Support and Trust

> My motivation was to bring to BiH the knowledge I gained, [as well as] the information and networks I built, both personal and organizational. We truly believed in what we were doing ... but it is important to give other women the opportunity and trust.

Jadranka's name in the post-war period and today is mostly associated with the feminist activities of the organization Women to Women,[20] which she founded with Nuna and Selma in 1997, and with the CURE Foundation that she and Taida, Danijela, and Andreja founded in 2005 in Sarajevo. The term *'cura'* in BiH languages means a young, unmarried woman; they chose this term because it is also used to denote disobedient girls and women who have a mind of their own.

During the war years, Jadranka built her identity as a Woman in Black, and she complemented that identity in Sarajevo with another important feminist identity, that of a disobedient girl with a mind of her own who opposes injustice. Upon her return to stay in Sarajevo, Jadranka decided to continue with her peace activism. There were some expectations that she would establish the Women in Black in Sarajevo, but the context was different and the political circumstances were much more complex, so she thought it not possible:

---

[19] Feministes contra la guerra, 2006, Barcelona: Dones x Dones; Done per la pace, Reti solidarita femminile nella ex Jugoslavia, a cura delle Donne in Nero di Venezia/Mestre, 1996.
[20] Žene ženama Sarajevo, www.zenezenama.org.

They expected me to organize Women in Black in Sarajevo. I said that it cannot be done due to the political situation; I cannot establish an organization in Sarajevo that will be politically active against the regime. In the end, we [the state and its society] were attacked. ... It wasn't a civil war, so how was I supposed to go against this state?

Aware of the context and the political climate in post-war BiH, Jadranka and her colleagues Selma and Nuna articulated the framework of action for the Association of Citizens "Women to Women" in Sarajevo, focusing on women's human rights. They became known for their empowerment of formal and informal groups in local communities, and these groups were later transformed into large organizations. Special attention to promote women's human rights was devoted to psychological counseling and women's political participation, and Jadranka recalls participating in and organizing campaigns such as "Women Can Do It" and "We Are in Majority." It was important to work with women voters, as women still do not support or vote for other women.[21]

Jadranka and her colleagues needed the initial funding, which she received from some Swiss women, to start implementing their dream. Registration of the first organization in Sarajevo with the word feminism in its initial subtitle proved provocative, and Jadranka was called explain what it was about:

As a lawyer, I was dealing with the paperwork for registration, and we were told that it would take months to get the court decision. Less than seven days later a certain judge, Senad, called and asked me to come for a meeting. He said: "Yours is the first organization—and we have registered 103 so far—that says it is feminist. I find it interesting and would like to know what kind of

---

[21] Zilka Spahić-Šiljak, 2010, *Women, Religion, and Politics: The Impact of Religious Interpretations of Judaism, Christianity, and Islam on the Status of Women in Public Life and Politics*, Sarajevo: IMIC. Center for Interdisciplinary Postgraduate Studies & TPO Foundation, 258-278.

women you are, because I see you are normal, even though you are feminists."

Jadranka commented with a smile that they were lucky to have a curious judge reviewing their documents, because it could have easily happened that their registration would have been rejected or postponed, as was the experience of some organizations. It was also a good indicator of the perception and understanding of feminism in a post-socialist context that even today feminism represents an identity feared by both men and women.[22]

But Jadranka wanted a different women's nongovernmental organization, because the existing organizations commonly had a national feature. She wanted a space for women with different identities, in which one's identity as a woman came first. She also wanted to share the knowledge she had acquired, as well as the support networks she had built in neighboring countries and in Europe, with the women in BiH and to be a bridge to connect them all. She was particularly motivated to work in small, rural communities that lacked the funds and administrative resources that women in large urban centers had available:

> Trust me, it is not the same thing to live in Sarajevo, Banja Luka, or even Tuzla, Mostar, Bihać, or Brčko as it is to live in a small town. Let's be honest, small towns have nothing. And you can't expect that these women have the same level of information as we do, or access to laws and legal protection.

Jadranka is grateful for the opportunity to obtain further education at various seminars, training sessions, and lectures. She was empowered in a way women from smaller towns were not, as they rarely had such opportunities and lacked funds as well as the

---

[22] Adriana. Zaharijević (ed.), 2012, *Neko je rekao feminizam? Kako je feminizam uticao na žene XXI veka* (*Someone Said Feminism? How Feminism Has Influenced 21th-Century Women*), Sarajevo: Sarajevo Open Centre, Heinrich Boll Foundation, CURE Foundation, 4th amended edition for BiH.

freedom to do anything for themselves. That is why she thinks it is her duty to assist these women, provide them with opportunities, and show them the same trust she once received from other women. "Were they [these other women] not there to believe in me, I wouldn't have been able to learn. I was helped, and now I help. My friends trusted me, supported me financially, and I want to provide the same support to other women." This is Jadranka's motto and the way she tries to teach young women at the CURE Foundation to act. Empowerment and sharing knowledge[23] is the essential feature of feminist leadership, something to which Jadranka vividly testifies through her work. In the post-war society beset with obstacles and divisions, it is important to create a base of supporters in one's field because only in this way, she says, is it possible to achieve change.

In January 2006, Jadranka withdrew from Women to Women and directed her energy into the work of the CURE Foundation. The focus of her work, however, remained almost the same: education, civic activism, culture, and women's human rights, only now the emphasis was more on culture and art. CURE is known today for its Pitchwise festival, where culture and activism mix. She explained her choice: "There are many cultural events but they are not accessible to everyone. Young artists do not have a space for action, and we have decided to open such a space in this way."

---

[23] Décosterd 2013, 118.

Fig. 3-5

Additionally, in her professional engagement with CARE International, she worked intensively on resolving problems that plague minorities, especially on accessing rights denied to Roma women. As a result of that work, a Roma woman, Indira Bajramović, is now chairperson of the Roma Board and handles the activities that focus on economic empowerment of Roma men and women and their employment by state institutions. Percentages are not yet high, but Jadranka is nevertheless satisfied, because Roma organizations and networks do now exist and people's awareness about Roma rights is slowly changing.

Always in Favor of Dialogue

It was not religion that motivated me to be a peacebuilder. I can't lie about that. My parents were partisans and I was raised in that spirit, which made it difficult for me to adjust to being placed in a [religious] box.

Jadranka clearly expresses her agnosticism, but is open to dialogue with people of different worldviews and affiliations. She never wanted to judge people first, but rather to give them a chance to present themselves—an important condition for any serious dialogue.[24] Of course, she also tried to prevent others from molding her or putting her into an ethno-national frame. As she says: "I am special, I am the way I want to be and I want to be recognized for it. I don't want to be placed in any box." Sometimes this attitude caused her problems, but she has also been invited to participate in various dialogues, including some on inter-religious topics.

She explains that her family was Orthodox only declaratively. They celebrated *slava*[25] such as Lazar's Saturday, in her grandfather's house, but did not practice the rituals or go to church for the liturgy. Jadranka had some knowledge of religion, but was always ready to hear the opinions of believers and work with them to promote peace.

She stresses that in the 1990s it was difficult to watch people start hiding behind religion and committing inhuman acts, while her understanding was that all holy books taught peace. Hypocrisy and the politicization of religion[26] made her move even farther from religion. However, during the war she met believers from Europe and discovered that religion can also provide strength for peacebuilding if interpreted and presented in the right way. She experienced a turning point in 1993, when she attended a peace academy in Switzerland:

> The first summer academy was held in Boldern. I was staying in the building of the Ecumenical Dialogue Church. But I did not find any belfries or ecclesiastical symbols. There was a Bible and a

---

[24] Leonard J. Swidler and Paul Mojzes, 2000, *The Study of Religion in an Age of Global Dialogue*, Philadelphia, PA: Temple University Press, 174-78.
[25] Ritual to celebrate a family's patron saint.
[26] Dino Abazović, 2006, *Za naciju i Boga*, Sarajevo: Magistrat; Mile Babić, 2000, *Nasilje idola*, Sarajevo: Did.

Qur'an in the room, in English. Thanks to that experience I started reading and researching.

When she overcame the ethno-national and religious feeling found in every single pore of life in the Balkans, she realized that religion, however abused during the war, could serve as an incentive and resource for people to come closer to each other, to reconcile and forgive. For more than a decade, along with Sabiha Husić, Jadranka has been active in the European Project for Interreligious Learning (EPIL),[27] because she cares about empowering women, religious or not, and she realized that it is possible to reconcile religion and feminism. She met great feminists among the believers who are fighting for dignity and equal opportunities for women and men.

Jadranka experienced and was aware of some of the prejudices that believers and feminists have toward one another. Through the EPIL project she wanted to offer the opportunity for both sides to meet each other in dialogue and to see that they have a lot in common. She feels that she learned so much from European Protestants, who she claims "have already adopted an attitude on women's rights. Everything they promoted is what you and I would support right away."

The problem, she says, is that people in the Balkans often face the dilemma of whether to act according to their conscience or as representatives of religious traditions. She was a witness to unhappy situations that developed in some families, and she comforted mothers who could not understand how their children became war criminals or accomplices to crimes when they had been raised differently. Jadranka tries to understand people, to see how they have been misled, deluded, or even scared. But she firmly thinks that true believers can never consent to evil. True faith and

---

[27] The European Project for Interreligious Learning (EPIL) is a Swiss initiative: www.epil.ch.

genuine humanity are, in her opinion, inseparable, and everything else is hypocrisy or escapism.

She has less sympathy for those religious communities and churches that allowed their rhetoric or their silence about the evils that were being committed to send messages of hate and exclusion; these groups sometimes even blessed war criminals. She mentioned the positive example of the inter-religious work of the friar, Ivo Marković, from St. Anthony's Monastery in Sarajevo; he was always ready to talk to anyone interested in reconciliation in BiH. Another person who impressed Jadranka was the Orthodox priest, Father Krstan Bijeljac, active in the Multi-religious Center, IMIC, in Sarajevo with Marko Oršolić, who suffered all the misfortunes of the war together with the citizens of Sarajevo, remaining upright in his faith and the goodness for which he is respected. The Jewish Municipality in Sarajevo also served as an amalgam of numerous peace activities, but because of its membership being such a small community, had the advantage that nobody cared if they belonged to the ethno-national triangle of Serbs, Bosniacs, and Croats.

She recalled a negative experience with the former Grand Mufti Mustafa Cerić, who in 2000 refused to receive a delegation of the Citizens' Assembly from Čačak, Serbia. Jadranka contacted him to ask for a meeting, and he angrily responded: "Shame on you! What do you want? You want to make bridges? There is nothing there for you." It was difficult to explain why the Grand Mufti refused to see the delegation, when a year later, he started communicating with everyone and became globally known for his inter-religious activities.

In Jadranka's view, religious leaders are mostly concentrating on their own interests and political goals, and much less on the welfare of believers and citizens in general. A strong interest of these leaders was the introduction of religious education in schools that, according to her, did not have a positive effect, as it only segregated children by ethno-national and religious belonging, thus deepening stereotypes. She also told about the outrageous groups of young hooligans using rhetoric bordering on fascist propaganda that can be found today in BiH. And these young fellows use church symbols and the words of national leaders to insult others, not only their sport opponents, but their political and national enemies. Exceptions do exist in religious communities of people who are committed to peace, Jadranka says, but they have no real power and very often are the target of oppression and criticism from within their own communities.

As for women as peacebuilders, she insisted that the peace in BiH has been accomplished by individuals with support from international organizations, including also UN Women. She would not want to claim that women are by nature inherently peaceful,[28] but she thinks women have more understanding and patience, and are not as violent and aggressive as men. "I think that more women than men have participated in reconciliation. Men sent women to restore their property after the war, because they were scared."

What Jadranka sees, however, as a problem and obstacle for women's equal representation in decision-making positions is men's persistent struggle for power. In addition, patriarchal gender roles still determine the lives of many women, and it is still important that men are heads of families, even though women get most things done. Women, on the other hand, do not have time to make their work visible or socially recognized due to the huge scope of work they continue to do. Women are partly to be blamed for this, as some of them do have positions in the legislature, and being gender unaware, send the wrong message to the public.

Jadranka is angry at the statements of some female politicians who are insensitive to other women and imitate men in the political

---

[28] Fiona Robinson, 2011, *The Ethics of Care: A Feminist Approach to Human Security*, Philadelphia, PA: Temple University Press; Sara Ruddick, 1990, "The Rationality of Care," in *Women, Militarism, and War: Essays in Politics, History, and Social Theory*, J. Elshtain and S. Tobias (eds.), Savage, MD: Rowman and Littlefield; and Sara Ruddick, 1989, *From Maternal Thinking Toward a Politics of Peace,* Boston, MA: Beacon Press.

arena. She mentioned a female member of parliament who recently said on TV: "What is important is to get the job done, by men or women—it does not matter. I do not consider myself underprivileged in this regard." Another female MP criticized women's human rights activists and told Jadranka: "What do you [feminists] want? We have as much as we need." Jadranka added, "Yes, she has as much as she needs because she has such a position and she is privileged." To maintain the positions they gained by being obedient to their party leaders, such politicians tend to thwart the work of those who promote women's rights and feminism, using stereotypes to portray these women as masculine-appearing lesbians. Jadranka concludes that this is due to a fear of competition, since the NGO sector has many smart and bold women who could serve well in those positions with much more accountability.

Despite such obstacles, however, Jadranka perseveres. For her, true peace can only happen in a process that includes all people and only when peace initiatives move from comfortable cabinets and offices to the smallest rural communities.

I Find Peace in Good People and in Nature

The years of continuous work in the field, of traveling and attending numerous events, have also brought fatigue and the need to stop occasionally in order to recuperate and continue. Jadranka admits there is little time for relaxation, but she does slow down from time to time to recharge her batteries, as she says, in order to manage the demanding tempo she has been experiencing for the last twenty years.

The best relaxation and repose for Jadranka is to meet and talk with good people. "My strength comes from the network of people I have built and from my way of life. Wherever I go, regardless of what I do, I have someone to talk to, friends and support." For her, friends are a form of spiritual refreshment, and her immeasurable humanity is fed by the humanity and goodness of others; in this intimate interaction, Jadranka feels her energy and strength are restored.

> Sometimes it is enough to just sit and talk with people I love. Sometimes we discuss films, books, global events, local circumstances, etc. It doesn't matter what we talk about, it matters that we are together and there is something I share with them.

Meeting friends brings joy to Jadranka and she describes it as a form of therapy that empowers her and makes her more enthusiastic about her work.

Jadranka also finds ways to relax in nature. She has learned how to combine work and relaxation, so she often uses her travels to take time for herself. Her soul relaxes in nature, be it on a mountain, by a river or the sea, in a city park or a hotel garden.

> Just the other day I had a seminar in Banja Ždrelo on the river Mlava, close to Petrovac in Serbia. When everyone left, I decided to stay for another night and enjoy nature by myself. It was the same thing—to spend the night there or pay for a hotel in Belgrade. It was such an amazing feeling not to have to talk to anyone.

In her rare moments of solitude, Jadranka gathers energy and prepares to continue on the path of building peace. Nature is for her a place of primeval peace and harmony, which reminds her that although everything passes, what remains are the good deeds people leave behind. Nature restores the harmony in her heart and soul. Jadranka has an immense energy and a strong will to work on peacebuilding, and a short respite in a good environment suffices for her to recover from fatigue.

Conclusion

Jadranka Miličević stands out as a peacebuilder who refuses to be indoctrinated or threatened. She focuses on informing herself and others beyond the media, beyond the political, and cultural rhetoric, which often promote ethno-nationalist agendas. During the war, when she was living as a refugee in Serbia, this meant being classified as a traitor for standing up against the opinions of her relatives and friends about what was going on in BiH. As a Woman in Black, rather than a Serb or even a Bosnian, Jadranka received threats and abuse for her activities against the Serbian government. As such, one could call her a rebel. She was a true agent of change through her bravery, creativity in tight situations, and impertinence toward the new and unacceptable rules and norms of the time. But she did all of these things as part of a community of like-minded people who strengthened each other.

Upon returning to Sarajevo after the war, this Woman in Black dedicated herself to the cause of women's rights, because the political situation was too complicated to simply oppose "the government." Jadranka initiated two NGOs, Women for Women and the CURE Foundation, and spearheaded other initiatives such as the effort for Roma rights. Again she placed her female and humanitarian/peacebuilder identity above any nationalist sympathy. She courageously introduced feminism to a society afraid of the unknown, showing that feminism is about equality, justice, and equal opportunities for women and men. Jadranka believes more women than men have been involved in peacebuilding activities in BiH, but says men are also capable of this work. In the same way, religious persons and communities may be complicit in wartime and postwar violence, but true believers resist evil, even if their efforts seem futile. Jadranka cooperates with all who have an orientation toward humanity and peace while seeking to understand those people who have been misled.

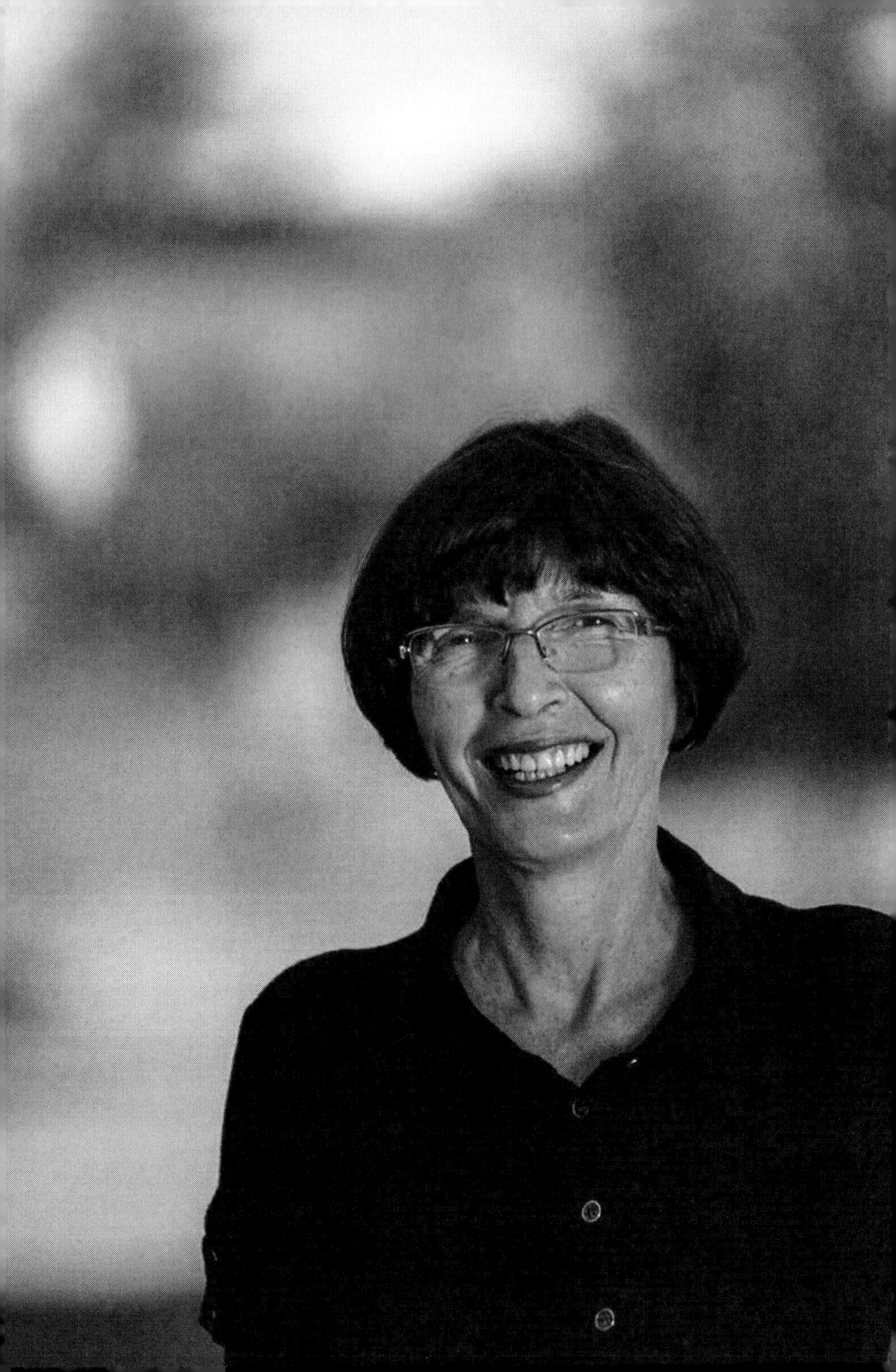

Story Four

Designing Civil Activism

Lidija Živanović

Biography

Lidija Živanović was born in 1950 in Kotor, Montenegro. She grew up in a traditional, that is, patriarchal, family where the father always had the last word. This was one of the reasons she decided later in her life to try to demonstrate that women, as well as men, have the ability to create their own lives, and this attitude led to great results in her private life, her business career, and her civic-minded activities. When Lidija was born, her parents were students receiving Tuzla Mine scholarships, so Lidija completed elementary school in Tuzla (Bosnia and Herzegovina) and high school and university in Sarajevo, graduating with a B.A. in Architecture. She married and moved to Banja Luka, where initially she worked in the construction industry as a specialist for interior and furniture design. Her sense of beauty and her creativity paved the way for her to take a position at the Museum of Bosanska Krajina, as a curator who worked on the permanent museum exhibition. Two years prior to the war, Lidija started her own design studio. She spent the war years with her family in Banja Luka, and immediately thereafter, she helped to launch a civil initiative for democratization and reconstruction of BiH. She was among the first women who crossed the country's internal borders and beyond to visit the neighboring nations of Serbia and Croatia to offer a hand of reconciliation, not waiting for the other side to take the first step. She was at the forefront of those who believed that the citizens of BiH could live together. In line with these beliefs, she initiated and supported all the actions targeted at bringing these citizens together. Her ideas and strategic thinking about peacebuilding in BiH were implemented via the Helsinki Citizens' Assembly (HcA) in Banja Luka, where she made her mark as the leader of the organization for sixteen years. For this work she was awarded a "Tolerance Charter" in 2009. Lately, she has withdrawn somewhat from activist work, but she still closely cooperates with the HcA in Banja Luka, for she believes that peacebuilding requires intensive daily effort and that all generations ought to be taught the basic concepts of peace, human rights, and democracy. She is the mother of three sons who were raised, as she notes, in the spirit of respect for diversity and gender equality.

Introduction

> Establishing communication in the territory of post-war Bosnia and Herzegovina was my priority. My target groups were young people and women, that is, marginalized groups, and my goal was their inclusion in the democratic processes.

Lidija Živanović's name is associated with a number of civic initiatives in BiH, the most important of which are certainly those targeted at linking women and youth, ensuring gender equality, and improving the position of minorities. Immediately after the war, together with her husband Miodrag Živanović, she joined in the discussions about the democratization process in BiH, about post-war reconstruction—especially the re-establishment of broken connections with neighboring communities, and about the establishment of new cooperation and support networks with a number of non-governmental organizations in the Federation of BiH and Republika Srpska. Lidija says that although she never planned to be an activist or to deal with human rights, but the post-war circumstances simply imposed on her such activity, so instead of investing in her architectural studio she focused her energy on mending human relationships. In order for that work to be effective and to approach the problems in a more systemic way, she established in 1996 the Helsinki Citizens' Assembly (HcA) of Banja Luka, supported by the International Helsinki Citizens' Assembly.

Occasionally I have had the opportunity to cooperate with the HcA on gender equality and peacebuilding projects, and I am very familiar with Lidija's work and achievements, as are the majority of people working in the non-governmental sector. Activists often refer to Lidija as "a doyenne of peace activism in BiH." This view was reiterated by other peace activists in this book. Lidija was among the first persons who launched peacebuilding and reconciliation activities, accomplishing very important results not only in Banja Luka but also throughout BiH at a time when it was unpopular to present such ideas publicly.

When I contacted her about doing this interview, she seemed glad to hear from me but asked, "Why, out of all the other women in BiH, have you recognized me?" We got together for the interview in Banja Luka, and at the outset she said: "Well, I do not know what to tell you. I did nothing special. There were many things I did over the course of the past sixteen years, but others did the same or similar things, so I do not know what to single out as particularly important."

It was a bit discouraging to hear that Lidija had nothing special to say about her long years of work, but then she started giving a few details about the beginning of her involvement, and her motives, dilemmas, and achievements, of which there were many.

Civic Activism Recognizes No Limits

> Had someone told me that I would be dealing with human rights and democracy ... I would not have believed their words.

As an interior designer, Lidija was very successful at her job, winning several prizes for her design solutions. It never crossed her mind, therefore, that she might close down her small design studio in order to work on something completely unrelated. However, the war changed many things, and people had to redefine themselves and their lives in accordance with the requirements of the time and the context in which they lived. That is what happened to Lidija, who after the war realized that something needed to be done to mend the broken connections that were preventing people from living together in harmony. This realization was a major turning point in Lidija's life.[1] She transformed her art from designing interiors and exhibitions for people to designing links and relations among people, people who were exhausted by the war and were seeking refuge after experiencing personal loss, trauma, and fear, people who were devastated and needed support to re-build everything that had been destroyed. The rich diversity of individuals she discovered outside her professional circle thrilled her, but at the same time she had a hard time accepting that the beauty of BiH was being neglected:

> It was such a thrill to meet people you never knew existed, to make new friendships. ... It was a context completely different from what I was used to, different from my professional circle, so to speak. It was beautiful to discover such a BiH. We have [here] a God-given beauty and it is shocking what we are doing with it. To be given such wealth and to waste it so ignorantly is really outrageous.

Together with her husband, Miodrag, she first established contacts with their pre-war friends, Lidija Mračević from Prague, Klelija Balta and Vehid Šehić from Tuzla, and Zdravko Grebo from Sarajevo, who were also engaged in launching civic initiatives in BiH. Then she established contacts with women from Sarajevo, Zenica, and Mostar who were organizing the first women's conferences and meetings.

Another reason Lidija abandoned her beloved job was to deal with the post-war transition, in which everything was turned upside

---

[1] Norman Denzin, 1989, *Interpretive Biography*, Thousand Oaks, CA: Sage, 70.

down. People were asked to do things in which they did not believe or with which they did not agree. In her story, Lidija does not name who restricted her freedom of movement at that time, but it is clear that she was referring to the government of Republika Srpska. She realized that people were divided according to their ethnic (i.e., religious) identities, but Lidija did not subscribe to such a division since her own family was ethnically diverse. She believed that the only acceptable division between people is between the good and the bad.

> Freedom of movement in particular ... it was horrible. To have someone to tell you where you can or cannot go. ... Nobody had [previously] asked me who I was and what I was, the way they did from the 1990s onward. Or to label me based on my first name and my family name, without asking what kind of a person I was.

Lidija was inspired by the needs of the people around her, all of whom had different troubles but a common need for help to move on and recover their lives. Caring for others outside of her community is what Martha Nussbaum calls the moral obligation to be fair and committed to preserving the dignity of another person.[2] With a deep sigh Lidija refers to what happened in Prijedor, which is near Banja Luka, and briefly comments on how awful and helpless she felt about the horror experienced by the survivors of prison camps there: "Prijedor and events in Prijedor and in the other places, for me, [raises] a terrible, terrible sense of helplessness, as if something heavy comes over you. I do not know how else to put it." Lidija simply could not understand the vulgarization of humanity that took place in BiH during the war: that people can stop being human and lose all their civility. Obviously some people had views of the world that differed from Lidija's, and by spreading fear via propaganda and by exerting pressure they managed to plant seeds

---

[2] Martha C. Nussbaum, 2000, *Sex and Social Justice,* Oxford: Oxford University Press, Pankhurst, 6.

of hate that culminated in terrifying atrocities. Lidija does not say much about it, but it is obvious that the war has left a lasting mark on her, threatening the value system by which she lived in the former Yugoslavia.

She used her strength to create useful things for her community and to re-connect people despite the imposed boundaries and identity policies. She recalls that she had always felt resistance toward divisions, even the small, local ones. Although people said they believed in coexistence, she discovered from moving around the former Yugoslavia that it was quite hard to be a stranger. It bothered her that people so often expressed their local patriotism and insisted on the uniqueness of their origins: "I was always a 'stranger,' i.e., a 'newcomer.' People would say to me, we are natives of Banja Luka, natives of Tuzla, natives of Sarajevo, etc." While Lidija remained sensitive to this, she would manage to find the strength to overcome such exclusive boxes and rather seek the advantages and beauty of diversity. Her resistance to being labeled with certain identities against her will was a strong motivation for her civic activism. In the post-war socio-political environment, in which it was extremely difficult to remain unbiased or outside the ethno-national groups and interests, Lidija focused her energy on positive things. In the first post-war years, her civic activism was focused on advocating women's human rights, because women were restricted from the political scene and had to struggle simply to retrieve their previous rights.

Crossing Borders

Since Lidija spent the war years with her family in isolation in Banja Luka, which had no electricity, water, or food, she missed communicating with her friends and colleagues in other parts of BiH. She suffered because of the war and its atrocities, but she does not speak as much about this as about being deprived of the freedom to move around and the lack of information. To her, the greatest suffering was to be imprisoned by the fear of others, separated from other people and unable to decide about one's own mobility, choice of friends, and associates. Her frustration speaks to the primal human need to be with other people and illustrates what Marshall Gantz calls "the ways of learning about how to become a complete and trustworthy human being."[3] For Lidija, life in the dark meant not only the physical darkness due to a lack of electricity, but the darkness in the minds of people who become victims of hatred:

> When the war broke out we lived like in a ghetto. Our movement was restricted, [there was] darkness. The villages around Banja Luka were glowing, while Banja Luka was in the dark. That was certainly a part of a strategy, because all the ugly things happened in the dark. No one could do anything because we were under a curfew regime.

Lidija compensated for the lack of electricity by the light of her heart and mind, which strongly resisted ignorance, darkness, fear, and hatred. Even in the war's isolation she found a way to retain her sanity, remain a human being, and resist impositions upon her opinions. She insisted on checking the facts prior to making decisions. She believed that one's own torch provided the best light. "I spent the war period trying to stay normal," she says. She listened to a radio connected to a car battery and closely followed the reports of Radio Free Europe and other stations: "In the end, I knew that something was going on. I did not want to subscribe to rigid attitudes. Even today we have media like those during the war, but they are just slightly more sophisticated."

---

[3] Marshall Gantz, 2009, "Why Stories Matter," *Sojournes: Faith in Action for Social Justice*, www.sojo.net/magazine/2009/03/why-stories-matter (accessed September 3, 2013).

Fig. 4-1

Lidija is very proud of re-establishing communication across both physical and imaginary borders. For a long time, she and a few other activists were alone in carrying the burden of public demonstration in Banja Luka for the promotion of civil values and reconciliation. She recalled a gathering in 1997,[4] attended by eighty-five persons from BiH, Croatia, and the former Yugoslavia. With her colleague, Zoran Levi, she organized the whole event. She dared to do what many did not have the courage to do for fear of the authorities. She had the support of her husband Miodrag and friends such as Zdravko Grebo, a law professor from Sarajevo and important humanist in BiH. Support from people who thought alike was very important at the time. In disbelief, Lidija described the grand rally she orchestrated and the courage she needed to stand

---

[4] The meeting was organized under the title "Economic, Social, and Political Aspects of Reconstruction and Development." It was the 4th session on "civil dialogue." The authors of the idea were the Belgrade Circle (Beogradski krug), the Civic Forum of Tuzla (Forum građana Tuzla) and the Anti-War Campaign (Antiratna kampanja) from Zagreb.

before so many people and speak publicly without any prior experience. She thinks her motivation at that moment may have been a sense of fulfillment at the gathering of her country-folk from before the war:

> In one place I saw again my country. I simply cannot forget who provided me my education, where I grew up, where I lived, and all that together. But it was simply too cramped a space for me to accomplish my goals. Sometimes I wonder, maybe we should have allowed all of this to completely fall apart to the level of the "*polis*," so we could then consolidate it in a new form.

Lidija believes that one's personal contribution is very important, which is why she has struggled first to do as much as possible at the level of her own community, and then to react to problems elsewhere: "I was always thinking about the phrase: 'Clean your courtyard first; react to the problems in your own house and support your house.'" From this statement it seems Lidija was oriented more toward solving specific problems in her community and the countryside around it than in building up her image as a human rights and peacebuilding activist, which is more effectively done at high-level meetings and gatherings of domestic and foreign political elites. Lidija was interested in working with ordinary people and solving their problems, and therefore she invested her skills and capabilities in such work. One important feature of Lidija's leadership was her focus on completing tasks, something Mary Lou Décosterd calls assimilative or directed force.[5]

When Lidija was invited for the first time to meet and cooperate with women in Sarajevo and Zenica (both cities lying within the Federation of BiH, although she lived in the other entity), she was immediately ready to travel across the newly established border in BiH. In July 1996, together with her friend Nada Golubović, and

---

[5] Mary Lou Décosterd, 2013, *How Women Are Transforming Leadership: Four Key Traits Powering Success*, Santa Barbara, CA: Praeger, 47.

upon the invitation and with the support of the OSCE, she organized the first visit of women of all nationalities to Sarajevo. She recalls, however, that the imposed conference program and style of moderation caused a lot of discomfort and dissatisfaction among women from Banja Luka, who wanted to go home on the very first day.[6]

> The conference began with a welcome speech by Alija Izetbegović and it continued in the fashion of a recital about the raped Bosniac women. The cameras were rolling, flashing on all sides. ... We spontaneously left the conference. Some other participants who felt uncomfortable soon joined us.

Lidija explained that the politicization of the conference through the appearance of Alija Izetbegović, who was not perceived as the state president in Republika Srpska, and the condemnation of the rape of only Bosniac women caused a lot of dissatisfaction. "We felt as if our presence was only needed to confirm the agreed-upon scenario," said Lidija. Nevertheless, after talking to women during the breaks they realized that there was a chance for their voices to be heard, which is what happened subsequently in the group sessions of the conference.

Thereafter, she met on a regular basis with certain women and families in Sarajevo, who hosted them. "The communication with them was warm and friendly," says Lidija. It was hard to see the wounded city of Sarajevo with so many scars both on the facades of the buildings and in the eyes of the people who had survived the siege. "It was my city as well," she adds. "I spent my high school and college days there, but just as in Banja Luka, the names of many streets were changed."

Lidija recalls a few comical moments that occurred as the women returned home from the conference to Banja Luka. At the

---

[6] Lidija recalled that the conference was organized by an organization called Žena 21 from Sarajevo.

time, there were still physical borders, ramps, and suspicious questioning at the border crossings. Nada and Lidija were in a bus full of women, and somewhere around Mrkonjić Grad they were stopped by a police patrol from Republika Srpska. With a big laugh, Lidija related the anecdote about a police officer. "Where are you going?" asked the police officer. "To Banja Luka," we responded. He then took a walkie-talkie and reported: "Some women are "going on" (conquering) Banja Luka."

In June 1996, before the Sarajevo conference, the Helsinki Citizens' Assemblies of Tuzla, Banja Luka, and Sarajevo, in cooperation with Medica Zenica, organized a conference called "A Room for Discussion," in which the problems of women refugees and displaced women were discussed, as well as the participation of women in the political process, reconstruction, and development of BiH. Laughingly, she recalls how she and Nada walked around Zenica and enjoyed eating bananas, because for a long time they could not buy bananas in Banja Luka, and even if someone had brought them bananas, they would have given them to their children.

In December of the same year, Lidija prepared "A Room for Discussion" as a women's conference in Banja Luka, and women from the Federation came for the first time as an organized group. She also extended an invitation to Biljana Plavšić.[7] Lidija explained this decision by saying. "I knew that she would not accept the invitation, but this was a way to inform everyone that the event is taking place. I requested approval from the police, because I thought that transparency ... would be some sort of protection. Of course, Biljana neither appeared at the conference nor did she speak

---

[7] Biljana Plavšić is the former president of Republika Srpska who was convicted before the International Criminal Tribunal for the Former Yugoslavia for war crimes and sentenced to 11 years imprisonment. Having served two thirds of her sentence, she was granted early release. http://www.haguejusticeportal.net/index.php?id=6084.

about it." Such a "smart flexible" strategy[8] helped Lidija survive irrespective of who was in power or what policies they proclaimed. She always made her work transparent. This was particularly important in the most turbulent and difficult times when the judicial system was highly politicized, while the court of public opinion was completely silent. Lidija recalls that women were very eager to do something about education, political participation for women, and the growing social problems; they have been busy doing just this for the past fifteen years. The most important thing, says Lidija, is that women are now networked, which means they can do so much more together. Such support and the first links, which were carefully built, empowered women to join together as a group to advocate, to develop strategies for, and to work on systemic solutions for a number of issues relevant to gender equality.

Fig. 4-2

---

[8] John Paul Lederach, 2005, *The Moral Imagination: The Art and Soul of Building Peace*, Oxford: Oxford University Press, 85.

Lidija and Nada traveled throughout Bosanska Krajina, bringing women in rural areas together through various democratization and reconstruction projects. Although the two were subject to many pressures for going to the Federation, Lidija continued to cross the border because she allowed no one to limit her movement. What Lederach writes about moral imagination captures Lidija's attitude: "That's the readiness to assume the risk of living out of the box."[9] By crossing the internal borders of BiH and seeing what was happening there, Lidija was able to reaffirm her belief that people everywhere can have good souls and can still care for one another. One such moment particularly encouraged her belief in the humanity of her fellow citizens: while traveling on her own to Sarajevo, she was caught in a storm, had a minor accident near Visoko, and had to find alternative transportation. An American offered her a lift, but first she had to take care of the broken car:

> When we reached Visoko, I went to look for a tow truck. A man who worked at a gas station found for me the contact information of a person who had a tow truck and asked if I wanted him to take me to that person. "No", I said. Instead, I gave him the car key and money for the mechanic. "Just have it fixed so that I can return home." ... I went on to Sarajevo with the American who had offered me the lift, not knowing if I would see my car again. The next day, the man phoned me to let me know that the car was fixed. I am so sorry that I never asked him for his name.

Lidija told me this detail because in Banja Luka, she had heard stories about people in the Federation that were quite different. However, since she had the direct experience of meeting both good and bad people in the field, she knew that there would always be people who are willing to help someone in need. When it comes to the enormous fear of others, she says: "It was more difficult to return to Banja Luka and recount that nothing bad happened and

---

[9] Ibid., 62.

that those other people are quite normal. Poor them! Fear is very powerful." Ultimately, these meetings motivated her to go further: "I think that those were the moments that motivated me, set me in motion, fulfilled me." That spark of humanity inspires those who are open to receive it, and Lidija demonstrated that even in the darkest of times she retained her open heart.

Referring to one of her trips across the border between Republika Srpska and the Federation, Lidija explained that good intentions do not necessarily mean good results. "Once, when I traveled from Doboj to Sarajevo I took a taxi." The taxi driver was from the Federation and he tried to make Lidija feel more comfortable: "As a good host from the 'other side,' he played [turbo] folk music for me [what he thought was] 'my kind' of music." Whereas the taxi driver's stereotype of Serbs included an appreciation of this style, Lidija, like many in BiH, finds such music anything but pleasant. Things are more complex than simple black and white. Rather than pass judgment, we should first consider our circumstances and the intentions of others, even if the results are not always favorable.

After the initial conferences in Zenica, Sarajevo, and Banja Luka, Lidija knew she would continue advocating for the rights of women in both the legislative and political arenas as well as at the practical level through the application of legal norms and standards.

Empowering Women through Strengthening Systems

Indeed, the laws are important, but achieving equality is much more important.

One of the most important post-war tasks for women's rights in BiH was to introduce a quota for women to make sure that women appeared on the candidate lists of political parties. In this regard, Lidija mentioned a very important campaign—"We outnumber you," which was conducted during the 1998 elections, as they advocated for a "women's quota." As a result of this campaign, three female candidates appeared on the list of the top ten candidates, significantly increasing the percentage of women running for parliament.[10] The BiH Election Law was adopted in 2001, introducing a 30 per cent quota for the underrepresented gender on the candidate lists. Campaigns for open lists and women's civic education were also introduced to encourage women's active participation in political life. A coalition of NGOs supporting gender equality was also established, bringing together about forty organizations and 130 civil society organizations to advocate for the adoption of the Gender Equality Act, which was made a law in 2003.

In addition to the new law, another important change was the establishment of national gender equality mechanisms, first at the level of the Federation of BiH (2000) and the Republika Srpska (2001), and subsequently at the BiH level (2005). However, Lidija is dissatisfied with the way these mechanisms function. "They are positioned in a way that does not give them any power. And, quite simply, very few people employed in these institutions went through the process of empowerment as did the women in the NGO sector." Lidija is concerned about insufficient cooperation between those who control the gender mechanisms and the NGOs that helped establish them, as well as by the lack of implementation of what the activists created:

> The institutional mechanisms we advocated for are now established, but in a way they have started their own story from scratch. Sometimes it seems to me that we appear as competition to one another rather than as groups playing for the same team. I am personally dissatisfied with it, but this will have to be settled in some way.

---

[10] Lidija claims that in the 1998 elections, 26% of the candidates listed were women, whereas the percentage of women elected grew from a single digit to numbers that are three,or in some parliaments, as much as ten times greater (e.g., from 15% to 26% women in the parliaments in BiH).

According to Lidija and other peace activists, the NGOs expected to partner in the institutionalization of gender mechanisms, but instead they ended up competing with one another in applying for funds and implementing projects in this area. The current situation demonstrates the insufficient level of solidarity and understanding between the women actors in the NGOs and the state institutions. Even though there are some examples of good cooperation, collaboration is only happening occasionally, says Lidija.

Fig. 4-3

The second aspect of the activities of Lidija and the Banja Luka HcA team was meant to empower women voters for political engagement. In this task, Lidija demonstrated an ability to empower other women and help them build self-confidence[11] in their struggle

---

[11] Décosterd 2013, 74.

for a place in the family and society. In addition, the team's successful campaign "To be visible, to be heard" focused on increasing the visibility of women in public and political life throughout BiH. It showed that much can be accomplished through joint efforts:

> We worked in local communities with women from Bratunac, Milići, Srebrenica, then Ljubuški, Mostar, Nevesinje, Tomislavgrad, Grahovo, Glamoč. One important mechanism we established through our work was a bridge of communication between these women. They all live in very small communities where it is extremely difficult for women to deal with any issue in public.

Women recognized the potential of election lists, notes Lidija, and focused their energy on promoting all women listed, irrespective of the parties they represented. As a result, the women who participated in the HcA training programs were elected councilors and MPs and often acted jointly in their municipal assemblies and councils. Such networking with a focus on establishing links between individuals and organizations is important to the peacebuilding process, according to Elisabeth Porter.[12]

The difficulty for women in small local communities is illustrated by the case of the deputy mayor of the Srebrenica Municipality, Milka Rankić, who was almost unlawfully removed from office so that her post could be re-assigned to a male candidate. However, women from the network "To be visible, to be heard" quickly assembled and voiced their reaction. "No kidding," Lidija exclaims, "a letter from Ljubuški [a Croat majority area] came to Srebrenica [a Serb majority area] opposing the deputy mayor's removal, because this was contrary to the statute [that was

---

[12] Elisabeth J. Porter, 2007, *Peacebuilding: Women in International Perspective*, London: Routledge, 33.

in force]. I kept insisting that we always react within the stipulated mechanisms." Lidija mentioned that some of the politicians from Srebrenica phoned her, shocked that women from some faraway NGOs were interfering. "But after the storm of our reactions, the deputy mayor remained in her position." For Lidija, this was the sign that because there are paths of power, it is possible to fight for the rights of women if appropriate efforts are made by the women as a group to have wide support. She was, however, dissatisfied that the women did not keep up the momentum, because many problems remain unsolved.

Lidija entertained us with an anecdote about her guest appearance on Republika Srpska TV on the occasion of the adoption of the BiH Law on Gender Equality (2003). It was during her appearance that she realized the young women of BiH do not understand the essence of the Law on Gender Equality. "I was watching the footage on TV. The journalist asked a young girl on a motorcycle if she deems men and women equal. 'Of course we are,' she responded. 'I am riding a motorcycle.'" According to Lidija, such comments from young women demonstrate that there is still a lot of work to do to change the culture and customs regulating both the sphere of private life and that of the education system, in order for the Law on Gender Equality to be fully understood, appropriately accepted, and functionally enforced. For this reason, over the past sixteen years Lidija and her colleagues from the HcA Banja Luka have constantly worked on implementing the law. With great pleasure, however, she pointed out that significant progress has been made in terms of women's political participation, mainly due to the intensive efforts of NGOs.

> We are not yet satisfied but we have now a woman who is the head of Elektroprivreda, and we cannot claim that she isn't powerful in RS. After all, this is an indirect result of our work. Many women politicians who attended our workshops are heavily involved in gender equality matters, and today they are holding high positions

... in the Government of RS we have never had as many women as we have now.

It is good that women finally have room to act, says Lidija, even though political parties tend to choose women who are obedient and would never question the policies of their party. A number of women who were empowered through the NGO workshops have found their place in politics and are now demonstrating the results of this work. A major problem, however, is that despite their involvement in politics, the work of the women is generally invisible and socially unrecognized, even though they contribute to peacebuilding and the development of society as much as men do. Women have different methods, says Lidija, but they are not inherently oriented toward peace. "Let's be clear, I think that women can be extremely radical. So maybe the difference is manifested in the methods applied, the ways of thinking, and patience." These differences in approach are something that Joseph Nye describes as an "ability to get what one wants by attracting rather than by coercion or payment."[13] While Lidija has always believed it is important for women to be represented in decision-making bodies, she also believes that both men and women can be good people. But as long as there is a power imbalance between men and women, one should use the mechanisms of "positive discrimination" and the international rules and standards that insist on equal inclusion of women in decision-making processes.

One such standard is UN Security Council Resolution 1325 on women, peace, and security, which according to Lidija, provides a solid basis for specific actions taken in BiH.

> In my view, a lot [of actions have] already been launched ... in relation to the police forces and the education of female police officers. There is increased interest on the part of the local

---

[13] Joseph S. Nye, Jr., 2005, *Soft Power: The Means to Success in World Politics*. NY: PublicAffairs, x.

community. They are reacting, responding, and undertaking certain measures. It is a process that will not happen overnight, but the Resolution clearly defined certain things, such as an obligation to eliminate the abuse of women in both war and peace.

Aware of the achievements, she still thinks much more time is required for all the instruments adopted in the national and international legislation to be applied in practice. Therefore, it is necessary to work with the young generations who will be the agents of change in society, a need Lidija recognized at the very beginning of her civic activism.

The Young Represent Hope

We succeeded in creating a youth network in BiH from the Helsinki Citizens' Assembly. The HcA youth network still exists today in that all the links between individuals and organizations are there, but it has transformed into different networks.

Besides her work on women's human rights, alongside Aleksandra Petrić and Bojana Mijić of the HcA, Lidija organized in BiH a set of youth activities, the most important of which established networks of young people, political academies for young politicians, and courses on reconciliation for teachers and students in primary schools. Youth networking was an important, but at the same time difficult, task in the post-war period; she worked a lot with Miralem Tursinović and other colleagues and associates from Tuzla who had established their own Helsinki Citizens' Assembly (HcA Tuzla) and supported the establishment of the HcA Banja Luka. In 1997, by combining their efforts, they managed to establish the first youth network in BiH with the aim of connecting youth initiatives from throughout the country and empowering the young, particularly in smaller communities. This network still exists and is recognized throughout BiH and the region for its activities aimed at improving the social position of the young.[14] Lidija is proud of this work and remembers how hard it was in the beginning to travel from one entity to another, despite the desire among the youth to do so, for the memories of war were still very fresh and people were afraid.

> Many young people who were already mobilized around some organizations took part in the activities, but for us it was more difficult to expand the youth network than the network of women. Namely, there were situations where parents would not allow their kids to join in. There were many barriers, both objective and subjective, in people's minds, which greatly depended on personal experiences. Later on, it all went well.

Working with young people, as Lidija describes it, laid the foundation for youth activism, such that young people lobbied together, fought to get office space for work in their local communities, and struggled to be recognized as partners in the processes of democratization. It was also important to build the capacity of youth organizations through initiatives such as "Let's restore gathering places for youth to the young," "You change it," and "Young people, be visible!" Lidija explained that the young people have analyzed the statutes of political parties to see how they can fight for better representation of youth within these parties, and they have also encouraged other young people to come to the polls and vote. This work has really paid off, because youth policies were adopted at both entity and local levels of government, thus enabling young people to become partners in dialogue with institutions concerning youth issues in BiH.

---

[14] HcA Tuzla and ORC—Omladinski resursni centar Tuzla, www.omladina-bih.net.

Fig. 4-4

The third important aspect of Lidija's work with young people was establishing the Academy for Young Leaders, which operated under the HcA Banja Luka until 2006. The academy embodied a new idea to educate young people about political parties and provide them with the skills they needed in political engagement that they could not otherwise acquire during a regular university education. The young people who worked on this project eventually moved to the Center for Youth and Community Development called Perpetuum Mobile, which is presently involved in youth education and has taken over the Political Academy for Young Politicians.[15] The transition, Lidija explained, resulted in no competition, often the case with NGOs. This transition is also an important indicator that young people are now capable of independently leading as big

---

[15] Perpetuum Mobile, Banja Luka, www.pm.rs.ba.

and significant a project as the Political Academy. The HcA Tuzla and Banja Luka sowed the seeds of youth activism that grew and branched into several projects and new organizations working with youth, the best outcome any activist could desire.

National Minorities

> Today, most people in BiH are members of minorities on some basis: ethnic, gender, or some other.

Work with national minorities was also an important segment of Lidija's peacebuilding work. Most neglected and marginalized were the Roma, but other national minorities also existed in Republika Srpska: Czechs, Ukrainians, Hungarians, Italians, Poles, Slovenians, Germans, Macedonians, Slovaks, and Jews.[16] Since 2000, Zoran Levi has led the work with national minorities in cooperation with the associations of national minorities in Banja Luka, and later a Federation of National Minorities in Republika Srpska was established. "In a way, this became a strength. Having us work with them has made them and their work visible and helped them fight for their rights, because it was not enough to restrict this work to the election process alone."

---

[16] The Law on the Protection of the Rights of National Minorities in Republika Srpska and a Decision on the Education of National Minorities were adopted. A National Minority Council was also established as an advisory body to the Republika Srpska National Assembly. Significant progress was made in terms of cooperation with media, resulting in an increased visibility of national minorities in the media.

Fig. 4-5

In the fight for minority rights, Lidija also advocated sharing experiences from BiH with neighboring countries such as Serbia and Croatia to empower their representatives of national minorities to better exercise their rights, and to connect cities in the region. Her stand for tolerance and peace in this regard was recognized, and in 2009 she was awarded a Tolerance Charter.[17] An important contribution to her work was ensured through cooperation with Igor and Mirjana Galo from the organization Homo from Pula, Croatia.

---

[17] At the 4th annual assembly of the Association of Multi-Ethnic Cities of Southeast Europe—PHILIA—which took place on 3-4 July 2009 in Sarajevo, Lidija Živanović, as the director of the Helsinki Citizen's Assembly of Banja Luka was awarded a Tolerance Charter. This Charter is awarded to outstanding individuals for their contributions to the advancement of multiculturalism and good inter-ethnic relations in their communities. In addition to Lidija, the Charter was also awarded in 2009 to Mr. Ivan Cenov, former Mayor of Vidin, Bulgaria, Mr. Alija Behmen, Mayor of the City of Sarajevo, and Petra Kovač from Hungary.

Indeed, successful regional cooperation was established with Croatia, and local authorities now even visit each other, says Lidija

> What is very important to me is that we managed to sign an agreement on cooperation with respect to national minorities[18] between Pula and Banja Luka. Now, on the occasion of the Day of the City when the delegations visit each other, we are no longer present. They took the baton. Usually that's what happens; our goal was to set things in motion.

As a result of long years of work with national minorities, these minorities now enjoy fairly good conditions in Banja Luka in which to conduct their activities. "They were given office space and the municipality or the city co-finances their work." This has enabled the national minorities to become engaged in promoting their cultural specificity. Every year national minority associations organize events in Banja Luka unique to their holidays.

However, the political engagement of minorities remains a neglected issue. Due to the constitutional setup of BiH and its existing limitations, ethnic minorities fall into the category of "others," and thus do not share the same rights as the three constituent peoples—the Serbs, Bosniacs, and Croats. Lidija ironically adds that not even all constituent peoples have equal rights because their rights depend on where in BiH they happen to live and which political option they support. In BiH, everyone is in some sense a minority somewhere in the country, and unless one

---

[18] A memorandum of cooperation between the cities of Pula and Banja Luka concerning the promotion of the culture and traditions of national minorities was signed in the City Hall of Pula on 28 March 2011. By signing this memorandum, the mayors of Pula and Banja Luka, Boris Miletić and Dragoljub Davidović, respectively, committed to a number of tasks targeted at promoting multiculturalism, intercultural dialogue, and the improvement of the position of national minorities with full respect of their rights at the local level. Signing of this memorandum was initiated by the hCa Banja Luka and the Association for the Protection of Human Rights and Civil Freedoms from Pula (HOMO) in cooperation with the Federation of National Minorities of Republika Srpska.

belongs to the ruling party, she or he does not have equal opportunities.

In order to draw attention to minorities and to other marginalized groups in society, HcA Banja Luka established the Srđan Aleksić journalism award in 2009, of which Lidija is particularly proud. The award is granted to journalists for professional reporting on marginalized groups in BiH (ethnic and religious minorities, the poor, women, children, returnees, sexual and other minorities). Lidija remembered how the award committee discussed the criteria and rules, but in the end realized they had no name for the award. While many proposals found their place at the table, the winning proposal was named the Srđan Aleksić award, in recognition of a Serbian soldier whose powerful wartime act in defense of a Bosniac cost him his life, as his own fellow soldiers in the army of Republika Srpska attacked him for defending that person.[19] Lidija claims that in 2009 it was still unacceptable to speak about this man killed by Serb soldiers for expressing such civic courage, although politicians later realized the value of his act and awarded him a medal posthumously.[20] In 2011, in memory of this act of civic courage, the HcA Banja Luka, Foundation CURE, and the Journalist Association of Republika Srpska awarded the first prize to the best and most professional reporting on marginalized groups. According to Lidija, this was an important cooperative action of the NGO sector and media whereby they drew attention to the problems of people who live on the margins of society.

---

[19] Srđan was a soldier in the army of Republika Srpska, when in 1993 he stood up in defense of Alen Glavović, a Bosniac, who was stopped in the street near the market in Trebinje by a group of RS Army members who wanted to see his ID. Alen managed to flee, but the soldiers brutally beat Srđan who subsequently died in hospital. For more about Srđan Aleksić see www.gariwo.org. For more on the Srđan Aleksić Journalist Award and the film about Srđan Aleksić, see www.hcabl.org.

[20] Boris Tadić, president of Serbia, awarded Srđan Aleksić the gold medal of Miloš Obilić, and Milorad Dodik, current president of Republika Srpska, awarded him the Republika Srpska medal of honor with golden rays.

Feminism under the Wings of the Family

I have always declared myself as one [a feminist], although perhaps I had no clear understanding of the essence of this concept. But I do see that people find this concept irritating and I like irritating people.

Lidija is a feminist and declares herself such publicly, whether people like it or not. As a person who cannot stand anyone imposing rules on her, she spoke publicly and openly about her feminist identity, thereby upsetting both men and women. Feminism is a word that still scares away many women, partly because they know little about it and partly because they cannot withstand the social pressure and stigma that surrounds it.[21]

She recalled one of her first live guest appearances on TV (TV Bel) at which, after her speech on feminism, a male viewer called the program and told her, "You'd better go home, make lunch, and give birth to children instead of telling such stories." In response, she told the viewer that she has children and knows how to cook, but she is still a feminist. Indeed, she learned about feminism and tried to use it theoretically to substantiate when she had a question about what was the right thing to do. In meetings and conferences with experienced scholars and politicians, such as Vesna Pusić and Biljana Kašić, Jasmina Tešanović from Croatia, Lepa Mlađenović and Daša Duhaček from Serbia, Nada Ler Sofronić, and many others, Lidija explains, we were learning "on the fly." She is grateful to all those with whom she worked, those from whom she learned, and those who learned from her.

Lidija's family support, namely that from her husband and three sons, is extremely important. "My eldest son says that he is a feminist and has absolutely no problem with it. My husband is perhaps the least progressive in this regard, that is, in terms of

---

[21] Zilka Spahić-Šiljak, 2012, *Contesting Female, Feminist, and Muslim Identities: Post-socialist Contexts of Bosnia and Herzegovina and Kosovo*, Sarajevo: Center for Interdisciplinary Postgraduate Studies, 138-45.

supporting my feminism." Lidija indicates that she has always worked on breaking patriarchal codes and hopes that she has succeeded in this endeavor. For her, the most important thing is to live in accordance with her beliefs so that she might demonstrate in her own family the changes she advocates in society. "If nothing else, I managed to raise three men outside the patriarchal code and now they share duties and obligations with their spouses."

In one way or another, most of the family was involved in civic activism and their participation helped Lidija to win support not only at home but also in public, appearing with them at various civic activities. "Through my work and the work of my husband, they became 'infected' and turned into activists. I think this … is very important to us as a family." Aware that their support was essential for her work, Lidija proudly says that she is a feminist who lives with four men. Of course, it was difficult to raise three kids and be fully committed to activism and all the travel that came with it, but her family's utmost understanding and support made it possible. In all this, she highlights the importance of the freedom she enjoyed in her family: no one ever hindered what she was doing. Her own responsibility for her family was based on self-regulation, which helped her balance her work with time for her family, the top priority.

Today, after sixteen years of work and numerous activities dedicated to empowering women for political involvement, Lidija claims that women are still poorly represented in the political scene in BiH (17 percent). Among the reasons for this, Lidija mentioned the difficulties that young women experience in balancing their political engagement with their family lives: "This kind of engagement requires additional effort and commitment. Family is often neglected as well as some of the personal needs of those … involved in public affairs." For Lidija, political engagement and civic activism have been additional obligations that can absorb one's whole day, without breaks, if approached professionally. This engagement has meant for Lidija not only being relieved of certain duties in her private life, but also being deprived of important moments:

> It happened occasionally that my family, for whom I care very much, was simply neglected. It is not about their not being able to function without me when I was on the other side of Bosnia and Herzegovina, but I missed them terribly. You yearn for those close family moments. It is a great challenge to balance this ... and it applies no matter if you're a man or a woman.

These are the dilemmas that many young women face today. Lidija does not have the answer but believes every woman must find it for herself. She found her way after the war, when she decided that it was important to invest in rebuilding her community. This decision was only made possible by the support of her family. Other women may have a harder time, especially those in small, rural communities where certain expectations of men and women prevail; such women generally choose to accept the imposed roles, following the line of least resistance.

Because of this reality, Lidija believes that making laws and establishing institutional gender equality mechanisms is not enough. Empowering women is also a much more complex process than that supported by the activities conducted by NGOs. Women do not live in isolation from patriarchal society in either the private or public sphere. Lidija sees that young women are not sufficiently prepared for what awaits them in family life, which is why they are unable to cope later on. "We wonder why young women are passive. They are not aware that they will be stretched ... they have no idea of what will happen when they start working, when they marry and have children. They simply do not comprehend the gap between reality and possibility."

Women struggle with this gap, according to Lidija, from the moment of public engagement. This is something that should be worked out through education where young women and men are taught about partnership relations based on a division of the workload in the house and mutual support. She expresses disappointment with the education system and the results evident in young people today.

Education for Peace or for Division

> So many things have been distorted by the education system and the young are the true victims of this all. We are not even aware of what has gotten into the young and what they are now thinking. ... I mean there are some who have never moved past the war.

Lidija spoke of projects implemented with young people and the good results achieved, but she is aware that these were just a drop in the sea of needs in BiH society where the public education system is not a democratic one. The system in place today is failing to prepare people for life together and for respecting diversity. Instead, it affirms and establishes ethnic divisions and segregation and increases fear. Lidija says that, "in my opinion, that's what is still wrong. And that is an important threat to our future in general, because our present life and government is fully based on ethnonational divisions." Lidija is surprised at how easily people still accept the ghettoization and divisions, because she knows isolation and alienation always give birth to bad things. That is why she could never accept restrictions on her own freedom of movement.

The educational system is organized in accordance with the constitution and laws of BiH, meaning that each entity and each canton has the power to determine how it will handle the education of its young people. For example, children are divided in school according to which group of "national subjects"[22] they choose to be taught: the Serbian, Croatian, or Bosnian curricula. Children learn one of three official histories, one of three languages—in reality a

---

[22] National subjects are: history, geography, language, religion.

single language,[23] and one of three religions: Orthodox Christianity, Roman Catholicism, and Islam. Such divisions by curriculum obviously segregate these children from their earliest years and provide them no experience of living together. Today, says Lidija, the situation is not far from that during the war. She thinks young people now are even more radical and that the situation was better during the period around 2000, when there was hope that things would change, when education would teach people about the value of living together, not about the importance of ethnic identity.

Local people are certainly responsible for their children's upbringing, but so are the national authorities and even the international community. "In my opinion," says Lidija, "a lot of things depend on the international community and the imposition of its priorities. In order to have continuity, new generations need to be raised to continue our work, but I do not think we have succeeded in reaching them."

On one hand, Lidija has put a lot of effort into working with youth, but she feels that essential change has failed to occur because of the education system, which refuses to entertain any deviation from ethnic schemes and divisions. The work of non-governmental organizations should supplement what the regular educational system cannot offer, but the system has fundamentally failed to prepare people for a democratic society. Consequently, according to Lidija, peace education is needed in public schools. "Simply put, until peace work or some kind of peace education is in our schools, there will be no change."

Religion can also have an important role in educating the young, and Lidija believes that religious communities are failing to put sufficient effort into promoting mutual dialogue and reconciliation. In fact, sometimes these communities directly oppose such efforts. Thus, she views religion as a subject in the schools as a negative

---

[23] The Bosnian, Serbian, and Croatian languages are basically the same language, but they have been given different names historically. They are a Slavic language with some regional variations and are written in either a Latin or a Cyrillic script.

influence that does not help to bridge differences or teach tolerance; it would be better to introduce religion in general as a topic of study for children while they are together in the classroom and then allow for discussion of the similarities and differences of various religions. "Or, if it has to be religion [as such], why not devote some classes to inter-religious dialogue and to learning about other religions; and why not have guests from other religions visit classes?" For Lidija, religion is *per se* not so much a problem; the problem is the way it is being presented in schools. In religion she sees a potential to stabilize society and achieve reconciliation, but she is skeptical about the religious communities' commitment to peace, because there are still too many divisions and a lack of readiness for true reconciliation.

Conclusion

Lidija, a successful interior designer from Banja Luka, invested her creative potential after the war in civic activism and re-connecting the broken links between the people of BiH and neighboring countries. Working with a group of intellectuals and humanitarians to build a civil society that would experience peace and reconciliation, she is rightfully considered by many a doyenne of peace activism in BiH. She expressed her resistance to ethno-national positions and compensated for her inability to move freely during the war by unearthing information about what was really happening at that time from European radio stations, and she did not allow others to determine where and with whom she would work and live. Immediately after the war, she started crossing entity borders and cooperating with women from other parts of BiH on the issues of education and the empowerment of women who might wish to take a more active role in social and political life. For Lidija it was important to work not only on establishing systems and mechanisms of gender equality, but also on empowering women for civic and political involvement. To this end she invested years in educating, advocating, and lobbying for the improved position of women and other marginalized groups in the community. A special challenge was working with young people and ethnic minorities who were given so little space and voice. Through the Helsinki Citizens' Assembly, Lidija managed to establish the first youth networks in Tuzla and Banja Luka, networks that are still active today. She also initiated the establishment of the Political Academy for Young Leaders, now successfully run by Perpetuum Mobile in Banja Luka. Lidija is one of very few women on the BiH public scene who speaks openly about her feminist identity. Her feminism grew with the support of her husband and her three sons of whom she is particularly proud. Although she has done much to empower the young, she remains concerned about their future, because their education has been fragmented along ethnic and national lines and thus does not prepare them for co-existence in a multiethnic state. She believes that each generation must be prepared to participate responsibly in civic life.

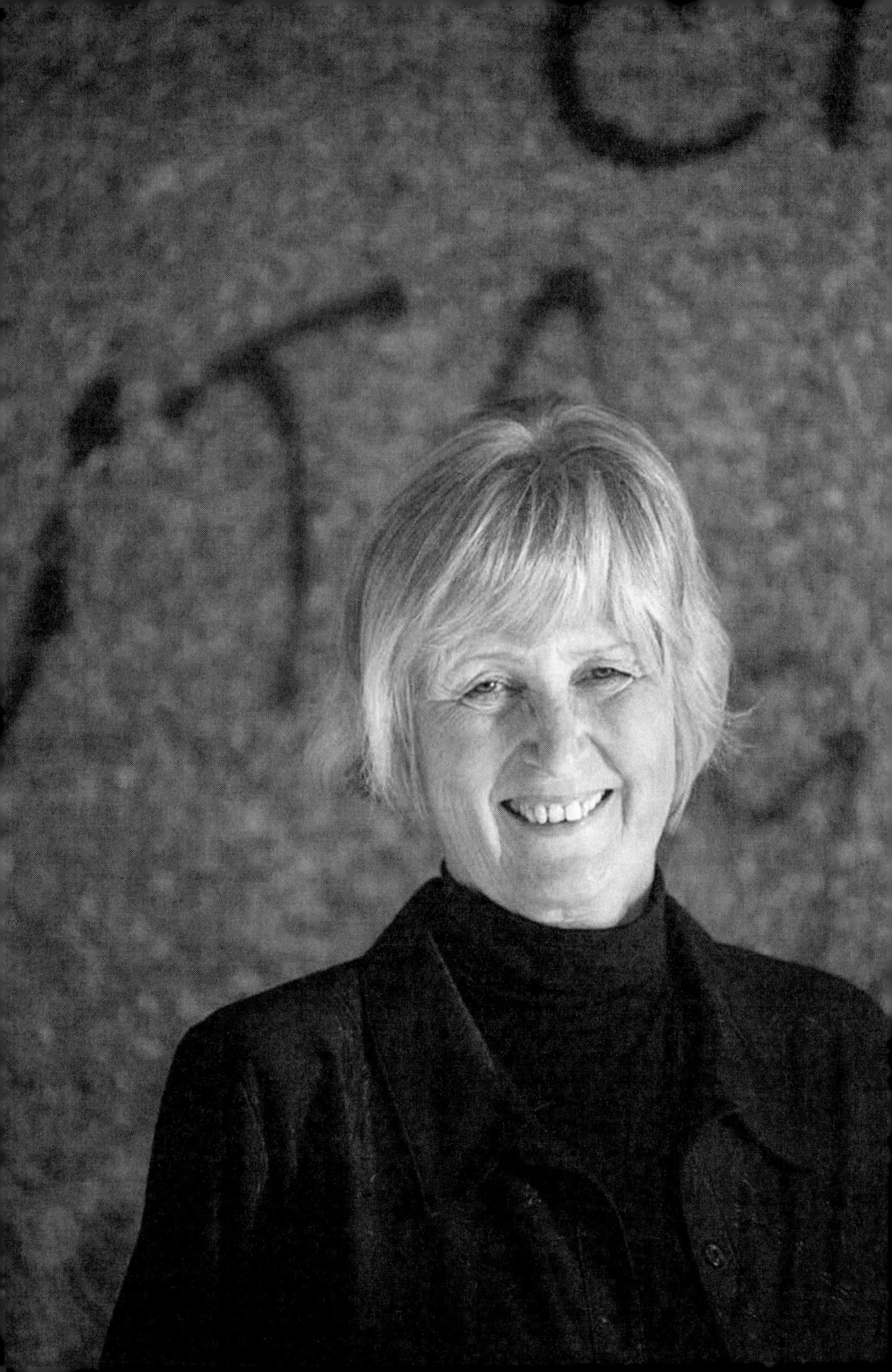

STORY FIVE

DIVERSITY IS A FORTUNE I NEVER INTEND TO GIVE UP

NADA GOLUBOVIĆ

Biography

Nada Golubović was born in Zagreb, Croatia, in 1946. She grew up in a traditional, middle-class family full of mutual respect and affection. From these beginnings, Nada absorbed the core moral values that were later reflected in her commitments and her peacebuilding activities, with special emphasis on respect for each and every human being, regardless of their affiliations or social status. Nada's parents placed great emphasis on their children's education, and Nada graduated from the Faculty of Biotechnology in Zagreb in 1971, following which she moved to Banja Luka, in BiH. There she started working in a hospital, having specialized in medical biochemistry at university. In Banja Luka, she met her future husband, a recent arrival from Belgrade, and they successfully managed to merge their two cultures (Croatian and Montenegrin) and religions (Catholic and Orthodox), and this in the very heart of former Yugoslavia. She feels she learned a lot from her husband's religious and cultural traditions and views the knowledge and experiences acquired as valuable assets in understanding people in her peacebuilding activities after the war.

Working in a hospital was an important job, but Nada also made it a humane endeavor as she transcended laboratory skills used to find the cause of a disease to people skills used to heal the trauma of war and violence. Because of her work in the hospital, she helped to found immediately after the war a non-governmental organization called United Women, Banja Luka, which she later chaired and works for to this day. For a while, she continued to work in the hospital as head of the laboratory, while also engaging in the non-governmental sector where she could do more to assist the victims of violence, especially women and children, returnees, and all others looking for a safe place to tell their stories and get help. Nada lives and works in Banja Luka. She has two grown sons and is a proud grandmother.

Introduction

What they should read about me is that I was an ordinary woman who did some ordinary things.

Nada modestly refers to her enormous dedication and contribution to promoting women's human rights, protecting women from domestic violence, and re-connecting people after the war as simply something necessary and the right thing to do. However, the citizens of Banja Luka and other towns in western BiH believe that she is no ordinary woman; consequently, they recognized her as a peacebuilder in both communities[1] Right after the war, alongside Lidija Živanović, she joined the first citizens' initiatives, whose aim was to reconnect and reconcile people. Therefore, both women are seen as doyennes of civic activism and peacebuilding in BiH.

Reviewing the activities of the women's movement in BiH, Nada Golubović and United Women are two names that repeatedly appear in the conversations of the participants in important national events. Nada's efforts have consistently been directed toward

---

[1] Zilka Spahić-Šiljak, Aida Spahić, and Elmaja Bavčić, 2012, *Baseline Study: Women and Peacebuilding in BH*, Sarajevo: TPO Foundation Sarajevo, www.tpo.ba.

bringing the people of BiH back together to live peacefully with one other as in previous times. On her journey of learning how to become a better, more complete human being,[2] Nada has created opportunities for herself and others to experience serious moments of awareness of the connections between people and their surroundings, to sense one's belonging to something larger than oneself, to experience life's fullness—the fullness of being human.

I have known Nada for years, but I got to know her better when collaborating with her on some projects promoting the political and economic rights of women in BiH who were seeking election to decision-making positions. What is most riveting about Nada is her dignified and professional attitude toward work and the people with whom she works. Those who know her better say that Nada promotes her feminist affiliation and views with a distinctive grace—unobtrusively, but clearly and consistently.

While she gladly accepted my interview invitation, she pointed out the many things yet to be accomplished to achieve absolute peace and gender equality in BiH. The interview with Nada was casual, and I had the impression that her narrative flowed just as smoothly as the Vrbas River that rippled and murmured its way underneath the restaurant in which we sat. She spoke of her life and her professional experiences with ease, and it was only occasionally that she paused to catch a breath when she remembered the difficult war times, her post-war experiences, and her attempts to help people in distress. Nada pointed to three things as being significant in her peacebuilding activities: reconnecting people for the sake of reconciliation, fighting against domestic violence, and promoting women's political engagement.

---

[2] Marshall Gantz, 2009, "Why Stories Matter," *Sojournes: Faith in Action for Social Justice*, www.sojo.net/magazine/2009/03/why-stories-matter (accessed September 3, 2013).

Story Five

We Looked After Our Neighbors

> My work as a conscientious peacebuilder began during the war and continued after the foundation of the non-governmental organization United Women in August 1996.

It is most often thought that peacebuilding starts after conflicts and wars have ended,[3] but Nada does not see it that way; she began her peace activism during the war in BiH (1992–1995). Of course, it was not an organized peacebuilding but rather an individualized, family-based attempt to save neighbors and friends who were going through hardships because they had the "wrong" names. In Banja Luka, this meant Bosniacs and Croats who were displaced, for the majority of them never returned after the war.[4] It was during this time that Nada first realized that people in BiH were noticing her accent (from being raised in Zagreb), which to be politically correct is now regarded as Croatian. Like many other people, Nada refused to believe that all of a sudden it was possible to divide people on the grounds of their national and religious affiliation, for she truly believed that diversity was enriching and could not be a reason for division:

> We used to be friends, we hung out with each other up until that ill-fated year of 1991. That was when people became aware of the fact that we were not the same. I spoke a language I had always spoken, but people started objecting—why did I speak the way I did? It made me realize to what extent people started noticing things that didn't matter to us before.

Nada saw what was happening in Croatia and throughout her former homeland, but she refused to believe the same thing could

---

[3] Johan Galtung, 1976, "Three Approaches to Peace: Peacekeeping, Peacemaking, and Peacebuilding," in *Peace, War, and Defense: Essays in Peace Research*, Vol. II, Johan Galtung (ed.), Copenhagen: Christian Ejlers.

[4] Serbs (54.58%), Croats (14.83%), Bosniacs (14.59%), Yugoslavs (12.08%), and others, uncommitted and unknown (3.92%).

happen in BiH. Her mother had already told her in 1991 that should there be a war, it would hit Bosnia the hardest, as was the case during World War II. Nada, however, never believed it would be possible to eradicate friendships and family ties so easily and she remains unshakeable in this belief despite everything that happened: "I still believe in true friendship, in love, and in the coexistence of all the people of BiH. We have never led parallel lives, but we have always lived together and shared a mutual space."

Nevertheless, the war that started in 1992 went exactly the way her mother had predicted, and in fact was even worse and bloodier. The first things Nada noticed were the departure of her friends and the arrival of new people. Nada described this in the following manner: "I ached for those who left and I sympathized with those who arrived. I felt lost and disoriented and yet I was trying to help them within my capacity and that of my family." Her mother was worried and insisted that Nada and her children come to Zagreb. However, Nada would not leave her husband behind, and says, "I simply thought I shouldn't leave the place where we built our home and where our children were born."

Staying in Banja Luka meant refusing to accept the general division by ethnicity as well as refusing the national division of her own family. Nada recalled some terrible events that took place at the time, omitting details and names, which demonstrates that it is still an unpleasant topic for discussion: "All the things that were happening to my friends, and all the horrible things that some people did, maybe even on my behalf, were a shock to me and it seemed as if I found myself in a nightmare after having … a wonderful dream." There were various problems with local authorities and warlords, as Nada calls them, because she refused to support them. People who truly believed in coexistence could not find their way in the new circumstances. The evil deeds done to neighbors and friends could not be justified and the transformation of some individuals into monstrous war criminals shocked Nada. It was as if they had become vampires, spreading darkness and leaving many numb with fear and helplessness. Using her simple human warmth, Nada facilitated a feeling of safety and protection, at least for a while, for her friends and neighbors.[5]

She recalls how, in 1992, young people were no longer to be seen on the streets of Banja Luka, which had once been renowned for the beauty of its youth. "All of a sudden, there were no more young people and we were only surrounded by death. Obituaries were being pinned on chestnut trees, and suddenly, caught in a moment of happiness, faces of young people were again smiling at you—they had been killed somewhere in Slavonia." At the beginning of the war, young men serving in the Yugoslav National Army were forced to shoot at the citizens of their own homeland, as it was splitting into smaller states.

At the same time, Serbian refugees from Croatia and western Bosnia were arriving in Banja Luka, and responsible citizen that she is, Nada tried to help them as much as she could while also assisting Bosniac friends who had been taken to a concentration camp in Kozarac. Nada and her husband tried to help a relative of her maid of honor who was in the Omarska camp, but they initially failed. The news that the man was actually being held in another camp put Nada's humanitarian work into high gear: "We [started] sending food, clothes, and parcels to that camp, the concentration camp in Manjača. The parcels were first brought to a mosque [but] that mosque was later destroyed."[6] On another front, as Serbian refugees from Croatia arrived and were accommodated in sports and cultural venues, Nada provided them too with food and clothes. Misery knows no identity or name, so it was very important for Nada to help all people in need, and there were so many—Croats,

---

[5] George Eliot, 1907, *Middlemarch: A Study of Provincial Life*, Edinburgh: William Blackwood and Sons, 467.
[6] The Ferhadija mosque was one of ex-Yugoslavia's cultural monuments destroyed in the war. Despite the extreme resistance of Serbian nationalists, this mosque has recently been restored.

Bosniacs, and Serbs. Then the conflict escalated; Serbian authorities banished Nada's Bosniac and Croat friends and even expropriated their property, which they have still not been able to recover.

> Some of our friends suggested that they transfer their property into our name, and I thought this was a horrible idea. Now I regret not having done so as it would have preserved their property. Some of them succeeded in recovering what was rightfully theirs, some Croats who traded their property for [escape to] Croatia have never succeeded, even though they would like to return to their homes.

Deep sighs occasionally interrupted Nada's recollection of that period, remembering how powerless she felt to stop the exodus of her friends. However, Nada and her husband made a moral choice and decided to help those who stayed.[7] One of the ways in which they helped was to receive humanitarian aid and serve as a channel of communication for their non-Serb neighbors and friends. "We sent letters, and [in turn] people sent us letters, and parcels from the outside world. A colleague of mine who was a Muslim sent parcels in my name to her sisters." Parcels were collected at the bus station, where people had to wait for a long time because the bus was always late. On one occasion, Nada and her Croatian colleagues Jasna and Milica went to collect some parcels. The bus was scheduled to arrive right before curfew, however, and the police were observing the people coming to the station. Nada was upset when her husband, who was walking past the station, said loudly, "'Hey you three Graces from Croatia.' With the police everywhere around us, it was no joy to be from Croatia, so we tried to hide ourselves. Now it appears funny, but we were really scared then."

They also defended the Bosniac and Croat neighbors in their building. Nada's husband, despite being Montenegrin, was considered to be a Serb and [therefore] a respectable person in

---

[7] Kathleen Barry, 1992, "Toward a Theory of Women's Biography," in Theresa Iles (ed.), *All Sides of the Subject: Women and Biography*, NY: Teachers College Press, Columbia University, 34.

Banja Luka. When raids were made during the night and paramilitary troops stormed the building, her husband would go out and speak on behalf of their neighbors, using his reputation as a university professor at the Faculty of Medicine to protect them. "It was then that he put a Cyrillic name plate on our door; we'd always had a Latin one that read 'Golubović.' The new plate read Srboljub Golubović, PhD—a title that would mean something to those military and paramilitary troops who walked into the building." Nada takes great pride in the fact that they managed to keep their friends and neighbors safe while they simultaneously helped Serbs who had fled to Banja Luka from Croatia and western BiH. For Nada, living with diversity is a way of life, something for which she continues to fight, for she wants to leave to her children an environment in which the person comes first and then the identity.

There is no Sustainable Peace without Gender Equality

> When I think of myself, I think about how ... and for what I may be recognized, and I conclude that it is first and foremost for my work with women who came from different political parties and then for my work on preventing and fighting violence, especially domestic violence against women. I am also recognized for being engaged in peacebuilding activities in my city and in [nearby] rural areas as well.

For a woman who says she was "only trying to do 'ordinary' things," Nada has refused to let others manage her life and has done everything in her power to ensure a better future for coming generations. Her story goes to prove that she has accomplished many important and positive things in her life, things that 'ordinary women' would never have had the vision to see, much less the courage or determination to do. In Jonathan Swift's words, "Vision is the art of seeing the invisible."[8] Swami Dyhan Giten similarly describes true leadership: "having the vision to see the whole person and not just a part of reality."[9] Nada realized that without the active participation of women in decision-making processes, there could be no permanent and sustainable peace. Equal participation contributes to the development of a political culture in which all social issues are also at the same time women's issues,[10] and that women should contribute to their resolution. She says she has worked hard to achieve women's participation and sees herself continuing to do so in the future, but notes that "it is also part of my history. I did play an important role in the women's political movement." Nada shares the credit for her achievements with her colleagues and friends from United Women, Lana, Natalija, and Aleksandra, with whom she learned how to overcome difficult moments and even traumatic situations, but also how to rejoice in success as a team sharing the same aim of building a society based on equality and peace.

Since 1998, Nada has been working with women from different political parties on educational programs that will enable them to share power in the public space. Gloria Steinem writes that "power can be taken not given. The process of taking is empowerment in itself."[11] Empowerment is also implied in the sensitization of women politicians to gender issues, since it is not only important to elect women, but also important that women knowingly work on gender equality issues. Nada does not intend to essentialize

---

[8] Jonathan Swift, 1857, *The Works of Dean Swift comprising A Tale of a Tub, The Battle of the Books with Thoughts and Essays on Various Subjects, Together with The Dean's Advice to a Young Lady on her Marriage*, NY: Derby & Jackson, 262.
[9] Swami Dyhan Giten, 2012, "On Intuition and Healing," in "The Silent Whisperings of the Heart: An Introduction to Giten's Approach to Life," www.selfgrowth.com/articles/GITEN2.html (accessed September 3, 2013).
[10] Beijing Declaration and Platform for Action, 1995.
[11] Gloria Steinem, 1995, *Outrageous Acts and Everyday Rebellions*, NY: McMillan, 385.

women's peace-making qualities,[12] claiming that both women and men can be insensitive to gender issues while being equally good peacebuilders. Until now, women have not had enough power to ascertain whether they have a natural inclination to peace: "I don't think that women are greater peace-makers than men. It is just that by protecting what was of greatest importance to me, my family ... my only wish is to ensure peace for my children." Due to family-based gender roles,[13] women seem to be more engaged and show more interest in peacebuilding. This awareness-raising, motherly care[14] is also visible in the engagement of certain female politicians for whom, as Nada says, socio-economic issues come first, as opposed to male politicians who primarily talk about nationalism.[15] Another important segment of Nada's work with female politicians provided the possibility for dialogue and reconciliation, which Nada feels was an important step, since female politicians from all levels of authority in BiH gathered to discuss problems faced by women and offer possible solutions.

Apart from these things, Nada advocated amendments to the election law at the time the OSCE established the temporary gender rule enforcing a mandatory 30 per cent of women on electoral party lists, a percentage that has now been defined in law and implemented. Opinions on quotas vary, and there are women who believe that it is not a democratic solution to favor one gender over another. However, as Nada explains, quantity, in spite of not guaranteeing core changes by itself, is still a good precondition for quality. Therefore, she maintains that visible changes can be expected only when a quota of 40 percent women in parliaments is

---

[12] Fiona Robinson, 2011, *The Ethics of Care: A Feminist Approach to Human Security*, Philadelphia, PA: Temple University Press, 120.
[13] Elisabeth J. Porter, 2007, *Peacebuilding: Women in International Perspective*, London: Routledge, 3.
[14] Sara Ruddick, 1989, *Maternal Thinking: Toward a Politics of Peace,* Boston: Beacon Press, 41-46.
[15] Asim Mujkić, 2008, *We, the Citizens of Ethnopolis*, Sarajevo: Center for Human Rights, University of Sarajevo.

reached. One must not ignore the significant achievements in this regard. In the first democratic elections in 1990, the number of women in leadership positions fell from 24 percent to 2-4 percent.[16] Thanks to the engagement of women's non-governmental organizations, the number rose again to 26.19 percent in 2000, but then fell to 17.9 percent in the following elections due to the introduction of open lists in 2010.[17] The reason for the current unsatisfactory state of affairs lies in numerous obstacles present in BiH ranging from structural patriarchy present in state institutions to certain cultural and customary practices whereby women, despite being well educated, lack support to engage themselves both politically and socially. Politics is still regarded as "men's business." A double moral standard for men's and women's jobs[18] also exists, as well as the phenomenon of "self-sacrificing micro-matriarchy" described by Marina Blagojević Hughson.[19]

---

[16] Jasna Bakšić-Muftić and Maja Ljubović, 2003, *Socio-economic Status of Women in BiH: Analysis of the Results of the Star Pilot Research Done in 2002*, Sarajevo: Jež, 17.

[17] Currently, women hold 13-17 percent of the seats in BiH parliaments at different levels of authority. In the government of Republika Srpska, apart from a female prime minister, five more women were elected ministers, but there are no women in the Council of Ministers of BiH and there are no women participating in talks on constitutional changes in BiH, which are being discussed by a small number of representatives of leading political parties.

[18] Zilka Spahić-Šiljak, 2010, *Women, Religion, and Politics: The Impact of the Religious Interpretations of Judaism, Christianity, and Islam on the Status of Women in Public Life and Politics in Bosnia and Herzegovina*, Sarajevo: IMIC, the Center for Interdisciplinary Postdoctoral Studies, TPO Foundation, 196-205.

[19] Marina Blagojević Hughson, 2012, *Rodni Barometar u Srbiji: razvoj i svakodnevni život*, Belgrade: U.N. Development Program.

Fig. 5-1

What seems to be particularly important is Nada's perception that some women, once in power, do not imitate men. Instead, these women try to develop their own political style, albeit there are very few doing so. A majority of women seem to be taking a lenient approach, as it is the only way for them to remain in their political parties:

> It is a frequent occurrence, that once a woman has grown enough to try to change something within her political party, men tend to regroup and remove that woman from the political scene. Only the obedient ones can survive the political scene.

However, Nada believes that there are women on the political stage who are willing to advocate for peace and for the well-being of all citizens and have not forgotten the roots of their identity as feminists. For a great number of these female politicians, it was the women's non-governmental organizations that helped and encouraged them to take up politics and develop skills as effective politicians.[20] For significant changes in politics to take place, women need more power, to be precise, more economic power. At present, what women's non-governmental organizations in BiH can objectively provide is inadequate. In BiH, non-governmental organizations are not supported by the government as may be the case elsewhere in democratic societies, so these organizations are still largely dependent on foreign donors, who in Nada's opinion, have played a very positive role.[21] Foreign donations are organized in such a way that a single person may be entrusted with the majority of tasks. Nada puts it this way: "Here, I am the manager, a shoulder to cry on, the organizer of events, and a participant all at the same time."

Furthermore, the economically unstable position of non-governmental organizations leaves no room for better networking and cooperation, because applications for funding take time to complete and organizations are very competitive. This is a serious issue in an economically weakened BiH, such that continuous advocacy for increased women's participation in politics is not possible. As a result such advocacy is occasionally done through ad hoc coalitions, as was the case in the 2010 general elections[22] and

---

[20] One of those female politicians is the Vice-President and Minister of Family, Youth and Sports of the Republika Srpska, described by Nada as a responsible minister who cooperates with women's NGOs in all aspects of the protection of women's human rights. In addition, there are a number of other politicians who are just as dedicated and engaged: Besima Borić, Katica Čerkez, and Ljilja Zovko, who are members of the House of Representatives of the Parliament of the Federation BiH; Snježana Jokić, Snježana Božić, and Rankica Panić, who are members of the National Assembly of Republika Srpska, as well as members of the House of Representatives of the Parliamentary Assembly of BiH, Ismeta Dervoz, Nermina Zaimović Uzunović, and Vesna Spremo.
[21] The OSCE, UNHCR, the Kvinna till Kvinna Foundation from Sweden, SIDA, as well as some other Swedish and Canadian sources and many other NGOs.
[22] A coalition of non-governmental organizations led by the TPO Foundation Sarajevo, Infohouse, and the CURE Foundation, and in cooperation with ten non-governmental organizations in BiH, including United Women, launched a campaign entitled "101 Reasons to Vote for Women" with the aim of motivating

the 2012 municipal elections.[23] While coalitions are important, it is necessary to work continuously in the field to achieve the best results to defeat the nationalist ideologies that threaten genuine democratization,

> I think that there is a serious task ahead of us if we want to create women whose awareness is raised and who will help our county become peaceful and prosperous, for our political scene is now full of politicians who raise national tensions, who keep us in some kind of fear.

Nada perseveres because she realizes that change comes to those who believe in change and persist through difficulties. The current situation in BiH is very difficult because the ethno-nationalistic rhetoric is so overwhelming that other voices can hardly be heard. Even though Nada believes that life is better now than it was right after the war, people are still frightened because the expected renewal of the country has never occurred while political elites continue to manipulate fears. Nevertheless, Nada has not let these threats scare her off, deciding to continue living with her former friends and neighbors.

Against the Boundaries that Divide People

> I became a peacebuilder and activist because I felt that other people were managing my life. I simply wanted to manage my own life and create a better future for my own [and] other children growing up at the time.

---

women to support female candidates. See: www.tpo.ba, www.infohouse.org, www.fondacijacure.org.

[23] Another organized attempt for women's non-governmental organizations was launched in 2012 within the project "Equal Opportunities for Women and Men in Politics" led by the TPO Foundation in cooperation with United Women and other partner organizations. More information can be found at www.tpo.ba and www.udruzenezene.org.

When the war ended, Nada and other women in Banja Luka and neighboring towns had to face numerous common problems. Nada directed her activities toward connecting women from the Federation of BiH and Republika Srpska, women from the rural areas of western Bosnia and urban working women of Banja Luka. The blatant injustice surrounding her was the trigger for her activities,[24] the discrimination her neighbors and friends suffered for having a different name, i.e., for belonging to a different ethnic and religious tradition:

> The difference between us was not visible ... we had different names but we spoke the same language. We were all white. And it was simply because you had a different name that people labeled you and singled you out. People were unjust and inhumane. There were some bullies who would attack you and you never knew why.

Additional motivation for Nada was, as she describes it, "that Balkan defiance against those who want to harm people." Her defiance was reflected in her rebellion against a retrograde state ideology that promoted ethno-nationalist divisions and ruined the coexistence in diversity in which Nada believed so wholeheartedly. "My parents raised me not to discriminate against people on the grounds of their religion, nation, color, or anything else." Nada believes that people who are divided and hate each other are worse off; only together can people live happily and peacefully. This conviction paved the way for her work to reconnect and reconcile people.

Visible and Invisible Boundaries

The first step in this process for Nada was to overcome the newly established borders[25] inside BiH. These borders were not

---

[24] Norman Denzin, 1989, *Interpretive Biography*, Thousand Oaks, CA: Sage, 70.
[25] Ghislaine Glasson Deschaumes and Svetlana Slapšak, 2003, "Žene Balkana za mir: Aktivistkinje prelaze granice," *ProFemina* 31-32, 126.

physical walls, but visible signs and symbols marking the territory, such as coats of arms with Cyrillic or Latin scripts that reflected the even more entrenched mental signs of ethnic and national divisions. Such signs were serious obstacles to the reconstruction of mutual life. If a "comprehensive peacebuilding process emphasizes the importance of a network of relationships,"[26] as Elisabeth Porter argues, then it "requires a vision of the relationship," explains John P. Lederach.[27] Nada emphasized the positive examples of communication and cooperation with women from the Federation of BiH who welcomed Nada and her associates from Republika Srpska warmly and helped them establish the first women's non-governmental organizations:

> I am proud to say that I was one of the first women from the RS who crossed the entity borders and I have to say that we learned a lot from our colleagues in the Federation, since we were under sanctions and we really did not know that non-governmental organizations existed and all that. ... We reached out a hand of reconciliation long before our politicians did.

Upon the OSCE's suggestion, Nada and her friend Lidija Živanović arranged a visit to the initial women's conference in Sarajevo in June 1996. Prior to that, the two of them had gone to Zenica to attend the conference titled "A Room for Discussion," organized by the Helsinki Citizens' Assembly and the women's organization Medica Zenica. For Nada, this event opened up new possibilities for organized peacebuilding activities. It is rather interesting how Nada describes crossing the internal borders of BiH as something completely normal, because she still perceived the whole area as her country and a space in which she had always felt free to move. "That was the first time the two of us crossed the entity border [and] I wanted to point out that not for a single

---

[26] Porter 2007, 33.
[27] John Paul Lederach, 2005, *The Moral Imagination: The Art and Soul of Building Peace*, Oxford: Oxford University Press, 35.

moment was I scared to step into the other part of the country. That was my country."

Fig. 5-2

With a certain nostalgia and sadness, Nada talked about Sarajevo. It was the city where she completed her specialization in medical biochemistry, a city she particularly loved, and a city that was renowned for receiving everyone who came with an open heart. Even though devastated and wounded, the city welcomed its true friends:

> I knew the spirit of Sarajevo too well. I knew what kind of people lived there—people from Sarajevo are different than people from Banja Luka. I always felt that Banja Lukans were warmer than natives of Zagreb, but I was convinced that Sarajevans had an even warmer heart than people from Banja Luka or Zagreb. Banja Luka appears to be simply a provincial city as compared with Sarajevo. … And when I first came to Sarajevo in June 1996 and saw how

devastated it was I felt really bad. I just couldn't believe that people could do that to other people.

Getting together with women from Sarajevo evoked nice memories as well as the hope that everything could be rebuilt if people worked together. As there were no hotels at the time, women from Banja Luka were accommodated in the homes of women from Sarajevo, "Everything was still in ruins, but people were so optimistic." There she met her former mentor for her specialist exam, a professor at the University of Sarajevo's Faculty of Medicine, Mira Winterhalter: "When we first saw each other, we shed some tears and then started talking as if we had never been apart." What still seems important to Nada is the power of women to talk about coexistence as well as to address the need to educate young people who had missed out on many things during the war, but as she says, "Unfortunately, neither they nor we now have the power to make decisions and that is why we are witnesses to the reality that in BiH there are still two different schools under the same roof as well as [two] different education curricula."

From what Nada told us, however, one can conclude that she and her colleagues who dared to cross the borders were put under a heavy strain: "There were problems [and] in 1996 and 1997, I was publicly warned in my hospital about my activities, because the former director of the hospital exercised great pressure over my husband and me." Moreover, Nada recalls headlines in the tabloid newspapers that reported that she and her colleagues had gone to the Federation to meet with generals of the Bosnian army.

Nada claims that crossing the border was no problem at all, but returning to her city afterward was a real problem, because the ethno-nationalists who were in power used provocation and threat to prevent others from doing the same. Swanee Hunt wrote about this as well, impressed as she was by the courage of women to expose themselves and their families to such a risk at a time when it was really dangerous.[28] Nada repeated this several times: "There were problems, but I wasn't afraid ... I simply thought that what I was doing was right and that the writings in a tabloid newspaper were completely irrelevant to me." Fortunately, her engagement was not considered so dangerous as to jeopardize her life, and the reputation of her husband still meant something. As was the case with other peacebuilders, women's engagement was perceived as less "dangerous" than men's engagement. The authorities' perception that whatever these women were doing would not have a strong impact or political significance at the same time provided Nada and all the other women peacebuilders great protection, especially in the first years after the war.

How Women See Democratization

The second step toward normalization was to work with women from rural areas. The enormous suffering, disorientation, and both human and material loss caused by the war resulted in a situation that the great majority of people did not know how to handle and that the state institutions were unable to solve. As a person with medical training, Nada regularly witnessed pain and suffering that she knew would not be healed by medical treatment, because trauma and mental and psychological problems require long-term treatment by those with additional knowledge and skills. Among the individuals most affected were the women who returned to devastated villages, trying to build a new life; it was for their sake that Nada accepted the invitation to engage with the non-governmental sector.

---

[28] Swanee Hunt, 2011, *Worlds Apart: Bosnian Lessons for Global Security*, Durham, NC: Duke University Press, 159.

Fig. 5-3

Her initial activities were directed toward women from the border regions of the Republika Srpska and the Federation of BiH. Supported by the OSCE and Mrs. Angela König from Germany, and alongside Lidija Živanović, Nada visited small rural communities in order to assist women in working cooperatively and to systematically help returnees to reconnect with their pre-war neighbors and friends. "It was only then that I realized how uninformed people were about one another and how little they knew about what others were doing." According to Mary Lou Décosterd, an important characteristic of leadership is empowering others,[29] giving them authority and confidence, the very thing these women needed after the war.

During her visits to the western parts of BiH divided by entity borders, Nada was able to witness the difficult state of affairs for residents. She met with women whose homes needed re-building and who needed basic assistance in organizing their lives, but Nada could not promise such things. She recalls that "reconstruction of homes was carried out through donations to which we as a women's NGO had no access." The donor policy in BiH in the first years

---

[29] Mary Lou Décosterd, 2013, *How Women Are Transforming Leadershi:. Four Key Traits Powering Success*, Santa Barbara, CA: Praeger, 74.

after the war insisted on certain democratization processes, but since a majority of people could hardly make ends meet, democratization meant nothing to them either as a term or a process.

Through the BiH Women's Initiative,[30] launched in 1996, Nada has started writing up projects that were compatible with the priorities and aims of donors, while simultaneously ensuring a significant financial incentive for returnees. For instance, women from rural areas were provided with livestock, since it was a way of ensuring sustenance for their families. Nada managed to find a way to bring democratization closer to women and to fit the problems and needs of returnees into the democratization framework upon which the donors insisted. Smiling in near disbelief at their success, Nada said:

> Property owners in rural areas are mostly men. Should a woman come into possession of a certain property, she would become equal in her household and in those cases women gain more significance in their families. Now that it's over, I have to admit that we could hardly believe that such things were written for the donors.

The presupposition was that women in rural areas were rarely property owners, even though the Law on Equal Inheritance Rights

---

[30] The Women's Initiative of Bosnia and Herzegovina was established as a program of the UNHCR with a primary focus on the empowerment of women through their reintegration into social and economic activities in post-war BiH. In 1996, the U.S. government launched the Initiative of Bosnian Women (IBŽ) with initial funding of $5 million. The initiative was implemented by the UNHCR and a number of partner organizations and was, until 2002, an important component of the UNHCR's programming in BiH. Its main aim was the empowerment of vulnerable women through providing support to them after the war, with a special concern for returnees and displaced persons, to rebuild their lives and contribute to long-term reconstruction and democratization of their communities and land, which would raise awareness in the community about the potential of women and their needs.

had existed in Yugoslavia since 1952.[31] Nada remembers situations when husbands complained about their wives coming into possession of a donated property, and thus it was very hard to make any progress at the beginning in a patriarchal family setup in which the man was the head of the household, the owner of the property, and the decision-maker. Nada recalls how some of them used to say, "Everything is mine, so that cow should be mine too," whereas 'wiser' men would advise them in the following manner, "You fool, be quiet! Your wife, your cow ... don't waste your energy on stupid things, let her sign what she wants, she's yours and therefore the cow is yours too." These examples best illustrate how the patriarchal family setup is entrenched, but may be slightly adjusted to new circumstances in which the man is still able to find a way to preserve his authority because he continues to see his wife as his "property." The goal of these democratization projects was empowering women and their families to help them survive the post-war years in their returnee settlements.

Apart from the economic benefits, these projects also contributed to the reconciliation of ethnically homogenous villages. To enable communication between people, Nada and her colleagues resorted to the "ethnic key" strategy, which basically meant that they would, for example, deliberately hire a project coordinator from one entity and a veterinarian from the other. The teams always consisted of both Serbs and Muslims, which communicated the particular message that people were working and living together again. And the method for facilitating this life together again was through employing ethnically mixed teams that travelled and worked together in the field.

Regardless of the fact that work in the field was done by professionals, Nada wanted to apply her medical experience in her direct contact with people,

---

[31] Spahić-Šiljak 2010, 144-52.

I participated in these projects and I directly talked to those women about the possibilities of mutual coexistence. We went through their traumas and suffering together. We worked on the organization of meetings and tried to discern the problems they shared and solve them together.

That kind of direct engagement meant a lot to both those women and to Nada because, as she put it, they were trying practically to establish new relationships and renew the old, disrupted ones.

One Should Not Diminish Other People's Pain and Suffering

The fourth and very important step in Nada's post-war peacebuilding work was dedicated to healing war trauma, the experience that blocked an individual from accepting the reality that other people had also gone through suffering and pain during the war. Nada continued working with women from villages around Prijedor, Banja Luka, and Kotor Varoš. The villages in question were mono-ethnic Bosniac, Serb, and Croat villages. In the former Yugoslavia, urban centers were usually ethnically mixed, while the villages remained ethnically and religiously homogenous. Nada pointed out that the people from the above-mentioned villages had lived next to each other as good neighbors[32] and then all of a sudden stopped communicating. Women from the three ethnic groups seemed to have varying perceptions of the war: "Every one of them has a different view of how the war began and why. It was extremely important to get them to talk to one another and then work together." Fear of a reunion, however, was so intense that women were afraid once they start talking to each another, they would forget everything that had happened to them. Nada says that, consequently, it was very difficult to start a dialogue. With her

---

[32] This is something Ambassador Swanee Hunt confirmed in her research: Swanee Hunt, 2004, *This Was Not Our War: Bosnian Women Reclaiming the Peace*, Durham, NC: Duke University Press, 104-14.

colleagues, she tried to convince these women that they didn't need to forget, but that forgiving would allow them to move on.

Nada used what Lederach calls the "smart flexible"[33] peacebuilding strategy. Instead of asking the women to face directly the horrors of their war experiences, she would find an indirect way to encourage communication, for example, through the common problems faced by their children regarding transportation, acquiring school equipment, providing a clean water supply in schools. "Women from different nationalities, with different war experiences were united by a joint action to improve the conditions of schools for their children." Even though this was a small step for them, for Nada it was a giant leap, because the women started working together on issues relevant for their future. The network of peace that Nada was persistently and patiently weaving was based on rebuilding relationships between people.

To make those meetings and dialogues even more productive, it was necessary to learn how to work on healing trauma in such a way as to facilitate the reconciliation process. It was particularly important to train educators in how to handle their own trauma before helping others. Assistance was provided by the U.N. expert on trans-generational trauma, Dr. Yael Danieli, who was working in BiH with the support of non-governmental organizations from Croatia and Germany.

> We worked on our personal traumas ... as well as on compassion for other people's trauma. I personally believe that it helped us all become better people. We learned to respect other people's pain and suffering, because the pain we talked about and the trauma we experienced and carried were always on an individual level. ... We learned to understand and feel the pain of others without diminishing our own pain.

---

[33] Lederach 2005, 85.

Nada was extremely appreciative of the experiences she gained despite the fact that she had always tried to understand the pain and suffering of others. The education helped her handle her own trauma as well as the trauma of others. Smiling, she added that she had become a better person due to this education process and working in the field.

How to Live Together Again?

The fifth important step was to work with women in the city of Banja Luka. Bearing in mind the emigration and deportation of masses from an entire region, the tensions in post-war Banja Luka between the population that remained in Banja Luka during the war, the refugees from Croatia and western BiH, and the returnees to Banja Luka after the war, Nada and other female activists initiated a media project called "How to live together again?" For some people, the very title of the project raised hopes of stabilization and a return to normalcy, while others found it confusing and frightening, since similar policies attempted to jeopardize the ethno-national divisions on which the power holders were counting with an aim to manipulate and govern the divided, displaced and tortured people.

Fig. 5-4

Bringing local, refugee, and returnee women together in her work was extremely important for Nada since their perceptions of the war's events were completely different. Nada's "moral imagination" was so powerful that not only did she think outside the ethno-national boxes, but she was also willing to risk living outside them[34] and so encourage women to start talking to one another:

> The local women believed that their fellow citizens who had left Banja Luka and now returned had had a great time somewhere else and did not suffer at all. The refugees believed that the local women and the returnees posed a threat to them. Those women who had stayed in Banja Luka, regardless of their nationality, believed that returnees and refugees were traitors and were not welcome in the city. In short, they were all "a threat" to one another.

---

[34] Ibid.

Nada tells us about that painstaking process in which the representatives of each group made appearances on radio shows where they talked about their biggest problems and tried to identify their mutual interests and solutions. This was the first joint presentation made by women from different nationalities on NTVBL, which enabled the message of reconciliation and dialogue to reach many people. It was a very important but also a very brave activity at a time when, in Nada's words, such activities were not in compliance with the ethno-nationalist rhetoric on division, difference, and vulnerability. "At the time, it was an act of bravery since our public spaces were reserved for the post-war rhetoric and little was said about mutual coexistence and the necessities of reconciliation in communities." Nada spoke of and did what many citizens secretly desired but had insufficient courage to do publicly. "After every show, citizens of Banja Luka from different national backgrounds would approach me and say, 'Thank God that someone has finally started talking about these things.'"

Nada continued on the path of dialogue, re-connecting, and reconciling because she and the women she worked with realized that in joining forces they could resolve numerous issues burdening BiH society. One of many issues they faced was domestic violence, which had escalated in dysfunctional families and society in general.

An (Un)usual Woman Fighting against Violence

Violence not only occurs in war and post-war societies. It can occur (to a greater or lesser extent) in any society, the question being how aware people are of that violence, to what extent is it socially acceptable, and whether it is still taboo to talk about it publicly. Prior to 1997, when United Women opened an office offering free legal aid, Nada had not contemplated addressing the issue of domestic violence. Whereas the issue of unresolved property was an obvious choice, to her surprise, she was asked to act on behalf of women who were victims of domestic violence. This was probably due to the fact that United Women was one of the rare organizations providing free legal aid to women, so it may have seemed women finally had a safe space[35] to talk about it openly.

Nada tried to explain that the phenomenon of violence did not appear abruptly and that it was not a product of war, despite the fact that war had greatly contributed to its escalation. The issue of domestic violence is deeper and much more serious than it appears, with a number of factors affecting it both within the family and the society itself.

The transitional period just before the war and just after it, influenced gender roles in the family:

> Male and female gender roles have changed. Women became stronger during the war and began looking after their families; however, they got no recognition for that since it was a role that has traditionally belonged to men. On the other hand, men who were fighting on the battlefield during the war and thereby enacting the gender role of defending the homeland returned to their homes to find closed factories and no opportunities for work, no recognition for their efforts and no valorization for their war labor. Such a change of gender identities might lead to increased violence in a patriarchal society.

A partial change of gender roles did perturb the traditional, patriarchal family, but could not have been the sole cause of domestic violence against women and children. Judging by clients who came to the United Women office and by the genesis of violence they talked about, Nada asserts that violence had always been present in some families and the war just deepened it. The

---

[35] Ristin Thomassen, 2006, *To Make Room for Changes: Peace Strategies from Women's Organisations in Bosnia and Herzegovina.* Johanneshof, Sweden: Kvinna till Kvinna Foundation, http://www.peacewomen.org/assets/file/Resources/NGO/kvinna_tomakeroomforchanges_2006.pdf (accessed September 3, 2011).

United Women team tried to analyze the roots of violence so as to be able to work on its prevention and protect women from it. "We came to the conclusion that the roots of violence were embedded in the family itself and that it was essential to work with the women … for in a patriarchal family, it is the women who raise the children." Nada went on to explain that while she does not wish to blame everything on women, but in her view, women bear enormous responsibility as they raise their children and they tolerate violence as a socially acceptable behavior, and it is something that mostly women are stigmatized for.[36] In the first years of United Women's work, the number of victims was enormous, which induced Nada to take up this issue more systematically. She launched various initiatives promoting a legal framework for protection from domestic violence, because until 2000 it was considered a private matter:

> We had so many cases of women being victims of domestic violence. Women victims started contacting us and we then realized that the victims [plight] actually had never been legally regulated, and then I really worked hard with the aim to amend the laws in BiH. Of course it was not only me, other non-governmental organizations worked toward that end [as well].

---

[36] Natalija Petrič, 2012, *Nacionalne politike u suzbijanju rodno zasnovanog nasilja u Srbiji, Hrvatskoj, i Bosni i Hercegovini: Položaj žrtava*, Ph.D. thesis, Novi Sad: ACIMSI University, 62-77.

Fig. 5-5

As a first step, they succeeded in defining domestic violence as a criminal act and including it in the RS Criminal Code (2000) and later in the Criminal Code of the FBiH (2003). This was just the beginning; an additional special law was needed to accommodate the victims of domestic violence. However, Nada believed that such a project should have the support of the state institutions:

> So we turned to the then-Prime Minister of the RS and asked him to allocate funds so that we could buy a house, not just for United Women. We thought we should form a network all over BiH and RS, and so we suggested the same idea to the women's center in Trebinje, which had been donated some funds at the time, and so United Women Banja Luka bought a house.

In this way, government institutions in RS started financing the safe houses that now exist in Banja Luka, Trebinje, Modriča, and Bijeljina. Since 2001, thanks to then-minister Besima Borić (see chapter 7), the Sarajevo Canton also received governmental support for maintaining a safe house.

Women's non-governmental organizations spent many years advocating for laws on protection against domestic violence that were finally adopted in both entities in 2005. In Republika Srpska, together with other female members of Parliament, Nada drafted a plan that safe houses in RS should be financed from the budget of both the entity and the local communities. That model served as a starting point for a similar setup in the Federation of BiH, where Nada collaborated with her colleague from Medica Zenica, Sabiha Husić (see chapter 1); they attempted to motivate the female members of the BiH Parliament to set priorities, develop a platform for action, and then to work on its application:

> I can also mention that this year, we are really in position to say that our platform has been one hundred percent completed, as it had been a priority on the state level to harmonize the Election Law with the Law on Gender Equality and that was completed at the end of this year. The priority in both entities was to introduce new laws on the protection against domestic violence and now both entities have new laws … so we can really regard it as a great success.

This success, Nada claims, is not only the success of United Women, but it is a success for the groups of non-governmental organizations who had been lobbying and working on it for many years. It was the first time that the issues around protecting victims of domestic violence and financing safe houses were legally regulated. Nada's work on this issue was also widely recognized, and she received the award of the *BiH Woman* (*Žena BiH*) magazine. Despite such recognition across BiH, Nada emphasizes that her field of work has yet to be fully accepted by society since "the issue of violence against women, the number of women engaged in politics, and the reconciliation of people in BiH are all topics that are [either] shoved under the carpet or used daily for political purposes by all politicians to support their own goals."

This form of civic activism still lacks the necessary support from both the state and the media, making systematic and continuous work very difficult. Nevertheless, Nada manages to find inspiration and strength in her belief in the goodness of mutual coexistence in diversity, which is the treasure of the Bosnian-Herzegovinian cultural mosaic.

Religion is Important for Peace, but what about Religious Communities?

Though raised a Catholic, Nada claims that for the purpose of her peacebuilding activities, she has behaved as an agnostic, never using religion as an argument for peacebuilding. This demonstrates once again that religion, while not initiating conversations about peacebuilding in Bosnia and Herzegovina,[37] nevertheless can pass on to its adherents the core religious postulates, such as those that have been visible in Nada's work: honesty, diligence, and sensitivity.

> Culturally, I belong to Christianity, and we Christians have a saying: "Turn the other cheek." I believe there's no reason why we should turn cheeks at all. I think we ought to share everything—if we have a loaf of bread we should share it justly and eat it together; that's what my parents have taught me.

Such equality is very important for Nada. She was taught to believe that the people of BiH belong to a single nation, but different religious groups. Her family also taught her that women and men are equal and that she should not favor a male child, as is often the case in Balkan families. "And so, by being equal within my own family, I saw all my friends from different religious and national groups as my equals."

---

[37] Ina Merdjanova and Patrice Brodeur, 2009, *Religion As a Conversation Starter: Interreligious Dialogue for Peacebuilding in the Balkans*, NY: Continuum, 108.

That deeply rooted sense of equality and the need to share everything with others made Nada commit herself to peace and reconciliation. While she believes that religions might serve as a factor in reconciliation, the reality is that religious communities may differentiate between people because of the interpretations of their teaching toward others. This happens, she explains, because politicians use religion to manipulate people. It is therefore important to her to recognize the difference between believing in certain religious tenets and belonging to an institutionalized religious group. All religions can help with the reconciliation process in their similar advocacy for tolerance and love. Every religion also expects its followers to be good people. Nada does not know why people would do horrible things on behalf of their religion, but she is certain that people who kill in the name of their religion are not religious but rather religious fanatics:

> I do not believe in killing in the name of any god, I do not believe in harassment and discrimination in the name of any god. We have to know the difference between true belief and true believers and those who are far from that but proclaim themselves to be leaders on behalf of their religious community.

For Nada, the role religious communities played during the war is highly questionable, because these communities blessed war crimes and failed to distance themselves from the violence. Moreover, they invaded the public space by introducing religious education in schools, which is now being taught to children in ethnically homogenous communities, a practice that does not contribute to peacebuilding and diversity. What Nada believes should be done is to dedicate more attention to educating children about different religious cultures to provide them with an understanding of religions' similarities and differences. The fear of the other that has long been nurtured in this part of the world is a powerful weapon in post-war BiH. Adding religion to the equation makes it even easier to manipulate people into hating, attacking, and banishing all those who are different from "us."

Conclusion

Nada is an ordinary woman, as she likes to point out, but she chose a path during the last two decades that was anything but ordinary. It was the path of recognizing the humanity in every person in need of help and support, both during and after the war. In the early nineties, when she realized how it was possible for warmongers to impose ethno-national divisions, she wholeheartedly opposed it in order to preserve her ethnically and religiously mixed family as well as other families who refused to accept these divisions. Immediately after the war she established the organization Udružene žene (United Women) in Banja Luka, circumventing the new boundaries in order to work with other women in BiH on restoring broken relationships and destroyed homes.

She is renowned for her efforts to politically empower women and to combat violence against women, and for her peace initiatives in rural areas, to which exiled people from all ethnic communities returned. Nada believed that it was crucial to connect women who remained in Banja Luka with refugees from other places and with returnees to Banja Luka, as they all had different perceptions of events during the war, but had to live alongside one another in the aftermath of the war. Nada also made a strong commitment to systematically address the issue of domestic violence, particularly in relation to the adoption of laws on the subject, as well as other concrete measures such as the establishment of safe houses for victims of domestic violence.

Although her Catholic values permeate her work, Nada never put that part of her identity in the forefront, instead accentuating humanist, civic values which she had learned through life in the former Yugoslavia. She critiques the many irresponsible churches and religious communities who were deeply involved in the events of the war. Because true believers are first and foremost good people, it was important for Nada to connect people so that they could experience one another's human spirit.

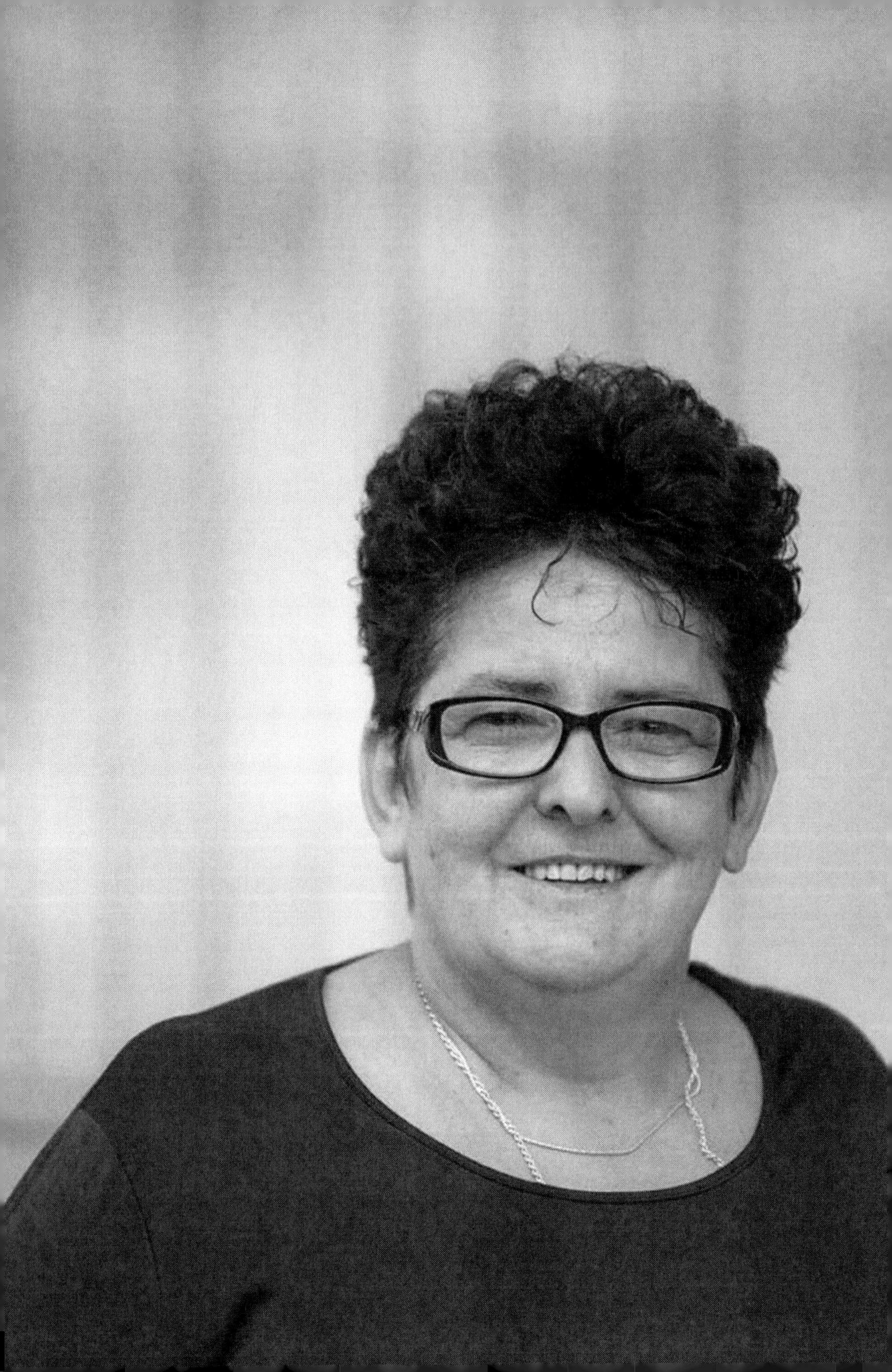

STORY SIX

PEACE RESTS UPON THE NEEDS OF ORDINARY PEOPLE

STANOJKA CANA TEŠIĆ

Biography

Stanojka Cana Tešić[1] was born in 1961 in Bratunac, eastern Bosnia, the third child of Serb parents. Cana and her three sisters were raised in a proletarian worker's family that did not observe any religion practices. Instead of icons, the walls in their house were covered with photos of the four daughters. Cana and her sisters were hard-working students and as such joined the Socialist Youth League. In the extra-curricular activities at their high school, the sisters had a chance to travel and be involved in the typical events that attracted teenagers of that time. Dancing in a folklore group took Cana to many cities where she met people from all over BiH. After marrying, Cana joined the Socialist Association of Women where she played an active role. She and her husband Goran launched a private business (in the food trade), which allowed her family to lead a comfortable life. She gave birth to two daughters, Gordana and Vladana, but the family's happiness was cut short with the war that started in 1992 in which eastern Bosnia suffered horrific killings of both its Bosniacs and Serbs.

After the war, Cana was engaged in work on behalf of the refugees and displaced persons returning to Bratunac, and in 1999

---

[1] Throughout her life Stanojka went by her middle name, Cana (pronounced Tsana) which is therefore the name used to refer to her in the chapter.

she founded the Forum of Women of Bratunac together with a group of co-workers. She wanted to connect former neighbors and friends and to open up the reconciliation process in this region, for which she toiled relentlessly with other NGOs to strengthen the women who had suffered the greatest burden in the post-war recovery. Despite the fact that there was and still is resistance to the activities of the Forum of Women, Cana does not pay attention to this, because she knows that she has done everything in her power to help people save their dignity and return to their homes.

Her engagement in the Forum of Women brought many obligations but it also made available to her educational opportunities in the field of civic activism and women's human rights, which was a novelty for most of the women in BiH. Through her own personal development, Cana helped a great number of women who became successful on the BiH political scene. Today, Cana lives and works in Bratunac.

Introduction

> Our mother inspired us [saying] that no one [else] should fight for our rights, but that each one of us individually should exert [our] selves. She somehow made us stable and strong persons.

Whenever I phoned Cana to ask if she would work with us on a project about strengthening the role of women in politics and peace activities, the answer would always be: "Count on us from the Forum of Women." She never missed the opportunity to cooperate and connect, and she was never too tired to come to a women's meeting in Sarajevo, Banja Luka, Mostar, or some other city. She has become a renowned activist promoting women's human rights, notably the rights of women returnees to eastern Bosnia, who are mostly single mothers attempting to rebuild their destroyed homes and lives and renew their torn neighborhood and its relationships.

When I invited her for an interview to talk about her life, she told me: "Oh why, dear Zilka, would my life be interesting to anyone?" I told her that some people in eastern Bosnia deem her life interesting because of the efforts she made to promote women's rights and the return of refugees,[2] so she should say something about this. In her good-natured way, she noted: "Well, I thank them for that but I have not done anything special except what I thought was right and humane." This is the answer that most women give, not because of false modesty, but because they sincerely believe that they are only doing what they know best and what is most useful at the moment for those in need.

"Oh, God, where do I begin? I do not have a lot to say and it would be somehow easier if you had questions." Nevertheless, even without leading questions, she began threading her life story to us over coffee, giving illustrative descriptions that she considered important to share. She talked about her family with great enthusiasm and also about her husband's family, who have all significantly defined her attitude toward life and her values of work, struggle, justice, and help for those in need.

Coming to the war years, she took a deep breath and asked if we could have a short break. She needed several minutes to gather her strength to recount the events that, like most people in BiH, she would prefer to repress. These events were aggregated traumas and accounts of being a witness to the fear and suffering of Bosniacs and Serbs in the region of Bratunac but also of standing in defense of the other's dignity regardless of the price. Sometimes this price was so great that she might have lost her family or died alongside the friends she protected.

---

[2] Zilka Spahić-Šiljak, Aida Spahić, and Elmaja Bavčić, 2012, *Baseline Study: Women and Peacebuilding in BH*, Sarajevo: TPO Foundation Sarajevo, www.tpo.ba.

The War Made Us Powerless, but It Did Not Defeat Us

It is easy to be good in good times, but it is hard to be a human being in hard times and lucky is the person who can resist the temptation.

Fig. 6-1

Those who know Cana will say that she is a great person with a huge heart. On the basis of her story, one can see that she has managed to preserve her humanity and protect the dignity and lives of her friends and neighbors during hard times. Her peace activism actually began in 1992, during the war, which is another indicator that peacebuilding is not only a post-war endeavor.[3] At the time, she lived in Bratunac with her husband Goran and her two daughters and worked as a private entrepreneur, enabling her to travel around BiH and establish new contacts and friends. This made Cana very

---

[3] Johan Galtung, 1976, "Three Approaches to Peace: Peacekeeping, Peacemaking, and Peacebuilding," in *Peace, War, and Defense: Essays in Peace Research*, Vol. II, Johan Galtung (ed.), Copenhagen: Christian Ejlers.

happy. Bratunac, like many other towns, was a multiethnic community[4] before the war, where Serbs, Bosniacs, and Croats lived together and where, according to Cana, one's value was not based on ethnic or religious affiliation.

However, at the beginning of 1992, Cana and her friends realized that the political situation had made it possible to impose ethno-national and religious identities on everyone, which resulted in division, hostility, and hate among the local population. Unfortunately, some people were more than eager to use this identity factor to benefit from the war and the associated deportations, while a great number of people silently watched the events in order to save their own lives and were unable to do anything meaningful. With a heavy sigh and arms spread as if wanting to show all the desperation that had overwhelmed them in those years she said:

> It is very difficult to go back to that time because whatever I say now that I felt then [is false], at that time I did not feel anything. I saw that my father-in-law and his admirable nobleness of spirit had simply disappeared, he suddenly looked like a decrepit old man as things went out of control around him.

Cana's father-in-law was a model of moral fortitude, a support but also an authority for the family and for others in the town. She appreciated him and tried to learn as much from him as possible. However, with the war, even her father-in-law, as a person of standing and an assured Communist, could do nothing. "It was then that I felt that he had no control over anything, he had even lost control over his children, because if they wanted to keep their jobs, they had to join one of the [non-Communist] political parties." After the disintegration of Communism in the Balkans, there was a great political turnabout; previously moral and political legitimacy

---

[4] According to the census of 1991, the population of Bratunac was comprised of 64.2% Muslims, 34.2% Serbs, 0.1% Croats, and 1.5% others. According to unofficial data, 78% of Bratunac today is Serb and 22% Bosniac.

as well as many jobs depended upon membership in the League of Communists of Yugoslavia. However, the ethno-national policies at the beginning of the nineties required people to have political legitimacy on another ideological basis. Watching the greatest authority figure in the family broken and defeated, she tried to remember his message on the importance of preserving one's humanity and honor.

Cana reiterates that in this period she strived not to buckle under the pressure, although it was difficult. In the war madness of 1992, Cana experienced the first great turning point[5] in her life when facing her friends' and neighbors' required exile as members of different ethnic groups. She mentions that at the time, ethno-national groups had already formed and that deportations and killing of innocent people had begun just because of their different name and surname. For Cana, her Muslim and Catholic friends and neighbors were primarily good people. The situation was hardest on those living in mixed ethnic marriages, but "We had truly decided to stay. Simply, our closest friends and everybody had decided to stay." This was their way of resisting the separation and division.

However, fear spread like a plague, and it soon also fell upon her house where a great number of women and girls had sought refuge. As the situation became serious, she requested support from her husband and her father-in-law, because she did not want to endanger her family should the army come to her door. Her father-in-law only said: "You know, Cana, everything that you are able to do and that you believe you can do to help, I am there for you and I am armed." This was strong moral support, and it was important for Cana to know she had allies in protecting her neighbors and friends. After several days, however, it became clear to them that they would have to part so as not to jeopardize their own and their host's safety. In those moments, Cana was thinking as a responsible mother facing difficult moral choices about her children:

---

[5] Norman Denzin, 1989, *Interpretive Biography*, Thousand Oaks, CA: Sage.

So, it was never a question of my own safety or the safety of my husband Goran; that was our choice. However, our choice also impacted our two young daughters. Did we have the right to endanger them and their lives? ... And believe me, we sat in front of our house and we all cried. For the first time, we felt powerless.

She therefore transported this community of friends and neighbors to different locations that might be safer, if there really was any safe place in eastern Bosnia at that time. Her closest friend and her family remained with Cana, but for safety reasons, they decided to move to the village of Uzovnica in Serbia, only a few kilometers from Bratunac.

Cana once again returned to the moral figure of her father-in-law. Although seriously ill at the time, he did not want to go to the hospital until the last of the neighbors, who were staying in their house and under their protection, had safely left Bratunac. Before leaving for the hospital, he drew Cana's attention to another important thing that was happening in Bratunac at the time in relation to their neighbors' property:

> "Do you see what is going on in our neighborhood?" I had not even paid attention to it. ... We noticed that they were carrying tapestries, flower pots, blankets, pillows, and some personal possessions from the Muslim houses. ... Suddenly some people who had come from other places—not our neighbor Serbs who remained in the town—were taking things and suddenly you only see chaos.

Attempting to take her friends and neighbors to a safe place outside Bratunac, Cana did not have time to notice people stealing her neighbor's possessions, the very neighbors forced to leave for fear of being killed. However, she claims that this was not done by Serbs from Bratunac but by "volunteers" who had come from places across the border in Serbia, choosing to profit from other people's hardship. Of course, all of this did not escape the watchful eye of her father-in-law who viewed this chaos as moral degradation. He said to Cana: "I may not come back [from the hospital] but you will return. You have to watch out that someone else's chicken does not enter our garden. If it does, you must drive it out of our garden." At first, Cana did not understand what he wanted from her, but it soon became clear when she saw a tenant in her house pushing some things in a small cart and she asked him:

> "Where are you taking that?" He said, "to my place." "Where is your place?" "To my apartment," he replied. "This is not your apartment; this is my apartment, my house," I said to him. "Nothing from other gardens must enter our garden." At that moment, I understood my father-in-law's last words to me. "Don't let something enter our garden."

Although everything was falling apart—the world in which they believed was disappearing—he wanted at least to maintain sanity and moral uprightness in his own house.

Real humanity and faith were always reflected in respecting one other's rights, and those words of wisdom and faith in just behavior were Cana's moral compass in the most difficult days when human life carried little value, when you could lose your life just by a word, a name, a look, an appearance, or your origin. This faith and hope helped her fight her own fears and to stand in defense of humanity and justice for her friends. Her father-in-law was a teacher and an ally who entrusted Cana along with his own children to preserve the dignity of his home. He must have seen in her a spark of humanity and goodness, such that he could count on her strength to preserve his family's dignity.

The Friendship and Support of Four Mothers

> What is more valuable? How much of a mother I am or how much of a mother my friend is? Or how much my child is worth to me or how much my friend's child is worth to her?

From the beginning of the war, Cana attempted to shelter her neighbors and friends, and when she was unable to provide a haven for them in her house, she helped them move to places that were not under the control of Bosnian Serbs. The first two years were difficult both for her and her children, because as she says, it was impossible to jump from a normal life into the darkness of hate and destruction, where all human values were smothered and devalued. For Cana it was like a life without air and water. Despite all the difficulties, the need to care[6] for her two daughters and the son of her friend was motivation enough to endure. Throughout the evil and tyranny and even in the toughest times, Cana looked for some goodness, some reason to be thankful. "No matter how difficult it was and no matter what we went through," she says, "if God is somewhere out there I am grateful to him ... for helping my daughters to accept life at that time in such an abnormal environment."

Cana continued speaking about the war period as if it was a surreal period in her life, a time full of paradoxes one had to endure to find a light at the end of the tunnel. The abnormality and disorientation caused by the turmoil of war, which the adults somehow managed to deal with, was very difficult for the children to accept. It was not easy to explain to them why they now had to pretend and hide and learn about things that were the opposite of everything they believed: brotherhood and unity and coexistence. In these surreal conditions, she had to teach her kids to call her friend's son Mile, because his real name was not a Serb name and would cause him problems:

> We taught him to sing Četnik songs, because if we got on a bus we could see all types of people there. There was once this case when one of the mercenaries (soldiers) put him in his lap and said ... OK, now you sing some songs to me ... Četnik songs, and the bus was

---

[6] Nel Noddings, 2002, *Starting at Home: Caring and Social Policy,* Berkeley, CA: University of California Press.

full of people. Imagine if he had just said, "I don't want to sing." We had to bring up three children and tell them from now on you [must] learn Četnik songs. They had never learned these before. You now had to teach them not to talk.

Cana chose the strategy of covering up her friend's identity and showing sympathy toward the people who imposed the Četnik ideology just to protect herself and her friend's son. Because her own and her husband's family had been Communists who fought against the Nazis, Četniks,[7] and Ustaša[8] in World War II, she could not imagine being forced to watch and even to participate in glorifying the Četnik movement. The children somehow understood that it was important to adapt to the war conditions, and they lived day by day in this surreal, schizophrenic existence. Evil was ever present in their life, and it seemed as if people's blood cells were even examined: their origins and identities were investigated in order to assess whether they deserved to live or die.

Hiding people in the village of Uzovnica in Serbia turned out to be a successful solution for the people Cana was trying to help, but as she recounts, there were occasional moments when it was necessary for those being hidden to appear in public, where they would be in danger of being recognized. The first time that

---

[7] Četnik songs were sung during World War II by Četniks who fought against Tito's Partisans. The Četniks were meant to represent the resistance movement after the capitulation of the Kingdom of Yugoslavia, but in reality they also collaborated with the Nazis. The movement glorified the Serb people as a divine nation asserting the right to all the territory where Serbs lived and where there were graves of their ancestors. See: Stjepan Mesić, 2012, "Serbia Endangers Region by Rehabilitating Chetniks," *Balkan Transitional Justice, Balkan Insight* (21 March); Sabrina Ramet, 2006, *The Three Yugoslavias: State Building and Legitimation, 1918-2005*, Bloomington, IN: Indiana University Press.

[8] The Ustaša fought against Tito and the Partisans in World War II and collaborated with the Nazis. They founded the Independent State of Croatia led by Ante Pavelić and occupied parts of Serbia and BiH. They committed horrific crimes against non-Croats including the establishment of the concentration camp Jasenovac, where the majority of victims were Serbs. See: Paul Mojzes, 2011, *Balkan Genocides: Holocaust and Ethnic Cleansing in the Twentieth Century*, Lanham, MD: Rowman and Littlefield.

happened was during a trip to the doctor to get a prescription for her friend's sick son; afterward, the two of them went to a shop. A woman recognized Cana's friend in the store and pointed: "'There she is ... it's her!' At that moment [fortunately] this woman stumbled and fell over some goods, and we used the commotion to flee to our car and drive away. This woman would probably have said, 'That's a Muslim woman,' or something similar." The example of the woman in the shop shows that plenty of women also accepted and served the ethno-national ideology, meaning that women should not be defined as inherently peaceful beings. As Fiona Robinson explains, it is important to recognize that the activities of women (and men) are limited by gender norms, institutions, and structures of militarism and neoliberal global restructuring.[9]

Fig. 6-2

---

[9] Fiona Robinson, 2011, *The Ethics of Care: A Feminist Approach to Human Security*, Philadelphia, PA: Temple University Press, 120; Elisabeth J. Porter, 2007, *Peacebuilding: Women in International Perspective*, London: Routledge, 57.

The second time someone recognized this friend who was hiding in Serbia was when the two of them had to go to Belgrade to get an important document that would allow her friend freedom of movement. Since at the time there was a serious shortage of fuel, the two of them took a bus to Belgrade. During the trip, some people on the bus were swearing, using the phrase "mother of a *balije*" (a derogatory term for Muslims), and Cana was scared that someone might start questioning them, so they got off the bus and continued on foot. They walked for kilometers, frozen and exhausted, but somewhat happy because they had evaded the pressures of hate and fear that the individuals on the bus had used to hold the others hostage.

The third time Cana's friend was recognized was the hardest test and provided a significant moral dilemma for Cana since it involved her children, whose endangerment worried her most during the war and influenced all her decisions. In the interview, Cana sat up straighter in her chair, illustrating through her posture the weight of the event she was about to retell. It was Christmas 1993 (Orthodox Christmas on January 7), and she had decided to go home to BiH with her friend and their children. Her husband was also home sick, and because he was not deployed at the front line, they planned to enjoy a family gathering for the holidays. They would take a short break, be together for awhile, and inspire each other to endure. The documents Cana's friend had obtained in Belgrade entitled her to move around freely. Cana and her friend set out on the journey: "We had roasted a piglet and carried it between the two of us in a bag as we walked … for six kilometers." Upon reaching Bratunac, where the local police met them at the army checkpoint, they passed through without any trouble: "We never had problems with our local people."

They all spent Christmas Eve in Cana's house, dreaming of the times they celebrated holidays together without any fear. The next day, however, there was bad news: "Kravice has fallen this morning. If you remain here, Cana, someone will kill you. … No one knows what happened there but you must leave Bratunac." The small town of Kravice, next to Bratunac, the birthplace of Cana's mother, had fallen into the hands of the Bosnian army, which meant that the Serbs had been expelled. There was no other information at that moment except that the Serbs in Bratunac might now retaliate with a killing spree. Fearing such a scenario, they decided to return immediately the next morning to their village hiding place in Serbia. Since there was no transportation they had to go on foot with their children.

Cana felt sure her friend's license to move freely was sufficient for them to return to the village safely, but due to the events on the front lines, the local Bratunac police force had been replaced: "There were some new soldiers, without a face. I mean they had something, a sort of a black mask over their faces, I really don't know, it was knitted and you could only see the eyes and the lips." Cana thinks they may have changed the border police to prevent men from fleeing to Serbia, forcing them to stay in Bratunac to fight. As soon as she saw new border guards with their faces masked, she expected problems. She prayed they would cross safely to the other side of the Drina into Serbia. When asked for their documents the thing she most dreaded thing happened:

> He asked for the papers naturally. My ID, nothing, he just had glanced at it. And he asked, "Your kids?" I said, "the two girls here and this boy." Then he requested, "Ma'am?" and my friend gave him her ID. The old, pre-war ID card, if you remember the one with the picture. He opened it and stared at it disbelievingly. He looked at her: "What brings you here, Turk, can you believe it, her father's name is Alija and she is walking around Republika Srpska."

Despite the fact that her friend's name was not identifiable by the categories of ethnic and religious identity and the fact that she dressed like all the other women in Bratunac, the name of her father, Alija, stirred a reaction. It was a typical Muslim name but more intriguingly, it was also the name of the president of the Republic of Bosnia and Herzegovina, Alija Izetbegović. The guards did not expect a Muslim woman to be walking around freely in Republika Srpska, so they sardonically labeled her a Turk, one of the names given to Bosniac Muslims to link them to the Ottoman occupation and to deny them their original identity. For the masked guards, the encounter was the perfect opportunity to exert power over the lives of others under the conditions of war.

Cana then went on to describe the moment further. While her friend held tightly to her son's hand, frozen with fear, the man in the mask shouted out: "'We have a *balinkuša* for the floor.' The floor meant that they would kill her." Labeling her with this derogative term for a Muslim woman, it was as if the masked soldier wanted to humiliate her even further. Cana recalls that they were already exhausted after their long walk and terrified at what might happen to them at the checkpoint. Upon hearing them threaten to kill her friend and her son, she suddenly resorted to using the authority of her husband's family:

> Even now I don't know where I got the strength, because suddenly I was not tired anymore. I was not scared. "What are you talking about?! Look at her! Do you know who she is and do you know who I am?!" He looked at me. "Who are you?" "I am Stanojka Tešić and this woman is with me. … [H]er husband is an officer at the health center. If she receives even a scratch, you and your whole family will be wiped out.

At that critical moment, Cana called upon her husband's family name, Tešić, hoping that the family's reputation in Bratunac would be enough reason to let them go. However, the soldiers obviously had different orders and they were not impressed by her performance. When she saw that neither her friend's license nor the authority of the Tešić family name meant anything to them, she did something else of which she still is surprised. Norman Denzin explains such a moment as one that "alters the fundamental meaning and structure in someone's life."[10] She told the soldier:

> "I am from the Tešić family so, hero, you would first have to slaughter my two kids" … and I took my two daughters and pushed them in front of his legs. "You would first have to do that." He stopped then. It wasn't really easy for him. Then he said: "Who is this woman? Who are you, woman?" And I said, "Go and check."

She called the guard "hero," thereby questioning the heroism of hiding behind a mask and exerting force upon women and children. Today, Cana cannot remember what he went to check, but after several minutes, which seemed to them like years standing at the doors of hell, the man came back and said: "We are sorry ma'am. We did not know who you were. Do you need a ride?" Still frantic, but with great self-confidence and authority, she refused the lift, maintaining her ability to move freely. The guard then kindly added: "Don't walk around with this woman any more. Not everyone will check."

Cana was visibly upset, and her voice was shaking from both fear and anger at being subjected to such humiliation and to the inhuman dilemma of having to pledge the lives of her children for the life of her friend. One can imagine she left the checkpoint flooded with emotion but also with pride for having saved two lives. She added with a sigh that this was the most difficult moment in her life, but the authority of the Tešić family had, nevertheless, been crucial. While this may have been true, her determination and her courage to shift the weight of her moral dilemma onto the guard obviously stunned him.

There was not much talk about this incident in her family, and as Cana explains, she did not want to burden her two daughters with war stories. However, several years ago when the older daughter gave birth to Cana's granddaughter, Cana was told that there is

---

[10] Denzin 1989, 70.

nothing in the world that the mother loves more than her own child. Her daughter then asked Cana:

> "How could you have given me and Vladana to that man on the bridge to slaughter us?" ... I was shocked at first, but then I turned to her and said: "Well, Goga, because my friend loved her son the same way you love your daughter and the same way I love you. And which is more valuable? How much of a mother am I and how much of a mother is my friend? Or how much is my child worth to me and how much is my friend's child worth to her?" Her eyes were full of tears, she cried for a long time and I cried as well.

Cana then learned that her daughters had discussed this together but had never shared it with her. She, on the other hand, thought that perhaps they had forgotten the event, or if they did remember it, did not want to stir up painful memories. The child expects that its mother will do anything to protect her, so Cana's daughters had somehow felt betrayed. Cana had shown them that in a moment when life hangs by a thread, the wish to save that life exceeds everything else. For Cana, motherly love is the greatest love in the world, but her motherhood had stretched to include her friend's child. This was the superhuman, unselfish act of a mother who was not only focused on her children but also exhibited "rationalized care" focused on others; her intention was to be protective and helpful to those around her regardless of any blood connection.[11] Summing up her war story, Cana also recalled two moments that may explain her unselfish love and commitment as well as her ethics of care.

The first occasion was the day after Christmas 1993, when they had saved themselves from the unknown guards at the checkpoint.

---

[11] Sara Ruddick, 1990, "The Rationality of Care," in *Women, Militarism, and War: Essays in History, Politics, and Social Theory,* Jean Bethke Elshtain and Sheila Tobias (eds.), Savage, MD: Rowman and Littlefield, 229-54; Sara Ruddick, 1989, *Maternal Thinking: Toward a Politics of Peace,* Boston, MA: Beacon Press, pp. 141-46.

The very next morning, after returning to Uzovnica, Cana's mother knocked on her door with news. Cana thought that something big must have happened, since her mother was not so young as to walk all the way to the village. In confidence, she told Cana that many Serbs had been killed in Kravice, including two of her cousins. She then leaned over and whispered: "You know, the Serbs also killed some of her [the friend's] family members up there [in Kravice], so [in retaliation] some Muslims killed [some of] your family. ... [But] don't you dare think anything bad about your friend [because of it], let alone say anything to her ... because if there is a God somewhere out there, he will not forgive you."

For Cana, her mother's words and act demonstrated great humanity and concern for others. Although she was not a very religious woman, Cana's mother believed in justice and wanted to make sure that her daughter would not insult her friend once she heard the news of her cousins' murder in Kravice—because her friend too had lost so much. The mother seems to have had a bigger perspective—that regardless of the war's events that were out of their control, they should still care for their friendship. She walked kilometers in order to be sure that Cana would abide by the moral postulates of her family. Although Cana had already proven her strong moral principles, her mother's act verified these deep family values.

The second instance demonstrating Cana's ethics of care is related to her responsibility for her friend's mother, Fatima. Cana explained that although her friend was four years older, her friend's mother had great trust in Cana who had married earlier and had more experience in raising children; therefore she asked Cana to take care of her daughter. Cana did just that, for example, treating her friend's son as if he were her own child. It seemed as if Fatima had had a premonition of the events to come. Cana recalls that she used to say:

> "My Cana, take care of my only child. You see what she is like. She doesn't know, she starts panicking over her child, maybe because she is a doctor and she immediately starts supposing what might be wrong with him." ... It is as if her mother had a premonition that there would be a time when I would really have to care for her only child.

Cana was therefore more than just a friend. The relationship became clear during the war, whose events brought Cana into a situation whereby she had to prove their friendship. In this way, four mothers: Cana and her mother plus Cana's friend and her friend's mother, Fatima, cared for each other, creating a circle of friendship and support strong enough to resist the darkness and killing that both families experienced. Cana says that even today she goes with her friend to visit Fatima's grave in Mostar. Fatima's remains as well as those of her husband and others in her family were found and buried after the war.

The war destroyed people in a material, a spiritual, and a mental sense, as can be seen from the isolation in which Cana lived in Bratunac during the first post-war years. Nevertheless, she devoted all her strength to re-establishing the links with her neighbors and friends.

We Did Not Know What Projects Were: We Simply Wanted to Bring People Together

> We primarily wanted to gain freedom, to emerge and free ourselves, so to say. And really we were wandering around at the beginning, but I know one thing for sure: this was the revival of coexistence. ... [even if we] did not know how to define it at that time.

When the war ended in 1995, Cana was in Bratunac expecting things to stabilize and thinking that she would soon be able to travel again and see the friends and neighbors who had fled, all the while assuming that these people would return to the homes from which they had been displaced. However, the physical isolation along with the political and media isolation was so strong in the first post-war years that it was very difficult to act and move freely.

Bratunac is a small town on the BiH border with Serbia and the sense of isolation there was even greater than in larger urban centers. She remembers the propaganda imposed by the authorities at the time as they tried to keep people divided, separated, and frightened so as to maintain control: "We did not have any way out except to Serbia. You only have one-sided news ... one [type of] information ... one truth ... everything [came to us as] one ["truth"]: that the Serbs are a divine nation and that everything else around us is dangerous."

Although she lived in an environment where the ethno-national propaganda was very strong, and she had almost no contacts with organizations and women from other cities in BiH, Cana decided in 1998 to set up and register an NGO, the Forum of Women of Bratunac. She did this with several of her colleagues who shared her views and who wished to emerge from the physical and mental blockade and begin restoring their torn neighborhoods and former relationships. At the time, there were some notions of change in the appearance of the new political social-democratic forces in the RS,[12] which for many stood as a sign of hope that the isolation would end. "At the beginning of 1998, we actually wanted to support [this] kind of politics that was emerging. ... We wanted to make an association. None of us had a way out of Bratunac, which was like a black hole."

The registration process for the Forum of Women in the regional court in Bijeljina did not succeed without difficulties, because Cana, her friend Mira, and other associates wrote in the proposed organization's statutes absolutely everything they truly wanted to do, which at the time garnered no understanding from existing government institutions. Furthermore, there was no will to register

---

[12] With the arrival of the SNSD party to power.

their association, because there was not support for its ideas of women's human rights and freedom of movement, and as Cana comments, "Probably the biggest roadblock for the Court was [our statement on] freedom of speech and opinion, which they stressed to us, needed changing. What to write then?! We did not wish to do charity work."

Fig. 6-3

In the end, they realized that they had to compromise, to use "smart flexible" tactics in order to achieve their goal. Lederach explains that this is "more [about] ... the creation of platforms for generating creative responses ... than [about] creating solutions."[13] Cana understood that if she wanted to do something for the women in the town, she sometimes had to choose a side road that would nevertheless bring her to the finish line. Thus, instead of stating

---

[13] John Paul Lederach, 2005, *The Moral Imagination: The Art and Soul of Building Peace*, Oxford: Oxford University Press, 85.

broad goals in the statutes, she agreed to simplify them to say that they would visit their neighbors in eastern Bosnia and other cities. She admits that they did not know how to articulate their request to promote coexistence in the best way. Their strategy was just to pretend to be inept and harmless and to claim that they only wished to organize meetings with their friends and neighbors. This was partially right, but their long-term goal was to bring coexistence back to the region:

> And really, this beginning was our wandering around, but we knew one thing even at the very beginning that we recognize also today—that we were actually working on some form of coexistence. We did not know how best to define it. We did not even think, but what the heck, we had to see each other, we missed each other.

People had not seen their relatives, friends, and neighbors for years, and they simply wanted to restore the relationships that they had known their whole lives. They were all so connected, that even the war was not a good enough reason to keep them apart forever. Remembering those first post-war encounters was painful to them.

As she recounts, visiting larger cities was less problematic. "I mean it is not written across your forehead who you are or what you are. When you go to Tuzla or Banja Luka, nobody knows who is who." People did not pay as much attention as was the case in small towns, where everyone knows each other and they immediately know if someone new arrives. "When one comes from a small milieu, there is no way to move around freely." For the first meetings, the plan was thus to drive the women in their own personal cars to the Forum of Women premises and then take them back the same way to evade attack or unpleasant situations in town. There was no freedom of movement. Fear and hate still prevailed, and Cana, aware of this, organized the first meetings incognito in order to avoid inconvenience and possible threats. It was an important strategy to provide some sort of protection from ethno-national thugs.

Although they managed to register the Forum of Women and to act as an NGO, Cana admits that at the time they had no experience in managing an organization, preparing and drafting projects. Those were new things that they had to learn and apply in their work in order to become competitive with the other more experienced NGOs seeking funding. However, they did know and understand the needs of ordinary people, such as the returnees who needed their houses rebuilt, in order to start their lives again in the ruined villages and to feel safe:

> We did not know what projects were. ... For us projects were like literally building a house and you ask an architect to make you a design. When the donors asked us what we thought was necessary, we would draw up a two- or three-page wish list with nothing material on it but rather what we believed should be ensured.

As she recalls, the beginning of the Forum of Women's work was very difficult, because they had fifteen women who were truly committed to that work, which is a lot for a small town. The other sixteen women needed to fulfill the legal requirements for registering an NGO came from their families—mothers, sisters, and aunts: "we could not have 31 women who would go with us." It was clearly difficult to provide support for such a large number of women for their activities, because, as Cana explains, at the time their ideas were seen as some sort of treason. But she says, "I never saw myself as a traitor. ... I thought that I was acting normally and that all the others were abnormal. Thus, every woman who was in on the founding of the organization knew why she was there, why she was a part of us."

Cana's persistence in working with returnees paid off, and the Forum of Women began working on the education and training of women to work on computers and learn the basics of English, which were preconditions for finding a job. This was obviously very important for many women who joined, because they saw it as their chance to gain new skills for working in state institutions. "And suddenly we were important, because all the women in the municipality wanted to learn how to use computers and how [to speak] English and get a certificate. And we used that … to bring women together." Cana believes that from the moment foreign donors began devoting more attention to the region the Forum of Women also gained importance, because it could offer certain services that were valuable and necessary for the community.

Certainly, Cana crystallized that momentum as another important factor in spreading the network of supporters and sympathizers both among ordinary women and among those who were influential in the local community. This is another indicator, as noted by Elissa Helms, that the donors aimed specifically at helping women and women's organizations who worked on issues of reconciliation and inter-ethnic cooperation.[14] The courses the Forum offered proved to be a good channel for making contact with women from Bratunac, refugees who returned to Bratunac, and later among women who came from the Federation of BiH. The education used to bring together women from Republika Srpska and the Federation of BiH became a place of encounter and the first steps toward reconciliation.

As Cana recounts, these first steps were the most difficult, because there were objections from all sides and nobody dared to be the first one to extend a hand, except the bravest women who cared most about this. For those who considered their own children's futures it was not important who made the first step toward reconciliation. It was important to establish and cherish peace and to bring an end to the isolation and fear.

---

[14] Elissa Helms, 2003, "Women as Agents of Ethnic Reconciliation? Women's NGOs and International Intervention in Postwar Bosnia–Herzegovina," *Women's Studies International Forum* 26, vol. 1, 15-33.

Persistence Pays Off

The Forum of Women of Bratunac, headed by Cana, can be seen as a forerunner for giving assistance to displaced persons returning to their homes, because the organization created a favorable environment so that everything "would go as painlessly as possible." It finally paid off, and a great number of refugees returned to the area. Cana notes that although today Bratunac is probably one of the poorest municipalities, it has the greatest number of returnees.

Cana is proud of her engagement in this field, because for her, returnees represented the hope that people could live together again and that people would reclaim their property and dignity. Believing that she must do everything in her power to enable people to return, she established cooperation with the women from the Association of Women of Podrinje, led at the time by Zejneba Sarajlić, a woman who rebuilt houses for both Bosniacs and Serbs and thus created preconditions for coexistence in the ruined towns near Bratunac. Both Cana and Zejneba were resolute and ready to help returnees from both ethnic groups.

Cynthia Cockburn[15] and Nira Yuval Davis[16] explain the core of the transversal identity policy whereby a person is ready to reconcile—to understand the sufferings of the other person—while maintaining different understandings and views on certain issues. Cana realized she must help any woman in need, because troubles struck every woman the same, whether Bosniac or Serb.

Together, Cana and Zejneba came up with the idea of organizing a conference on returnees, to be held in Bratunac in 2001. The attempt failed, however: "The first arrivals were not well organized, prepared. The Bosniac women were stoned at the entrance to the

---

[15] Cynthia Cockburn, 2004, *The Line: Women, Partition and Gender Order in Cyprus*, London: Zed Books, 186.
[16] Nira Yuval-Davis, 1994, "Women, Ethnicity, and Empowerment," in Kum-Kum Bhavnani and Ann Phoenix (eds.), *Shifting Identities, Shifting Racisms: A Feminism and Psychology Reader*, London: Sage, 179.

conference." Cana believes they should have prepared better by lobbying the authorities in Bratunac. They were the ones who obstructed the conference via media attention and called for banning the Bosniac women from entering the town: "The local authorities called upon citizens to prevent the women's entrance." The project of return and encounter between returnees (Bosniac women) and locals (Serb women) was an idea well thought out, but as Cana can see now, the time was not yet right for benign returns.

This was a great defeat for Cana. "We realized then that nobody in the town respected us." They did not receive support from the authorities or from the citizens but rather open resistance to the encounters and reconciliation. However, Cana is not a woman who gives up. She was not impeded by the open antagonism of the authorities but continued working on reconciliation and linking people together, because she believed that not all the people in her town were like the media portrayed them:

> We felt very bad. ... All the reports read, "women stoned," and I could not explain to anyone how bad that is for all those who live there, because Bratunac is not like that, we from the inside see it differently. We wanted to show that to outsiders as well, that was our motive, and [eventually] we did succeed.

Strongly motivated by the wish to show ordinary people's capacity for mutual understanding and reconciliation, she continued working with her colleagues on organizing a new conference on returnees. As a leader, Cana was true to her intuition that by continuing to work on refugee returns and by encouraging frightened people and helping to rebuild their destroyed houses, their relations with their neighbors would improve. Here one sees clearly two characteristics of a leader according to Mary Lou Décosterd: intuition and a focused power to complete the job.[17]

---

[17] Mary Lou Décosterd, 2013, *How Women Are Transforming Leadership: Four Key Traits Powering Success*, Santa Barbara, CA: Praeger, 27, 47.

Experience had shown that it was important to obtain support from the authorities, so once again Cana used the smart flexible platform and strategically focused on lobbying the mayor, who only six months earlier had expressed open antagonism to the idea of organizing the conference. He was asked to be the guest of honor and to address the women at the beginning of the conference. Creating such a platform for constructive social change[18] helped Cana and her co-workers to change relationships and interactions among the very people who were against the notion of becoming allies. Her success with this strategy was visible in the man who first openly opposed the idea of refugee return but eventually allowed the conference to take place.

Other resistance to their work came through obstruction to the organization's activities. When they could not contest the reconstruction of houses for returnees, certain individuals within the local government institutions attempted to hinder the work of the Forum of Women by tapping their phones, cutting off their electricity supplies, or failing to provide consents for electricity and water to some of the members who had returned to their reconstructed homes:

> That was the obstruction of the state institutions toward victims, because they could not take away anything else from them except their own lives. Once again, the displaced persons were subjected to threats and once again they were being punished by different forms of obstruction just because they had come back to their town and their homes.

Cana and her colleagues endured all these pressures and continued to fight for the rights of returnees, helping them organize their lives, most notably in rural areas. Even today, there are still people who do not like what Cana is doing, but she proudly notes that it is not important, because she and her colleagues know how to

---

[18] Lederach, 2005, 43.

fight for the right of all people to live where they want and to exercise their fundamental freedoms, including the right to political participation.

Peacebuilding Means Women in Decision-making Positions

> We will realize only later that we had worked on some projects that were peace oriented as we [increasingly] perceive women's participation in politics as a peace project.

Like many other activists at that time, Cana did not know how to define peacebuilding, feminism, and gender equality. These were new terms for newly established NGOs. She worked on building peace and only later learned through various training efforts how to define her activities. An important segment of Cana's peace work was promoting women to decision-making posts, because she understood that any form of change requires cooperation with the authorities whose positions are often occupied by men. "We somehow thought that the war was a male thing, but after the war everything was again in their hands [and] for too long and it was important to have more women in these places." Men who fought in the war and had been part of the ethno-national political establishment once again held authority in most of the towns in BiH, including Bratunac, and according to Cana, it was difficult to establish cooperation with these men and recruit them to get involved in her intended changes. For this reason, Cana and the Forum of Women were engaged in helping women with electoral candidacy and winning a decision-making post. The Forum wanted to boost women's confidence and help them build authority, which is another important characteristic of leadership.[19] The first woman they directly supported was Vesna Ivanović, who was elected in

---

[19] IDEA leadership characteristics are: intuition, focused power, strengthening, and assimilative/transformative power (Décosterd, 2013, 74).

2000 to the local parliament—a great victory for their efforts. Cana acknowledges that the Forum of Women deemed it important to have their voice heard in politics and to know firsthand what was happening there in order to influence decisions relating to women and men in their communities.

However, Cana and her associates from the Forum of Women faced patriarchal prejudice when the elections came.

Fig. 6-4

> [T]here were insults. There was this local municipal radio, and authority was in the hands of the radicals, so imagine now when a candidate from another party comes there, takes the microphone, and says: "Don't vote for Doctor Vesna, she is barren." Barren is the most derogatory word for a woman.

This was one of the old, tested ways of disqualifying women in politics—using their marital or family status to delegitimize them, using the expectation that women should primarily fulfill the role of wife and mother before doing anything else.[20] They could not contest Vesna's candidacy except for the fact that she did not have children, which was of course never used as criteria for any male political engagement.

Moreover, the women who supported her party (SNSD) were considered to be enemies of the Serb people and of Republika Srpska, which was also a reason to silence their voices. Despite all the objections, however, Vesna won in the elections, as did many other women for whom Cana and the Forum of Women lobbied to get the support of the electorate. They also worked on providing these women with the education and training needed for a political career, because the women did not have enough experience in political engagement. The number of women increased at all levels of government institutions, and in the last general elections in 2010, a great number of women entered the state and entity authorities in BiH, where they work on the empowerment of both women politicians and the electoral body.

Cana characterizes this segment of her organization's work as peacebuilding, because "we see women's participation in politics as a sort of a peace project. If there are more women, the services will be better for all citizens but especially for women and children, for education, health and the social aspects of life in general." In this way Cana expresses in her own words how peacebuilding involves a wide spectrum of activities, activities, as Elisabeth Porter says, "that build positive relationships, heal wounds, reconcile antagonistic differences, restore esteem, respect rights, meet basic needs, enhance equality."[21]

---

[20] Zilka Spahić-Šiljak, 2010, *Women, Religion and Politics: The Impact of Religious Interpretations of Judaism, Christianity, and Islam on the Status of Women in Public Life and Politics in Bosnia and Herzegovina*, Sarajevo: IMIC, Center for Interdisciplinary Postgraduate Studies, TPO Foundation, 312.
[21] Porter 2007, 42.

Fig. 6-5

Cana directly links women's political engagement with the improvement of women's and children's quality of life and once again reiterates that the world would be a better place if women were in power: "We believe that there would be fewer wars everywhere if women ruled." Cana also glorifies women via their ethics of caring for the family and society, which probably is a result of her experience working with women. She truly believes that women could improve the conditions of society and take care of people's needs better than men do currently. Maybe one of the reasons for this is her deep faith that all the women gathered around the Forum of Women, regardless of when they joined the organization, truly believe in what they do and have not succumbed to hate. "Not each activist in the Forum of Women has been an activist since 1999 when the organization was officially founded. She has [rather] been an activist or a peacebuilder from the moment she was born. ... For this reason there was no hate coming from us." Cana mentions one of her friends who remained in Bratunac and survived both the good and the bad times while never succumbing to the prevailing hate and fear. "And my friend … I wouldn't say that she is a victim, she is a great human being. To remain sane and not hate anyone: that is a great value."

Finally, Cana added that everything she did was also done by the other women in the Forum of Women, and thus all their accomplishments had been achieved jointly. Although she is not completely satisfied with the results and believes that they could always be better, that more could be achieved, she says, "I can look at myself in the mirror and sleep well because I do not hate anybody and I do not wish anyone anything bad." Moreover, she adds that it was easier for those women who had support from their families, something she also had from her own and her husband's family: "You have to have someone in your family to support you, yet we still have not [reached] good times. It is hard to stand up and say that [everything is not yet perfect]."

After all that she had been through during the war and afterward, Cana is aware that it is still difficult for those who wish to speak openly against injustice and stick up for the rights of others. Moreover, the sovereign rule of fear is still largely present, holding people back from making more significant changes for themselves and the society they live in. The critical edge of opinion has abated but was distorted so much that it is difficult to animate a wider citizens' front for change. The creators of war and division know this and count on the fact that over time, people will lose their strength and their impulse to change the status quo. Although aware of it herself and pretty exhausted, Cana is still fighting, believing that the road of peace is the only right path.

My Peace Oasis

> Good people and nature can always strengthen and invigorate me to continue.

When she gets tired of it all and when the obstacles lining the road of peacebuilding stubbornly refuse to move, Cana finds ways to relax and gather strength to go on. The conditions in which she works do not allow her to take long breaks, because someone always needs help and because people are used to the fact that the Forum of Women is one of the few places where they can receive advice, legal aid, medical aid, and a kind word. Therefore, in order to work successfully all these years and to be able to resist numerous temptations and challenges that arise from working in the NGO sector, Cana has found a peace oasis in her family, her garden, and her friends.

Her family is her biggest source of strength, her stronghold and her support, because without her daughters Gordana and Vladana and her husband Goran, who passed away when I was concluding her story (June 2013), Cana would not have been able to endure the difficult years of work and the numerous sacrifices on her path toward peace and coexistence in eastern Bosnia. When she came home exhausted and upset, she could always count on love and support from these three. Cana explains her work as a deposit for the future of her children and grandchildren: she says that goodness is paid off with goodness. "What my mom deposited for me I now have, and my children will have tomorrow only that which I deposit now on the road to goodness and peace."

Her second oasis of peace is nature, which sooths and restores her strength, as for a tired traveler. For this reason, she and her husband built a garden full of flowers and fruit trees, where they spent happy moments together. They brought flowers into the garden from their journeys, reminding them of some important moments in their lives. They brought a Vietnamese vine tree from their first holiday together in 1981, and with tears in her eyes she says: "We restored it last year because it had dried out and I almost had a premonition that he wouldn't be with us anymore." Her garden has been a sort of a shrine where she would go to think and meditate in silence; this has helped her find internal peace and harmony with nature and people. Cana reiterates that she believes in God, but her faith exceeds the walls of churches and institutions: "I can stand in a valley and pray to God, because God dwells in everything nice and is beheld in the eye of each good person."

Good people, especially her friends, are another important peace oasis for Cana. Her talks with good people are beneficial, relaxing, healing, and they give her strength to continue. For Cana, goodness and humanity reflect the divinity in each person, regardless of religion or ethnic belonging, because everyone is first a person and then a Serb, Bosniac, Croat, or something other. Cana has been working her whole life to bring people together, and when she gets tired her friends are there to encourage her with a kind word; sometimes they only sit in silence over coffee and sometimes they laugh and enjoy—moments to invigorate the most tired of souls.

Conclusion

The story of Stanojka Tešić is marked by the war and suffering in eastern Bosnia and by her attempts to testify to her humanity in moments when it was necessary to protect the lives of friends and neighbors who were targeted for having a different ethnic and religious identity. She had great support in her efforts from her husband's family, notably her father-in-law, a man whose moral authority was vital at a time when it was important to preserve one's dignity. Sometimes covering over her feelings for the nationalistic ruling ideology in order to protect the life of her friend and her son, she portrays the strength of a kind of motherhood not limited to her own family. She managed to save two lives, while faced with a shameful dilemma of pledging the lives of her own children in exchange. Although she lived in isolation in Bratunac after the war, her wish was for displaced persons to return to their homes and to reestablish coexistence. As soon as the political situation changed, she and her friends established the Forum of Women of Bratunac in order to connect with pre-war friends and neighbors to work together on tasks facing the region. There was and still is resistance to these efforts, but Cana believes that through perseverance and persistent commitment to realizing the rights and freedoms for all who live in her surroundings, she can achieve this. She learned that it is important to be both clever and patient in overcoming the barriers facing women's issues. Notably, she helped women return to their homes in Bratunac and surrounding areas. She also worked on empowering them economically and politically so that they can improve their own lives and also support other women in the public sphere. For her, gaining more women's participation in decision-making roles is a true peace activity, because women typically advocate for education, social and health protection, and other issues important to each family unit. In her work, she relies on her own family's support and love but also on the support of her friends and co-workers who have inspired Cana not to give up.

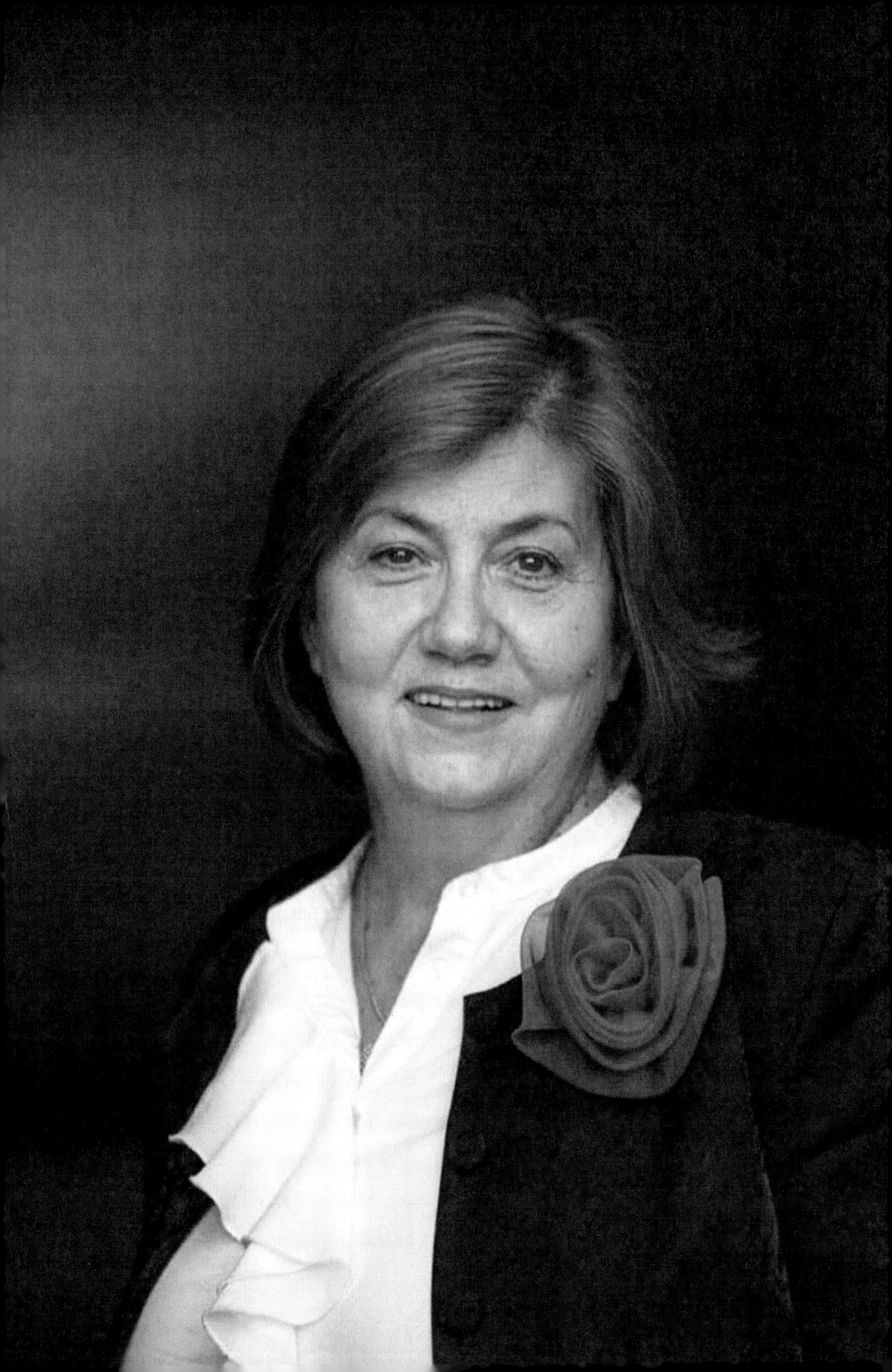

STORY SEVEN

WOMAN OF TRUST

BESIMA BORIĆ

Biography

Besima Borić was born in 1950 in Jajce (central Bosnia) and raised there in a Partisan[1] family. Her parents were active in the Communist Party, instilling in Besima and her sister the socialist values of brotherhood, unity, and equality. Nominally Muslim, her family did not observe their religion but rather declared themselves Yugoslavs.

In 1965, the family moved to Vogošća, a suburb of Sarajevo, to give their children better educational opportunities. Besima attended high school in Sarajevo and later received a teaching degree in Serbo-Croatian language study at the University of Sarajevo. She married in 1973 and together with her husband moved to Algeria, where she worked as a teacher in a school for Yugoslavian expatriates. Upon her return to Yugoslavia in 1976, she settled in Vogošća, where she still resides. Besima's professional career is extensive. A professor of languages, she was socially and politically engaged and, just prior to the war, became involved with the Socialist Alliance. She was the president of a municipal confederation from 1986 to 1990, and in 1989 she became an

---

[1] The Partisans were an antifascist movement in World War II Yugoslavia. Their fighters made up the army headed by Tito and led by the Communist Party. After liberating Yugoslavia from the Nazis, the Partisan movement continued in the postwar period, greatly influencing Yugoslav culture, including literature, art and film.

official of the Vogošća Municipality. She was elected to the Municipal Council there in 1997 and in 1998 entered the Federal Parliament. During this time, she was also the president of the municipal organization of the Socialist Party. In the past ten years, Besima has assumed important political functions. In the period of 2001-2002, she was the Minister of Labor, Social Policy, Displaced Persons, and Refugees in the Sarajevo Canton. Today, she serves as a representative in the Parliament of the Federation of Bosnia and Herzegovina.

Besima Borić has contributed to the process of institutionalizing women's human rights. In addition to her political duties, she is engaged in fighting against the oppression of minorities, and is working to improve gender equality and social policies.

Introduction

Besima Borić is one of the rare politicians in today's BiH who is respected throughout the country. She has been working with the people and for the people, always ready to answer their calls and discuss social and political issues in their communities. Her activism is not only related to her political engagement within the Social Democratic Party (SDP), but also includes a willingness to collaborate with others who are interested in improving the lives of citizens, providing jobs, protecting workers, and ensuring gender equality. For this reason, people of all ethnic and religious backgrounds recognize her as a trustworthy politician, an extremely unusual recognition in BiH's post-war political realm, burdened as it is with corruption and nepotism. Most people have only the lowest regard for political parties[2] and therefore appreciate individuals like Besima who show sincere concern and interest in other people's lives.

---

[2] Paula M. Pickering, 2007, *Peacebuilding in the Balkans: A View from the Ground Floor*, Ithaca, NY: Cornell University Press, 155.

My communication with Besima started years ago when I became involved in academic discussions about gender equality. I wanted to discuss some ideas and findings from my research with experienced intellectuals and politicians. Her dedication, energy, and compassion in dealing with social and political issues impressed me, and I was honored to collaborate with her on various occasions.

When I called her about an interview, she exclaimed: "Come on, me?!" and then added: "It is because of my pursuit of the rights of workers, women, refugees and socially vulnerable citizens, which is in fact real peace work." My colleagues, Aida Spahić and Elmaja Bavčić, conducted the first interview with her, reporting that she was very enthusiastic and had shared many stories. She readily spoke about her peace activities with refugees, women's organizations, and state institutions.

Be a Good Minister to the People!

> Whatever I do in my life, it is always very important to me that my actions are meaningful and that my work and the "sacrifices" I make are useful in some way and lead to a certain goal; otherwise, I wouldn't know how to do my job.

Besima's political and activist career is all about social and economic rights and gender equality. She believes that her work is meaningful and useful for her people and for her country. Working with trade unions, supporting returnees, and empowering women in politics has been fulfilling for her. She reminds one of Jane Addams, who was a model of someone dedicated to the rights of workers and trade unions in the United States. Clearly, these are important issues in every post-war context, and there is a tendency for male politicians to overlook or avoid them. This work takes patience, time, and energy and does not bring prestige or power. She says that if political parties or governments do not know how to deal with an issue, for example with companies and institutions that are close to bankruptcy, they often appoint a woman to the leading position. She reflected on how, recently, the public transportation system in Sarajevo was blocked for a week because the state transportation company, Gras, was on strike. When the newly appointed female director did not succeed, she published this perspective in the media: "This is exactly what happens when those in charge do not have the courage to deal with accumulated problems, they appoint a woman to run it, and then blame it [the failure] on her. It is easier for them to sacrifice a woman." Besima is aware of these political games and of politics being a particularly difficult space for a woman if she is not ready to be obedient and silent. She commented that women struggle more than men to stay upright and responsible in the eyes of the public, because of the gender-based double standards in public life. Politicians have influenced this dichotomy, which is why many people do not hold them in high regard.[3] Besima has been involved in politics for a long time, building her own political style as a woman:

> I'm fully aware that I am a woman … with this glass ceiling that does not allow a woman to go farther … I have been taking notes throughout this process. Being aware of these mistreatments has helped me to get through certain hardships, to analyze them and explain them. … If I were a man, these things would not have happened to me. But since I am a woman in politics and I am the way I am, many of these things happened. And this realization made it much easier for me to go through many difficult situations.

Besima analyzes the appropriate contexts to understand the multilayered obstacles for women in politics, from structural to cultural to personal. Rationalizing the challenges she has experienced both within the structure of her political party and

---

[3] Zilka Spahić-Šiljak, 2010, *Women, Religion, and Politics: The Impact of Religious Interpretations of Judaism, Christianity, and Islam on the Status of Women in Public Life and Politics*, Sarajevo: IMIC, Center for Interdisciplinary Postgraduate Studies & TPO Foundation.

within the broader social and political discourse has helped her understand and keep going. She describes herself as a woman with high energy and a strong character, both of which prove useful in facing danger: "I never run away from troubles, but instead meet them head on, but not in a way that provokes danger. ... This is one of the reasons why there aren't more of us [women in politics]."

For Besima, accepting her leadership position has meant being responsible to the people who elected her and being ready to work hard to justify their trust. It has been like that from 1997, when she was first elected to the Municipal Council in Vogošća, to her first ministerial position in 2001 in the government of the Sarajevo Canton (one of the ten cantons in the Federation of BiH). She was appointed to the Ministry for Labor, Social Policy, Displaced Persons, and Refugees, a position that includes one of the toughest responsibilities in the post-war government because there are so many immediate needs and such insufficient funding. Once again, the political party appointed a woman to the post that was the most difficult but had the least amount of power. Besima was aware of this, but she accepted the job because she had worked previously with refugees and wanted to make structural changes[4] in the government to better assist these individuals. She was reminded of why she had taken this job when a woman wrapped in a wool scarf (worn traditionally the way people from the Bjelašnica mountain area do during the winter) approached her:

> And she came to me as I was walking into the building; she took me by the sleeve, startling me, and she asked, "Are you the new minister?" I said I was, and I waited to hear what else she had to say to me. She put her hand on my shoulder, and said: "Be a good minister to the people." I'll never forget that. I said I would, and I thanked her and walked into the building.

---

[4] Structural change and work within institutions is described as track-one peacebuilding. See, Louise Diamond and John MacDonald, 1996, *Multi-track Diplomacy: A Systems Approach to Peace*, 3rd ed., West Harford CT: Kumarian Press, 26-36.

Being a good minister resonated throughout her work: from the very beginning she made it a priority to keep promises and answer the needs of the people first, and only then attend to administration. Thus she did not go to the office on her first day, but rather to Mostar, where she gave a speech at the women's NGO Žena BiH: "There was public debate there and I told them that today I was supposed to be in my office working, but I had come here to be with them. ... I had told them I would come and I could not betray them." Being honest with people and being there for them when they need you makes one a good politician.

Her deep sense of responsibility, her ethics of care and politics of compassion[5] were supported by serious training, seminars, and workshops organized by many domestic and international organizations. From her days as a schoolteacher, she had learned that preparation is crucial for good results, and she wanted to learn more to be able to provide better support to the people in her jurisdiction. Most women peacebuilders are not in a position to make structural changes, but Besima has used the power of her ministerial position to make formal networks between institutions and relevant NGOs. This was quite a new approach to resolving social and political issues. Besima has the capacity "to understand the patterns of the present, imagine the desired future, and design the process of change."[6] She worked closely with ordinary people and therefore was able to imagine how to best help them.

---

[5] Elisabeth J. Porter, 2007, *Peacebuilding Women in International Perspective*, London: Routledge, 103.
[6] John Paul Lederach, 2005, *The Moral Imagination: The Art and Soul of Building Peace*, Oxford: Oxford University Press, 138.

Fig. 7-1

Among her biggest achievements at the ministry was the work she did helping refugees and displaced persons return to their pre-war homes. At that time in Sarajevo, many families were without social support or health care. There was a need to organize the return and the re-building of the homes of Bosniacs in eastern Bosnia, and of Serbs, Croats, and others in Sarajevo. Besima therefore worked with all relevant institutions and returnees to make it happen.

> I am the first minister who went to Montenegro to meet with refugees from Sarajevo. I went to Belgrade to meet with Bosnian refugees in Serbia who wanted to return, etc. This was the first time that this happened in such a way and I was the person who did that; of course, it was under the auspices of the international organizations of the UNHCR and OSCE.

She notes that these international organizations played a positive role in assisting the return process and provided the logistics for meetings, trips, and exchanges between BiH and neighboring countries, Serbia and Montenegro. They supported, mediated, and monitored all of these activities, but wanted to encourage local institutions to negotiate the return of displaced persons.[7] Besima was ready to travel, to talk, to negotiate, but she always took time for direct contact with the people who mattered the most:

> When I went to Montenegro to meet with refugees from Bosnia and Herzegovina, mostly from Sarajevo, the auditorium was full to the brim and I sat down at the table and said, "Hello, Sarajevans." I got an amazing response: an ovation. It was such an unbelievable situation. And I had said it because it was the most natural thing to say.

She spoke to the people who left Sarajevo during the war, mostly Serbs or people from mixed marriages. "They could not believe that somebody came and addressed them in that way." This occurred just a couple of years after the war, and it was praiseworthy to do such a thing, even if official politics did not approve. Besima responded by saying that she was a minister to all citizens notwithstanding their ethnic or religious identities or their displacement. Some of her colleagues were surprised at her openness and her dedication to her work: to invite all to come back and live together. After the siege of Sarajevo, some people were not ready to hear that Serbs should come back to live there again. Besima knew that most people had left because they had to or because they did not want to be involved in the war, and she did not wish for them to be associated with those involved in war crimes.

Her deep desire to re-build multicultural life in Sarajevo motivated her to invite all displaced Sarajevans to come back to their city. To show them that they were welcome, she worked with Serbian associations assisting their return and helped them start small businesses and get jobs. She particularly emphasized her care

---

[7] Adam Fagan, 2006, "Civil Society in Bosnia Ten Years after Dayton," in David Chandler (ed.), *Peace Without Politics? Ten Years of International State-building in Bosnia*, London: Routledge, 101-2.

for the Serbian elderly population: "Thanks to my engagement with the government, retired Serb returnees got bonuses for public transportation, which made it easier for them to travel." Croatian returnees were also supported.

Before any of the official initiatives and protocols, she began communicating with municipalities in Republika Srpska about the most effective way to help returnees. Besima believed that open dialogue would be the best way to start helping returnees. She never waited for an invitation but searched for opportunities to initiate dialogue around important issues such as refugee return. Her ability to envisage the whole and not just the current interests of a group, party, or government were characteristic of her leadership skills.[8]

At that time, nobody dared to go to Višegrad, Foča, Bratunac, or Zvornik in eastern BiH to ask their mayors to support the reconstruction of returnee's homes. But Besima dared to go. She visited these municipalities and got their support. Dialogue with those who have different views than one's own about the war, the refugees, and the state helped bring them to reciprocal recognition of their differences, which Seyla Benhabib claims is an important step in coming to an agreement.[9] Although it was not easy because of the prevailing ethno-national rhetoric, Besima was able to soften some of the hard-line attitudes:

> There were funny encounters, for instance in Višegrad, when the deputy mayor started to lecture me, raising his voice about the suffering of Serbs, saying that in the municipality of Vogošća, they were not allowed to return to their pre-war homes. When I told him that I spent the war in Vogošća and that I knew everything that was happening there, he lowered his voice and became cooperative.

---

[8] Mary Lou Décosterd, 2013, *How Women Are Transforming Leadership: Four Key Traits Powering Success*, Santa Barbara, CA: Praeger, 27.
[9] Seyla Benhabib, 1992, *Situating the Self: Gender, Community, and Postmodernism in Contemporary Ethics*, Cambridge: Polity Press, 9.

Fig. 7-2

Besima consistently spoke to those who did return in order to find ways to help them, both officially as a government minister and privately as an individual. Another way to support the sustainable return of refugees was to secure their employment. One such endeavor entailed the Ministry incentivizing teachers to re-build schools in Žepa by giving out bonuses for this work. It did the same for the first police officers in the Višegrad municipality. In this way, refugees who lived in the Federation of BiH entity were encouraged to go back to the Republika Srpska entity and re-build their lives there.

Besima's work in the Ministry was informed by her experience in the non-governmental sector. Right after the war, she worked with refugees in Vogošća, where thousands of families, mostly women with children from Srebrenica and Bratunac, lived after the exodus to eastern Bosnia. Besima did not have a job at that time because the new Bosniac leadership was in power, and she was not viewed as a desirable teacher in the school. As a woman from a mixed marriage who had spent the war in Vogošća under Serbian rule, she was not welcome in the school under its ethno-national Bosniac leadership. Therefore, she volunteered for the Marie Stopes International from the United Kingdom, helping the organization connect with refugees who needed psycho-social support. The staff and volunteers worked with women of different ethnic origins and supported them in challenges they faced in their local community. Above all, the organization provided a "safe space"[10] for them in which to tell their stories and heal their traumas. Besima has countless stories from that period, including those that relate the challenge of bringing together refugee women with local women from different ethnic backgrounds. She explained how the organization provided psycho-social support and formed culturally and ethnically mixed groups of women in order to encourage interaction. But there was one group of women, ten refugees from Srebrenica with the same surname, who did not want to work with anybody else. "It took so long for them to open up and reveal the traumas they experienced during the Srebrenica exodus," she said, "and at the beginning they felt more secure within their own group." When Besima gained their trust, she noted how much they laughed together and how much spirit these women had despite everything they had been through. Knowing that many of them had lost dozens of family members, it is understandable that they remained insular at first and only later became involved in mixed groups.

Besima is proud of the friendly relationships she established with everyday people, and these people seemed to like her non-hierarchical approach and her human touch, a characteristic feminist approach to leadership, according to Jean Lau Chin.[11]

---

[10] Ristin Thomassen, 2006, *To Make Room for Changes, A Report by Kvinna Till Kvinna*, http://www.peacewomen.org/assets/file/Resources/NGO/kvinna_tomake roomforchanges_2006.pdf (accessed September 3, 2011).

[11] Jean Lau Chin, Bernice Lott, Joy Rice, and Janis Sanchez-Hucles (eds.), 2007, *Women and Leadership: Transforming Visions and Diverse Voices*, Hoboken, NJ: Wiley-Blackwell, 6.

Besima's style of politics was far from the image of the untouchable minister who is distant from the needs of the people. Her own style was to be people-friendly and approachable. People used to say to her: "You are somehow different from the others [politicians] ... we can't lump you together with them." She showed another face of politics, a human face, to gain the trust of the people. Building relationships is especially important for Besima, because as Elisabeth Porter says, "peacebuilding is a comprehensive process with an emphasis on networks of relationships."[12] Lederach explains, "Relationships are at the heart of social change."[13] Besima understood the importance of good relations that can only lead to positive change. These all point to her view that understanding and patience are gained through respect.

> I've always said that no politician or officer or anyone can do their job properly if they are not involved with people and their lives. You can be immensely clever and make idealistic plans and policies, but without immersing yourself in the every-day problems of the people you won't make a real difference. Real politics is the one thing that takes into account people's lives.

After her ministerial mandate, Besima became a parliamentarian, and one day in front of the Parliament building, a familiar woman approached her. Besima thought the woman was looking for help, so Besima told her that she was no longer the minister, but "if you need something I can help you reach the new minister." The woman looked at her with a smile and said: "No, I just came to tell you what a good minister you've been, I will never forget your support and humanity [ljudskost]." These reflections from ordinary people serve as confirmation that Besima did her job well, as she commented: "this is the most important for me, this is the beginning and the end, what you have done and what kind of

---

[12] Porter 2007, 33.
[13] Lederach 2005, 86.

impression you made on people." Such recognition always motivated Besima to keep going: the sparkle of happiness she saw in the eyes of the people touched her heart and re-energized her. Especially during the days when she felt helpless to change the situation, or when her colleagues did not want to collaborate, or when they even made things hard for her, because she was working "too much."

Fig. 7-3

Besima's biggest accomplishment was gaining people's trust: "I came to the point where people believed me, which is rare for politicians." Deserving this trust took years of patient work. Besima's motto was *being good and doing good.* This helped her survive and make a better world for her family and her community. The war traumas she witnessed, her political engagement, and her concern for the future of her family and community determined the course of her peace activities. She knew that people needed smiles, verbal support, and understanding after all the trauma they had experienced. She came to understand that being kind and good was crucial to making life easier, even if she could not always provide material support. Sometimes just shaking hands, giving a hug and a few words of encouragement were what people needed. This attitude guided her through life and became a norm for her. Although she does not expect gratitude, people come to her with deep appreciation for her support.

Another important achievement during her ministerial mandate was signing the protocol of cooperation between the government of the Sarajevo Canton and the NGO AD Barcelona (today's Foundation of Local Democracy) in 2001. Besima was the first minister to ask for a shelter for victims of domestic violence in Sarajevo, and this shelter was the first to be supported by state institutions. She knew that financial support needed to be accompanied by legal protection for the victims of domestic violence. At that time (2003), the only possibility was to include them under other laws. Thus, "the next year I proposed the law on social protection and protection for civil victims of the war, which also involved victims of domestic violence, granting them financial support." Lack of proper legislation did not discourage her, but led her to search for other options. In the process of drafting the new Law on Social Protection, Besima decided to involve NGOs in the discussion. "It was novel and everybody, both the Ministry employees and NGO representatives, were surprised. But they were happy that I introduced this practice." Knowing that more was needed to enable structural changes for the protection of women's human rights, she also managed during her mandate to get the Law on Domestic Violence adopted in 2005.

Two Wings of Peace: Institutional and NGO Approaches

Besima knew that it was important to institutionalize women's human rights requests within a strong legal framework that had mechanisms for implementation. Therefore, from her first moment in the Parliament of the Federation of BiH in 1998, she worked alongside other female politicians and with women's NGOs to establish gender-based state mechanisms that would promote equality, peace, and justice. Thanks to these efforts, government gender centers in both the Federation of BiH and the Republika Srpska were established.[14] Their role is important in the implementation of the international human rights standards and norms and gender equality principles underlined in the Beijing Platform for Action (1995).

She said that it was not easy to do this work because male politicians wanted to control the process. At that time, in 1998, the government of Finland provided donations for gender equality projects as preparatory activities for the formation of gender centers. With other female colleagues, she requested information from the president of the Federation of BiH about the donation and the plan for the project's implementation. Under their pressure, the president provided the information and formed the first governmental body for gender equality, appointing as its leader a woman who was his chief of staff. "We were offended and frustrated, but we understood that he wanted to control the process. As I was the loudest in these requests, he hated me. But what was important is that we got what we wanted: state support of gender equality projects."

This was not the first time Besima butted heads with male politicians who wanted to control women's activities and women's rights. Among the many battles, one in particular resonated in her memory: a battle that was won in old Yugoslavia but that now years later threatened women's reproductive rights:

> I remember that the group of conservative politicians proposed that the Parliament of the Federation of BiH adopt a declaration on the

---

[14] More about FBiH's Gender Center can be found at: http://www.fgenderc.com.ba. More about Republika Srpska's Center can be found here: http://www.gc.vladars.net.

unborn child. I came to the podium and defended the freedom of a woman to decide about her pregnancy. I was motivated and emotional and the speech was well received. ... I was applauded, which is not usual in Parliament. I was surprised, but proud of myself.

After the struggle to establish gender centers in the two entities of BiH, Besima and others knew that they had to push for the enforcement of the Gender Equality Law of BiH (2003). This was the first state-level legal framework, and it resulted in the formation of the State Agency for Gender Equality, the highest state agency to represent BiH on this subject in international organizations and institutions. Dozens of women's NGOs, plus female politicians in the Federation of BiH and in the Republika Srpska, as well as in the BiH Parliament, all advocated the law. These women were met with resistance and lack of understanding. It was hard for some politicians to accept the clause, which mandated equal participation of men and women in politics and in the Parliament. During one discussion, a male parliamentarian posed the question: "If 50 percent of women come to the Parliament what would we [men] do?" Besima and the other women laughed and answered: "The same thing that we [women] do now." This mindset, refusing to imagine what it would be like to share Parliament equally with women, was held by many men, illustrating how patriarchy, wrapped in a democratic robe, resisted the move toward gender equality.

Besima, however, was aware that having better gender equality legislation and female representatives within state institutions was not enough:

> We were the first in the [Balkan] region to establish these gender equality state mechanisms. We spent years walking around praising our work ... how we had the best mechanisms. ... But if you stop [working] and just talk about great mechanisms and the small accomplishments ... it is a problem.

She knows that a national legal framework is an important first step, but the laws need application and efficiency. For that to occur, one needs gender-sensitive people in government, channeling the legal norms into practice responsibly and conscientiously and communicating the message of gender equality to the people. Besima pays tribute to some of her colleagues in gender centers who are doing their best to achieve these ends, but she thinks the short-term projects and action plans that have been implemented thus far have not brought the desired results. They have just stirred the surface. Therefore the majority of citizens, even those employed at the municipality level, do not know what the Gender Equality Law is about.[15] She also mentioned the newly adopted UNSCR 1325 Action Plan on Women, Peace, and Security (2011),[16] saying that although it is a great document, it does not offer any long-term solutions. "Everything is somehow short-term oriented, which is a problem. I am not satisfied with that." Besima wants to see consistent dedication to the work, rather than the project-based approach, which does not include the continuity necessary for more profound change.

As an experienced politician, she knows that only if one is ready to question, analyze, and criticize will she or he make lasting progress: "I would be naïve after all my years of experience to say anything else ... there is a chance to repair something, to improve things, but not if we keep telling ourselves that everything is just fine." Unsatisfied with small achievements, Besima always looks ahead for new challenges and expects her colleagues to do the same. There are no breaks on this journey, because the roads are beset with challenges. Women and men therefore need to be aware and not take for granted any of the hard-won accomplishments, because as in 1990 when most of the women were expelled from

---

[15] Jasmina Čaušević (ed.), 2012, *Rodno inkluzivne zajednice u BiH* (Gender Inclusive Communities in BiH), Sarajevo: TPO Foundation Sarajevo, www.tpo.ba.
[16] This document is available on the website of the Agency for Gender Equality, www.arsbih.gov.ba.

politics, these gains can be lost.[17] Besima believes that working on human rights and gender equality is therefore a life-long endeavor.

Fig. 7-4

The systemic approach of her peace work is not unrelated to women's non-governmental organizational work, and she has actively maintained these bonds. For Besima, the two wings—institutional and non-governmental—are equally necessary for enlivening and sustaining peace. Thus, she has participated in hundreds of discussions, workshops, forums, and public demonstrations organized by women's NGOs in order to demonstrate her support and to gain allies to enforce laws and policies.

This activism was always important to me, an important link with NGOs, especially with women's organizations in this whole history of feminism in Bosnia and Herzegovina, in which I was active

---

[17] Jasna Bakšić-Muftić, 2006, *Ženska prava*, Sarajevo: Law Faculty, University of Sarajevo.

since the beginning. I think that while I still breathe and work I will always have the same attitude toward this issue.

Besima mentioned that she had many offers to make her life more comfortable, without its everyday challenges and disappointments, but she could not sit in her office as an unapproachable minister; she would rather look for opportunities to help, to find solutions, and to bring people together. Collaboration with women's NGOs after the war had enabled her to cross the imposed borders and boundaries that divided BiH. "It was crossing the borders, both physically and mentally, that enabled early connections with politicians from the two entities." She mentioned the Helsinski Assembly of Citizens in Banja Luka and its director Lidija Živanović—considered by many in BiH as the doyenne of peace activism in BiH—who dared to cross ethnic boundaries. Besima revealed that it was unsafe to travel across the borders at that time, but she was not scared:

> So during that time, when it was perhaps dangerous, when it was practically unimaginable, I went to the other entity [Republika Srpska]. There I visited certain regions along the borders [within and outside BiH], communicated and maintained connections with people, and I knew they were just like us.

Her desire to return to normalcy after the destruction of war and ethnic division motivated her to meet with friends and neighbors who wanted the same thing—to live together again. Women's NGOs were good channels for these encounters, and she used every opportunity to make connections. During the first meeting devoted to the topic of tolerance, which gathered NGOs and female politicians in 1997 in Mostar, she remembers the tension and awkwardness that was felt at the beginning of the session:

> I remember thinking about what I should say to break the icy atmosphere. Then I began: "I am a politician, a social democrat, a Bosniac who has two children—a daughter with a Croat and a son

with a Serb, and you can think whatever you want [about that]." I started laughing and others did the same. This released steam. ... We shared all the stories we could think of about tolerance, and that helped unite us to work together on re-building these relationships.

Based on her experience, women and women's organizations did the most peace work, although they were not visible enough in public life. "There are many women who work [for peace], because they are motivated by what is happening in their lives. We bear children ... and it seems that the peace work somehow is in our nature, but is often not visible or recognized in the way it deserves to be." Despite the silence about their work, women's contributions to peace are crucial, according to Besima, because they are relational foundations built and re-built within the informal networks in their local communities. She also mentioned, although reluctantly, the role of international organizations that contributed to peace because they supported women's organizations. Without that support, most of them would not have been able to survive, to provide the services that BiH is still not able to provide for all its citizens. She was reluctant, because on one hand, international organizations were important and are still important for BiH, but on the other hand, they could have done more with the funding and power they had. She claims they hid behind their mandates and jurisdictions.

Although Besima highlights women's contributions to peacebuilding, she does not want to essentialize this work as inherently feminine,[18] because men were also involved in peacekeeping activities. However, Besima describes men as being more inclined to simply be present, whereas actively raising the issue or even talking about it is difficult:

---

[18] Sara Ruddick, 1989, *From Maternal Thinking Toward a Politics of Peace*, Boston: Beacon Press, 41.

Men perceive peace activities as some kind of theater, where they can show up, say that they are doing some kind of [important peace work in] politics, speak about the huge efforts they are undertaking, when in fact things can be resolved in a simpler way, a more human way, through dialogue.

As with many other peacebuilders in this book, Besima also spoke about the importance of recognition and visibility, something that men know how to achieve when presenting their work to the public. Women, on the other hand, she says, do not have the time or the opportunities to do the same, and furthermore many women do not find this important, because there is so much to be done. She is one of them, waiting for retirement as a better time to present to the public her journey in politics and peace work. Before retirement, she will continue to work and contribute to peace as she always has. But she would like to see politicians and religious leaders take more responsibility.

Politics and Religion are (not) for Peace

Besima did not speak extensively about problems and obstacles, but rather focused her story on the positive achievements and future prospects of peace activism. However, she criticized those whose work should be oriented toward peace and yet who don't contribute to it. She specifically talked about the need for politicians and religious leaders to build trust among the people, and not keep them imprisoned in their ethnic/religious identities.

Although Besima is intensely engaged in her political role, she does not give much credit to politics for building peace in BiH, citing the ethno-national ideologies that keep people divided and the selfish interest of politicians from other political parties:

> A politician will make up problems, sometimes consciously, in order to have something to deal with, to show how big and important a politician he is. He walks around loudly negotiating about things that could be negotiated in a much easier way.

The Baseline Study on Women and Peacebuilding in BH[19] showed the same results. Respondents said that they did not trust politicians and political parties to build peace, although they appreciated the rare individuals who tried to stay humane and care-oriented. Respondents shared similar attitudes about religious leaders and institutions. They respected religion *per se* as a valuable factor in peace and reconciliation, but not the religious leadership, especially the highly positioned authorities who allowed religion to be politicized and nationalized, reducing their universal messages to narrow ethno-national identities.

> Generally speaking, religious communities did so much evil, and their role [in the war] is questionable … they did not take the chance to do the good things they should have done according to their mission. It is a dark blemish and although I am not a believer, it is hard for me to accept this. I want to believe that those who belong to religious communities can be honest … religion is about that.

As such, Besima argued that reaffirming religion in public life and politics is a stumbling block for the peacebuilding process since religious communities carry a huge responsibility for the past. She does, however, make a distinction between believers, on the one hand, and the religious leadership on the other, which did not work to bring people together but instead, supported ethno-national ideologies. She reflected on her encounters with religious leaders on various occasions during 2001 when she was in the Ministry. Once she participated in a conference attended by such leaders discussing the return of refugees. "I spoke about the role of religious communities in the return process and boldly told them that they had missed the chance to do something. Cardinal Puljić and Grand Mufti Cerić could not believe that anyone dared to tell

---

[19] Zilka Spahić-Šiljak, Aida Spahić, and Elmaja Bavčić, 2012, *Baseline Study: Women and Peacebuilding in BH*, Sarajevo: TPO Foundation Sarajevo, www.tpo.ba.

them such things," she complained. Besima believes that in the future, when their work is evaluated, these leaders will feel ashamed because they could have done much more in terms of return, peace, and reconciliation.

Acknowledging religions' potentially positive role in peacebuilding, she exclaimed:

> They [religions] could help so much, because people in adversity and danger turn to faith, they go to churches and mosques, they believe, and religious leaders are trusted authorities. People follow them not only during times of personal dilemmas but also during the collective tragedies we face.

She thinks that religions could create and build peace, but this depends on their leadership, on how their leaders communicate the faith. Many have argued that the religious leadership of BiH was not there for people when it was needed during and after the war. People would have survived their hardships much more easily if they had been given a hand to lead them and been provided spiritual support and hope. People, including Besima, expect this of religious leaders and their communities. "The entire post-war process we have been going through would be easier, shorter and better, if religious communities had given their genuine and expected contribution."

Instead, they have been preoccupied with their own interests and power in public life. Besima believes that this was reflected in the introduction of religious instruction in public schools during the war, which divided children according to their religious traditions. "I do not support this kind of religious teaching in public schools ... it would be better to have one course that would teach children about all religions." Besima does not find the current approach to religious instruction useful for the peace and reintegration of BiH. Rather than dividing people, religions should connect them and encourage their sense of hope, because the people of BiH desperately need hope after the war and the years of unsuccessful recovery.

Besima's idea of peace is about doing good for a broad circle of people, which in turn will make life easier for everyone: "Peace is attained when people are satisfied, ... when they are frustrated and suffer there is no peace." So this is Besima's passion: to bring hope, happiness, and at least a minimum of social and economic security to normal human life, for all citizens whatever their ethnic or religious identity.[20] Being a good and productive person is her personal first commandment. After that comes the understanding of ethnic and religious identities. Imagine if the religious and national leadership followed these commandments. Besima has demonstrated how believers and non-believers could work together and share the same ethical principles.

My Little Family is a Mini Version of Bosnia and Herzegovina

> I have a daughter with a Croat and a son with a Serb. They have names typical for those groups, and the three of us are one awesome little family, a mini-version of Bosnia and Herzegovina.

As a single mother with two children, Besima was motivated to build a place where they could live with all three of their identities. Her mixed marriage and family background guided her political affiliation and activism. She experienced hardships in 1990 when ethno-national identity (Bosniac, Serb, Croat) became the most important issue in BiH. Besima's family story is representative of many Bosnians who lived in mixed marriages when the war started. These mixed ethnic identities, however, were no longer allowed; being able to check only one identity box was imposed by the new

---

[20] Porter 2007, 42.

Constitution.[21] Because Besima had been raised in a Partisan family (skojevci) with a Yugoslav identity, mixed marriage was an accepted part of her worldview.

Her first marriage to a Yugoslav of Croatian origin was happy but did not last long. She became a young widow with a nine-month-old daughter and had to build her life alone. At the same time, it was a moment of self-empowerment: "I worked in the school in Vogošća … and it took some time to calm down, to finish my house. … Everything in this house is built with my own hands. … I still do not have tiles on my balcony, but never mind."

Besima was not discouraged, but rather determined to make a good life for her daughter. In the following years, she gained a measure of economic stability, and then she re-married. "In the moment when I did not need to be married … I fell in love. … There was no need for financial support, because I had a job, a house, a car, and I had freedom. I had everything, but I got married and had a son with a Serbian man." She faced many difficulties both during the war and afterward, especially in terms of her identity and in surviving in ethnically homogenized communities.

The war was one of the biggest turning points in her life. She had to decide whether to stay in BiH or to leave. Her mother and her two children (Besima's daughter was twelve and her son was two) left for Croatia, and Besima stayed in Vogošća with her father. Her husband left for Belgrade with his mother, but as she explained later they did not divorce because of ethnic relations, but because of his alcohol addiction. She remembers her neighbors commenting: "You're a Muslim who stayed in Vogošća [under Serb control], and your Serb husband escaped." Her husband, however, contacted her and asked her to leave Vogošća, but she did not want to, saying: "No way, out of the question, better kill me right here and get it over with. I stayed and spent the whole war in Vogošća." She

---

[21] Asim Mujkić, 2008, *We, the Citizens of Ethnopolis*, Sarajevo: Center for Human Rights, University of Sarajevo; Ugo Vlaisavljević, 2006, *Etnopolitika i građanstvo*, Mostar: Udruga građana Dijalog.

thought she would not survive the war, but she made the decision to stay. She could not accept that the world as she knew it was falling apart. Staying in BiH during the war was her way to resist, despite warnings that she could be killed.

Although many did not identify themselves ethnically at that time, they were nevertheless put into or "returned" to their ethnic boxes, as Besima's neighbor did when commenting on her husband's "escape." Her marriage was perceived as a marriage between a Serb and a Muslim, not a union of two Yugoslavs. Whatever identity one had at that time, he or she was perceived by their pre-Yugoslav identity roots, with funny questions such as, "Which Yugoslav are you: Serb, Croat or Muslim (later Bosniac)?"

Besima noted that although she always declared a Yugoslav national identity, during the war in Vogošća, which was under Serb control, she began to think about her identity and roots:

> It was Eid before Labor Day … and my neighbors had slaughtered a sheep for Kurban, and I was standing there at the window in the kitchen and I watched them, and felt a wave of sadness for the first time in my life. … You start to wonder, not only regarding the sense of religion, but in general, regarding national identity, because it was never a primary thing for me.

Having been raised by parents who lived according to the socialist values of brotherhood and unity, she felt somewhat perplexed. Her grandfather, an educated man in Jajce, was not a believer, but her grandmother was, and she kept all of the customs found in a typical Muslim neighborhood (mahala). The sounds and scents of such a neighborhood reminded Besima of her origins and of the familiar Muslim culture. Although she was not a believer and did not know much about religion, Islam was an important part of her cultural identity.[22] In 1992, when Serbs took control of the

---

[22] Enes Karić, 1998, "Naše bošnjaštvo i naše muslimanstvo," *Ljiljan* 6, no. 264 (February).

municipality in Vogošća, the new officials made an address list of the citizens. One day soldiers appeared at her house, asking:

> "What is your nationality?" I said, "Muslim." He wrote that down, we finished, and I was thinking. For the first time in my life, in the most dangerous situation possible, I identified myself as Muslim. Of course, I didn't even think about it at that moment, the word just came out spontaneously.

Besima explained how circumstances like war make people rethink their identities, their lives, and what is important to them. She described it as: "Awakening myself or something inside me, something [I] did not think about, but was somehow very important to me." Afterward she began to realize what this meant to her, when she had to communicate it to other people.

During the war in Vogošća, she expected to be expelled or killed any day. Therefore she had a bag packed with all the basics next to the entrance of her house, but then one day, something happened inside her. She decided to live: "At one moment I told myself: Why am I doing this? I am going to sit in my house, prepare everything, and I am going to live … we did not have electricity and water but I found a brazier, lit the fire, and all my life was there around it." That epiphany[23] was crucial for her survival during the war. She made food in the pressure cooker for her elderly neighbors who did not have a brazier, and she prepared vegetables from among what she had planted in her garden. Taking care of each other in her *mahala* and sharing everything with her neighbors was how she remained sane. She briefly mentioned that she had heard about murders and torture of Bosniacs, but she skipped that disturbing topic, saying that the bad time was over and that her neighbors were a great support to her.

Her children were in Croatia, but her son wanted to come back to be with her, and his father brought him back to Vogošća in 1993.

---

[23] Norman Denzin, 1989, *Interpretive Biography*, Thousand Oaks, CA: Sage, 70.

Her eyes were full of tears when she recalled their encounter after a year and a half, when she thought that the two-year-old boy, who had had to leave her, might have forgotten her. He had not, and when they finally hugged he said: "You look the same as in the photos." His grandmother had shown him photos to keep his memories alive. Besima recalled for him how they had walked through the town to her house: "He asked me, 'Whose house is that?' 'Where is our house?' It was as if I were bringing him home from kindergarten. I will never forget that conversation." With her son Nikola and her Muslim neighbors, she survived the war under Serb rule in Vogošća.

The next challenge for her was figuring out how to survive in the postwar peace with her family background. The war ended in 1995, and Vogošća was re-integrated into Sarajevo under the control of the new Bosniac/Croat federation called the Federation of BiH. Besima described the atmosphere after the war as terrifying, first because of the territorial jurisdiction over Vogošća when the Serbs were leaving. She sounded anxious when she remembered what might have happened in those moments. "All of them [the Serbs] were packing and leaving, they were taking off windows and doors from their houses. … We [Bosniacs] were advised to stay inside our houses, because one could only imagine, how these people felt … and what they might have done if you crossed their path." Besima remembers that they burned a couple of Croats' houses, tortured some Croats, not Bosniacs. She explained that this was because Croats had somehow betrayed them, but she could not recall what exactly had happened.

The second reason she found the environment so terrifying at the moment of transition was because of the new dynamic that had developed between the Bosniac population that had returned and the Bosniac refugees from eastern Bosnia who had settled in Vogošća. Besima had initiated the local branch of the Social Democratic Party (SDP) in 1996. "Back then, the Social Democrats were seen here as Četniks.[24] It was inconceivable that someone could be anything other than a member of the Party of Democratic Action (SDA) in Vogošća, in such atmosphere."

Besima entered politics very consciously, and with a strong desire to lessen the tension and bring about peace. When her children asked her what she was doing, she replied: "I've tried to do this, I don't know how all of this will turn out, but these are my motives." When she decided to run for office in the elections after the war, her son challenged her, saying, "How do you think you can do this in Vogošća when you have a son with the name Nikola and a daughter named Dubravka. ... It was terrible at that time. ... It seemed equal parts Četnik and Ustaša.[25] Today it is better, normal." She did not expect such a question from her son, but it was exactly the reason she decided to enter politics—to make Vogošća and BiH the place where families like hers could live in peace and coexistence. These values of multiculturalism and peace were what motivated her, as she proudly explained: "I would not allow anybody to make me uncomfortable about my identity and push me to the margins."

Her son and daughter started school in Vogošća, where the majority of the population is Bosniac. Children called them *Četnik*, and *Ustaša* because of their names. Her daughter suffered so much that she had to change schools. Her son also did not want to go to school, so Besima and her father drove him to Sarajevo every day. The following year, however, he decided to come back to his school in Vogošća: "Something happened to that child, he was somehow stronger, it took some time, and it was all very traumatic, horrible." Besima added that her family did not get through it unscathed, but "as people say, what doesn't kill you makes you stronger." Even when she spoke about the difficulties and traumas they experienced,

---

[24] The term "*Četnik*" refers to a hardline, nationalist Serb.
[25] The term "*Ustaša*" is a name for a hardline, nationalist Croat.

she would quickly skip to the bright side and the aspects of life that encouraged her to go on.

Fig. 7-5

Besima re-discovered her national Bosniac/Muslim identity during the war and had the courage to stay in Vogošća and continue living there with her two children from Serbian and Croatian fathers. A mini-version of Bosnia and Herzegovina was nurtured in her family. She admitted that she experienced terrible moments and misfortune, tragedy, and fights, but she says:

> I am a person who remembers a different time. I lived in peace. I can't say that I lived in prosperity, but I had a normal life. ... That was a huge motivation for me. I believed that everything that has happened to us, and all the consequences of it, cannot become permanent conditions. So I think that we should be doing something to change it, for my children from mixed marriages, for their future. What I am thinking of is the generations ahead that need to live here, about where they will live, with whom they will live, how they will live?

As a public figure engaged in politics, she could not escape judgment about her personal life: "Your private life is always out there open to the public. And that is hard to handle, but thank God, it all affected me in such a way that it made me better than I was, it helped me to be good." Her passion for continuing this work is for the sake of her family and the future generations that need better conditions and a life without ethno-national tensions and divisions.

She has survived both war and peace, and it is up to the new generation to continue making room in BiH for different identities to be nurtured, respected, and celebrated.

Conclusion

Besima's story communicates the way in which even someone from the so-called elite and privileged political sector of society has struggled to overcome the same divisive, prejudicial forces that have subjected so many residents of BiH to insecurity, danger, and suffering. She is also an individual who has fought against the new ethno-national politics, but from within the political system. This has provided her advantages—the ability to shape policy—but also challenges, which others did not have to face. While she does not dwell on the negative parts of her life, we can see that her stand for the vulnerable, such as Serb returnees to the Sarajevo Canton, and her own life choices as a Yugoslav who did not care about ethnic identity have damaged her own and her family members' lives. Nevertheless, she maintains the ethical practice of doing good for others, which has meant prioritizing the needs of the people who elected her minister, opening the political dialogue to NGOs, defending women's rights in a man's world, and even speaking well of religions (as a faith with a universal message of peace) despite the fact that religious leaders and institutions have compromised themselves through nationalist politics. Besima has a clear mind that analyzes her situation without illusions or idealism. Perhaps this is what has enabled her to face reality and its challenges with a sense of strength and the will to do the right thing. She maintains faith in a Bosnia-Herzegovina that can reclaim its past treasure of the mutual appreciation of diversity and of living together with respect. Her own family is a living demonstration of her belief and practice.

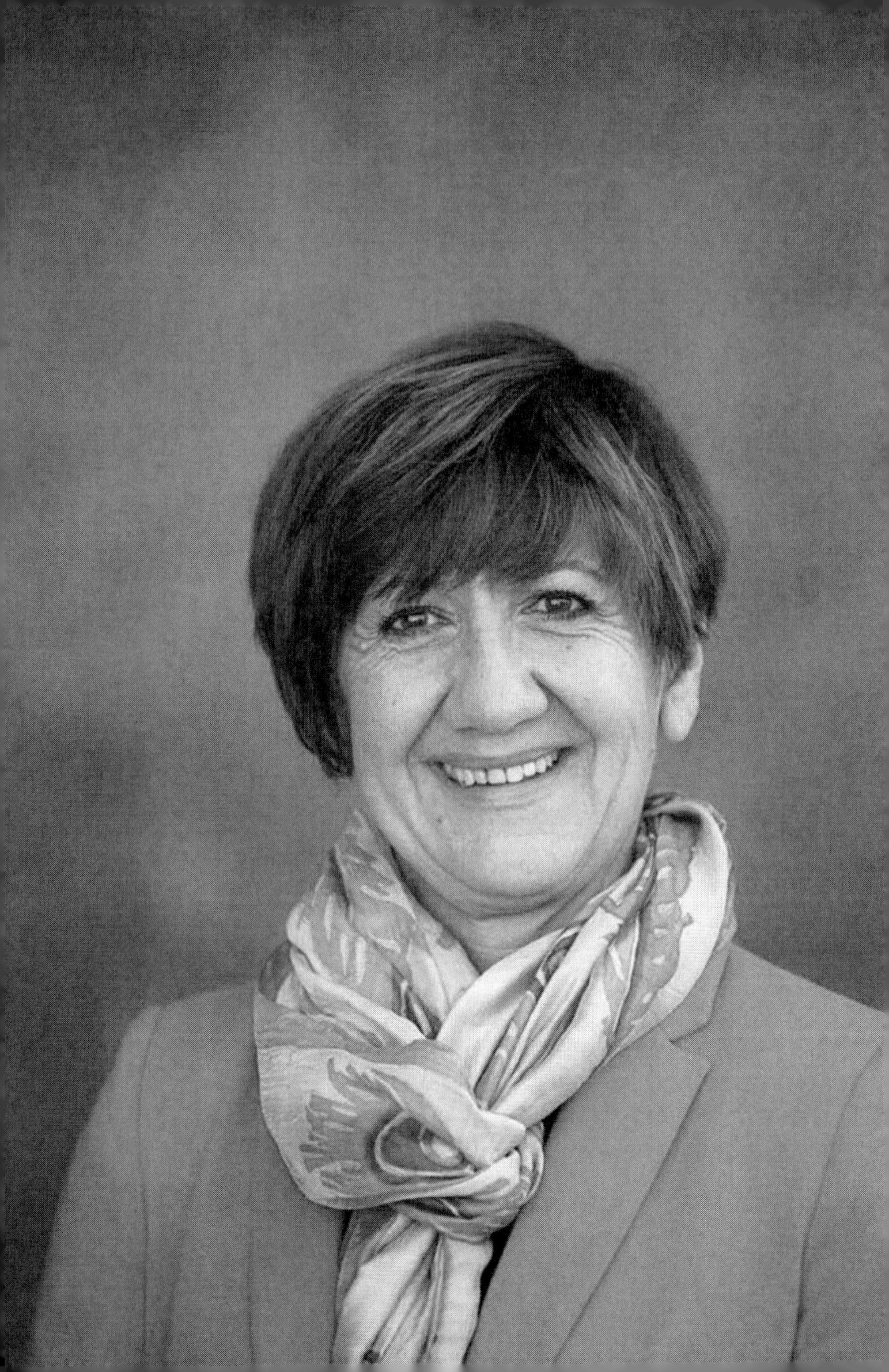

Story Eight

Civic Education: A Safe Platform for Communication and Understanding

Rahela Džidić

Biography

Rahela (Levi) Džidić, born in 1955, was raised in Sarajevo in a family that cherished its cultural and religious identity as residents within the Jewish Municipality. She grew up with two sisters and two brothers in a liberal family that helped nurture her personality and develop her value system. Her motto became: contribute to both one's personal good and to the common good.

As a successful student, Rahela had the opportunity to go to the United States as an exchange student, and while there she stayed with the Kollin family. Returning to Sarajevo, she graduated from university in electrical engineering (in 1978), then married a fellow Sarajevan, and later gave birth to two sons. Before long she became manager of the Automation Department of PTT, a local telecommunications company.

In 1992, the war came into Rahela's life. Not wishing to leave the city, she and her husband, Atif, decided to stay, while her father, a Holocaust survivor, insisted the couple take the children away from the besieged Sarajevo, first to Belgrade and then to Israel. During that difficult period, Rahela found it was the support, love, and understanding in her marriage that enabled her to become the person she is now. Rahela and Atif reconciled their religious differences and family expectations and created a happy family life in which everyone was respected. War atrocities and life as refugees only strengthened their relationship and they decided that rather than live off someone else's help, they would seek work to maintain their family independently. Rahela was persistent in studying Hebrew, and soon her skills were good enough to land her a job in an Israeli telecommunications company. This job represented a huge personal and professional success. Atif also found work in Israel, and their sons Haris and Denis did so well that the best schools in Israel were open to them. At that point, Rahela's family decided to return to Sarajevo.

Rahela was able to go back to her post at PTT, but due to changes emerging in the postwar cultural landscape, she went to work for Civitas in 1998. Civitas was a rather new organization promoting democratic citizenship in the Balkans. Today, she works in the American Embassy[1] in a position that enables her to devote her postwar life and work to civic education aimed at reconciling and uniting war-torn communities. She has two grandchildren.

Introduction

> If I believe that my cause is noble and if I believe that my mission is important, there is no one who can make me doubt these things.

Books have always been Rahela's great love, supporting her passion to learn and discover things, a passion that had started in childhood and one that became especially important in her professional life after she began working in youth education. After the war, Rahela could not come to terms with the fact that as social life in BiH crumbled—split by ethnicities, the children and youth of Bosnia were distanced from one another as a consequence. From the very beginning of her educational work, she strove to enable

---

[1] All opinions expressed in this story are personal and do not represent the U.S. Embassy in Sarajevo.

children in BiH to have the kind of quality education that would make them honest citizens, unafraid of neighbors or friends from different ethnic groups and religions. This was her mission, to build a society in which her own children, raised in the multicultural environment of her Jewish tradition and her husband's Muslim background, could live freely no matter what their affiliations and differences.

Relying on her prewar experience in the United States and her later refugee experience in Israel, Rahela knew she had to do something to enable the younger generations to build a civil society that respected human rights not through an imposition of such respect (as if this is possible), but as an important element for the country's progress and for the well-being of every citizen. Convinced from the start that education was crucial, she applied to work in the organization Civitas. Rahela knows that the war in BiH proved the need for civic education: "I think my generation did too little to stop the war and the atrocities that followed, because it believed that power and authorities are distant concepts. We simply did not have the knowledge or the tools to stop the authorities and comprehend the ongoing processes. This is exactly what I want to prevent."

I have known Rahela for years, but we never directly cooperated on educational projects. I learnt of her work from her colleagues, who were inspired by her devotion, patience, and ability to build bridges for dialogue between the divided people of BiH. When I proposed to interview her, Rahela was surprised; she smiled and said: "Is it really the case that people have recognized my commitment to civic education as peace work?[2] I am honored and, of course, happy to tell you about it, but I share my success with all members of the big Civitas family." My colleague Aida Spahić and I visited Rahela in her apartment where she greeted us with coffee,

---

[2] Zilka Spahić-Šiljak, Aida Spahić, and Elmaja Bavčić, 2012, *Baseline Study: Women and Peacebuilding in BH*, Sarajevo: TPO Foundation Sarajevo, www.tpo.ba.

juice, and cakes. Her small, warm home, which was filled with countless memories from travels and photos of her family, was the most comfortable place for her to tell us her life story.

Engineering in Civic Education

> Something that should be a universal principle, and which is found in every religion as well as being present in the founding documents of every democracy, is the notion that all human beings are equal and have equal rights to realize their potential. … This is a difficult principle to put into practice, for it is always too easy to neglect the rights of the person next to you.

Rahela believes in the general principles of democracy, the principles that refer to the equality of all persons and the opportunity for all persons to exercise their freedom, potential, and talent. For her, equality does not stand for sameness, but rather for equal opportunity for all. It was this belief that informed Rahela's decision to abandon her telecommunications engineering work in postwar BiH and turn to work in designing educational tools that would knit together the broken lines of communication that had cut off the people of Bosnia from one another. Rahela sees her greatest achievement as the creation of a curriculum devoted to democracy and human rights that came to be used in high schools all over the country. Together with the Civitas team, she managed not only to offer something new and necessary to the devastated country, but also to unite a divided people in such a way that they supported the need for quality education for all of their children. Rahela, being an effective leader, had the ability to see the big picture in a particularized situation and work toward the realization of that vision.[3]

---

[3] Mary Lou Décosterd, 2013, *How Women Are Transforming Leadership: Four Key Traits Powering Success*, Santa Barbara, CA: Praeger, 27, 47; Swami DyhanGiten, 2012, "On Intuition and Healing," excerpt from "The Silent

Rahela says she herself had received a high-quality education in former Yugoslavia, an education in which students were not segregated according to their ethnicity, and thus she believed that when people differ in their identities in such settings it can be an advantage. These beliefs came not only from her family upbringing, but also from the society she lived in, a society and culture that was ideologically oriented toward equality, brotherhood, and unity. Although there was little equality in practice, she thinks the existing value system did ensure a stable foundation for education and gender equality. The war destroyed the old education system based on Marxist concepts, but a new system of universal values did not replace it. Rahela recalls the postwar ethno-nationalist authorities who did not know how or did not want to modernize the education system:

> It is difficult to modernize the study of humanities ... the old system was based completely on Marxism. When you pull the foundations out from beneath a building, nothing is left. However, the problems of the educational system in BiH have never been addressed, maybe because those who replaced Marxism with democracy or religion did so only nominally and have now assumed positions of leadership in BiH politics. The situation has been particularly stressful due to the frequent changes in government, and quality as a measure of good education has still not been introduced as a pressing need.

Part of the turbulence can be explained, Rahela explained, by the fact that the people who knew how to manage the education system were no longer in BiH. Some had been killed, others had left and had never returned, and the next generation was not sufficiently prepared: "Our education was devastated by war, and in the meantime the rest of the world made progress on many educational fronts."

Whisperings of the Heart—An Introduction to Giten's Approach to Life," www.selfgrowth.com/articles/GITEN2.html (accessed, September 2, 2013).

After returning from Israel and assuming her old telecommunications job, Rahela grew dissatisfied with the situation because people without experience or the will to learn were being employed there through family or party connections. Looking for other jobs, she found employment as the executive director at Civitas,[4] where she could use both her English language skills and the knowledge of civic education that she had obtained from her time in the United States and her years in Israel as a refugee. Having read a lot about the topic of civic education and being a person dedicated to improving the local educational system, she was seriously committed to creating a civic education curriculum for BiH schools. In her words, it was a big challenge, learning for the first time how the government functions and how representatives are elected, both of which provided yet another sign that civic and political rights had not been practiced to their full capacity. Socialism did not allow such questions: "I was convinced that it is a big deal. When you go to the municipality or anywhere similar, it is torture. [It has] nothing to do with paying for their services, and the fact that the authorities are supposed to serve you, not vice versa."

---

[4] Civitas in Bosnia and Herzegovina is a nongovernmental organization founded in 1996 at the initiative of the Center for Civic Education, the Council of Europe, and the United States Information Agency. The Civitas Education Network in BiH was established to promote democracy, human rights, and efficient citizenship. The U.S government has funded the project from the beginning. For more details, see civitas.ba.

Fig. 8-1

Rahela recalls the difficulties that arose in implementing the ambitious civic education program in BiH. As she remembers, "Not many people believed it could work." Those who were ideologically against it claimed various things, such as that she was an American or Israeli spy, that democracy failed to meet expectations, that democracy is disputable and inefficient when it comes to government functioning. People expected democracy to mean a life such as one in the United States or Germany or some other western country. Rahela commented on this:

> It disappointed them greatly. It is true that in most countries of the world, democracy maybe did not meet expectations in terms of bringing huge economic progress. But that is linked with so many other things, [including] the quality of the decisions taken by the majority; when people are free they must know how to use their freedom for the purpose of common, not only individual, good.

In the beginning it was difficult for the young people in BiH to understand that civic education is important and can serve as a solution to the current crisis. Young people have only a partial knowledge and understanding of the democratic changes that have been made in their country, and these are mostly based on the experiences of the 1990s, a period that brought division and misfortune to them because of the war in the Balkans. The challenges Rahela described are many and profound: the lack of a language for democracy, the failure of political, business, and academic elites to accept democracy, an absent middle class to implement genuine democratic change, the positions taken by those in power who frantically guard against democratic measures, and the ignorance among young people of the rights provided to them by democracy, such as their right to hold the government accountable. With the support of the Center for Civic Education in Calabasas, California, and the example of her role models, Charles Quigley and Margaret Branson,[5] Rahela was certain that what they were doing was right and important and could help the people of BiH.

However, Rahela also faced her own expectations, expectations that were inconsistent with reality. For instance, she expected people to be more civic-minded after the war; she expected goodness, helpfulness, and understanding to prevail, and she adds with sadness in her voice: "I finally realized that evil had taken over, and that there was bitter hatred in everyone." War trauma was so tangible that you could feel dissatisfaction everywhere you went. As well as hatred of the "enemy," other divisions were soon apparent. Those who had stayed in Sarajevo during the war felt that they were "morally right" in all things, compared to those who had fled and later returned. Rahela nevertheless tries to understand such behavior: she explained that people's expectations were not met, they felt cheated and exhausted by war, they had suffered a great loss and been brought to the edge of poverty.

In their overall frustration, people resisted any and all progress, saying: "'I do not need to reconcile with anybody; I am not in a fight with anyone.' [But] this was not true; they were in a fight with themselves. And the fight, or restlessness, was obvious in all segments of our social life and relationships." There was no excuse for inaction, however, and Rahela was determined to do something to begin the process of peace and reconciliation. She spoke to as

---

[5] Center for Civic Education, www.civiced.org.

many people as possible, starting with teachers and students in schools. She met people throughout BiH who had done much good in the past, but whose circumstances during the war may have caused them to become involved in a compromising situation; and who therefore felt it necessary to defend their actions when criticized. Rahela saw that what was needed was a space where such people could be accepted, listened to, and understood, without criticism or judgment. The civic education program run by Civitas opened such a space for meetings and reconciliation.

Rahela personally experienced the need to face the differences among Bosnians when she worked on integrated education in the Brčko District, a place with highly divided schools and three national curricula. She recalled the beginning of her encounter there with the teachers, parents, authorities, and students in a setting saturated with a sense of fear. These individuals were so deeply divided because of the war's atrocities that they all wanted to hold onto their own national curricula.

Fig. 8-2

Such a beginning meant that in order to create any sense of trust, there would have to be a public discussion in which all wartime terrors could be disclosed, and this would best take place in a common space where everyone could say publicly what they thought. When a safe room[6] was established, not only for parents and teachers but also for the students, they slowly started realizing that it was possible to work together. "It was a huge problem. If children cannot study together, they will not be able to work together in the future, let alone live together. How could a town of 80,000 citizens progress in such circumstances?"

Being with people and among people was the motto of Civitas under Rahela's leadership. She deemed it most important to work in the field and be in direct contact with people in order to discover their fears and the problems they faced, and then together to look for solutions. "Every novelty causes some sort of resistance and fear … perception is sometimes much more important than reality. The way people see things is for them the truth." Fieldwork enabled divided schools to begin tentative communication with one other, then cooperate further and begin the reconciliation process in which everyone could speak openly about their pain without minimizing the pain of others. This type of communication is a skill that must be learned, for people tend to speak only of their own suffering and fail to acknowledge or even deny the suffering of others. In Rahela's view, the Civitas program excelled in helping teachers and students overcome their prejudices and limitations and respect the pain and perception of others, even while not necessarily agreeing:

> You do not have to agree with another person to be able to see that person's emotions in relation to a certain event. I think that is the essence of democracy—there are so many different perceptions of the world and we are not to judge them, but to teach the youth to

---

[6] Ristin Thomassen, 2006, *To Make Room for Changes: Report by Kvinna Till Kvinna*, http://www.peacewomen.org/assets/file/Resources/NGO/kvinna_tomakeroomforchanges_2006.pdf (accessed September 3, 2011).

develop the skill of presenting arguments, of being able to reason and reach compromises.

In Bosnia, an educational system that fails to provide a space for the other side to be heard consciously limits its students to a closed ethno-national environment. Rahela stresses that, "We have no right to allow a fearful environment to exist in our schools, an environment in which young people not only feel no need to meet others but also do not have any wish to meet others." The parents of these students have had the experience of living together in diversity in the past, but most young people in BiH today live in homogenous ethno-national communities and are gripped by a fear of others. In conversations with young people, Rahela realized how important it was to eliminate this fear and open the door to communication and reconciliation:

> For young people, it is completely irrelevant if their father died as an attacker or as one who was attacked. They are the orphans of war; they are the ones whose fathers died for freedom. Those who killed their father were the enemies in any case, whether attackers or attacked. The young generation lived in such a narrow and fearful world that it was important for someone to open up this world and offer them something sensible, something sustainable.

Rahela was convinced that civic education made sense and was sustainable, and she invested her full energy into the program, not shying away from the many obstacles that faced her. She was recognized by her fellow citizens in BiH not only for her fieldwork but also for her work in schools, as well as being applauded by international institutions.[7] She emphasizes that through her efforts in bringing reconciliation to Bosnia, she learned to understand that

---

[7] In 2010, Rahela received a letter from the Deputy High Representative of the Brčko Office of the High Representative, Gerhard Stonheim, in which he acknowledged what Rahela had done for Brčko—how she had brought together children of different nationalities through civic education.

there are no good people or bad people, or even genocidal people. "Germans are not genocidal people, regardless of what they had done to Jews; it was Hitler and the Nazi movement." In an attempt to find an explanation for the horrors that happened in the Balkans, Rahela says that although it was difficult to face life after the war; to figure out how to move on, how to trust people again, and what to do in certain circumstances, her vision of civic education as a means to ensure equal opportunity and access to education for all children in BiH yielded good results and was sustainable as a program, so she decided to work on domestic capacity building:

> Only with our own experts can we further develop and improve education. On the one hand, we had to have a massive training program in order to include as many people as possible, and to create a critical mass in schools, and on the other hand, we had to train the trainers—to have a pool of our own trainers and experts.

She believes her engineering experience helped her to establish a systematically structured approach to the work and in a few years to build a whole network of teachers and students all over BiH. This network provided not only ambassadors for civic education, but also trained educators for schools and local communities. It seems that Rahela demonstrated a feminist approach to leadership, one that is both inclusive and transformative,[8] and is based on sharing knowledge with the purpose of empowerment.[9] The Civitas office and its coordinators played a crucial role, as Rahela explains: it was not easy being pioneers of civic education in their communities for those who wished to cooperate with others in BiH. These were brave people who had a vision of a better life for the younger generation in BiH, a life based on a good education.

---

[8] Paula D. Nesbitt and Linda E. Thomas, 1998, "Beyond Feminism: An Intercultural Challenge for Transforming the Academy," in Elizabeth G. Peck and JoAnna Stephens Mink (eds.), *Common Ground: Feminist Collaboration in the Academy*, Albany: State University of New York Press.
[9] Décosterd, 2013, 74.

Citizen Identity

> Our intention was to add an additional layer, an identity as a democratic citizen, an identity that would be universal everywhere. … Our laws and practice should be directed toward these equalities.

Rahela spoke about the importance of perceiving one's identity beyond the limits of ethnicity and religion. In her mind, people's lives and volitions are much more complex and rich than the imposed ethno-national trinity: "If you are Serb, Croat, or Bosniac, that determines your core, but it's not the only layer. … So we started introducing the notion of searching for one's identity and the need to expand this identity by adding layers to it."

Coming from a family that celebrated diversity enabled Rahela to transpose the idea of multiple identities into the Civitas program. Aware that the educational system in BiH did not produce responsible citizens, but rather yielded dissatisfied ethno-national groups, she decided to do something to loosen the grip of these ethno-national identities to enable people to be more than just Serbs, Croats, or Bosniacs. She dared to show that it was possible to overcome even the strongest boundaries, both visible and invisible, between the divided people in BiH, and to awaken a hope that things could be different, not by reducing anyone's identity, but rather by enriching and improving it. As Lederach notes when describing peacebuilders, Rahela embraced even this complexity and did not avoid the seemingly insurmountable challenge it posed.[10]

Rahela's was motivated a number of sources in her desire that there be quality education for the young. Many teachers and students remain dissatisfied with the state of education in BiH, which is in Rahela's opinion a result of the irresponsible approach

---

[10] John Paul Lederach, 2005, *The Moral Imagination: The Art and Soul of Building Peace*, Oxford: Oxford University Press, 33.

of those in power who fail to value their citizens' welfare. She wanted progress for Bosnian young people so they would feel a sense of hope in the future, because she claims, very few people advocate for programs that provide inspiration for the nation's youth. She never lost faith, however, because she believed so strongly that young people should be given a chance. She realizes that such work requires sacrifice and a belief that things can be different:

> Many people think you are crazy or just pretending. But you know in your heart that it is true and you let them criticize you and spit on you … whatever they do—you ignore it, and continue working and looking into the eyes of children who meet [each other] and want to meet again. And you say: I'll make that happen. Then the light bulb goes on … and you think, "why hasn't anyone told me this before," and you just know you have to have the strength [to continue].

What Rahela saw in the eyes of children was a real hope for things to be different, a hope that someone could help them, could open the doors of closed communities and take them to a better, safer future. Civic education was one of the paths to achieve this, and Rahela worked tirelessly to realize this hope, to bring people closer and release them from the fears and prejudices they brought to their first training sessions.

In addition, Rahela's motivation came from a sort of rebellion against the prevailing practice of collective identity, discrimination, and exclusion. She has always promoted women's rights, which is reflected in her ongoing representation of all parties equally, be they men and women or ethnic and religious groups. She believes relations in a society should be based on meritocracy, and that one's identity, though important, is second to one's competence and capabilities. Thus she was ready as Joseph Nye would say, to take the risk of living outside the imposed identity frameworks[11]—

---

[11] Joseph S. Nye, Jr., 2005, *Soft Power: The Means to Success in World Politics*, New York: PublicAffairs.

ethno-national boxes. However, in postwar BiH, the political elites teach that everything should be divided into three—for Bosniacs, Croats, and Serbs, while others, i.e., minorities, have almost no rights.

Fig. 8-3

She recalled an anecdote from Mostar in 1999. It was the first meeting of Civitas coordinators and a number of them thought that Rahela, a Jew, should not be their leader—it should rather be organized like BiH, with a three-headed presidency.[12] Rahela explained in disbelief that there were still people who wanted to regulate everything according to the imposed ethno-national trinity: "They were completely unable to remove themselves from the

---

[12] Pursuant to the Dayton Constitution, BiH was established with a tripartite Presidency, unlike the general practice of a single president, and thus each member represents his/her constituent people. There is no place for the category of *others* (minorities) in these presidencies, according to the Constitution. They are simply not represented and therefore have become less equal citizens.

three-nation matrix; the individual did not exist, only the collective."

The issue of belonging and identity burdened Bosnian society to such an extent that Rahela, as a member of a minority in an ethnically divided state, was often exposed to both direct and indirect questioning related to assumptions and judgments about who she was. Which nation did she belong to, which political option did she support, what were her goals, who did she work for, and what was she promoting under the guise of democracy. Her every encounter meant the unavoidable question: who are you (in terms of ethnic belonging)? If she refused to respond, or if her name did not clearly indicate her ethnicity and religion, as was the case of course, the intrigue grew, and various conspiracy theories developed about her work, her supporters, her authority, and her legitimacy:

> It often happened in training sessions that people were more interested in who I was; they read between the lines, tried to assess me by what they thought I wanted to say. I come from Sarajevo, and the program is American [so the questions and critiques begin]: "they are trying to sell us some democracy" and "look what they've done to African Americans" and similar things.

Rahela experienced this personally but sometimes pretended to be naive and not notice the evaluations and assessments. She resorted to a "smart flexible" strategy summarized as: "the ability to adapt to, respond to, and take advantage of emerging and context-based challenges."[13] She believed that people would, once they got to know her, accept her and focus on results more than on concerns about her origin. And time has proven her right, showing that it is possible to think and act outside the scope of imposed matrices and that the identity of a person as a human being can come before all other identities. In the ongoing work of Civitas, the program Project

---

[13] Lederach 2005, 85.

Citizen was very helpful because it opened doors to the development of a civic, political culture that assisted many in enriching their identity by adding a citizen identity component symbolizing the universal value of citizens living in a democratic society.

Project Citizen

> We can establish democratic institutions, but what moves them are human beings. [What to do however] if they are not sufficiently aware, if they lack sufficient moral qualities to care for those they represent? ... We see this happen at all levels of authority.

Rahela underlines the importance of human beings as the key factor in democratic processes. Governments may change, and it is difficult each time there is a change to establish a functioning government suitable for citizens. Rahela brought her belief in the strength of an individual to the project. One of Civitas's educational programs, Project Citizen, was implemented in schools in BiH. This program trained teachers and young people in the skills and knowledge needed to become responsible citizens.

Although many in BiH have misunderstood democracy and abused it by their irresponsible behavior, Rahela stresses that people need to be taught how to be ready to face the consequences of expressing their beliefs in acts of civil disobedience. "It often happens that people want to break the law, but are not willing to face the consequences," she says. In the process of building a democratic society, citizens should be informed and equipped with a set of skills that will enable them to demand their rights legally and to require accountability from governments that violate laws.

Rahela recalled that, despite all the obstacles to common action in an ethno-nationally divided education, it was the understanding of individuals that helped society see that civic education was a human right. In addition, Rahela explains, schools and teachers began to realize that it was no good to keep promoting one-track politics, because young people had access to the internet for all kinds of information and knowledge. Thus, it was necessary for these young people to develop critical thinking skills: "That's why we always say that this program teaches both the young generation and the older people not *what* to think but *how* to think." Project Citizen[14] has encouraged young people not only to take responsibility for their communities but also to learn how the state functions so they can try to change things when necessary. Rahela notes:

> Project Citizen does not teach a problem-solving skill but rather a capacity to impact public policy measures. We think that if young people fail to influence the creation of public policy measures and don't work on the implementation of these measures, a remnant of the political and national elite will be able to manipulate the overall process to their own advantage.

This project is of great importance for Rahela. She remembers one of the initial years of the project when her son Denis was in primary school and tried to help his class prepare for the Civitas competition. Rahela was involved in Project Citizen, so Denis could not be part of the team, but he helped his school to participate for the first time. She was pleased to say that they both found it challenging; students were not used to work that required such activism, nor were the teachers. His school's project was well received, and Rahela adds: "the experience brought us closer and proved that individuals truly can contribute to the betterment of the situation."

---

[14] The Citizen Project is the practical part of the Civitas Program. Students (60,000 annually, making up over 2,400 teams) are encouraged to select a problem in their communities, assess the existing policy measures, develop their own solutions, present them to the authorities, and create action plans to implement them. Each year, 32 winning teams—more than 400 students and teachers from all parts of BiH come to Sarajevo for the final ceremony, and during the summer they visit Brčko Summer Camp. The U.S. government has been financing the project since 1996.

Project Citizen also made possible the affirmation of young people, who longed for opportunities, competition, achievements, and the valorization of the results. After all, humans are competitive creatures who would not achieve anything much were it not for their driving competitive spirit. Rahela explained that Project Citizen is competitive for two reasons.

One reason is the fact that democracy is itself competitive. People gather around common interests, and those who advocate best for their interests get what they want. Rahela says the message for young people is that failing to achieve the desired result is not only caused by an unjust society, but also by insufficient effort on the part of the individual to fight for a goal or interest. She encouraged young people to follow their goal and not give up before even trying.

The second reason is to ensure continuity for teachers and students to understand that the project is serious in providing opportunities and an equal chance to all participants and to their project ideas at local and regional competitions and events. In addition to the visibility the competitions provided in schools and communities, everyone looked forward to these events as the occasion for meeting old friends and making new ones:

> We somehow managed to unite them toward the same goal and bring them closer. We always looked for creative ways to bring young people closer, because we realized there were not too many personalities in popular culture, film, even sports, that connect young people. It really was difficult to come up with a common denominator, something around which they could unite.

Competitions and festivals of knowledge and skills have succeeded in bringing people closer, and Rahela says that even today when she visits some towns in BiH, she meets people who say that Project Citizen was their ticket to making new friends and being able to socialize with them.

However, in spite of the benefits of the competitions and the associated socializing, both young people and teachers had difficulty at times in defending their attitudes, accepting the arguments of others, reaching a consensus, and changing their opinions when it was necessary for the welfare of the community.

Consistency Versus Consensus

> How can we reach a minimum of consensus, when they taught us to be consistent?

Rahela reveals how a faulty value system can greatly limit democratization. She tackled an important characteristic of local people who proudly promote consistency as virtue. In BiH this usually means that people should remain static in all their actions and attitudes, for only those who would "betray their own" allow themselves to change. In such an environment, regardless of the strength of an argument in favor of change, it is difficult to actually make change happen. Rahela faced this situation when she tried to introduce what was seen as a novelty in the BiH education system. She believes, of course, that "to remain consistent is not a virtue. A virtue is to listen to arguments, to weigh them, and to offer better solutions with regard to the argument, to come up with one's own solutions." She particularly remembers a philosophical essay entitled "In Praise of Inconsistency"[15] by the Polish author Leszek Kołakowski from which she learned that thought evolves as it relates to different situations. While every person is bound at some point to change his or her opinion, "we are taught consistency and keeping to a single direction."

Due to this conventional notion of consistency as a value, there was a lot of resistance to a civic education that required constant

---

[15] Leszek Kołakowski, 1964, "In Praise of Inconsistency," *Dissent* 11, no. 2 (April), http://search.opinionarchives.com/Summary/Dissent/V11I2P201-1.htm (accessed July 2, 2013).

deliberation and change. Rahela, however, thought that if being consistent keeps children physically divided in different worlds, it cannot be right. It continues to separate children who "cannot even imagine things that were normal for us: to sit together and socialize, to marry amongst ourselves, and to meet new cultures and strive to make life more beautiful by being richer in a new custom or knowledge about those who are different from us." However, this was exactly what perpetrators of war and division wanted—to distance people, to alienate them so they could only think of their differences, not their more numerous similarities. Rahela's motivation was to bring people together, to connect and reconcile them, and this required sensitivity for the feelings and needs of others. Martha Nussbaum draws attention to the importance of developing such virtues for the achievement of justice,[16] as does Elisabeth Porter, who stresses that without respect for and acknowledgement of others, it is difficult to be sensitive to their needs.[17] In order to master these virtues and the feeling of respect for others, it is necessary to change any existing relations in society that fixate on the welfare of one's own ethnic group.

Many education experts in BiH, Rahela claims, thought that it was sufficient just to live in a system that calls itself democratic in order to actually achieve democracy. However, her experience shows that each new generation must be taught the principles of democracy and human rights. The process never ends, but needs constant renewal. That's what makes her proud of Project Citizen: it has been teaching new generations of citizens for years, citizens ready to introduce the principles of democracy into a postwar society with a non-democratic constitutional framework.[18]

---

[16] Martha Nussbaum, 1999, *Sex and Social Justice,* Oxford: Oxford University Press, 6.

[17] Elisabeth J. Porter, 2007, *Peacebuilding: Women in International Perspective*, London: Routledge, 103.

[18] BiH Constitution, 1995 (part of Dayton Peace Accords) recognizes first and foremost the ethnic identities of the three constituent groups, which is itself a limitation of democracy.

One of the ways she sought to teach young people democracy was to insist that they develop empathy and responsibility for other members of the community, because according to Rahela, the public good must be evenly distributed. "It is not [now] as it was in communism [where] all people were entitled to the same things. It is [now] about those of us with more helping those with less."

Another way of witnessing to the principle of democracy was in society's treatment of minorities. After the war in BiH, each of the three major ethnic groups constituted a minority in one or another part of the country. Wherever a particular ethnic group was in the majority, other ethnic groups were completely neglected. In trying to understand the consistent support of one's own ethnic group over the needs of others, Rahela, herself a minority Jew, says that people have gone through such traumatic experiences and suffering (based on their collective ethnic identity that it is now difficult to move them from what has become an entrenched position as victim. To encourage them to support transitional justice or to take individual responsibility is nearly impossible. After a war, a traumatized generation lives in fear of another war and thus it is difficult to move them toward change. This generation supports all the things their ethnic group imposes in the way of norms, for they have experienced the hardship of being a minority in BiH. Rahela says that even in Sarajevo, which used to be a paradigm of multiculturalism and openness, there is less and less space for minorities regardless of ethnic background:

> We really tried to maintain Sarajevo in as multicultural a way as possible. But in circumstances of an extremely large majority and a very small minority, there was little understanding of minority opinion. You are not allowed to share it in public. It is simply impermissible and unacceptable.

It was therefore a huge challenge for Rahela and those she worked with to resist ethno-national divisions in a way that would not abolish differences among ethnic groups. Rahela's understanding of democracy acknowledged and respected the differences, provided they did not serve as grounds for discrimination, because "democracy is the rule of the majority, but one in which minorities are well protected." It is important for young people to learn how to build their own systems of democracy while offering a place for those who hold a different opinion, who disagree with the majority, but who can also serve as a corrective to the majority. Rahela compares this to her upbringing in socialist Yugoslavia, which as she says, did not allow for full equality and freedom but did provide sufficient space, freedom, solidarity, and security.

The Values We Have Lost

> I am not one of those who regret times gone by. I look to the future too much. But I try to learn from the past—to take the best from it.

Rahela's story contains a comparison of socialist and post-socialist contexts in the Balkans and BiH not because she longs for times gone by, but because she wants to stress everything that was good in the past and could now serve as a basis for further improvements. In her opinion, the socialist system was not ideal, but with all its disadvantages and flaws, it was a system that provided social and economic security. "I think that socialism or communism, whatever we call it, had three outstanding components: equal access to education, gender equality, and health protection."

In terms of equal access to education, Rahela says that we need a system in which all children from all parts of the country attend primary school. After that, scholarships should be provided to both the poor and the talented to go to secondary school and university. Comparing past opportunities with today's post-socialist options, Rahela says with concern:

> Any child that wanted to go, and was capable, could go to school. It is not the case today, and I am afraid that if we continue like this our education will lose its quality. And we are not even aware of how many children do not have access to education nowadays.

Rahela believes that a majority of children did have access to education in the previous system, because the state cared for those who were unable to pay for school. The quality of education used to be much better, the state invested in it, and criteria ensuring a certain quality of instruction were applied. In her long years of work at Civitas, Rahela visited many rural areas and saw poverty and failing schools: "It is such a huge problem for kids to reach high school … we who live in the cities have no idea how hard it is for people in rural areas to live and how many people lose their right to education."

Rahela is nostalgic about the solidarity found among individuals in the socially oriented state that cared for its people in the old days. She speaks of those values with pride: "The upbringing we received from our parents was very important—it made us think about others, to have minds of our own, be responsible, be hard-working, always do our best, and never think we're better than anyone else." Her father Isak was the one who particularly insisted on a strong work ethic and a critical spirit; he was an entrepreneur, which enabled him, as Rahela says, "to have a bit more freedom."

Fig. 8-4

The second important achievement that should have been carried over from the previous system was gender equality as a social value. Rahela says that because she could study what she wanted, she chose electrical engineering, a profession not pursued by many women at the time. Before that, she had been selected to spend a year in the United States with a wonderful American family that she is close to even today. She recalled jokes about communism and capitalism, and the prejudice people had against both these systems:

> I defended communism and Yugoslavia, and Sarajevo and all that was important to me. It was 1974. We joked a lot, they [the Americans] called me a communist, and I called them capitalists. My American colleagues first thought that communists selected me as a *wunderkind* to show them how smart we were. As we started knowing and understanding each other, we all felt much richer.

Rahela explains that she was knowledgeable about science, and even though Yugoslavia did not have computers, she soon mastered basic computer language and was outstanding in advanced mathematics. After completing her studies, she was appointed head of a department in PTT, a position usually occupied by men. She was given a managerial position despite the fact that she was not much of a communist. Aware that high-ranking positions were reserved for prominent party members, she assumed that the coming Olympics in Sarajevo played a role, as experts were greatly needed. "Everyone knew I visited the Jewish Municipality and that that was an important part of my identity. Maybe I was lucky that we were selected for the Olympic Games and they needed people who spoke foreign languages." During the Olympics, however, she experienced an incident in which prejudice against a woman in a leading position was expressed with regard to her own position. As a young engineer, she had been tasked to work on behalf of PTT with the International Communications Committee of the CCIT (Consultative Committee for International Telephony and Telegraphy). Representatives of the American Broadcasting Service, the chief media sponsor of the Olympics, were present as well, and they assumed a man would be working with them. Rahela laughed while she was telling us the story:

> So I, a tiny woman—I was even skinnier then—came to talk with them … and I asked them at one point: "Shall we go?" And they looked at me and said: "We're waiting for the engineer." And I asked them: "You mean a big guy with a moustache?" And they replied: "We were told an engineer will accompany us." Then I said: "And who do you think I am?" They thought I was an interpreter. It was unimaginable to have a woman engineer, particularly one so young and tiny. We joked about it all the time.

The third important achievement of the previous system was access to healthcare for all Yugoslav citizens. Rahela felt that the old system "created empathy among people and a wish to help those who were ill. Today such empathy almost doesn't exist. Of course, the lack of empathy is detrimental to society, and I have witnessed this when my husband was ill." She criticized the current situation on the matter, for she believes those who have empathy have achieved the highest level of development of their personality. Such a level of compassion requires, as Elisabeth Porter and others have written, the development of a politics of compassion that includes a sense for the sufferings of others, active listening, and wise responses to certain needs.[19]

Rahela recalled how careful her family was about not hurting the feelings of those who had less, and they never publicly showed that they had more or lived better:

> In the beginning my parents lived a humble life; they created everything themselves and they taught us to feel compassion. I remember we were not allowed to wear anything expensive, although our father was a private entrepreneur. We were not allowed to take anything to school that could not be shared with others.

Ethical values from the legacy of cultural and religious traditions found in regions of Yugoslavia were added to the ethics of a socialist society that emphasized justice, fairness, solidarity, and caring for fellow citizens. Rahela thinks it is a pity that these values have not been maintained today, because the impoverished society now found in BiH makes more and more visible the gap between the rich and the poor, and the ever-present insensitivity to others' needs.

Rahela is also proud of the cultural life and openness that enabled Sarajevo to welcome non-Bosnians and make them feel at home. With its rich cultural and artistic programs and diversity, Sarajevo was an attractive city. Rahela spoke fondly of the events that were organized within the Union of Jewish Municipalities, which everyone loved coming to because they enjoyed being in

---

[19] Porter 2007, 103.

Sarajevo so much. It was a city in which things happened all the time and everyone felt free:

> There was no need here to pretend you were something you were not. Everyone accepted everyone else as long as there was no pretending. [The idea was] "Here, take all the space you want, but leave me to my own desires. If you accept me as I am—I will accept you as well." That's why we had such a rich cultural and artistic life.

She remembers an Arab student who studied electrical engineering with her and who kept saying that BiH "lives" the true Islam; he felt good, he was free and he could be a Muslim without being looked down upon. Rahela added that this attitude was true toward other faiths. "We should feel close to all religions."

Rahela's favorite periods were the 1970s and 1980s. She described it as a time of prosperity, optimism, faith, and love. She believed that love was enough to overcome all obstacles. She was married to a Muslim in an ethnically and religiously mixed family: "We were all mixed. My godmother is Dubravka (a Serb), Atko (Atif) my Muslim husband served as the best man for Zlatko (a Serb), one of my daughters-in-law is a Serb, one a Jew … all mixed and all living together." These are the values Rahela embodied and still embodies, but she is aware that the war burdened people with identity differences and politics such that opportunities for community are now scarce.

Fig. 8-5

Successful Women as "Honorary Men"

Rahela finds gender equality very important and she has consistently advocated for it. In the Balkans, the emancipation of women stagnated in the 1990s. After the war, women struggled for the legal regulation of equality issues, but also tried to raise the awareness of both women and men about the essential changes needed for emancipation and equality. Rahela notes, however, that the efforts of nongovernmental organizations and the newly established gender equality institutions, as important as they are as a framework, have not been sufficient. The actual situation in society shows that there are few women in senior and decision-making positions and that the traditional, patriarchal understanding of the role and position of women in the family and society still prevails:

> A lot should be invested in raising awareness of men and women, particularly women, and also emphasizing women's capabilities. Very often nothing is done about their role in society. The rare women in senior positions are in fact "honorary men."

Rahela regrets that many women in political positions have accepted being "honorary men" in institutional or business positions, thus showing a lack of sensitivity for women's issues. "It seems to me that women who are free and equal do not do enough for those who are not. They lack empathy. Not everyone is as lucky as they are and it takes a lot of effort to really achieve equality."

There is an unwritten rule that women who succeed in life and prove they can be good leaders are no longer called women but rather referred to as men, claims Rahela. In the BiH context the word *čovjek*[20] should denote both male and female, but its grammatical gender is male and culturally it is used to denote men. When her husband passed away, a respected member of his family paid a tribute, saying: "And Rahela, she is not like a woman, she is a man of some sort—and in their mind, this was the greatest possible acknowledgement I could get."

According to Rahela, it was one thing to be a good person and another thing to accept, as a woman, the role of "honorary man." One can find similar thinking in studies that confirm the indecisiveness of women in questioning such acquired positions.[21] In their defense, they often claim they have achieved these positions because of their knowledge and experience. They do not understand why they should deal with gender equality and feminism when they are already equal. Maybe some women have succeeded in this way, but other women do not often have such success.

Changing the general awareness of both women and men should be a goal in the long-term process of changing the socially expected

---

[20] The word for "man" (not including women) is *muškarac* in Bosnian.
[21] Zilka Spahić-Šiljak, 2012, *Contesting Female, Feminist, and Muslim Identities, Post-socialist Contexts of Bosnia and Herzegovina and Kosovo*, Sarajevo: Center for Interdisciplinary Postgraduate Studies, 232.

and acceptable gender roles, she says. The reason often quoted for the lack of engagement on these issues is shortage of funds, but Rahela thinks that a lot can be done without money, once there is a social system and structure that values equally the potential of all people:

> It is not true it can't be done because of [a lack of] money. We have so much unused potential. When people retire at the age of 55 they are erased from the picture, the state sees them only as individuals who spend public money for pensions and medicines. In local community centers these people play chess and cards, drink coffee ... we haven't put in place democratic social structures.

Rahela is very critical of such relations and the politics that fail to use human resources for socially beneficial work and assistance. For example, the CVs of politicians, business people, or even youth do not contain any reference to their volunteering or contributing to society—only their professional engagements are mentioned. Rahela would like to see the programs of nongovernmental organizations more involved in working with the elderly, with parents, and with unemployed women and youth—because they also need education to understand equality and peacebuilding.

Rahela thinks that women are not inherent peacebuilders; they are capable of discrimination just like men. However, she uses affirmative essentialism[22] and differentiates between women and men because "women are mothers and life is holier for them; they know how hard it is to give birth, raise a child, and then lose the child. They are thus more inclined to find other possible solutions and to look for some sort of consensus." Therefore, biological and gender roles influence to a certain extent the greater commitment of

---

[22] Elissa Helms, 2013, *Innocence and Victimhood, Gender, Nation, and Women's Activism in Postwar Bosnia-Herzegovina.* Madison, WI: University of Wisconsin Press, 9.

women to find ways to solve conflicts and misunderstandings, both in family and in society.

> Men are wrongfully taught that they are the ones carrying the burden of tradition. They are taught heroic poems from an early age, taught not to cry, to be responsible. ... It is discriminating, and it does not teach them tolerance. It teaches them to be hard, unchanging.

Due to the socially constructed roles and expectations set for women and men,[23] Rahela concludes that women are more inclined to peace work, for the type of behavior expected of men is not expected of women. She gave as an example the Project Citizen program in schools, a program for which mostly girls apply, "because boys are in sports or other things that bring awards, money, and prestige." But taking the example of her sons, she says that such a characterization might be unfair to men, because one's upbringing plays a great role. This statement seems consistent with what Fiona Robinson says about socially constructed gender roles: "it is important to recognize that women's (and men's) agency is constrained by the gendered norms, institutions, and structures of militarism and neoliberal global restructuring."[24] Therefore, true emancipation and equality requires women to understand their roles and responsibilities. "Women, as mothers and to a great extent as educational workers, accept these gender roles and they mostly continue raising children according to traditionally divided roles."

Although Rahela has almost always been in favor of change and introducing novelties, she is on the other hand equally devoted to keeping the old ways in terms of culture, tradition, and religion. However, she supports maintaining traditions only to the extent that

---

[23] Elise Boulding, 2000, *Cultures of Peace: The Hidden Side of History*, New York: Syracuse University Press, 71.
[24] Fiona Robinson, 2011, *The Ethics of Care: A Feminist Approach to Human Security*, Philadelphia: Temple University Press, 57.

they are not in the service of discrimination or exclusion. Her approach in this regard is quite selective.

> Where there is the presence of God there should also be the presence of the universal good and equal welfare for everyone—that is the essence of faith. If people have God in their souls, then God is present in the way that he loves all his children equally, and is good to everyone. I think this can never mean hating someone who is from a different ethnicity or speaks a different language or does something differently.

In the end, Rahela admits that war trauma still makes her fear those who designed the horrors of the early 1990s. She explains that BiH did not go through the process of facing the truth about the war, which could serve as one of the foundations of justice and reconciliation. Therefore, many people are not yet ready to face their mistakes. Despite this, she says she will not give up: "I can use what is left of my life to try to enable, both individually and within the system, as many people, youth, and educators as possible to recognize human warmth and love." Rahela is concerned not only with the future of BiH but also with the future of her family. Her love for her sons, daughters-in-law, and grandchildren dictate her attempts to leave BiH in as good a condition as possible, for people in Bosnia have an additional work to do on reconciliation, and reconciliation is only be possible when the truth is fully accepted.

Conclusion

Rahela's story shows the power of the love she exhibits for her primary family and for the family she created with her husband. Her love of knowledge and openness as a means to transform diversity into richness show how ready and committed she is to share with her children and with all children in BiH the results of her work in peacebuilding. This work resulted in her three separate careers—two in telecommunications and one in education. But everything she did, she did from her heart and from the conviction that she was doing the right thing.

Her latter career in education is the focus of this chapter, specifically her work against singular identities within the changed system of values that prioritized the collective needs over individual needs. She pursued this goal through teaching civic education to residents of the new "democratic" BiH, providing both a safe space for revisiting past traumas as well as opening the door to air new ideas. Because she believes the essence of democracy is people striving for the common good, civic education is essential to the improvement of the new political and social system that was put in place after communist socialism failed. Among many other things, civic-minded thinking there is challenged by a local resistance to change, but Rahela asserts that the true virtue is to deliberate on issues and propose solutions, rather than remain wedded to the old ways.

Less pronounced but also a part of her worldview is her feminism. She is an advocate for women's equality and can see how this value was eroded in the 1990s after great inroads had been made toward women's rights during the communist regime. She resists the category of "honorary men" for women like herself who have advanced professionally, but she also recognizes her privilege in even having to deal with this stereotype, when most women are simply cut off from public influence altogether. Rahela wisely asserts that women cannot inherently be peacebuilders, for they are just as prone to discriminate as men, but she does acknowledge the biological and social roles that attract women, perhaps more than men, to this arena of work. All in all, Rahela relishes diversity of religions, ideas, and personalities, and can envision her country returning to its previous value system of solidarity, care, education, and equality as its best course.

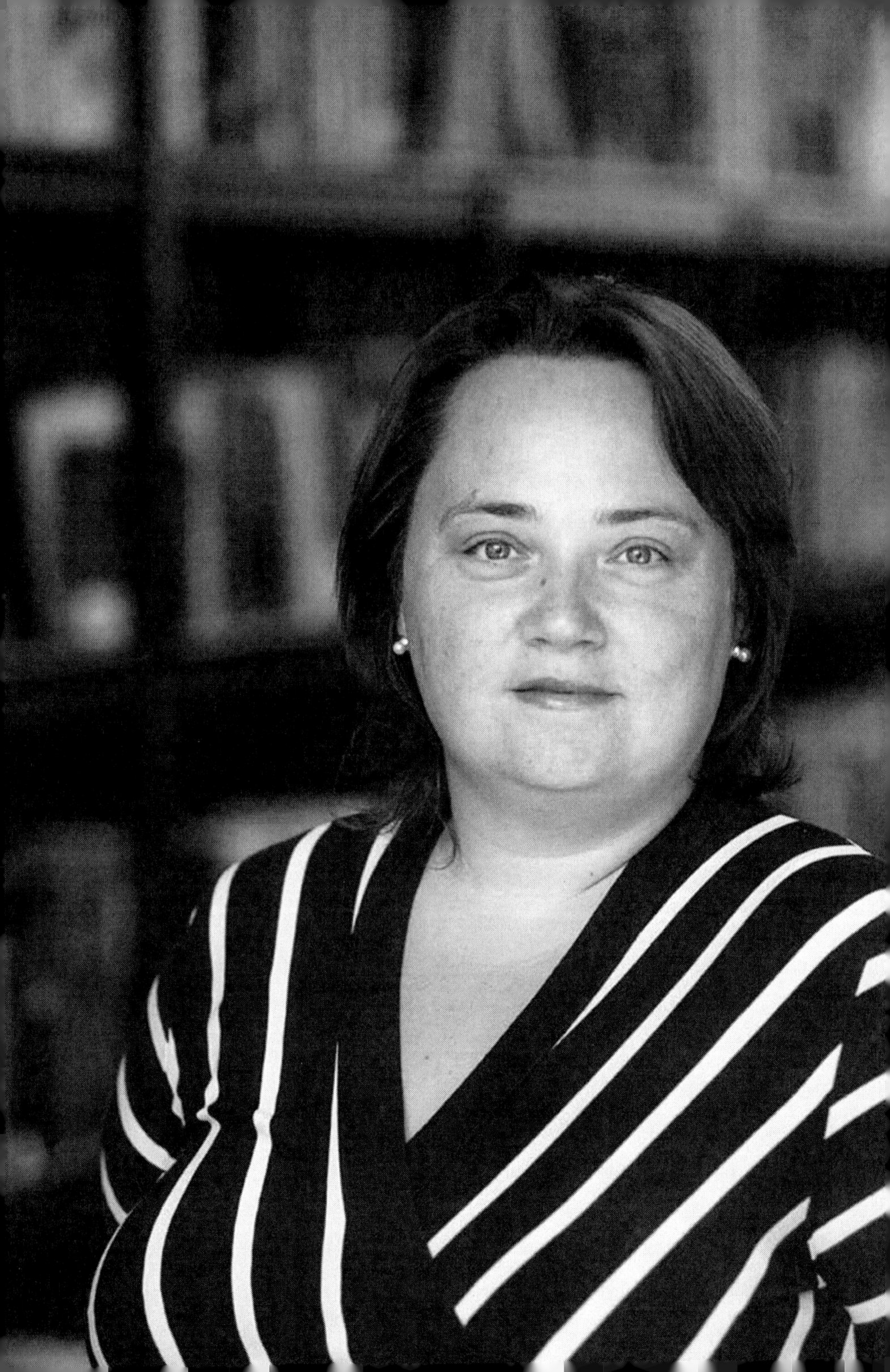

STORY NINE

PEACEBUILDING IS MY LIFE CALLING

AMRA PANDŽO

Biography

Amra Pandžo was born in 1970 in Sarajevo into a family of secular Bosniac Muslim intellectual family who nurtured socialist values of brotherhood and unity and who had a long tradition of highly educated ancestors. Because of her family's longstanding intellectual traditions Amra was exposed to the ideas of peace through her family heritage, specifically through the literature of her grandfather Šukrija Pandžo, a renowned children's author. Growing up in this intellectual hub, Amra learned about concepts such as dialogue, the importance of respect for others based on dialogue and communication. Having lost her father at the age of twelve, she came to view her mother and the other strong and successful women in her family as great role models.

Amra studied at the Faculty of Philosophy at the University of Sarajevo and holds a diploma in Comparative Slavic Literature and Librarianship. After the war, she continued with her graduate studies at the Faculty of Political Science. When the war started, however, she was still a young student, and for the first time, she found herself face to face with challenges to her ethnic and religious identity. The war period was marked by encounters with people from different cultural contexts who came to Sarajevo. During the war, Amra met her future husband, but her family and the people around her found it difficult to accept their marriage because her husband was a Serb.

Her professional experience in the field of peacebuilding began at the Helsinki Committee for Human Rights (HCHR) of BiH, where she was in charge of the Centre for Information and Support for NGOs. In 2001, she attended a seminar by the Centre for Non-violent Action of the HCHR—a ten-day training session aimed at sensitizing the participants working in the area of peacebuilding—and from that moment on, each of her subsequent actions was clearly taken with the idea of peacebuilding in mind. Additionally, Amra was the founder and a board member of an inter-religious organization called Abraham. Currently, she runs a faith-based organization called Small Steps (Mali Koraci) and a similar association named Dialogue in the Family and Society, and she works in the city's public library. She lives in Sarajevo with her two children, Uma and Imran.

Introduction

> If people are predisposed to work in peacebuilding, they cannot make a clear break between their private and public discourse. They simply have to be holistic, in the sense that they approach peacebuilding the same way. It is *vocation*, it is a calling. It is not something you choose to be, such as a typist or an accountant. ... It is a way of life.

Amra is a young woman with extraordinary energy and vision. She leaves everyone she meets astonished by her level of commitment to the activities of peacebuilding. Her life trajectory has been anything but ordinary. From her early days as a student, she was challenged by the war, which shook her life dramatically and negated the values nurtured in her family. In the middle of the war, she started to question her identity and worldview. After many ups and downs during this time, she found herself drawn to religion, which seemed to provide her with an inner strength for what she had come to see as her life's work: building peace in her community. Amra is one of the rare peacebuilders in BiH who has dared to use religion as a platform in her work. The post-war socio-political context and politicization of religion[1] have made her work truly significant, for it is a brave initiative to include the voice of religion in peace discussions. However, most of the examples of peace work inspired by religion, such as Abraham or the interreligious service Eye to Eye, were initiated after 2000, when secular NGOs started to provide more space for these kinds of activities. Although there were some faith-based NGOs established before 2000, like IMIC Zajedno in Sarajevo (1991), their work was more focused on humanitarian activities. Medica Zenica was the only secular women's NGO that used religion as a way to heal the traumas of wartime rape victims, but its first interreligious activities also started after 2001.[2]

I met Amra when she was active in Abraham, and from that time on, we would occasionally collaborate on projects together. In 2005, she became involved in designing a religious studies program in Sarajevo, the first such non-theological program in the post-socialist Southeast European context.[3] After learning of the interview I wanted to do with her, she felt happy and honored that her fellow citizens recognized her peace work, and she readily accepted. When my colleague Elmaja and I came to her home, we chatted with her and her children for a bit, and then she calmly sat up, straightened her back, and positioned herself to begin the

---

[1] Neven Andjelic, 2003, *Bosnia and Herzegovina: The End of Legacy*, London: Frank Cass, 140-153.
[2] Zilka Spahić-Šiljak, 2013, "Do It and Name It: Feminist Theology and Peacebuilding in Bosnia and Herzegovina," *Journal for Feminist Studies in Religion* 29, no. 2, 178-186.
[3] The M.A. Program in Religious Studies at the University of Sarajevo was initiated under the leadership of Prof. Stephen Batalden of the Melikian Center at Arizona State University. He recognized Sarajevo as an important site in Southeastern Europe to develop a graduate program for academic study of religion. The Program in Religious Studies enrolled its first class of students in 2007 with the helpful support of Marko Oršolić, director of the IMIC Center (Zajedno Sarajevo); Prof. Zdravko Grebo, Faculty of Law, University of Sarajevo; and the financial support of the U.S. Department of State and the Norwegian Ministry of Foreign Affairs.

serious and powerful part of the conversation. As an articulate woman who has experience in public discussions and conversation, she easily narrated her rich life experiences and her journey as a woman who becomes fully sensitive to the needs of other human beings.[4]

All Voices Should be Heard

What is crucial for peace is that all the voices be heard ... everybody has the right to bring her/his own perspective and story.

Fig. 9-1

Anyone who knows Amra is aware of her determination to enable different voices to join together to discuss even the most painful of issues. In this way, she creates room for dialogue and

---

[4] Marshall Gantz, 2009, "Why Stories Matter," *Sojournes: Faith in Action for Social Justice*, www.sojo.net/magazine/2009/03/why-stories-matter (accessed September 3, 2013).

reconciliation and a "safe space"[5] for telling stories based on traumatic experiences. Even for her though, it is not always an easy and productive endeavor; she admitted that she has made mistakes and had difficulties, especially when she had to accept that she was going to live with those very individuals who had held her under siege in Sarajevo. Even so, she learned that making room for dialogue was the only way to come to peaceful understanding and show that there was an alternative to violence and evil.

In the middle of the war in 1993, when Sarajevo was under siege, surrounded by Serbs, Amra was faced with her first moral dilemma—to talk or not to talk with a Serb from Belgrade who wanted to visit Sarajevo. Together with some of her colleagues, she attended a student gathering at the University of Sarajevo. There the matter was discussed—whether to allow the voice of a young man from Belgrade to be heard in the midst of terror and killing in Sarajevo:

> There was shooting around us, there were bombs going off, and the president of a youth organization from Belgrade called us. He wanted to come to Sarajevo. Opinions were quite divided ... I stood up and said, "No!" And then a guy in the group reacted: "If you do not receive him, you are the same as Karadžić.[6] If a man wants to come, then that means he does not support the policy of Greater Serbia and that not all Serbs are the same!" I then said that if he comes, I will take him to my house in Kovači, a *mahala* neighborhood that is one hundred percent Muslim.

Among the students in the discussion there were Serbs, Croats, and others, who remained together in the city with Bosniacs/Muslimss, or more accurately, with Sarajevans (people

---

[5] Ristin Thomassen, 2006, *To Make Room for Changes: Report by Kvinna Till Kvinna*, http://www.peacewomen.org/assets/file/Resources/NGO/kvinna_tomakeroomforchanges_2006.pdf (accessed September 3, 2011).

[6] Radovan Karadžić is an infamous war criminal currently being prosecuted in the Hague. He was the first president of the Republika Srpska entity of Bosnia and Herzegovina.

from Sarajevo used this name, which emphasized their Sarajevan identity first). What convinced Amra to offer assistance was the statement by her fellow student who asserted that they could not allow themselves to be like the cowardly war criminals who shot at them from the hills above the city. She became intrigued by the young man who had expressed himself so tellingly and was told that he was a Serb from Sarajevo. "I walked over to him to say: 'You're really brave. You will lose your head if you keep this up,' because the atmosphere at the university was not really suitable for the language he was using. He replied: 'I'm not afraid ... I stayed here to fight for this city,' and that is how our love story began." This encounter was a turning-point for Amra, one that changed the course of her life and her world.[7]

Amra's memory of that time taught her that being a Serb in Sarajevo during the war was not easy, and she was struck not only by this man's courage, but also by his striving to allow every voice of goodwill to be heard. She accepted his attitude as a morally correct position. New love began out of that courage, that remarkable humanity (ljudskost). Two young people under siege in Sarajevo found each other, and despite all the rules and expectations, decided to fight for their love. They married in 1994, according to Amra, "to the horror and dismay of everyone else. ... My aunt said that it was the same thing as marrying a German in 1943." Although Amra was raised in a communist family in which religion had not played a significant role, marrying a Serb during the war was outrageous and completely unacceptable. Such an act had significant social consequences. It was seen as a kind of betrayal, not only of her family, but of the entire Bosniac community that was suffering under the siege of Sarajevo. Amra spoke about the reaction: "There were instances when we'd approach a group of people, and they would fall silent. ... It was clear that I was a Serbian daughter-in-law, it reverberated through

---

[7] Norman Denzin, 1989, *Interpretive Biography*, Thousand Oaks, CA: Sage, 70.

my family like an echo, and they struggled to make peace with that."

She had a hard time convincing her family and the community that her husband was not a fascist, that he would not cheat on her and leave her as many spouses did at the beginning of the war. The many bad experiences and betrayals of friendships and marriages that occurred during the war made her family and many others cautious in trusting him. Her father-in-law said about her: "She was a brave woman; she married a Serb in 1994." Amra laughed at that statement. She said that her marriage marked her life permanently, because they now have two beautiful children.

Living in an ethnically mixed marriage taught her that she always had to be mindful of hearing different voices and perspectives and to provide a space for the ensuing dialogue. Life in an ethnically homogenized post-war country, however, had many challenges: "Being in a mixed marriage today means that you will, as a rule, be subjected to discrimination and you will have so many problems that you can easily slip into the role of victim and do nothing with your life." Amra knows that many people in mixed marriages steer away from their ethnic and religious identities and make compromises to overcome differences, but for her, this was not an option.

She wanted to keep her identity and to nurture her newly rediscovered religion after the war. The transition from wartime to postwar Sarajevo presented Amra with the opportunity to embark on a search for her identity.[8] In Amra's case, every life situation, when read correctly, was important for her growth. One of these situations occurred when her son told her: "I'm really sorry that I am not a full Bosniac, from only one ethnic group." Much to his surprise, she responded to him: "I'm glad you do not have a chance to be from only one ethnic group. You would fall so easily into the

---

[8] Amia Lieblich, 1998, "Looking at Change: Natasha, 21, New Immigrant from Russia to Israel," in Ruthellen Josselson and Amia Lieblich (eds.), *Narrative Research: Reading, Analysis and Interpretation*, Thousand Oaks, CA: Sage, 93.

old cliché of disliking another ethnic group, of thinking that your people are better." Amra's children were a great motivation for her to stand firmly in favor of peacebuilding after the war, because she wants them to live comfortably with all their identities.

Amra's first official calling to peace activism came when she got a job at the Helsinki Committee for Human Rights of BiH in Sarajevo. This job provided a chance for her to become a professional in the field of human rights and peace work. When she started in 1998, the committee's aim was to create the first center for information and the first umbrella center for dozens of NGOs that were scattered throughout BiH: "This organization created the first BiH network and it still exists today; it now has about 110 organizations, and it is called the B-H Council of NGOs." As the head of the Information Center, Amra was pleased that the organization was fundamentally about peacebuilding. It was not preoccupied with mere data collection. Instead it bridged the gap between the two BiH entities, as well as the cantons in the Federation of BiH, and it enabled encounters between the divided Bosniacs, Serbs, and Croats in BiH. Amra's task was to design a database of non-governmental organizations in BiH. More than that, however, the Center was to give a voice to both secular and religious people and organizations engaged in human rights work and peace activism.

> For me, the third sector and civil society became my way of showing that it is possible for all of us to exist in this society despite our vast differences, without crowding each other, and that we can understand that there is a completely different perspective, both with this new religious identity, and with that [past] socialism, with these relics that remained.

One of the first project visits was to Bijeljina, in northern BiH, to meet fellow colleagues from the Helsinki Committee of the Republika Srpska entity. With her colleague, Amra brought up the issue of rebuilding the destroyed mosque: "Duško took out a brick, put it on the table and said: 'I have brought the brick for the first mosque, for the renewal of the first mosque in Bijeljina.' And then about ten police officers barged in through the door, because it was 1998 and it was insane to say such a thing." Right after the war, says Amra, it was hard to travel to some regions to bring attention to issues like the rebuilding of religious sites. At the beginning of the war, terrible crimes were committed in Bijeljina including the devastation of its cultural and religious heritage. Duško's gesture, as a Serb lawyer who was active in the protection of children's rights, stirred ethno-nationalist feelings among the local authorities. Amra noted that Duško wanted to take steps toward reconciliation, but obviously the timing was bad and those in power were not ready to hear such a proposal.

Another such encounter took place in Mostar, a city symbolic of the ethnic divisions between Croats and Bosniacs and the destruction of cultural heritage, which involved the demolition of the famous Old Bridge built five hundred years ago. Amra emphasized that the meeting took place in west Mostar, the part of the city controlled by Croatian authorities. She was proud of that meeting where they brought the victims of crimes together with the perpetrators of these crimes, both of whom were searching for healing. In this space, they were able to hear one another and even come to forgive one another, which is usually a long process:

> We had a situation in which those sitting together were, for example, ... a guard at Omarska war camp and a mother from Prijedor who had lost her two children and who still did not know where they were buried. [When] she heard his story, she stood up and said, "I forgive all of you, for all that happened."

The entire social fabric of BiH was so torn up after the war that many felt lost and did not know their identity. For Amra, civil society was "a certain form of constructive chaos that I envision being an ideal scene in which all of us can have that voice." Having a voice, as John Paul Lederach[9] explains, "is about meaningful conversation and power ... our voices are heard and have some impact on the direction of the process and the decisions made." Amra was able to imagine the possibility of peace in that constructive chaos through bringing different and opposite voices together and making some changes. Her vision and willingness to cross the supposed "borders" oriented her firmly toward working to understand different voices. She demonstrated an "assimilative leadership trait," which means "bring[ing] people and constructs together,"[10] and is close to the transformation of conflict into peace that interested Amra.

As a woman who became religious after the war, Amra was interested in providing a religious voice at the peace tables and gatherings. She explained that the Helsinki Committee was a secular human rights organization that gathered people together who generally did not strongly identify with ethno-national politics or religion. This is one of many examples that confirm the hypothesis that the peacebuilding process in BiH was not motivated by religion and was not initiated by faith-based organizations and faith communities,[11] but rather by secular human rights organizations. Amra states:

> The civil sector was separated from anything that was this ethno-national mainstream. In other words, these were the organizations that mostly inherited some of the socialist and communist and atheist ideas. Everything related to nationalism or, God forbid, religiosity was removed from civil society.

---

[9] John Paul Lederach, 2005, *The Moral Imagination: The Art and Soul of Building Peace*, Oxford: Oxford University Press, 56.
[10] Mary Lou Décosterd, 2013, *How Women are Transforming Leadership: Four Key Traits Powering Success*, Santa Barbara, CA: Praeger, 98.
[11] Ina Merdjanova and Patrice Brodeur, 2009, *Religion as a Conversation Starter: Interreligious Dialogue for Peacebuilding in the Balkans*, New York: Continuum, 108-124.

Amra collaborated on dozens of projects with secular human rights activists like Vehid Šehić from Tuzla, Srđan Dizdarević from Sarajevo, and Lidija Živanović (Story 4) from Banja Luka, but still succeeded in making room for faith-based initiatives in the peace process: "Because I instinctively felt that it was a platform for peace." She said that on the peace platform, all voices should be represented, including the voices of religious women and men, except those involved in war crimes. Amra built coalitions, as Elisabeth Porter describes, through fostering confidence, opening dialogue between unreconciled viewpoints, and enabling different stories to be heard.[12] Slowly, she moved toward working with a faith-based organization in order to be more profoundly involved in peace work motivated by religion.

Small Steps Brought Me to Myself

Peace is the spirit, and the spirit is free to go wherever it wants.

Although Amra is a woman who is filled with the energy of activism, she has learned over time that working through the peace process requires dedication and patience. For her, peace is beyond political divisions and laws. Referring to the Bible, she says peace always seems to find a way to proliferate (Galatians 5:22-23). Peace is a state of mind that starts inside one's heart and then, while searching for fertile ground, plants its seed. Amra also was searching for the appropriate ground to sow her vision of peace, and she gradually realized that focusing on small steps brought results. In this regard, Elisabeth Porter argues: "peacebuilding is a comprehensive process with an emphasis on networks of relationships."[13] But it also "requires a vision of relationships," as Lederach explains,[14] which is crucial for sustainable peacebuilding.

---

[12] Elisabeth J. Porter, 2007, *Peacebuilding: Women in International Perspective*, London: Routledge, 83.
[13] Ibid., 33.
[14] Lederach 2005, 35.

Amra's journey had several important stations along the way that helped her acknowledge the importance of small steps in achieving understanding and reconciliation.

One of these steps included her journey into interreligious work. Because Amra was interested in bringing all voices together, and because she was an observant believer, she turned from secular to faith-based activities. With her colleagues, the young Franciscan theologian Alen Kristić and the Islamic theologian Samir Beglerović, she founded the NGO Abraham and invited religious people, mostly from younger generations, to join them in peace initiatives. Working together enabled them to get to know each other better, but more importantly, to model peaceful coexistence and to help to rebuild multicultural life in BiH.

Fig. 9-2

Another important step brought Amra back to her family heritage. She wants her personal accomplishments to be included in her family legacy.[15] In 2001, she attended the first seminar of the Centre for Non-violent Action. It was in this organization, run by her cousin Adnan Hasanbegović, that she became better trained in skills and theoretical knowledge for peace work. With Adnan, she tried to revive the spirit of the messages their antecedents had entrusted to them. Amra's aunts told her the story of their great-grandfather Smailbegović, a professor at the Shari'a school in Sarajevo, who stood up to violence against the Serb people after Gavrilo Princip's assassination of the Austrian heir to the throne, Franz Ferdinand.[16] There was a terrible persecution of the Serbs in Sarajevo, and it was thought that the entire Serbian people were somehow responsible for the outbreak of World War I. Some Muslim groups even started destroying Serbian-owned shops on the main street:

> When they started tearing down whole streets up there, our great-grandfather came unarmed before these people, with a full beard and a fez on his head, he lifted his hands and said, "Here, kill me first and attack these innocent people over my dead body. These people did nothing wrong, there is an organization who claimed responsibility for it," and so on.

Amra commented that in her family the spirit of Islam was nurtured as a reflection of the values of justice, compassion, and peace. These values extended throughout the socialist world, underlining the egalitarian rights of the working class and everyday people: "We were brought up with the thought that the human being is important." Her great-grandfather was an Islamic scholar and a

---

[15] Kathleen Barry, 1992, "Toward a Theory of Women's Biography," in Theresa Iles (ed.), *All Sides of the Subjects: Women and Biography*, New York: Teachers College Press, Columbia University, 33.
[16] Gavrilo Princip was a Bosnian Serb who joined the secret nationalist society of the Black Hand that sought independence for Bosnia and Herzegovina from Austro-Hungarian rule in order to unite with Serbia. The assassination is considered the beginning of the First World War. See also, Noel Malcom, 1996, *Bosnia: A Short History*, New York: New York University Press.

strong family figure, a person who stood up to defend human rights and dignity. Her family could easily relate to his legacy of peace and justice within the new socialist system that stood for the well-being of humankind, and its social and economic rights and security. Another important figure in her family history was her grandfather Šukrija Pandžo, a prominent children's poet who was constantly talking to children, encouraging them to be more engaged with good literature and poetry. Amra describes him as great teacher who was able to make children, including herself and her brother, feel important by allowing them to pose questions: "And we were constantly asking questions, and answering questions, we talked, and talked, and talked, and truly ... this dialogue influenced me greatly and provided a framework for my life. These were some of the formative first steps in my journey." In the patriarchal culture, however, such relationships are rare, as is the kind of upbringing where children are encouraged to be free spirited.

Amra depicts her grandmother as somewhat avant-garde, because few women before World War II had access to education. As a teacher, she was respected in her community, impacting a new generation of women, including her daughters. Amra's mother and "the council of aunts" (the proud name Amra gives to her mother's sisters) were successful women holding prominent positions both professionally and in the community. They served also as role models. Amra pays special tribute to her mother, because it was her mother who kept the family together after the death of Amra's father:

> She was able to spectacularly prove herself in her professional life, because she managed to be a true authority to us, to be father and the mother to us at the same time, and because she managed to somehow maintain this family, this love, so much so that the three of us are still very close today.

With this heritage, Amra turned out to be a person of quite liberal views and open-mindedness, and she stood against ethno-national exclusivity. She is an empowered woman, ready to embrace people's differences. Her education at the Centre for Non-Violence, under the leadership of her cousin Adnan, reclaimed her family's legacy of dialogue and peacebuilding, becoming in structural form an NGO that is one of the prominent peacebuilding organizations in BiH.

> From that moment in 2001, everything I did was clearly articulated toward peacebuilding. For me, that primarily meant fighting against discrimination, advocating for non-violence, and serving as a sort of a paradigm in which we act preventively to avoid the terrible, bloody conflicts we've seen here in Bosnia and Herzegovina.

Because of her education in non-violent resolution and transformation of conflict, she was able to better articulate her peace work as a struggle to eradicate patriarchal and structural violence against women and other vulnerable groups and to build a culture of peace for all. As she puts it: "to be able to breathe freely and not to shove everything under the carpet." She learned how important it was not only to resolve conflict, but also to transform it, to deal with it, to sort it out and not suppress it until the next eruption. According to Lederach, "peace-builder[s] must embrace complexity, not ignore or run from it."[17] The transformation of conflict is important in the Balkans, because as Amra underlined several times in her story, unresolved issues had been swept under the carpet until they reappeared in 1990, devastating lives, culture, and coexistence.

---

[17] Lederach 2005, 33.

Fig. 9-3

Finally, after benefiting from all this training, gaining her master's degree in social sciences, and accumulating a remarkable amount of the knowledge and skills used in peace activism, Amra decided to launch the NGO called Small Steps (Association for Dialogue in Family and Society). The small steps she had taken during her life brought her to the point of establishing this organization, which would be primarily focused on faith-based peace activities. She decided that all her future peace activism would be informed by her faith, a sector of formal peace work that is not well developed. One of her goals is to help families overcome pain and suffering and jointly commemorate their losses.

Amra works hard to bring together Bosniacs, Croats, Serbs, and others. For her, it is especially important to bring Serbs to the table, because as she explains: "after the genocide and all that happened, we effectively shut their mouths in a way, but we were unaware that we had just swept the enemy under a societal carpet, meaning no revolutionary changes were made." She is trying to open up a dialogue about crimes, genocide, rape, and different kinds of torture that people experienced during the war. She admitted that it is hard and painstaking, but people have begun to talk and commemorate certain events together, an important first step in recognizing the suffering and pain of others:

> There were times when they were arguing so much that we had to interrupt them, in front of the media and everyone else, and I would say: "Come on, please, can we just remember why we are here, to commemorate all those people who are not alive anymore? All of you are sitting here now, and you philosophize about this, and then we'll go to lunch and you'll return to your homes, and your nearest and dearest [but these] are not with us anymore. So let us have a little bit of dignity and get back to what this is about."

With her strong and powerful voice, Amra was able to mediate these encounters and channel the discussion, which at the beginning seemed like an impossible mission. Her education and training helped her navigate these interactions and to imagine that it is possible to bring people together and come to reconciliation. She said that it was helpful to remind people why they were talking together in the first place. During a visit to Brčko, in the northern part of BiH, a commemoration took place for all the victims in the city, and two choirs were invited: an Orthodox Christian choir that sang *Our Father* (The Lord's Prayer) and a Muslim religious choir that sang *Allah Is the Truth*. Women dressed in black were crossing themselves. Next to them Muslim grandmothers sat reciting *Al-Fatiha* (the first chapter of the Qur'an). They were all together in the square in Brčko. "So, we had a dignified memorial service, which was in common, it was from Bosnia and Herzegovina." Through such memorials, Amra has sought to show the spirit and strength of BiH. She admitted that these activities were demanding and inconceivably hard, which exhausted her but also renewed her hope in peace work. It reminded her that it is indeed possible to bring all these voices together.

Amra is aware that building a culture of peace is important and that BiH, a post-socialist society, needs to learn the skills essential for peacebuilding. She explained that the inequality inherent in its patriarchal culture makes acquiring these skills a challenge, because they are not taught or promoted as they could be. Instead of prioritizing equal rights, active listening, dialogue, and personal responsibility, people are more accustomed to suppressing, manipulating, and avoiding conflict and things that are disturbing. Amra criticized the socialist legacy in this respect, because it had suppressed freedom: "In the most recent period of socialism we filtered only the correct and incorrect answers, while in peacebuilding everything has the right to exist, to be heard, and we were drilled for 50 years that the only truth is what is heard."

Unfortunately, the ethno-nationalists have been doing the same, only they have changed the forms for and the targets of suppression. Amra has therefore invested a lot of time in teaching people the values of religion and how to distinguish between religion, religious leadership, and individuals who claim they are doing something in the name of God while committing atrocities.

One of the most important projects for Amra's work was the conference *Tragom vjere i mira* (On the Path of Faith and Peace), held in 2009, for which she brought together 40 educators, university professors, journalists, and others. They networked, got to know one another, and figured out ways to create a society in which they would not necessarily be bound to a leader, but could try to make their personal contributions instead and provide their own answers to dilemmas. In a culture accustomed to following leaders, whether religious, communist, or ethno-nationalist, it is hard to change the local mind-set and expect people to be open and ready to act alternatively toward the existing leadership monopoly in religious and political life. "We are constantly working on demystifying faith as a violent framework that serves only to be adopted by a great leader and then misused, to awaken the worst in people," says Amra. She is determined to remove from the face of religion the marks of tyranny and bullying and to raise awareness of its role as a bearer of values that are good for humans: justice, truth, and peace. Temporary individual or group interests and motives are not relevant for her, and as a believer, she attempts to move people away from their selfish interests and comfortable positions, hiding behind some kind of authority and not wanting to risk anything on their own. Peace work is not a comfortable job, it requires someone "to embrace complexity without reliance on dualistic polarity, the belief in the creative act, and acceptance of the inherent risk required to break violence and to venture on unknown paths that build constructive change."[18] Amra was definitely ready for that, with small but important steps.

Changes from within the System

> The organization I run, Small Steps, is in a difficult social position as it falls somewhere between a religious institution and the civil society, which is essentially, deeply anti-faith and anti-religious. I am proud of this role. In a society that is essentially divided, we are smack in the middle.

As a religious person, Amra is interested in overcoming the secular-religious divide and finding proper forms of religious identity in the public sphere. She is aware of the role of faith communities during the war and after. She does not give these communities any credit for bringing peace: "They worked more on the disintegration of peace ... they are trained here to be toys in the hands of ethno-nationalist elites, some political options, individuals in power ... some general principles of peace and justice are not visible." She added that the only good thing these communities did

---

[18] Ibid., 20.

was not disturb those individuals in their communities who were engaged in peacebuilding activities.

Amra decided to lean on these uncommon individuals, imams and priests in local communities who supported peace activities and who gave her hope that within the system of faith communities in BiH, it *is* possible to make changes. One of them, Sulejman Bugari, is a very active imam in Sarajevo who works on something she calls the "Islamic answer for the world [which] is to be an inclusive place for all." He is that rare imam who does not reduce his work to territorial jurisdiction over his congregation or concentration on the ethics, morality, and goodness that he insists are found not only in Islam. His mosque is a place where Amra feels at home with all of her ideas and work. "It is a completely inclusive spirituality." She has brought her non-Muslims friends there to sing songs together about the prophet Muhammad, and about Jesus, and just to be together despite their different faiths and paths of spirituality. She has experienced similar moments of inclusiveness with Ivo Marković, a Franciscan priest engaged in interreligious dialogue through his amazing work with a choir called Pontanima, helping to nurture and promote spiritual music that can bring people together.

Another friend who brought religious leaders together to promote peace from within the system is Father Danilo, an abbot in the Serbian Orthodox Church, who comes from the famous monastery Žitomislić in Herzegovina, close to Mostar:

> He brought back my hope because the Serbian Orthodox Church, as well as other churches and faith communities, have not done much in peacebuilding. The Serbian Orthodox Church obviously was involved in protecting war criminals, hiding them in monasteries … and in general there were not so many Orthodox priests involved in peace and dialogue.

Amra finds that one reason Orthodox priests did not take part in peace activities, like some Catholic priests and imams, is the specific structure of the Orthodox Church, which requires special approval and blessings for priests to be involved in certain activities. When Father Danilo opened the door of his monastery for interreligious activities, it was a sign for Amra that the time had come to introduce change, albeit with the support of the religious authorities that enjoy recognition and support among people. When she asked Father Danilo how he had earned the respect of both Catholics and Muslims, he told her: "Because I am at home here ... my home is not in Republika Srpska nor in Serbia or Vojvodina [his birthplace] ... the closest persons to me are my neighbors across the street — Croats/Catholics." Keep in mind that Croats killed Serb Orthodox monks there during the Second World War and during the last war, and they destroyed the monastery. This was consequently a brave decision. He was determined to live there among his Catholic and Muslim neighbors, and the neighbors accepted him as their own priest.

Besides collaboration with other religious leaders, who nevertheless have limitations in their communities, Amra decided to work on structural change (track-two diplomacy)[19] within the religious education system in the public schools. Most human rights activists, including Amra herself, were against formal religious education in public schools, considering it an obstacle to the democratization of BiH and to reconciliation of the ethnic groups therein. "Everyone understood that this was a rather negative phenomenon in our society because it introduced division. I was the first to fight against the segregation of children in schools in Sarajevo two to three years before that." Based on research, religious education was perceived as a stumbling block to reconciliation and increasing social reintegration in ethnically mixed communities. Some authors conclude that the only result of

---

[19] Louise Diamond and John MacDonald, 1996, *Multi-track Diplomacy: A Systems Approach to Peace*, 3rd ed., West Hartford, CT: Kumarian Press, 87-93.

religious education "can be deepening the gap between different ethnic and religious groups."[20]

Essentially, Amra would like to have more interreligious studies that will bring children together, but understands the reality of the majority of people not wanting that type of religious education for their children. The fact is that 95 per cent of children attend religious instruction in public schools in BiH,[21] which means that parents support it and consider it relevant for their children's upbringing. Their voices are also important in the matter. Knowing this, Amra did not want to spend her energy and time in unproductive discussions about what would be better for children and the divided society of BiH. Instead she looks for ways to assist and help those who teach these courses to reduce exclusionist perspectives, the biased portrayal of others, and contents that imply hatred. She decided to turn the ambiguous role of religion into constructive change and to show that religion can also be part of the solution[22] if it is presented in the proper way:

> I simply love my religion so much that I was horrified by the fact that it was exclusively bound to fascism and nationalism, so I prepared a guide for teachers of Islam that actually talked about the position of "others," the position of women, the position of all those things related to peace.

---

[20] Petar Atanacković, 2007/8, *Religijsko obrazovanje u javnom školstvu: Prilog razmatranju problema ideološke ofanzive Crkve u društvima u tranziciji*, "Divided God," Project of Intercultural Dialogue, http://www.pozitiv.si/dividedgod/index.php?option=com_content&task=view&id=206&Itemid=68 (accessed April 25, 2013), 6.

[21] Ahmet Alibašić, 2009, "Vjersko obrazovanje u javnim školama u Bosni i Hercegovini: Ka modelu koji podržava suživot i uzajamno razumijevanje," in *Religija i školovanje u otvorenom društvu: Preispitivanje modela Religijskog obrazovanja u Bosni i Hercegovini*, Sarajevo: Open Society Foundation, 17.

[22] Liam Gearon, 2004, *Citizenship through Secondary Religious Education*, London: Routledge, 1; R. Scott Appleby, 2000, *The Ambivalence of the Sacred: Religion, Violence, and Reconciliation*, Lanham, MD: Rowman and Littlefield.

Amra is worried about closed classrooms where only one religion is taught, how they present these topics and how they prepare children for future coexistence with others. She decided that instead of criticizing existing textbooks and pedagogical approaches, she would offer guidelines, texts, and exercises to help teachers bring different perspectives into the classroom regarding the genuine message of Islam. The team engaged to produce this guide were those who wanted to sensitize teachers toward peaceful approaches in Islam. "We wanted to build a narrative that will lead our children toward peace ... and to sensitize the teachers of religion so that they understand and accept the truth in Islam—peace [*salaam*]." During the meetings with teachers of religious instruction, she would start by explaining the root of the word *Islam* (s-l-m), which in Arabic signifies peace. She wanted teachers to remember that "Islam is, therefore, reconciliation, and a Muslim is one who is a conciliator."

Fig. 9-4

In the spirit of the Sufi tradition that nurtures and emphasizes peace as crucial in the interactions one has with others, Amra thinks that Muslims should not have difficulty accepting differences. According to Amra, Islam, claiming to be the last revealed religion, historically respects previous monotheistic traditions (Qur'an, 24,49; 3,84), and there is no place for exclusivity over other religions (49,13). But she is also aware of different interpretations that emphasize exclusive elements of Islam and portray it as the only right path toward God, an interpretation obviously not in compliance with Oneness (tawheed), the key principle of Islam that includes everything created as a part of the revealed reality.[23]

It was in this understanding of Islam that Amra designed the guide for teachers and structured it as a small textbook with accessible exercises and examples of equality, respect, and peacebuilding activities. She wanted to lay a foundation for peace principles to be accepted and applied to all and to train teachers to be torchbearers of peace in their communities. Theorizing about Islam and peace was accepted well, but then teachers posed concrete questions like: "What about the genocide, crimes, immense pain, and suffering that the Muslim population went through in the previous war?" People wanted to know why they should be peacebuilders after everything they had experienced and why they should take the first steps in the process.

Amra mentioned an interview she once gave to the media, in which a journalist challenged her with questions about victims and why Muslims should be the ones initiating peace. She answered that clearly the roles of the perpetrator, the victim, and the bystander in conflict only represent a momentary role; they do not contain each person's entire identity:

> Whoever might start the reconciliation, it is good to start it and then to step outside that role for a bit ... and say, "yes, I was a victim,

---

[23] Sachiko Murata. 1992, *The Tao of Islam: A Source Book on Gender Relationships in Islamic Thought*, Albany: State University of New York Press.

but now I'm not, and now I have a voice. I can stop and ask: Where do you get the right to be a perpetrator of violence? What were you thinking about doing? Let's have a little chat about it."

According to Amra, those who are able to step outside of that cycle of victim and perpetrator are winners in a spiritual sense. For every ethnic group who experienced terrible suffering, like the Bosniac Muslims did in this war, it is important that they prevent themselves from becoming perpetrators and falling into the trap of the cycle of violence.

Fig. 9-5

Amra is motivated to teach people to understand the cycle of violence and build new relationships. It was not easy to get permission to work with teachers of Islamic religious education, because she did not request funding and compensation from the Islamic Community. "[the Grand Mufti of BiH] told us that he did not have funding for that, and I replied, 'okay, Christians will provide it.' I could not help myself from showing sarcasm, and finally we got permission." After that, since the Islamic Community is decentralized, she had to talk to each and every mufti in the provinces (muftiluk) to get their permission to work with each particular Canton and region. With the support of the RAND organization (Regional Address for Nonviolent Action) and her colleagues Ana and Otto Raffai as well as Randall Puljek-Shank and his wife Amela, she provided educational sessions for 950 teachers of religious instruction in BiH. She helped them to modernize and improve their teaching methods with more interactive work with children. It was an incredible journey for her and she enjoyed working with bright young people who were eager to learn more about the peace perspective in Islam.

After these training sessions, teachers were expected to do something about peacebuilding work in their schools and communities. In schools, clubs were formed to deal with non-violence and peacebuilding. For most of the students, it was the first time they had heard about active peacebuilding efforts, which made them pioneers in preventing future conflicts. For Amra, empowerment for peace is very important, especially in light of the global portrayal of Muslims:

> Do not forget that Muslims today are globally discriminated against because they carry the stigma of being tied to terrorism, to something [that's] bad ... [or] violent. When they return to their roots and when they are enlightened, when you shine such a light in their direction, it represents a very important alibi for them in their inner world, so much so that they happily stand in front of these children and talk about how important it is for them.

Amra is aware that not all teachers who attended peace education sessions would actively continue working on peacebuilding activities, but she mentioned that out of 950, about 30 continued their education. They attended the RAND training workshops and took part in regional peace conferences in Macedonia, Kosovo, Croatia, and Northern Ireland.

For Amra, working for peace is a constant effort and a constant transformation of conflict. There is no break. "You can imagine this as being like an ideal marriage: things always come up, people are constantly working on it and trying to reach an agreement. But it can be done in such a way where nobody is pushing their own agenda [and] they are very honest about their goals."

As a peacebuilder and an activist, Amra figured out that she had to be within the system in order to change it. An impact can be made only if one is a part of something bigger. She is aware that in BiH, independent voices or public opinion do not exist as relevant factors: "Of course, then you have to put up with a lot of structural violence within those systems, but I've chosen some of these systems within which I can and want to do this." This is her way of making change within a system that is not favorable either for women or for different opinions, but she has been attempting to find the best channels of communication to enable her voice to be heard through meaningful conversation[24] and through those who work with children in schools.

Serving Peace as a Muslim and a Feminist

Amra emphasized that her work is primarily oriented toward a religious perspective of peace and a dismantling of ethno-nationalism as an obstacle to reconciliation. Gender equality was just one of the themes she has worked on. But when she narrated her struggle to reconcile gender equality and Islam, she brought forth interesting details about how her two identities, as a Muslim and a feminist, firmly root her in both religion and human rights.

Amra's journey into religion was similar to that of many others during the war. They too rediscovered Islam through the channels

---

[24] Lederach 2005, 56.

of Salafi groups[25] who came to BiH and offered refresher courses on Islam. After the war, Amra started searching for spirituality and came into contact with missionaries who offered an interesting group dynamic and socialization for Muslims, something that was missing within the regular Islamic Community. However, during our interview, she did not reveal much about that part of her life. She just mentioned that she carried some positive and some negative memories. As a woman, she said she could not understand or accept the gender segregation imposed via Salafi interpretations of Islam, and therefore she found a new direction in her life oriented toward faith-based peace initiatives within which she could learn more and offer more. However, she respects all approaches and interpretations of Islam from the most conservative to the most liberal and is determined to be in dialogue with all of them for the sake of peace. Amra is also thankful for acquiring the training and discipline in that period of her life to pray and fast, something that is not easy for many Muslims to accept and observe. It helped her to persevere during times of both personal and professional challenge:

> For me, changing myself is not a problem. … In that period I also received many wonderful gifts, such as training for prayer. … If someone wants to pray five times a day, it's a serious training; it requires discipline, and if you are not brought up that way from early childhood, you need a special system to help you learn how to do so. … I remember that lifestyle helped my own growth in my own personal training.

Amra speaks about the importance of change and how every new piece of knowledge and experience brings change to a person.

---

[25] In BiH these Muslims, usually called Wahhabis, are a new addition to the Bosnian Islamic scene. Salafis claim to represent an Islam that is "pure and free from any additions, deletions or alterations" (according to "An Introduction to the Salafi Da'wah" http://www.qss.org/articles/salafi/text.html).

However, it is considered a failure in BiH, because being persistent is so strong a virtue in this region. (see Story 8)

In time, Amra learned how to build her own feminist identity. A new understanding of women's human rights and how they intersect with Islam came through education and collaboration with women's human rights activists and Muslim feminists. Gradual empowerment convinced Amra that it is possible to search for gender equality within Islam, and therefore, she started to declare her Islamic feminist identity. During her work on the guide for religious teachers, Amra was particularly interested in gender equality because regular religious textbooks limit women's issues to motherhood and family roles.[26] She commented: "We tried to talk about the fact that the Qur'an offered gender-sensitive language in the sixth century. To talk about this is to touch upon things that are important to women's issues."

However, having a feminist identity was not perceived as desirable for Bosnian Muslim women, and she faced discrimination when she started working in schools with teachers of religious instruction. When she entered these schools, she would always be given two important tests, one about her religious identity and another about her feminist identity. The school representatives had two main questions that could discredit her: "They asked me if I was a member of the Bahá'í religion, because Bahá'ís are often connected to the peace movement. And I said that I was a classic Muslim."[27] At that time, a woman who was working in religious education had to wear a *hijab* to prove oneself as a Muslim, and

---

[26] Zilka Spahić-Šiljak, 2008, "Analysis of the Image of Women in School: Religious Textbooks in Bosnia and Herzegovina," in Michaela Moravcikova and Lucia Greskova (eds.), *Ženy a Náboženstva: Women and Religions* 2, Bratislava: Ustav pre vztahy statu a crkvi, 8.

[27] The founder of Bahá'í is Bahá'u'lláh, considered the last of God's messengers (including the Buddha, the Jewish prophets, Jesus, and Mohammed). According to the international website of the world's Bahá'ís (http://info.bahai.org/), "The central theme of Bahá'u'lláh's message is that humanity is one single race and that the day has come for its unification in one global society."

therefore Amra did so. Interestingly, the majority of Muslim women in BiH at that time and today do not wear a *hijab* nor do they find it relevant to their faith.[28]

Their second question was always about her feminist identity. "They asked me if I was an Islamic feminist because they had found my statement on the internet saying I was an Islamic feminist, and in this context it reverberated as if I had dropped a bomb." She could not deny this, because her statement was available online, and the only thing she could do was to explain what she meant by this statement, based on the Qur'an and the Sunnah of the Prophet. They then accepted her and thereafter she had great experiences and friendships with these teachers.

Despite these questions designed to check her legitimacy for working with teachers, she thinks that it was easier for her as a woman to get permission to enter schools. They did not fear her, but participated in order to demonstrate cooperativeness, she thinks. It was only important for them that Amra wasn't a feminist, because: "If I were a feminist, I would be perceived as dangerous." Being a Muslim feminist in line with the Qur'an's teachings was somehow acceptable, whatever that might mean to them. Explaining the patriarchal culture of BiH, she said that men in leadership rarely take women seriously, only reacting to women behind the scenes. Thus, ignoring woman is the strategy for excluding them from public life:

> In our society you really can step out, write any kind of text you want and criticize anyone you want out there, because our institutions and our closed systems have a fantastic way of dealing with it, and that's by ignoring it. So, no one will bat an eye if you say whatever in the world you want to say. The dogs bark, but the caravan goes on.

---

[28] Zilka Spahić-Šiljak, 2012, *Contesting Female, Feminist, and Muslim Identities: Post-Socialist Contexts of Bosnia and Herzegovina and Kosovo*, Sarajevo: Center for Interdisciplinary Postgraduate Studies.

Ignorance and lack of recognition are reasons why peacebuilding activities and women peacebuilders, in particular, are not recognized in BiH. The concept of peacebuilding is still something fluid, without a clear definition. Amra's mother always tells her: "My dear child, I never know what your occupation is, what you are working on."[29] Amra thinks that in general people have the same attitude when they learn that one is involved in peacebuilding work. Most of this work is done in the civil sector of society mostly by women, and their work is still not recognized.

Amra is full of respect for women, because they show consistency and honesty in their work. She uses affirmative essentialism[30] to underline these female characteristics in contrast to men who are in her opinion, different: "From an early age they are trained to say one thing in public [and] another, completely opposite thing, to their wife, a third thing to their children, and a fourth to their father and mother. Everything is legitimate for them." Amra's experience with men taught her that they are like actors in every part of their lives, with different texts to read, which they do not find disturbing. Women are more inclined to advocate for social justice and human rights, to be those who keep the civil society scene alive and demand fair play. It should be added that despite this glorification and essentialization of women[31], Amra does not think that peacebuilding is something all women are prone to or something that is women's inherent characteristic.

---

[29] Renowned peace practitioner and scholar John Paul Lederach often hears the same response: "when I say 'I work in support of conciliation processes,' it is rarely sufficient to give people a sense of what I do ... if I endeavor to explain the actual heart of the experience of what I do, people soon have a lost and perplexed look on their faces," 2005, 95.

[30] Elissa Helms, 2013, *Innocence and Victimhood, Gender, Nation, and Women's Activism in Postwar Bosnia-Herzegovina.* Madison, WI: University of Wisconsin Press, 9.

[31] Fiona Robinson, 2011, *The Ethics of Care. A Feminist Approach to Human Security*, Philadelphia: Temple University Press, 120.

One of the issues with women's peace work is the lack of cooperation and information sharing between secular and faith-based organizations about their activism. Amra, for instance, did not know anything about the UNSCR 1325 despite the fact that numerous women's NGOs have been working for more than a decade on its implementation. Similarly, secular women's NGOs are not familiar with her faith-based initiatives. A need remains for intra-sector communication and cooperation. It is through bridging this gap that the two may overcome the secular-religious divide and benefit women and men, believers and citizens.

Conclusion

A committed peace activist, Amra believes that all variety of voices must be heard for a sustainable peace, and she herself brings voices of faith to the table, despite their provocative nature. She believes faith is, contrary to general opinion, a potential platform for peace. Amra manages to do this as a strong Muslim believer who works within her own religious community while at the same time advocating for inclusiveness and the richness of diversity. This diversity also includes the so-called victims and perpetrators, because she sees these categories as dynamic, changing. She follows in a line of peacebuilders in her family, realizing such work through the public space of civil society in an NGO called Small Steps, which captures the essential philosophy of her peace activism. Examples of small steps include: networking with religious leaders who are also peacebuilders in order to share experiences, helping each other, and building up the foundations of peace that exist in all of BiH's religions. In this way, she works from within her own society and community, strengthened by these networks, for example, to reform the controversial religious education system or to emphasize the feminist aspects of Islam. In her very person, she weaves the liberal communist values modeled by the strong women in her family with the teachings of Islam that provide her with a framework for life. Despite being essentially ignored as a woman who builds peace in a patriarchal culture, she does not measure her success through these standards but listens to her heart to know what is really valuable to the believer. As such, Amra's story is an important one to be heard.

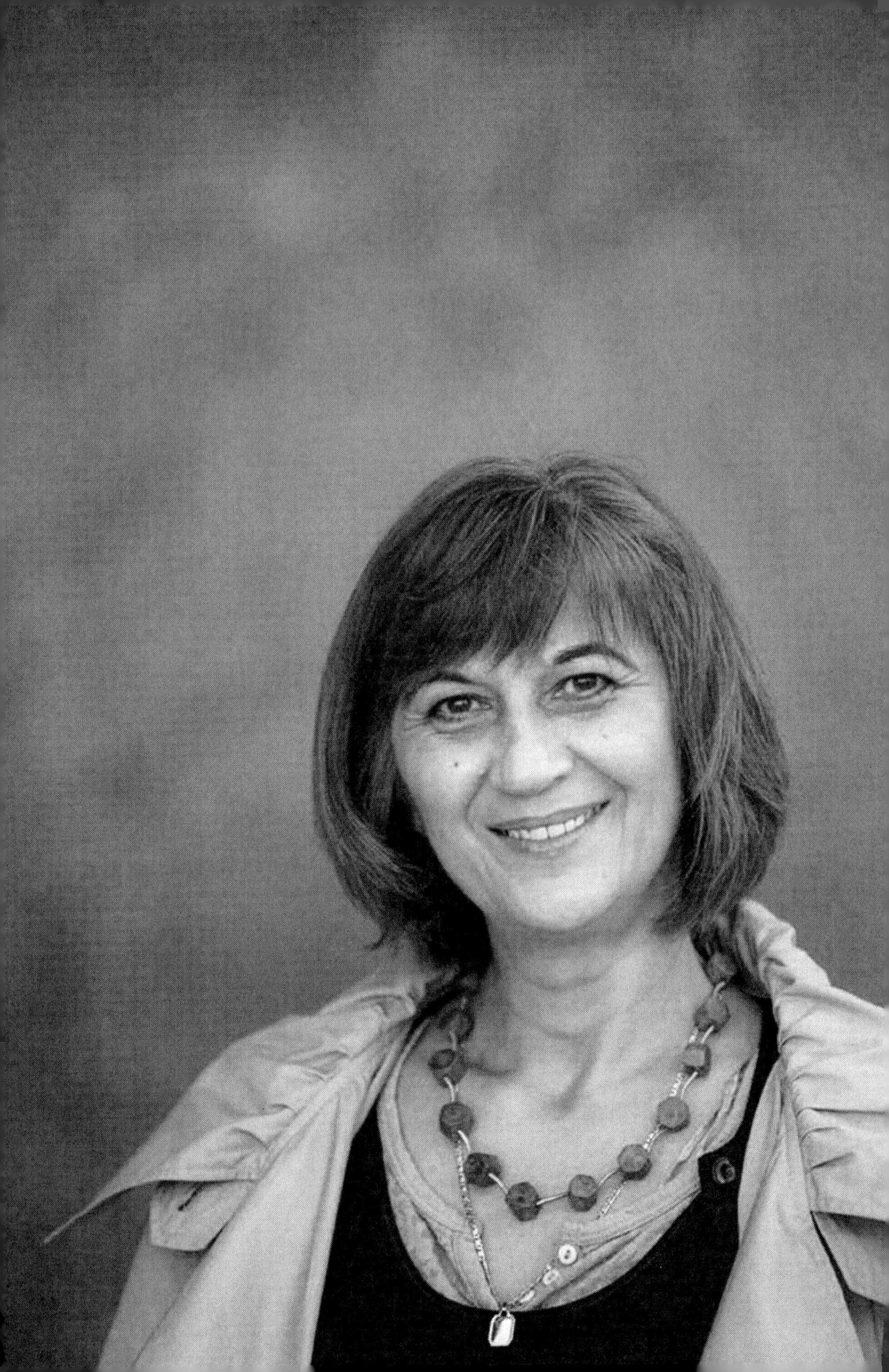

Story Ten

The Power of Voice

Radmila Žigić

Biography

Radmila Žigić was born in Lončari in 1960, in the northern part of Bosnia and Herzegovina to a Serbian Orthodox Christian family. Despite the unemployment and economic difficulties of that time, Radmila's family managed to encourage and support the education of their children. Ever curious, Radmila took advantage of this and studied hard, making daily trips to Brčko in order to attend high school. After graduating, she moved to Belgrade to study journalism. The move to the "big city" was a turning point in Radmila's life; the move fulfilled her childhood dream of becoming an educated intellectual in the urban milieu. Spurred on by this dream, Radmila wanted to pursue further education, but she returned to BiH and in 1985 began working as a reporter for Radio Orašje, later becoming its editor in chief. In 1992, at the beginning of the war, she moved from Orašje back to Lončari to be with her family.

Her restless spirit and journalistic curiosity drove her to join the magazine *Extra* in Bijeljina, the only opposition newspaper in the territory controlled by the Bosnian Serbs; soon after she joined the magazine, it was banned as a "political provocation." In 1996, after *Extra* was disbanded, she and two other independent journalists established a new oppositional magazine, *Panorama*. Together with her colleagues, she then started a local radio station in 1997 so that their information could reach a larger audience.

In 1998, while continuing to work as a journalist, Radmila, along with Mara Radovanović and a group of women activists, formed the NGO Lara in Bijeljina. Lara remains one of the most prominent and recognizable women's organizations in BiH and the surrounding region. Journalism brought Radmila closer to the feminist movement and women's rights activism, and her activism enabled her to continue working as a journalist on Pan Radio and on the Lara website.

Introduction

My work has always been focused on freedom of expression, respect for human rights, and law. These things are, in effect, advocacy for a stable society in which peace is the most important value.

Radmila is well known in the eastern and northern regions of BiH as a local peacebuilder and for her activism on the issues of human trafficking and reconciliation.[1] Radmila herself is very modest about her story and how it reveals the power of female leadership in the post-war period. When we met in Sarajevo for the first interview she was surprised to be recognized as a peacebuilder in her local community. In fact, she told me, "I was just trying to be the voice of those who were less privileged and oppressed."

As the interview began, Radmila was visibly nervous, and asked for my permission to light a cigarette. Pain and sadness were written in the lines on her face. It seemed to me that her narration of the war opened up old wounds that had never fully healed, and that she felt this pain as we spoke. Like many women in the post-war era, Radmila was busy providing support for others, so her trauma and sufferings were buried. She had never been given the opportunity to tell her story and, in the process, to fully heal. Much

---

[1] Zilka Spahić-Šiljak, Aida Spahić and Elmaja Bavčić, 2012, *Baseline Study: Women and Peacebuilding in BH*, Sarajevo: TPO Foundation Sarajevo, www.tpo.ba.

of our conversation therefore revolved around the war and, in particular, Radmila's struggle to survive and yet stay fully human in the darkness of war and destruction. However, as she began to speak of her early childhood, she became relaxed and softened visibly.

After her studies in Belgrade, Radmila worked at the local radio station of Orašje, in northern BiH, and it was a time of both personal and professional fulfillment. Although she eschewed talk of her personal life, noting that it was not so relevant to her peace work, Radmila emphasized the importance of women's subjectivity and wanted to be recognized and known for her work and activities,[2] not for her private life, which is what people are usually interested in when it comes to women engaged in the public sphere. Nevertheless, her life story exemplifies classic themes of wartime experience such as the need to plan strategies to stay alive and the obligation to make the right moral choices during the chaos. It also sheds light on her work as a human rights activist and feminist after the war. Most important to her renown as a peacebuilder is the power of her voice in anti-trafficking activities and promotion of women's human rights and peace.

Against Trafficking of Human Beings

My power was small and limited, but I did not want to relinquish it.

Radmila is known best for her anti-trafficking activities and for protecting victims of domestic violence in the post-war period in the Brčko and Bijeljina regions. Since 1998, she has been active in the woman's NGO Lara where she has advocated for human rights and democratization with a strong emphasis on women's human rights. While all the activities of Lara are noteworthy, the

---

[2] Kathleen Barry, 1992, "Toward a Theory of Women's Biography," in Theresa Iles (ed.), *All Sides of the Subjects: Women and Biography*, New York: Teachers College Press, Columbia University, 33.

achievements of this organization and its activists in the struggle against human trafficking are an enormous success.

Radmila confessed that she did not expect she would be dealing with trafficking of women after the war, because she thought that the biggest horror has passed and that people in Bosnia and Herzegovina would have had time to recover and to build new state institutions and establish the rule of law. But, as people in BiH say, "evil never comes alone." The post-war society and in this ethnically divided country with its permeable borders turned out to be the perfect place for the criminal activities of human trafficking:

> I remember how I reacted with horror to [the information about] the trafficking of women, to the cruel and degrading treatment of women from Eastern Europe who came here out of poverty to look for a job and a better life, but who have been trapped in slavery and experienced probably the harshest moments of their lives. I had to stand up and say that, "I cannot tolerate this! I will not allow this!"

She added, with a pain-filled smile, that if she could not speak freely during the war, she would nevertheless after the war fight with all the means at her disposal to stop the trafficking of women. Except for the war, this was the biggest turning point in her life, one that brought change to her and her community.[3] She emphasized that it was important to know that the international community at that time provided significant funding for these activities:

> And we really did many, many things in this area. If there is anything I am really proud of, then I am proud of those activities that were purely voluntary and during which I honored a specific principle: for all my involvement in direct assistance to victims, for everything I did in the field of assistance to victims, I never received any payment.

---

[3] Norman Denzin, 1989, *Interpretive Biography*, Thousand Oaks, CA: Sage, 70.

Radmila was firmly determined to free and protect the enslaved women who had been trapped in criminal networks. Her story is about the journey "of learning to be a full human being and faithful person,"[4] in which a legacy of strength, dedication, curiosity, passion and strategies emerge to provide the best solutions against the trafficking of human beings.

Trafficking started immediately after the war in 1995 when women from Eastern Europe were brought to BiH for the purpose of prostitution.[5] Madeleine Rees from the Office of the UN High Commissioner for Human Rights (OHCHR) explains that trafficking became an important business within an emerging market for sexual services: "The Dayton Peace Agreement brought to Bosnia and Herzegovina over 5,000 international personnel, the vast majority of them males. They constituted such a market."[6] Based on the data of the International Organization for Migration, many of the clients in the brothels that developed were internationals, and they could afford to patronize such places.[7] Kathryn Bolkovac elaborated on this trafficking business in her book *The Whistleblower*.[8]

---

[4] Marshall Gantz, 2009, "Why Stories Matter," *Sojourns: Faith in Action for Social Justice*, www.sojo.net/magazine/2009/03/why-stories-matter (accessed September 3, 2013).

[5] Madeleine Rees, 2002, "International Intervention in Bosnia and Herzegovina: The Cost of Ignoring Gender," in Cynthia Cockburn and Dubravka Zarkov (eds.), *The Post-War Moment: Militaries, Masculinities, and Peacekeeping*, London: Lawrence and Wishard, 51-67.

[6] Ibid., 59.

[7] Ibid., 64. As part of the Dayton Peace agreement, the UN Security Council mandated the creation of a mission in Bosnia and Herzegovina to provide an International Police Task Force and a UN Civilian Affairs Office. Together, these two bodies were tasked with humanitarian relief and refugee aid, de-mining, monitoring human rights issues, facilitating elections, rebuilding infrastructure, rebuilding the economy, and providing civilian police to train and monitor what was left of the diminished local police force.

[8] Kathryn Bolkovac, 2011, *The Whistleblower: Sex Trafficking, Military Contractors, and One Woman's Fight for Justice*, New York: Palgrave Macmillan.

In 1999, Radmila became one of the first journalists to publish a piece about human trafficking in BiH. She wrote a story about six women in a brothel in the village of Dvorovi, near Bijeljina, where she discovered that the police, under pressure of the International Police Task Force (IPTF), had written down the women's testimonies but never reported them to the prosecutor, because both domestic police officers and members of the international forces located in BiH were involved:

> I disclosed that inspectors from the department in charge of foreign residents were involved in trafficking and that they actually enabled it, they were the very ones who made the slavery of these women possible. Two inspectors were suspended because of my article.

One of the bar owners involved in this dirty business threatened both Slobodan Marković and Radmila, the editors in chief of the magazine *Panorama,* to prevent them from publishing the story. But the story was published, and as Radmila continued to publicize the issue and campaign against the trafficking, brothels were closed down. It was not easy to go against the system; human trafficking was a plague that infected all layers of society and the structures of government and power. Radmila argued that: "Politicians tolerated it; officials who could benefit from it took the racket money, while ordinary people kept quiet."

Since trafficking was mixed up with voluntary prostitution at that time, which is also illegal in BiH, there was an attempt to criminalize the victims rather than the perpetrators.[9] It was therefore a huge struggle to make sex trafficking visible and recognized as a criminal act. With the support of relevant international organizations,[10] feminist human rights lawyers like

---

[9] Rees 2002, 60-64.
[10] The UN Office of the High Commissioner for Human Rights (which came to BiH in 1993 with special rapporteurs on human rights), the Organization for Security and Cooperation in Europe, the International Organization for Migration, and others.

Madeleine Rees and Jasminka Džumhur from the OHCHR, and other colleagues from BiH state institutions (parliaments, courts, police, prosecutors), women's NGOs managed to make criminal these activities before the BiH courts. Radmila herself submitted her research to Martina Vandenberg from Human Rights Watch for the U.S. State Department Report on Trafficking, where Lara is mentioned as a source of information.

Lobbying and raising awareness about this social problem has certainly helped to gather more support. Radmila and her colleagues from Lara dared to imagine an end to trafficking and create a new front of local activists to stand against this crime. Elisabeth Porter points out that such networking is important for peacebuilding[11] in order to make permanent change. These actors had the capacity to embrace the complexity of the post-war context and work on bringing constructive change through rebuilding relationships. Just as Lederach describes the spider web as a model of relational webs, which can be woven together for change that sticks, Radmila and her colleagues from Lara built a network for anti-trafficking. In terms of peacebuilding, this meant creating "relational spaces, the ability to keep sets of people in creative interaction."[12] Their network began its anti-trafficking program with small grants obtained to help victims of trafficking. However, the victims' unwillingness to speak about the problem openly created big problems, and Radmila had to be doubly careful about taking statements from them. She explained how giving such a statement to the police did not necessarily mean it would be used in trial proceedings, and if that happened, the criminals could go free:

> The police took statements, the victims were returned to their homes, the traffickers continued with their activities. We insisted

---

[11] Elisabeth J. Porter, 2007, *Peacebuilding: Women in International Perspective*, London: Routledge, 33.
[12] John Paul Lederach, 2005, *The Moral Imagination: The Art and Soul of Building Peace*, Oxford: Oxford University Press, 85.

on victims testifying before the investigating judge, so that their pimps and traffickers could later on be legally prosecuted. ... There were very few results as far as court decisions, but some cases were processed and adjudicated.

The small number of court rulings against criminals did not discourage Radmila because she succeeded in publicizing her cases and gathering both sympathy and interest in her cause. Despite the limitations of the judicial system to bring about radical change or swift justice on the issue of human trafficking, she hoped that by following the legal procedures her work would pave the way for other organizations and groups to achieve justice within the existing BiH legal system. She was able to imagine, to create, and to keep alive the art of relating to the web of interactions between local institutions and organizations relevant to the problem. Her leadership provided a personal example of women's empowerment, as did making coalitions with other NGOs and local institutions that wanted to collaborate on these issues.[13] Oriented toward outcomes in the struggle against trafficking and violence, Radmila showed another important characteristic of her leadership, which Mary Lou Décosterd defines as "directive force"—focused to finish the task.[14]

One way she increased support for anti-trafficking measures was through the media. As a journalist, Radmila intimately understood the power of the public voice, and she believed that the visibility of her and her colleagues' actions in the media provided some kind of protection (against violence or death) for them. In her own words:

> I realized that the only way we could be protected was to publicize our work and then I also relied on the post-UDBA[15] psychology of

---

[13] C. Cryss Brunner (ed.), 1999, *Sacred Dreams: Women and Superintendency*, Albany: State University of New York Press.
[14] Mary Lou Décosterd, 2013, *How Women are Transforming Leadership: Four Key Traits Powering Success*, Santa Barbara, CA: Praeger, 47.
[15] UDBA (Uprava službe bezbjednosti Yugoslavije) stands for the State Security Administration of Yugoslavia, established in 1946 and abolished in 1990 with the dissolution of Yugoslavia.

the people, which means if one of us does something that goes against criminal activities, people tended to believe that powerful [political] circles protected us and that nobody would harm us. Fortunately, nobody did, but we also took care as to how we behaved.

Radmila felt ashamed that after the war and its depredations her own ethno-religious group was involved in the new horrors of trafficking, and she wanted to eliminate it: "I considered that this kind of behavior should not be considered normal and that we needed to get it condemned by the public ... [so] we collaborated with all who wanted to hear about this problem." For example, Lara's 2001 campaign, "Stop modern slavery," was run through radio messages, posters, and street actions that were broadcast on local radio programs to raise awareness that trafficking was an organized criminal activity going on in cooperation with the government, police forces, and other institutions. Public protests in the streets of Bijeljina further expanded visibility, especially when the famous actress Jelisaveta Sablić from Belgrade joined them. Lara also organized public debates in Bijeljina and Brčko, where representatives from all relevant state institutions were invited to discuss the issue. Bar and nightclub owners were another very important target audience; Radmila mentioned Milorad Milaković from Prijedor, convicted for trafficking by the Court of BiH, who organized the association of bar owners in order to advocate for the legalization of prostitution. They came to the public debate in Brčko to oppose Lara's goals and to represent the "rights" of bar owners. As a result of their activities, from 2001 onward, the municipality of Bijeljina stopped issuing licenses for nightclubs and bars. It was the first concrete action of state institutions to stop and prevent trafficking.

Fig. 10-1

Radmila concluded that they were able to mitigate public prostitution in that region of BiH and help end the public exploitation of women. This was a big victory, and she felt relieved that in the post-war period, she was able to use her voice to its full capacity, even though it was suppressed with other voices against the war during that time.

The Suppressed Voice Finds its Way

> My voice against oppression and tyranny during the war was like a running river, sometimes it disappeared and was not heard, but then it would appear again in a place where it was possible to make a change, even a slight change.

Like all the peacebuilders in this book, Radmila also spoke about the war (1992-1995) as a big turning point in her life and a time when her voice was not only suppressed but that threats were also made on her life. As mentioned above, before the war started she had moved from Orašje to be with her family in Lončari, in large part because her mother worried about her staying in a city where the Croatian Democratic Party (HDZ) had come to power. Radmila claims that as a journalist, she would have been in danger if she had stayed in Orašje amidst the rising nationalist sentiment. Since she had always expressed her opinions against the nationalists and since she did not belong to the SDS (Serbian Social Democratic Party) or approve of the HDZ's actions and words, her family thought that it would be better for her to leave Orašje.

She learned later that some extremists from HDZ saw her as a "dangerous person" who collaborated with the Yugoslav National Army (JNA) and the SDS. "Maybe 20 days before the war began, I organized an anti-war rally with a group of young people, and a group of people from the HDZ stood some 50 meters away from us and watched us, frowning." Feeling unwelcome in Orašje, she quit her job as editor in chief of the Orašje public radio station and moved back to northeastern BiH, where the majority of the population was Serbian. Despite the apparent safety of being in the majority, Radmila felt suffocated by the Serbian ethno-national political leadership that silenced any voice against the war. She stayed with her family in Lončari but in 1994 moved to the city of Bijeljina.[16] She says, "I stayed and began another kind of struggle: the struggle to preserve my own integrity and not to do anything that would go against my moral code during this war, as bad as it was."

Radmila tells us that the war brought to the surface all of the tensions hidden in the social fabric of Yugoslavia under the communist regime:

> Today when I think about the first months of the war, if I had not seen how people changed, I would not have believed it. I had a

---

[16] The city of Bijeljina is located in the northeastern part of BiH on the border with Serbia. Before the war, according to the census of 1991, the majority population was Serb (57.39 percent), with fewer Muslims (30.22 percent), Croats (0.50 percent), and other minorities.

feeling of living in a parallel reality, that what I saw with my own eyes was not real, somehow, but it was.

She does not elaborate much on this notion of parallel realities, but it is clear that the war had released feelings and attitudes that had been suppressed under the previous regime because they were not socially and politically acceptable. These prejudices erupted volcanically, destroying all previously stable conditions in their wake. It seems that the brotherhood, unity, and equality[17] celebrated by many in urban centers of the former Yugoslavia were understood and lived superficially by some groups that easily slipped into nationalism, claiming a historical right to territories. Or perhaps it was time to revive old national pride and the prominence of one nation over others.

Radmila's story reveals the tension of her personal battle: she had to walk a difficult line between not endangering herself, on one hand, and on the other, not becoming a tool in the war propaganda of the Serbian regime. In light of this struggle, she explained:

> I cannot say that I have seen certain war crimes, but I was aware of them and what was going on there. And very soon I made the decision not to work for the state media. I knew that the war would be over and that one day we would face each other and it would matter to all of us what we had done.

Her strategy to get through the war was to postpone some of her activities for better times, when life would again be valued and the rule of law would once more be enforced. She knew she could have been killed if she had protested against war crimes directly: "I felt I could only sacrifice myself, if it were to die but nothing else. In addition, my parents needed me and I wanted to survive the war."

---

[17] 'Bratstvo i jedinstvo' (brotherhood and unity) was a slogan of the Communist Party of Yugoslavia and was the official policy for ethnic relations after World War II, in which South Slavs carried out atrocities against each other. The idea was to subsume national identity under Yugoslav identity, but in practice, injustices committed during the Second World War remained unaddressed.

Radmila does not deny the war crimes, executions, and torture that happened in territories under the control of Bosnian Serbs, but she emphasized her powerlessness to undo the suffering, crimes, and injustices against non-Serbs:

> knowing that they were not guilty of anything except having a different first or last name, or being of a different religion. This feeling of powerlessness stayed with me for a long time, the feeling of not being able to help those people or to prevent those things from happening to them in any way, except to do what Srđan Aleksić[18] did, because that was the only possible option at that time.

The madness of the war and the cruel reality of their ongoing powerlessness forced many, including Radmila, to be careful in their actions, because ethno-nationalists did not want any interference in the mass-killings, rape, torture, and deportation that were part and parcel of the war: "I am aware that I belong to the side in the war that committed terrible crimes, and having said that I do not count how many crimes were committed on the other side. I simply feel the need to say that." She said that she has felt the need to talk about these things, but the room for that had narrowed. She learned to be patient and to make compromises, because she did not want to burn out, adding: "I know that I live in a place where there is no civic public [sphere] and if I die, nothing will be changed." Raising her voice against crimes in the middle of the war might have been understood as a betrayal of the nation and religion, which in the Balkans, is the most shameful act one can commit. Her moral choices and strategies were conditioned by the immediate context

---

[18] Srđan Aleksić was a Bosnian Serb from Trebinje who protected the life of a fellow Bosniac/Muslim citizen in Trebinje and was killed by the Army of Republika Srpska. More in *Večernje novosti* online, http://www.novosti.rs/vesti/naslovna/aktuelno.293.html%3A416474-Srdjan-Aleksic-je-zivot-dao-za-coveka (accessed March 7, 2013).

and social reality, and she describes her choices as those she could live with.

Radmila expressed not only her moral choices and dilemmas, but also provided insight into the complex social structure of the war, with its own dynamic and norms.[19] She could not speak up against war crimes without risking her life, so she turned her energy into criticism of the corruption and terror the Serbian people suffered from the war government in Republika Srpska. Together with two fellow journalists, she launched the magazine *Extra* in 1993 and raised her voice against tyranny and oppression in Republika Srpska. They decided to launch an opposition newspaper, because as she says, "we could not stay silent about war profiteers and the irrational rejection of the peace agreements. ... But we knew that if we were to write about war crimes, we would soon become victims."

The magazine was distributed all over Republika Srpska with the support of Radmila's colleagues from Banja Luka and other cities, enabling people to expose the hidden or overlooked problems through the state media. As such the magazine helped to restore freedom of speech and freedom of thought, but unfortunately it was abolished and erased from the register in 1995 by the Ministry of Information in Pale. At the beginning then, she says: "We understood that we were marked for elimination: Maybe I was in less danger than my male colleagues, because they could have been sent to the front line and no one knows where bullets come from."

---

[19] Julia Chaitin, 2002, "How do I ask them about the war? Collecting and understanding the stories of soldiers and victims of war," *Social Science Research Network Electronic Library.*

Fig. 10-2

Speaking out against the regime was dangerous because it disturbed the power structure. Radmila was aware of this danger, but she did not allow her voice to be fully suppressed. However, she paid the price for her courage, independence, and the justice she fought for by being made a *persona non grata* in Serbian media circles after the magazine was banned. When the war ended, she had no job, no apartment, and was not viewed as desirable in any media circles in Bijeljina. After the magazine *Extra* was banned, she commented:

> Most of my colleagues who worked in national newspapers, on national television or radio would cross to the other side of the street in order to avoid me. ... One can never really fathom the effects this has on a person. It took me a long time to forget this feeling of being ostracized, as if I had to be socialized anew.

Radmila perceived her journalism career as a way to bring about positive change in society, such as respect for democracy, human rights, and civic order. In other words, she wanted to bring back a system of values and lawfulness to a war-ravaged society, something she described as part of her peace activism.[20] Despite isolation from other journalists, her love for journalism inspired her to launch a new magazine, Panorama, in 1996. The small staff of Panorama soon received support from international organizations, but she reported that the state media in Republika Srpska did not want to advertise the magazine and newsstands did not want to sell it: "There was a period of isolation until 1998 when the power structures changed in Republika Srpska."[21] From 1998, Radmila claims they had more freedom with new politicians in power: "The atmosphere had changed and we could work in normal conditions." But she soon came to understand that freedom of speech was not sufficient for an independent media in BiH without the economic and social well-being of a society that could afford to buy newspapers:

> Bosnia today is not a profitable market for independent media, especially for media that do not want to submit to political influence. ... *Panorama* had as its mission and role the democratization of public thought; I was not interested in making a

---

[20] She clarified that her real peace activism began in 1995 when she was going to the international corridor called Arizona (the "wild, wild west," a gray marketplace established during the war for illegal trading by merchants who sold untaxed goods, and located in northern BiH on the road between Orašje and Tuzla) to look for her pre-war friends: "When I decided that official politics and the entity borders would not limit my life, I started a dialogue with those whom I knew before the war and new friends even ... when I was criticized."

[21] The international community had great expectations of Milorad Dodik, a leader in the Serb entity of BiH called Republika Srpska, and his political party the SNSD, in terms of the democratization of BiH and diminishing nationalistic rhetoric and politics. It turned out, however, that Milorad Dodik, who remains in power today in Republika Srpska, found nationalism was the best way to maintain his power.

tabloid of it. ... Newspapers without the backing of political parties can hardly survive.

Although the political realm was finally more favorable for free media, there was still not full freedom or a sufficient market to support independent media without foreign funds, which also declined after 2004. This was the time when Radmila formed and began managing the NGO Lara and became a journalist on Pan Radio. Her feminist and journalistic engagements were merged in her peace work, but her new focus was on reconciliation and women's human rights.

Fig. 10-3

Being a Feminist in My Own Way

> Every one of us has the right to be a feminist in his or her own way. I do not like boxes. We are not the Salvation Army that does everything [according] to rules.

It is hard to distinguish between Radmila's journalistic activism during the war, her anti-trafficking activities after the war, and her feminism. She did not know much about feminism before 1999, and two key factors were crucial for her feminist formation. First, when she began her NGO work, she felt she was not sufficiently equipped to explain theoretically what feminism was, even though she was uncomfortable with the existing gender roles. The second factor was her family's acceptance of the way she lived her life, without judgments. She emphasized that as she was growing up they never criticized her for preferring reading rather than going out to play with other children or doing something in the house: "I spent my childhood and adolescence before university in my own world. My parents gave me the freedom to form my own opinions as I saw fit." Her mother tried to teach her some traditional women's skills like crochet embroidery, but Radmila recalled, with a smile, that the lessons did not stick:

> There was a custom that a child should learn a new skill on the second day of Christmas, as he or she will supposedly pick up that skill the fastest on this particular day. My mom tried that one Christmas, and I did not do well in knitting, then she tried another Christmas, and then she gave up. She said: "Never mind, I don't do that either, she doesn't have to do it. She's good in school; we will provide an education for her, for as long as she wants to learn."

Living in a rural area in a patriarchal society, Radmila's mother knew that her daughter deserved better, and that she could only get it with education. As Radmila said, "I have grown up in poverty: I practically had to fight for everything on my own. On the other hand, I was unchained." Radmila's education and family support enabled her to follow her dreams and to survive in a society that was judgmental of women who were "too liberal." Radmila spoke about patriarchy and the subordination of women as something unreasonable and unacceptable, describing herself as a rebellious person:

> It was my instinct that led me to feminist activism in which the first thing that bothered me was the absolute exclusion of women in decision-making positions. I simply felt that I could not be excluded from the process of making decisions that would affect my future. If I should not be excluded, then no woman should be

excluded; they should at least be included in the same proportion as men. I had a very developed sense of partnership and equality [from a young age].

She was inherently a feminist, as she says: "I felt there was something wrong, but did not have enough arguments or was not able to understand the causes for these things." She was motivated to read and learn more about women's history in order to understand the extent of woman's subordination. She started with a book by Neda Božinović, a doyenne of the feminist movement in Yugoslavia, who depicted the struggle of the anti-Fascist movement against the Communist Party. Having been introduced to the Yugoslav feminist movement, Radmila began studying the European or Western feminist movement by reading authors such as Gisela Bock and others. She comments: "My education about feminism came at a later date, but I would say I was a fast learner."

She started understanding feminism as a wider struggle against the patriarchal system that governed women's lives not only in Yugoslavia, but also elsewhere on the globe. Most women around her did not read about feminism, and feminist conversation was a privilege of female intellectuals, primarily university scholars and artists in Belgrade, Zagreb, Ljubljana, and Sarajevo, who spoke foreign languages and were connected to feminist circles in other parts of Europe. Feminism was not taught in schools or universities and there was no literature available in her mother tongue, so Radmila did not have insight into that dimension of women's human rights: "We did not learn about it in the school system. Even though I was a diligent student who read many books, feminist literature was not available."

However, she noticed major differences between life in Belgrade and life in the small towns in northern BiH in terms of gender equality and gender roles. Her liberal ideas about life and gender relations acquired during her time in Belgrade did not correspond to that patriarchal mindset where women were forced into traditional gender roles and their public lives were curtailed. As an example, she told me a story about arriving early at a café in Orašje and sitting down at a table while the friend she was meeting waited for her fifteen minutes in front of the café and finally left. "She did not even think to enter the café," Radmila commented, laughing, because she was alone as a woman. In rural areas, a double moral standard existed in which men were free to do things denied to women.[22]

Fig. 10-4

Despite the more liberal approach to gender in big cities, there was no official promotion of feminism, equality of rights, or equality of opportunity for women. In fact, Radmila notes that there was a strong current of anti-feminism in post-socialist Yugoslavia.

---

[22] Spahić-Šiljak, 2010, *Women, Religion and Politics: The Impact of Religious Interpretations of Judaism, Christianity, and Islam on the Status of Women in Public Life and Politics*, Sarajevo: IMIC, Center for Interdisciplinary Postgraduate Studies and the TPO Foundation Sarajevo, 254.

One reason for this resistance is the fact that gender equality was established at the time of Communist Yugoslavia based on the rejection of all things bourgeois. Radmila says:

> The Communist Party adopted all the ideas of equality for women and all of the feminist principles ... thus practically taking the credit for the emancipation of women. Feminism became the collateral damage of the collapse of the total communist ideology, which was based on the rejection of everything deemed as capitalist.

On one hand, the Yugoslav state rejected any feminism alien to Marxist ideology,[23] but on the other, it was a social welfare state that provided gender equality and recognized the value of unpaid work such as child care. Radmila clarified that women had equal salaries for equal work, the right to have an abortion, the right to an education, and the right to maternity leave. She concluded, saying, "Communists granted women so many rights that the communist state took over the responsibility for family life."

Social and economic security was important to women and they did not question gender equality in family relations. For Radmila, feminism means structural changes both in private and public life to establish partnership-oriented gender roles, rather than the patriarchally assigned and socially acceptable roles and obligations for women and men in BiH society. Although the socialist state provided room for women in politics and the notion of women as *drugarice* (comrades) was very strong, women continued to follow the patriarchal norms.[24] When Radmila compared the Yugoslav period with the post-war era she noted that it was easier to work in

---

[23] See more in: Jelisaveta Blagojević, Katerina Kolozova, and Svetlana Slapšak (eds.), 2006, *Gender and Identity: Theories from and/or on Southeastern Europe*, Belgrade and Skopje: ATHENA: Advanced Thematic Network in Women's Studies in Europe.
[24] Elissa Helms, 2003, "Women as Agents of Ethnic Reconciliation? Women's NGOs and International Intervention in Postwar Bosnia–Herzegovina," *Women's Studies International Forum* 26.1, 15-33.

a society where the rule of law functioned and where a certain code of conduct was maintained, but she says "the [post-war] transition has unraveled all the relationships and destroyed all the values as well. There is much more freedom for women and many things that were anathematized in previous times are now considered completely normal."

She underlined that today, despite ongoing patriarchal attitudes, women have more freedom and it is a bit easier to go against social norms and survive the social stigma and exclusion that follow such rebellion. She offered an example of a single woman having a child out of wedlock, who once would have been socially stigmatized, but today is more or less accepted—particularly in bigger cities—as normal. Today, Radmila openly identifies herself as a feminist, a rare identity in the circles of BiH intelligentsia. Being a public feminist is, for Radmila, an important way to raise awareness and to promote feminism and feminist action as a socially recognized value. She concluded that "each of us has the right to be a feminist in her own way. I do not like boxes. ... I am a feminist in my own way and respect different types of feminism."

Recognition of Women in Peacebuilding

> Women may collaborate more, but could we have done more? ... I am sure [that] yes, we could have.

According to Radmila, peacebuilding is still not a widespread social activity, but she claims that more women became involved in this after the war, especially at the grassroots level. The fact is that women were the first ones to cross the entity borders, and as Radmila narrates, they erased that border with more courage than men showed; they also established communication more easily. She adds: "We [women] did not wear guns and were not afraid that we might be arrested or that we would experience a higher degree of violence." After the war, women initiated meetings and collaborated on different peacebuilding projects together.[25] While women were more ready to collaborate, they also remained the prisoners of their ethnic groups/nations,[26] because as Radmila says: "We are afraid, and fear is the prevailing emotion in the region." Ethno-national elites in power nurture fear, and therefore activities for peace and reconciliation are not welcome. Any move to rebuild a multicultural, open society in BiH leaves the activist vulnerable to the accusation of disloyalty to his/her community, a serious claim that can precipitate violence and exile.

Another very important question for women, Radmila explained, is gaining support, support from other women and men, and from other communities. "There is the fear that we will not have allies." She thinks that there is not yet a critical mass of women, a group substantial enough to enable serious political change. However, she reported that women's organizations cooperate with one another, and although they operate in the ethnically divided society of BiH, they do not allow these divisions to prevent them from working together across the country's internal borders:

> Divisions exist, but they do not dominate our dialogue. We somehow spontaneously accept that we do not necessarily have the same thoughts about every issue ... but do we work together all the time? We have never had problems implementing some projects together and collaborating ... we do not work in the tripartite political divisions.

Women's organizations were also active in the implementation of the UN Security Council Resolution 1325 on Women, Peace and Security (2000) and the UNSCR 1325 Action Plan for BiH (2011). Despite these seemingly positive steps, Radmila cautioned that the weak BiH Parliament often adopts new action plans under pressure

---

[25] Zilka Spahić-Šiljak, 2013, "Do It and Name It: Feminist Theology and Peacebuilding in Bosnia and Herzegovina", *Journal for Feminist Studies in Religion* 29.2, 178-186.
[26] Helms 2003, 15-33.

from the international community, but that such plans are rarely implemented. She emphasized that the big problem in BiH is the lack of political responsibility by those in power. The elected representatives tend to put everything behind them and only struggle to stay in power and manage the state's funding. She noted that, "implementation of the UNSCR Action Plan 1325 for BiH would significantly change the structure of the power centers, and at first would also change the tone of the public dialogue."

Fig. 10-5

Radmila believes that implementing the laws and action plans adopted so far in BiH would enable women to be involved in negotiations and decision-making processes. To date, they do all of the peacebuilding work in local communities, but do not have the power to negotiate the very peace that they stand for and that they so carefully nurture in the local communities. When I pressed her for a solution to this unfair situation, she blamed it on the lack of a common attitude toward the rejection of ethno-nationalist divisions:

> Since we do not have any public space other than the ethnic/national one ... we lack a public voice that can analyze our dialogue and assert that it is a dialogue for peacebuilding ... and in this dialogue more women participate and we should provide more space for them. Peacebuilding should become a [social] value ... in order to support those who build peace and direct their activities [there].

In other words, for women to be recognized as peace actors there should be a strong public voice supporting a culture of peace and dialogue. The apparatus of the government and especially the actions of local politicians should follow the law and action plans in order to bring systematic change to BiH society. Also, women rarely participate in the public dialogue of BiH because, as Radmila notes, this "public dialogue ... should be civic, and our entire dialogue is political and ethnic/national." Thus, most of the voices for dialogue and the strengthening of civil society were not strong enough to be heard above the voices promoting collective and ethnic rights in BiH.[27]

Radmila claims that males dominate BiH and if women tried to express their requests louder and bring different ideas to the table they would be punished: "They might take this away [rights and access], what we have now. But the question is, can the voices of reason find any place in a country dominated by fear, fear about tomorrow, about [mere] existence?"

In addition to the reasons given above, poverty also limits women in BiH. Women were the first to lose their jobs during the war and the last to get them back. Women's work in NGOs is further affected by the limited foreign funding they receive compared with what state institutions receive. Radmila confirms

---

[27] Asim Mujkić, 2008, *We, the Citizens of Ethnopolis*, Sarajevo: Center for Human Rights, University of Sarajevo.

that the support women's organizations receive is small, and that the organizations live between writing reports and writing applications, always struggling for funds and for work places. In a poor, post-war society like BiH, she says: "We do not have the luxury of full-time volunteers to do this work, rather this work is intertwined with the volunteer women's personal struggle to survive and the huge administrative requests from the state. The state does not [generally] support us, and when it does it, it gives small grants."

Radmila concluded this part of her narrative by saying that women are more involved in peace work than before, but they still do not have the necessary political power, media presence, and funding to gain better results. This is a problem many peacebuilders face, because they do not have a voice in decisions that affect their lives.

She is not sure whether women are in fact more peaceful than men,[28] because since women simply do not have the power that men have, it is impossible to evaluate the question. "Only future generations will be able to answer the question, when women have a similar amount of power as men." However, she believes that women should continue their work and weave their threads in the tapestry of peace in BiH.

The Role of Religion in Peacebuilding

> I do not have anything against any of the religions in this region, or against any other religion, because they all preach about peace, love, and positive values among people. If of all those who declare faith are true believers we would have finished with our conflicts long ago.

---

[28] Nel Noddings, 2002, *Starting at Home: Caring and Social Policy,* Berkeley: University of California Press; Fiona Robinson, 2011, *The Ethics of Care: A Feminist Approach to Human Security*, Philadelphia: Temple University Press.

One of the themes Radmila discussed with me was the role of religion and religious communities in peacebuilding. She said that she did not have much to suggest about religion because she does not go to church, although she is not an atheist. She has read the Bible and knows the basic facts about Orthodox Christianity and some other traditions, but she was not raised a practicing believer. Like many in BiH, Radmila is secularized and believes in God but does not belong to a church or attend services—"believing without belonging."[29] She reasoned that because churches were involved in the war and sided with the ethno-nationalists currently in power, and furthermore remain closely connected to these politicians, they are not perceived in public as peace actors. In fact, she argues, occasionally they can even be seen working against the goal of social reconciliation:

> Church structures were strong supporters of the war elites, political elites, and they are present in the political life [of BiH], and since the voices of our political life are not voices of peace, I do not believe that voices of religious communities are much different …

Due to the ties between ethno-national leadership and religious leadership, as well as the interference of religious communities in politics within BiH,[30] Radmila questions BiH's status as a secular state. One of the key arguments against its secular nature for her is that religious education is imposed in public schools in BiH. "I would like this state to become again secular and religion to be a private matter. … I have never agreed with the introduction of religious education in schools." Radmila is not against religion *per se* and she advocates for freedom of religion, but she believes that

---

[29] Grace Davie, 1994, *Religion in Britain since 1945: Believing without Belonging*, Hoboken, NJ: Wiley-Blackwell.
[30] Neven Andjelic, 2003, *Bosnia-Herzegovina: The End of a Legacy*, London: Frank Cass; 140-153, Michael A. Sells, 1996, *The Bridge Betrayed. Religion and Genocide in Bosnia*, Berkeley: University of California Press; Paul Mojzes, 1994, *Yugoslavian Inferno: Ethnoreligious Warfare in the Balknas*, New York: Continuum.

religious teachings should remain within churches/mosques. Further elaboration on this topic disclosed another argument: Radmila believes that religious instruction in schools is actually nurturing ethno-religious tensions and divisions as well as stereotypical and biased portrayals of other religious groups, atheists, and minorities, as some research has shown.[31] She commented:

> Considering how long religious instruction has been in school [almost two decades], we should have today a generation of young people marching the streets singing: "Let us give peace a chance," but it does not happen. Youth are sometimes even more hot-blooded and clearly divided alongside ethnic lines.

Radmila's recipe for getting back to the secular state and building a culture of peace is to redefine the school curricula—not only the courses on religious education, but other courses like history and language, all of which should promote tolerance, coexistence, and peace: "something that would bring us together, that would place us next to each other, to talk like human beings, to listen to each other, would be better than [the divisions] we have now."

---

[31] Dženana Husremović, Steve Powell, Ajla Šišić, and Aida Dolić, 2007, *Obrazovanje u BiH: Čemu učimo djecu? Analiza sadržaja udžbenika nacionalne grupe predmeta,* Sarajevo: Open Society Fund of BiH and ProMENT; Zlatiborka Popov-Momčinović, 2009, "'Male' religijske manjine u sistemu verske nastave u BiH: Između nevidljivosti i negativnih stereotipa," in *Religijsko i školovanje u otvorenom društvu. Preispitivanje modela religijskog obrazovanja u BiH,* Sarajevo: Open Society Fund of BiH, 51-68; Emina Abrahamsdotter, 2009, "Preispitivanje modela religijskog obrazovanja u BiH," in *Religijsko i školovanje u otvorenom društvu: Preispitivanje modela religijskog obrazovanja u BiH,* Sarajevo: Open Society Fund of BiH, 81-100; Renata Stuebner, 2009, *The Current Status of Coexistence and Religious Education in Bosnia and Herzegovina,* Washington D.C.: USIP.

This latter USIP report concluded that: "Despite 15 years of sporadic efforts, religion today in Bosnia and Herzegovina is more of a hindrance than a help to promoting peaceful coexistence. Polarization and extremism make religions other than one's own even more distant, strange and threatening. Physical interaction that existed before the last war is now almost completely lost because of political division".

She is also very suspicious of formal religious identification as it is measured in BiH; she feels that if people adhered to the messages of their faiths, "we would have finished with the post-war conflicts a long time ago." Instead, the war discourse dominates public life, and for Radmila, religions have become ideologies that do not fulfill their missions to connect people to God and people to people. She reported that not enough people organized to reconsider the role of religious communities in the war and their co-responsibility for peacebuilding. She contextualized the role of religious communities in today's society: they struggle to keep their positions, to have enough congregants to belong to churches/mosques, but they are not interested in raising the consciousness of believers who would reflect upon their own aims and work in society. She concluded by asking, tongue in cheek: "who needs conscious believers?" Obviously the elite religious leadership does not, because conscious believers would presumably also be responsible citizens who would not stand for the nationalist emotional manipulation and segregation of citizens from different groups.

When asked why religion is not a conversation starter for peacebuilding in BiH,[32] Radmila said that religious leaders are reluctant to enter into dialogue with those of other faiths. As Lederach portrays in his pyramid of decision-making, they are at the top of the pyramid, with their public activities and visibility. "They are under tremendous pressure to maintain a position of strength vis-à-vis their adversaries and their own constituencies."[33]

However, she compared religious institutions with state institutions, which also need a great deal of time to start working together to take responsibility for social ills such as human

---

[32] Ina Merdjanova and Patrice Brodeur, 2009, *Religion as a Conversation Starter. Interreligious Dialogue for Peacebuilding in the Balkans*, New York: Continuum. 108.
[33] John Paul Lederach, 1997, *Building Peace. Sustainable Reconciliation in Divided Societies*, Washington D.C.: United States Institute for Peace Press, 40.

trafficking and domestic violence. Radmila believes that it is time to start communicating with religious communities more profoundly and to make them partners in the elimination of violence. "I have been thinking for a long time, what would it be like if a priest, during a prayer or homily, invited believers to refrain from committing violence in their families because it is not in accordance with religious laws?" She thinks that it is possible to build a common platform with religious institutions against domestic violence and other important social issues. Since Lara has not cooperated very much with religious communities, Radmila tells me that it is time to enter into this dialogue and expand the network for promoting a culture of peace and non-violence in BiH.

Conclusion

Radmila's story is a testament to the difficult struggle against the trafficking of women and domestic violence in post-war BiH because both domestic and international police forces have been involved in the activity and therefore were uninterested in prosecuting perpetrators. Against these odds, she and her colleagues from Lara managed to sensitize the public and to create a network of contacts in various institutions and organizations that helped criminalize modern slavery and sanction perpetrators.

Although her voice was suppressed during the war by an ethno-nationalist government and she could not speak about war crimes as she felt compelled to, she decided to use her voice after the war to create a platform for reconciliation. Her story is a demonstration of the daily moral dilemmas and choices necessary during the war. Though she used her voice as a journalist and her role at the magazine *Extra* against the corruption and single-mindedness of the regime that kept her own Serb people isolated, she was unhappy to be silent about war crimes. Her resistance against becoming a tool for war propaganda cost her the job, and she was ostracized after the war. Nevertheless, she persevered in her work both in the NGO and media sectors. Today she continues to pursue dialogue, peace, and reconciliation within Lara and Pan Radio.

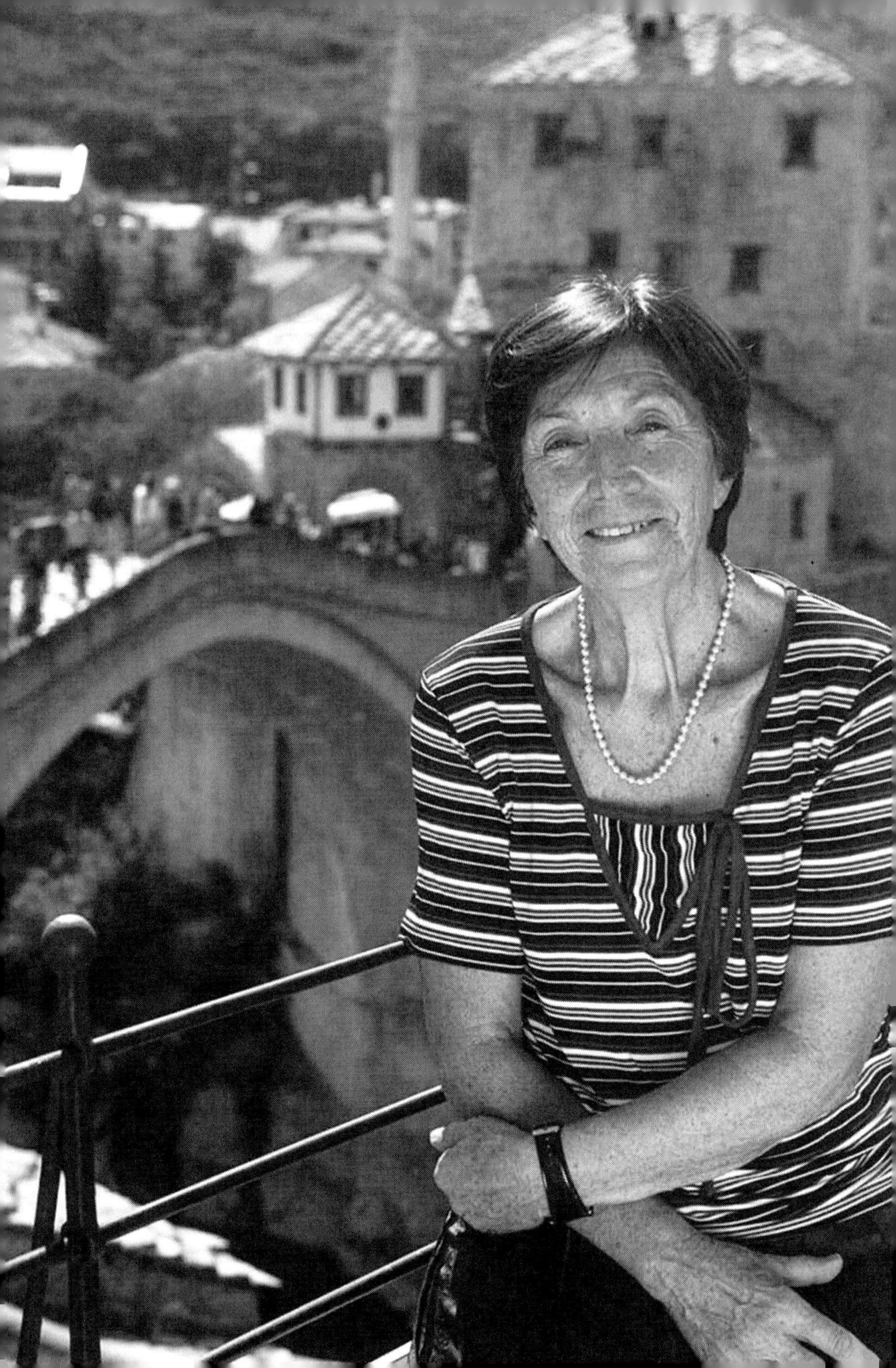

STORY ELEVEN

UNDIVIDED CARE IN A DIVIDED CITY

JASMINKA REBAC

Biography

Jasminka was born in 1947 in Mostar, Bosnia and Herzegovina, to a Bosniac/Muslim family, a family skilled in tackling the challenges of the time in which they lived. One of the ways they did this was by ensuring a university education for their children. Thus, at the age of 18, Jasminka completed her education at a teacher training college and was subsequently directed by state authorities, the practice in socialist Yugoslavia at that time, to take a teaching post at a rural school in the vicinity of Mostar. Eight years later she was transferred to the city of Mostar, where she worked at *Bijeli Brijeg* (White Hill) school until the beginning of the war. During this time, she also graduated from law school and met her husband Emir, who supported her philanthropic work with those who were materially disadvantaged. Jasminka had grown up with a great love for people, especially for children, a quality that came to define her professional life. Believing that every person deserves to live with full dignity, Jasminka began working in classes for children with special needs or, as she likes to say, with special gifts. During the war (1992-1995), Jasminka spent three years in Croatia, where together with the association *Povratak* (Return) and the support of many kind-hearted people, she established a school for refugee children, who did not have the right to enroll in regular classes in Croatia. As the principal of this school, she helped many children avoid an interruption in their education.

After the war, in 1996, she started working in a "special school," which subsequently was renamed the Los Rosales Center for Children and Youth with Special Needs, in recognition of its being funded by the government of Spain. It is still operational and active in Mostar. For her work there, Jasminka received the Order of Civil Merit award from the king of Spain in 2004.

Although she is now retired, Jasminka continues to be active in the Los Rosales Association for Women, which helps support children with special needs. She lives in Mostar, where she has a son, Miro, and a daughter, Mia, and she is the proud grandmother of four—Emir, Arman, Neira, and Rean. She also considers herself a mother to the children with whom she worked in the Los Rosales Center (The Rose Garden).

Introduction

> I learned that people are worth just as much as they believe they are worth, and that they are worth this much because of their basic humanity. And all people can be real and fully human beings (pravi ljudi) if they are in relationship with other people, and if they know how to get up again if they fall down.

Jasminka is a woman with a special love for people and, in particular, for those with special needs. One rarely finds a person so able to embrace everything and everybody, a person whose constant smile offers comfort, understanding, and support to all who approach her. Her career in education has enabled her to show care and compassion to the most vulnerable group of children in society, especially those in rural areas who were legally entitled to education, but often lost that right due to their parents' social and economic status.

Working in the countryside in 1960s Yugoslavia was a huge turning point for Jasminka. She was used to the comforts of city life, yet here for the first time she faced sheer poverty, lack of education, and ignorance, but also the kindness of people who knew how to accept an outsider and make her feel a part of the community. Jasminka showed that same kindness and acceptance later to children in the school for special needs in Mostar, becoming in the process an iconic figure in the whole region for her work, dedication, and advocacy for human rights and the dignity of children in the local school.

My acquaintance with Jasminka began in the context of empowering women in public life and politics in 2004. Her strong support of women's organizations, and her good will and persistence, motivated many. Looking at how much she was able to accomplish, others would say: "If Jasminka can do this despite all the work she has in the school, why can we not do the same?"

When Jasminka learned that some citizens in the Mostar region recognized her activities as important for peace work and that she had been selected for this interview, her reply reflected her humble personality: "Well, thank you, I am honored, but among all of these women in BiH who have done so much, why is it that I deserve such respect?" She readily accepted the interview, however, and her talent to narrate her story immediately captured my attention. She always related her rich life experiences to the empowerment of people through education, an empowerment that brought people in the Mostar region together to work toward the common goal of helping children with special needs.

Care Does Not Have Ethnicity

> My life story is a story about children with special needs and I have been living this story for the past fifteen years. Soon you will understand why.

Before the war, Mostar was an inspiring symbol of multicultural life and tolerance. Its beautiful and famous Old Bridge dating from the sixteenth century attracted visitors from all around the world. By the end of the war, Mostar had become an entirely different kind of symbol, one that represented the tragedy of ethnic division[1] and the destruction of cultural heritage, including even the exquisite Old Bridge. Everything in the city is now divided between the east and west sides of the river, between Bosniacs and Croatians, respectively. Rather than producing a better life, this separation has created a situation in which people act as if they had not previously ever lived in peace together.[2] Although many efforts have been made to reconcile the two ethnic groups and integrate the city, none have been successful, and today there seems to be an invisible, rarely crossed line dividing the population and the city they live in.

One woman who had to leave during the war showed great courage in coming back and doing something politicians, international diplomats, and various human rights activists were unable to do. This person was Jasminka, and she literally did the impossible, managing to keep together one group of people, one segment of social life, undivided. And she did this in an environment where everything is measured by ethnicity, where ethnic identity dictates one's destiny. Jasminka decided to act, and as Kathleen Barry explains, "to translate received reality into her

---

[1] Daria Sito-Sucic, 2012, "Mostar: One family, three armies, a divided city," *Reuters* (April 2), http://www.reuters.com/article/2012/04/02/uk-bosnia-mostar-idUSLNE83102N20120402 (accessed September 12, 2013).
[2] Kai Vöckler, 2010, "Politics of Identity: The Example of Mostar Bosnia and Herzegovina," European Workshop "City and Diversity – Challenges for Citizenship Education," 24-26 June, Barcelona: "In 1992 the city was occupied by the Serbian-controlled Yugoslav People's Army and by the Bosnian-Serb paramilitary. Fighting bands of Bosnian-Croats and Bosniacs (also known as Bosnian Muslims) opposed them successfully and eventually drove out the Serbian military, along with the Serbian population of Mostar. Then, in 1993, more armed conflict ensued, this time between the Bosnian-Croats and the Bosniacs, over who would rule the city; this was not ended until the United States' military intervention in 1994" (2). Network of European Citizenship Education, www.bpb.de/syste,/files/pdf/2G5U1B.pdf (accessed July 12, 2013).

life."[3] The choices she made are a testimony to her extraordinary leadership qualities and vision.

Jasminka invested most of her post-war activism in convincing local authorities and fellow citizens, both Bosniacs and Croats, to keep children with special needs together. She knew, of course, that their need for care and love surpassed all ethnic divisions, requiring instead basic justice. If labeled by ethnicity, the children's care would not be adequate, but rather it would be a fragmented care that neglected their needs and feelings as human beings because they belong to this particular group, and thus have different capabilities and needs within their social and cultural contexts.[4] Jasminka's moral reasoning derives from her caring attitude toward these children and her concern for the fair and just treatment she believes they deserve.[5] Elisabeth Porter calls this the politics of compassion,[6] seen as an important part of acknowledging the relationships and the rights of those who are dependent. The main goal for Jasminka and her colleagues was to ensure that all local children with special needs benefit from the Los Rosales Center and that employees of the center represent all religions and nationalities. Thus, Jasminka's work fits into the frame of track-two diplomacy, as explained in the work by Diamond and McDonald.[7] She has long advocated for structural change to the existing legal system and better policies in the social and health care systems. It seems like a simple goal for any functioning democratic society, but it is tremendously hard in a place like BiH, where society is

---

[3] Kathleen Barry, 1992, "Toward a Theory of Women's Biography," in Theresa Iles (ed.), *All Sides of the Subjects: Women and Biography*, New York: Teachers College Press, Columbia University, 34.
[4] Martha Nussbaum, 2000, *Women and Human Development: The Capabilities Approach*, Cambridge: Cambridge University Press, 5-7.
[5] Fiona Robinson, 2011, *The Ethics of Care: A Feminist Approach to Human Security*, Philadelphia: Temple University Press, 62.
[6] Elisabeth J. Porter, 2007, *Peacebuilding: Women in International Perspective*, London: Routledge, 100-103.
[7] Louise Diamond and John MacDonald, 1996, *Multi-track Diplomacy: A Systems Approach to Peace*, 3rd ed. West Hartford CT: Kumarian Press, 87-93.

disenfranchised and sees only through the lens of ethnic and religious identity.

Jasminka's peace journey continued in 1996 when she returned to Mostar after three years as a refugee in Croatia with her family. Her former colleague Fadila ran into her on the street and asked her to come to work for a "Special Elementary School" (Specijalna osnovna škola) for Disabled Children, which later became The Los Rosales Center for Children and Youth with Special Needs. Jasminka accepted the offer and began working as a teacher in the school. She admitted that the first two years were a difficult adjustment in learning how to help the children: "I cried for a whole year. ... But after starting this job, working with special needs children became a part of me. I cannot separate myself from it."

As soon as she adjusted to the school and children, a new challenge arose. She was faced with a difficult decision that would determine her further work in education. The school principal approached her one day, saying: "You know, Jasna, I can no longer be the principal. My son is ill. ... And the job of a principal is demanding, so I had a talk with the school founders and it turns out that the only person they can identify who could continue this job right away is you." Jasminka was surprised and answered modestly that she did not know how to be a principal. The principal did not give up, however. Recognizing Jasminka's potential, she continued to encourage her and reminded her of what she had undertaken during the war:

> You knew how to be a principal at a time when you were not allowed to be a principal. ... In a context where you were not really accepted ... you established many strong relationships [in Makarska, in Croatia], so why wouldn't you use them for the advancement of this school?

Jasminka had been a good principal and demonstrated much leadership and managerial skill in exile in Croatia, but as a responsible person she did not want to accept the job before she learned if she had the support of her fellow teachers: "When I realized that they really believed I could do it and that I would be working on their behalf, I accepted the tasks set before me."

She did her job well, and she was grateful for the support she was given to upgrade her managerial skills. "Thanks to the education programs within Civitas [Educational Center for Democracy and Human Rights[8]], I learned about basic democratic managerial skills." For example, she discovered that teamwork is crucial to success. She is just one of many teachers who benefited from the Civitas programs initiated and managed by Rahela Džidić (see Story 8). Jasminka also invited her colleagues to attend the training sessions with her, because she knew that no one can succeed in such a job all on her own. As manager of the Los Rosales Center, Jasminka was overwhelmed by its immediate needs, but with proper distribution of tasks and responsibilities, she was able to win some very important "battles" in the local community.

---

[8] Civitas BiH, http://civitas.ba/obrazovni-programi.

Fig. 11-1

Among her first tasks was changing the school's name, a procedure that would be just a formality in most cases, but in BiH nothing is simple. The renaming of the school had to be negotiated with the new local authorities, who did not care much about children with special needs or about social welfare issues in general. Jasminka commented that the name Specijalna škola (Special School) communicated preconceived notions of its pupils being different and disabled, when in reality they were like any other children in the ways that mattered. So, the name was changed to School for Children with Special Needs. A secondary issue related to the renaming was the wish to recognize the sponsoring Spaniards, who had benevolently supported the school, by giving it a name in Spanish, Los Rosales.

Another more important challenge was to transform the school into a Center, a facility that would provide services in addition to education. This idea became a huge battle, because as Jasminka explained, there was no precedent in BiH legal practice for transforming a public school into something more. It took nearly all her energy to convince local authorities that Mostar needed the Center. Finally, the last of the challenges was the decision to use the word Center: "How were we supposed to convert a school for children with special needs into a Center? … It took seven years … seven years of permanent struggle: administrative, legal, human, and inhuman."

Seven long years is what it took for her to sensitize the politicians and those who ran the government institutions in the Mostar region, seven long years for them to understand and approve the request. Jasminka explained that the reason the process took so long was twofold. First, education, social welfare, and health care lie within the exclusive jurisdiction of the cantons in the entity known as the Federation of BiH, and these cantons adopt their own legislation and policies. Second, Mostar as a city had a special status, and as a special administrative unit it had been struggling to find a balance of power between the Croatian and Bosniac ethnic groups. Politicians in the Herzegovina-Neretva canton, on the other hand, were not interested in forming the Center, which in theory might serve as a bridge to connect people in the region, a prospect they feared. Therefore they postponed the decision as long as they could: for seven years. But Jasminka is a woman who can find inspiration even in obstacles:

> Barriers can often be motivational. I am a very persistent person … persistent and stubborn, and I can stand suffering because I see the light at the end of the tunnel. What I think is most important in my situation, however, is the tremendous love I have for children.

When somebody loves children, she or he is willing to do everything to protect them. Thus, Jasminka was strongly motivated to help children obtain the right not to be further marginalized, excluded, and neglected based on their ethnic identity. The image of a united Mostar made her take the "risk required to break the violence and to venture on unknown paths to build constructive change,"[9] to live outside the imposed ethnic boxes and create a small island where everybody could live and work together. The last legal battle she needed to fight was that of ensuring health care for youth with special needs. She succeeded in convincing the canton's parliament in Mostar to declare that all persons older than eighteen who had special needs must have health care. Jasminka says "This particular victory really pleases me, it makes me really happy."

Alongside the legal, administrative, and political battles, Jasminka envisaged building a multi-ethnic team of teachers and volunteers from the entire region of Herzegovina. Evaluating her last fifteen years of work, she spoke proudly:

> When I think back to our early days in 1996, the Center had 42 children and 11 employees ... yet by the time I retired in 2010, 160 individuals had been benefitted by the Center ... and 42 employees staffed the place, of which a vast majority ... were well-educated people with university degrees in pedagogy, psychology, social work, disability health care, therapy education, physical education, music ... with an average age of thirty two. I think that says it all.

With a team of experienced specialists and teachers, accompanied by young colleagues and interns, the staff improved the Center's service using the latest methodological approaches to educating children with special needs. The children who were served in the Center usually had parents, but since the Center is outside Mostar, many parents could not make the necessary commute every day. Furthermore, many children came not only for their education, but also to get a proper meal: "What I want to say is that these projects not only raised the capacities of these children, they also raised their standard of living ... Our children are not on the verge of poverty ... but below the poverty line, together with their families."

---

[9] John Paul Lederach, 2005, *The Moral Imagination: The Art and Soul of Building Peace*, Oxford: Oxford University Press, 29.

Jasminka gathered children from all the ethnic groups in Herzegovina and her goal was to bring them together in the Los Rosales Center to love and enjoy the pure spirit of humanity. These are "the biggest gifts children with special needs can offer to all of us." Jasminka explains that the important thing to keep in mind while helping children improve their capabilities and capacities is simply to be human. In return, one receives unconditional love, a special gift that can be found particularly in these children. Because children were her biggest love and her true motivation, success for her was to make them happy and show them they are not alone, that people are there for them.

When Jasminka retired, she did not become inactive, "I am no longer the director of the Los Rosales Center, even though I will be its member for as long as I can walk, and even if God makes it so that I can't walk, I'll be with them in my thoughts." Her membership is a life-long commitment.

A Teacher with a Special Gift of Caring

If you give love, you will get love in return, and if you care for somebody, it will empower you to be a fully realized human being.

How did Jasminka come to appreciate and recognize the special gift of love and humanity in children with special needs? What made her so deeply connected to these children and their needs? The answer is simple: Jasminka is a woman who is able to make the most complicated things accessible and understandable and to make one feel comfortable with them. She is, as John Lederach explains, willing to accept complexity and yet to find a simple way to shape her work promoting peace in the region.[10]

Jasminka has a special gift of being able to care for others: to love them, teach them, and embrace them. Her maternal care goes beyond her family and includes what Sara Ruddick calls a

---

[10] Ibid., 33.

"rationality of care,"[11] which means that she is absolutely attentive to the needs of others. When she graduated from the Teacher Training College and was appointed to a village school near Mostar: "Teachers ... had to be the pioneers, those who created a more positive perspective. ... I think this is a role teachers should play even today." To eradicate illiteracy, socialist Yugoslavia appointed teachers to spend seven or eight years of work in the most remote villages, and afterward they were relocated to an urban area, to help satisfy them not only in their work, but also in their place of work. Jasminka's first assignment was a challenge, and her family wanted her to reject the job and search for something more appropriate for a city girl. Her mother, who was working in Mostar at the time because she was an active participant in the World War II, and her older brother Sejo tried to convince her not to go and work in a village, explaining that it was a job for someone born and raised in a rural area. Life would be too hard for her there.

Jasminka, however, accepted the challenge, because she wanted to be a teacher. Once she learned that large numbers of illiterate people lived in the rural areas, she became eager to teach there, in settings for both children and adults. She went to work in the village called Ravni (in English this means flat). As a young girl of eighteen, she did not at first associate the name, geographical location, and appearance of the village, but she laughed and explained: "It did not take me long to realize it was probably a symbolic name because there was absolutely nothing flat in that village." She was shocked when she arrived by bus at the base of the hill and was instructed to climb up to the village. From that moment on she knew that she would have much to adjust to in her life there. Even though the village lifestyle in the 1960s was completely different from city life, she accepted the challenge, and

---

[11] Sara Ruddick, 1989, *From Maternal Thinking: Toward a Politics of Peace*, Boston: Beacon Press. 41-46.

in return enjoyed the respect of the community in the village of Ravni:

> I started wearing *opanci*, a type of peasant sandal, which the villagers made for me using the best, most white leather. Then I went on to wearing wool socks. I was always up there with the villagers, at all their weddings and baptisms, I was there with them in times of tragedy, joy, and birth. A teacher was highly respected in the village, respected and appreciated.

Life in the village affected her health; the well-water was not of good quality, and she started losing her teeth. It amazed us during the interview to hear her explain this: "Pulling out a couple of teeth didn't really bother me that much. Even though I was young, I couldn't waste time going to Mostar to fix them." Coming down to the city from the village of Ravni took her about 45 minutes, but she felt it was not a priority to take time from her work to go to town. Her huge sense of responsibility put her children's needs over her own health and beauty. Despite all the difficulties, she liked her work and enjoyed being with these people. She wanted to help them educate their children, and she became more and more integrated into their society, enjoying the benefits of rural life.

Ravni consisted of three *mahalas* (neighborhoods), populated according to surnames. "Back then the residents were divided on the basis of their ethnic and religious identity, but I did not realize it at the time." Other female scholars have claimed similar attitudes in their research.[12] Jasminka, however, was not exactly ignorant about the ethnic and religious identities in the village because she participated in so many religious holiday gatherings. However, these ethnic identities seemed otherwise irrelevant to her since she views people first and foremost as human beings deserving all the fundamental human rights owing to them.

---

[12] Swanee Hunt, 2004, *This Was Not Our War: Bosnian Women Reclaiming the Peace*. Durham: Duke University Press, 125.

Fig. 11-2

Jasminka was not happy with the teaching arrangements in the school, which included four grades of students in one classroom. There were so many children that she felt she could not complete the appropriate daily lessons for each grade while enduring the four-in-one classroom structure. Children were not able to learn in such circumstances, and she asked the school principal to allow her to separate the children so as to work with each grade individually, even though her workday would be longer. Her request was approved and the principal told her: "I am proud of you ... you do not need any approval, everybody will be happy with your request to spend more time with children." So, she worked the whole day with these children separately, grade by grade, and got better results.

Jasminka wanted more for these rural children, for she knew that city kids had much more available to them. Therefore she lobbied to bring in a mobile cinema at a time when the village had no electricity and thus no TV. She organized extra-curricular activities: sports, choir, and school drama performances. She spoke of the excitement of preparing children to act in these school performances, especially when they celebrated important socialist holidays, wearing red scarves and white caps. She also organized visits to cities and urban centers and to the Adriatic coast. Her brother helped her with transportation and the organization of these trips, because the children's parents could not afford it: "He was the manager of a large company in Mostar and he arranged for busses for these kids free of charge." She devoted herself entirely to this cause, which helped her fulfill her duties as a teacher as well as a human being. The trust and support of her family and friends brought life to her vision.

Jasminka was raised within a family that embodied an ethic of care, compassion, and justice, making her an activist for the rights of the less privileged. However in 1992, she learned that not all people had been raised with these values, nor did they believe in brotherhood and unity like she did. She faced a painful realization about friends and colleagues whom she considered brothers and sisters.

Masks of False Humanity

> We don't choose war, war befalls us, war happens, and then we have to think about what to do under the circumstances, what is it that I can do for my family, for myself, and for others?

When the Yugoslav National Army attacked Mostar in 1992, and the conflict between Croats and Bosniacs subsequently began in 1993, Jasminka was absolutely astonished. Because she lived in this multicultural city,[13] she had friends from all its ethnic and religious backgrounds. The beginning of the war turned out to be a very sobering time in terms of people's unexpected behaviors, and Jasminka had to face the betrayal of some of her good friends and

---

[13] According to the census in 1991, the ethnic composition of Mostar was: Muslims 34.6%, Croats 34%, Serbs 18.8%, and Yugoslavs 10%.

colleagues at the school. She recalled: "It just so happened that my work colleagues revealed a real inhumanity ... [and even] my friends, whom I referred to as my sisters up until that year. ... We had spent every day together, our children were raised together and did their homework together."

Fig. 11-3

Jasminka was devastated and could not fathom how people could so quickly transform themselves. How could they have been her close friends all those years and one day wake up as nationalists. It felt like her whole world was falling apart. This was the first big turning point in Jasminka's life.[14] Shortly thereafter, she was further shocked to be fired from her job without explanation. All teachers of non-Croatian background were fired and nobody could explain to her the legal arguments for this. As a graduate of the law school, she knew something about legal procedures,

---

[14] Norman Denzin, 1989, *Interpretive Biography*, Thousand Oaks, CA: Sage. 70.

commenting: "During that time there was no respect for laws or procedures. All you had to do was not belong to the majority group and you lost your job."

But she recounted that not all her friends abandoned her. Some went through life-threatening situations with her, situations that might have jeopardized their families, because they helped her to survive in the western part of Mostar where a majority of Croats lived. Her friend Vesna told her it might be best to leave Mostar, because some parents and students could use the occasion of the war as an excuse to "question" her teaching: "The grade you gave them, or maybe they were not satisfied because they felt you didn't give them enough attention or affection. Perhaps it would be good for you to get out of here." Jasminka could not understand why she had to leave when she had not done anything wrong: "I must have cried for seven nights in a row." At that time, mortar shells were falling all over the eastern side of Mostar where Bosniacs lived, and recalling this in the interview, she started to cry:

> One day, more than three thousand shells fell on the city. My mother was living in a *mahala* called Cernica, a neighborhood not far from where I lived. It was a ten-minute walk to reach her, but now it was a whole eternity away from me. My mom lived in this other part of town and she was killed there. I could not help her.

After her mother's death Jasminka finally decided to leave the city. Her friends, those who remained friends, helped her move to Makarska, in Croatia. She was completely exhausted by the pain and the loss, and yet she still had two young children and a seriously ill husband to care for in exile. While in exile, she met both good and bad people: "There were those who were bothered by someone's first and last name. There were those who understood your trouble and knew you had left your home not because you wanted to, but because you had to." She mentioned only a few good friends in Croatia, among them a German language teacher and the manager of a restaurant where she worked.

As a teacher, Jasminka could not accept the Croatian policy barring refugee children from attending school. Just a year before, Croatia had been part of Yugoslavia with a common curriculum and the same language, yet now the schools were politically divided by three languages (Bosnian, Croatian, or Serbian). Nevertheless, stubbornly seeking a solution for her own children, she recalls: "I will never forget the German language teacher, a remarkable woman who advised me on how I could find legal loopholes in order to enroll my children in school." Keeping the woman's name a secret for safety considerations, Jasmina praised her as one of the righteous people who wanted to help, but could not do so publicly.

Another good person remaining in Jasminka's memory is Grma, the manager at the restaurant where she worked. Grma helped in any way he could. At the time, Jasminka had a twelve-year-old daughter who was allowed to help in the restaurant kitchen after school. One day, Grma brought two envelopes with pay inside, saying: "Mrs. Rebac, one of these envelopes is for you, and the other is for your daughter." Jasminka noted that although there was not a significant amount of money in her envelope, it was her most valuable and most proudly earned paycheck ever. Jasminka asked Grma to give the money to her daughter himself, but he could not, saying: "'No, please, you give it to her, I don't have the strength to do it, I have a daughter her age. I can't give it to her' ... I didn't understand him then, but now I do."

So Jasminka enrolled her children in school and worked to provide what she could for her family. But she could not stay silent about the hundreds of refugees who were unable to find a solution for their children's education. She soon joined the association Povratak (Return), which had attracted a large number of intellectuals from BiH, of all religious and ethnic identities. Povratak supported the refugees in helping each other, because they faced so many problems in common. For example, refugees from BiH were immediately recognized by their accent and therefore avoided speaking in public, a situation that led to many embarrassing encounters, especially on public transportation. Muslim refugees were scared to go to Islamic organizations for support: "Someone might see you entering such a place," thus identifying oneself as a Muslim and risking trouble. Jasminka noted that this behavior occurred during the height of nationalist tension in Croatia, a time when people thought about every last detail that might jeopardize their security.

Consequently, it seemed best to stick with one's own, to create an NGO and do something cooperatively. Povratak, therefore, decided to contact staff from the BiH embassy in Zagreb with a proposal to open a school for refugee children. Such a school was duly established under the leadership of Ms. Maida Cabrera from Sarajevo, and Jasminka became the principal of this "Extraterritorial High School" for three years. Professors representing many different religious and ethnic groups from BiH, mostly from Sarajevo, taught there without any compensation. Because of their relationship with the Pedagogical Institute in Sarajevo, Mrs. Mira Merlo and Mrs. Atija Fako helped the school fulfill all the requirements and standards for high school graduation and issued valid diplomas to graduates. Jasminka felt strongly that no generation of refugees should have to miss school because of the newly imposed ethno-nationalist exclusionary rules. The top seven graduates from this high school were sent to Spain to study and Jasminka proudly noted:

> Today, they are doctors, economists, computer scientists, and I am happy that after several years spent in Spain, and having received a good education there, five of them returned to Bosnia and Herzegovina to continue their university education, while two of them stayed in Spain.

Fig. 11-4

After the war, Jasminka's mission with refugees was finished, and she wished to return to Mostar. Her seriously ill husband and her children stayed in Croatia while she went ahead in 1996 to prepare the apartment for their return: "I arrived in the western part of Mostar, the part of town rumored to be completely shut off, where no one could come in or go out. If a Muslim person went there, he or she could be killed." She had heard all of these stories, but she still wanted to go back. The good people, her friends who remained true despite the nationalist politics, helped her to get back into her apartment. She needed to paint it and find furniture for it, but those things seemed totally irrelevant to Jasminka. What she wanted was something she could not have: her mother and her lost friendships. With pain in her eyes, she explained that, "perhaps this war was needed so that all of us could take off our masks and show our true faces. I call it a 'masquerade with victims.'" Although she had suffered, experienced loss, and faced the challenges of refugee life, she admitted that the awakening in 1992 helped her to learn who was truly a friend and who just pretended to be. The war became an opportunity to see people's true colors.

The good people and friends who were there for her and for children were able to preserve one small island in divided Mostar, a place where children, parents, and teachers of all religious and ethnic backgrounds could come and be safe. Many women who needed support were thus motivated to continue working and were able to express their own compassion thanks to this community. The first supporters and collaborators were women from both sides of the river who had no time to wait for the politicians to do something in their city.

The River Neretva: Where Women Started to Sing Again

Jasminka was one of the few Bosniacs to return to the west side of Mostar to reclaim an apartment and is one of the few who continues to live there today. Her biggest challenge was not the return itself, but rather the necessity of convincing people on each side of the Neretva River to communicate with one another again to rebuild their lives and relationships. The Green River is what Herzegovinians like to call the Neretva. Spanning its depths and symbolizing the city is the Old Bridge, destroyed during the war and thus making the river a barrier that divided the citizens of Mostar according to their ethnic community: Croats on the west side and Bosniacs on the east.

After the war, Mostar was filled with refugees, mostly Bosniacs and displaced persons from neighboring cities in Herzegovina who had been in the war refugee camps organized by Croats. As these individuals were waiting to get their property back, Jasminka was struck by their suffering and the inhuman treatment they endured at the hands of the local authorities. The refugees had no access to health care or other social services, and they needed housing and adequate food. She reports that, at that time, however, their overriding concern was to stay alive. Jasminka was courageous enough to come back to her apartment and initiate communication with her pre-war neighbors, because as she argued, she was innocent: "I returned to my apartment and I greeted my Croatian neighbors with my head held high. I met people in the courtyard and I socialized with them. I offered my help to anyone who needed assistance and they accepted."

Jasminka staunchly refused to approve of the unnatural division and imprisonment of Mostar's residents in ethnic boxes. She was looking for individuals with whom she could initiate the kind of dialogue that could lead to reconciliation. Her vision remained, as always, to help people and in particular to help children with special needs.

Courageous women appeared from both sides of the Neretva, and they arranged the very first meeting of women from East and West Mostar: "Several women met up at the Swiss House and started talking about what we could do." They did not know where to start but had the goodwill and drive to do something, for themselves and for the city. Jasminka reminisces about these women who were looking for a way to survive with their families:

> So, Jelena, Želja, and Devleta were our presidents. They were very energetic and very motivated women, educated women with university degrees. Before the war, they had worked in leadership positions in their companies and now they were nothing. None of them was politically active back then, none of them was employed. ... They had their families and started bit by bit, little by little.

A small nucleus of women envisaged a plan for working on rebuilding personal connections and relationships and encouraged other women to join them. The effort was not easy. They built a "network of relationships"[15] with their friends, acquaintances, and people they believed would trust them, "strategically and imaginatively weaving relational webs across social spaces within

---

[15] Porter 2007, 33.

settings of protracted violent conflict" for constructive change.[16] The first thing they did was to organize a social event to enable initial post-war encounters. At that time, they had to prepare everything on their own, devise a schedule, and divide up their duties. Jasminka described the atmosphere as similar to the preparation for a school party including a pot-luck dinner: "One made a loaf of bread, one made a pie, one made a cake and cookies. We bought sodas, coffee, and we arranged it all nicely, as only women know how do. We even found a few flowers." The women who came to that first meeting were mostly unemployed and had nothing.

Jasminka spoke excitedly about how hard it was for them in those days to find hair color to dye their gray hair. Instead, they used a certain soap that was meant for washing clothes. It was called Kabaš, because it was so strong, so full of soda. She laughed, explaining the procedure: "It would turn a brunette into a blonde. We'd melt this soap and put it on their heads to equalize the color, so they'd have no dark parts in the middle." Women also lent each other their most beautiful clothes so they could get dressed up for an evening. They tried to bring back a little normalcy and a little glamour into the midst of the post-war struggle to provide the more mundane necessities of life, such as water and electricity.

Jasminka remembered how they used to greet each other at the door with the sentence: "Just because I am sad does not mean I have to look bad" (Ako sam tužna, ne moram biti ružna), thus articulating the desire to overcome the unbearable deprivation of post-war Mostar with a spirit of optimism. They were trying to revive the spirit of care for appearance that characterized their dignity and resistance to the violence and destruction around them. The gatherings were successful and they even sang together. As the meetings continued, they started to share their stories and fears. Some women attended for several months, but came furtively,

---

[16] Lederach 2005, 84.

reporting that they were scared to tell anyone they were coming. Eventually a number of them came openly, but by then the women in Swiss House had begun working intensively on peacebuilding as the mission of their women's organization.

Fig. 11-5

Jasminka is proud of these individuals because they showed their husbands and neighbors that women could initiate change. After a while, the group was formally registered as the NGO Žene BiH. Jasminka sought cooperation with other NGOs, and she visited a large number of less-developed local rural areas: "There was a need to talk to women. I always say that women have their eyes open, but they just need to open them wider." Women need to be empowered so that they know they are a force to be reckoned with. She believes that women understand their own family needs as well as society's needs better than men do and are genuine and natural-born peacebuilders.

Despite disappointments at the beginning of the war and the betrayal of friends and colleagues, Jasminka did not allow herself to be defeated and instead found ways to overcome the challenges. She was not one who wanted to leave Mostar, as many others did, just because they could not stand to live with "pretend friends." Jasminka's desire to return to Mostar and work on behalf of children was stronger than anything else. Fortunately, she was able to find supporters and collaborators with a similar vision.

My Feminism is about Empowerment

Although Jasminka's work at the Los Rosales Center was demanding, she always had time to work with women and for women, knowing well their challenges. In doing so, she did not emphasize her feminist identity, but rather her dedication to empowering women. As Mary Lou Décosterd says: "To empower means to give authority or to make someone more confident."[17] Empowerment is also one trait[18] important for every successful leader, of whom Jasminka was definitely one. After her retirement from the Center, she became president of the Los Rosales Youth NGO. Through this association, she continued to try to empower women to seek the same opportunities and rights that men had.

In her work, Jasminka specifically focused on empowering women with disabilities: "Women with disabilities, young women and girls with special needs, can easily become victims." She noted that all women could become victims, so at the very least they should know how to articulate their needs and rights. Women with disabilities, however, need support and somebody to speak on their behalf. Jasminka was able to take on the leadership of this NGO, which is small and without financial support, because she has an incredible faith and vision that help her persevere.

One example from the Los Rosales Youth Association, as related by Jasminka, is about a girl with special needs who has been able to

---

[17] Mary Lou Décosterd, 2013, *How Women are Transforming Leadership: Four Key Traits Powering Success*, Santa Barbara, CA: Praeger, 74.
[18] One of the IDEA-based leadership traits (Ibid.)

move into her own apartment on an independent basis, all because Jasminka and her colleagues were so effective in advocating for her. She had previously lived in an orphanage and had had psychiatric issues. With proper support and encouragement, she recovered and was able to take care of herself. These are the types of cases that motivate Jasminka and keep her going, just to see one more smile and make one more person strong. It defines her feminism:

> And for the first time in her life, after 21 years, no one else is deciding for her what she will wear, what she will eat, where she will sleep, with whom she will hang out, what her curfew will be, and so on ... And such a girl now calls on the phone and says: "Auntie Jasna, can you come tomorrow to have a cappuccino with me?"

She believes the obstacles encountered in one's life are not accidental, but God-given, and that therefore people should accept them and learn from them. She accepted the challenges in her life and built an amazing Center for children with special needs, and later for women with special needs. Jasminka's life work is about peace, education, empowerment, relationships, and reconciliation. She pays tribute to those women who did the bulk of the peace work in their own local communities, describing their caring qualities[19] as a matter of biological pre-destination, confirmed also by various theological arguments:

> A woman inclines toward peace because of her genetic makeup: her mind, emotions, and sensibilities, those character traits that only women have. Women are less war-mongering, though there are exceptions ... Women cannot stay mad for very long, by their very nature. God has given them that. They look more favorably upon reconciliation. They do not see better, and they do not have better vision than men, but they are more ready to forgive. And without forgiveness there is no reconciliation.

---

[19] Robinson 2011, 120.

Jasminka does not want to say women are superior to men, but she emphasized inborn qualities they have that are relevant for peace work and in that way she uses affirmative essentialism.[20] For her women are the key element in peace and reconciliation efforts in BiH, because in the family, in the workplace, in the community, and in society women are the conciliators. Above all, women are able to forgive more easily than men, and forgiveness and action go hand by hand. As Hannah Arendt says: "Forgiving is the only reaction which does not merely react but acts anew and unexpectedly, unconditioned by the act which provoked it and therefore freeing from its consequences both the one who forgives and the one who is forgiven."[21] Jasminka added that women are inadequately recognized for these qualities.[22]

Among the reasons for this lack of recognition is women's vulnerable position in family and public life. Women, especially middle-aged women, have the highest rate of unemployment, because no one wants to hire them. And if a woman does have a job, she still must spend many hours doing the household chores, work that is not recognized because it is not paid.[23] For Jasminka, women are at risk because they do not have the space to sufficiently organize themselves to show their strength. She added that the traditional patriarchal values dominating BiH society tend to silence women and relegate them to the shadows. Most women, however, seem to accept the role of "self-sacrificing micro-matriarchy" in the

---

[20] Elissa Helms, 2013, *Innocence and Victimhood, Gender, Nation, and Women's Activism in Postwar Bosnia-Herzegovina.* Madison, WI: University of Wisconsin Press., 9.
[21] Hannah Arendt, 1958, *The Human Condition*, Chicago: University of Chicago Press, 241.
[22] Zilka Spahić-Šiljak, Aida Spahić, and Elmaja Bavčić, 2012, *Baseline Study on Women and Peacebuilding in BiH*, Sarajevo: TPO Foundation Sarajevo, www.tpo.ba.
[23] Jasna Bakšić-Muftić and Maja Ljubović, 2003, *Socio-economic Status of Women in BiH: Analysis of the Results of the Star Pilot Research Done in 2002*, Sarajevo: Jež, 17.

private sphere.[24] Her experience from the field—during her travels to work with women during the elections—speak best about that silence and invisibility. Jasminka points out the strong cultural and traditional influences that control women's behavior while they are raising a family. Women seem to be more subject to these influences than men: "During any event, a husband just comes home and says what he thinks, and does not ask his wife what she thinks, or if she has a different opinion. He acts like someone with two heads, who thinks and makes decisions for both of them."

Jasminka demonstrates that it is possible to step outside the assigned gender roles, but when doing so, women face structural violence, rejection, and ignorance. Thus, it takes courage, faith, and persistence to follow such a pattern. Jasminka's work is well-recognized among women activists in BiH; she has twice been awarded the woman of the year prize in the Herzegovina-Neretva Canton, and she was awarded the medal of the Order of Civil Merit from the king of Spain. Nevertheless, she was faced with political pressure, reflected in "doors closing" to her in certain settings. She could not understand the resistance from the municipal and cantonal authorities when she was chosen for the medal. Although she received it as the principal of the Los Rosales Center and asked the Spanish Embassy to organize the ceremony in the Center, some people could not bear her being recognized. This may illustrate the old Bosnian saying that people will tolerate everything except someone else's success. She was quite disappointed after receiving the medal, because so many doors were really closed to her by government officials. But she came to work with a smile on her face, pinching herself at times in order not to show that she had noticed their dislike: "I still walked through that door and greeted with kisses those people who had accepted me before. I did that very consciously."

---

[24] Marina Blagojević, 2002, *Rodni barometer BiH,* www.vladars.net/sr-SP-Cyrl/Vlada/centri/gender%barometar%20BiH%202002.pdf (accessed September 5, 2013).

Fig. 11-6

Jasminka was not defeated by these rejections, but acted in the same professional manner as always, continuing to invite the mayor, ministers, and other representatives of state institutions. She refused to think of them as individuals who liked or disliked her work, and she deliberately "opened all doors" in the belief that any barrier could be overcome with honest communication. She employed again and again a "smart flexible" strategy[25] in her communication with local authorities and eventually won them to her side again.

While women have a great capacity to empower themselves through education, to encourage each other through friendships, to work together and trust each other, Jasminka believes such qualities are missing among women in BiH. They still do not support each other, do not vote for each other,[26] and most of them remain

---

[25] Lederach 2005, 126.
[26] Zilka Spahić-Šiljak, 2010, *Women, Religion and Politics: The Impact of Religious Interpretations of Judaism, Christianity, and Islam on the Status of*

subjugated by their ethno-nationalist political agendas and identities.[27] The only way out of this situation is to create associations, coalitions, and networks that encourage individuals and youth to learn from those who have such qualities and expertise, and to refuse to pay heed to their ethnic and religious identities.

This advice applies equally to women's NGOs, according to Jasminka: although they have done an important job in empowering women, they have not yet united enough around a common cause. Many women's NGOs just do not seem able to overcome existing rivalries and to partner with others who also work on behalf of women.

Jasminka has also been occupied with promoting the UN Security Council Resolution 1325 on women, peace, and security in Herzegovina, especially in rural areas where her NGO is striving to improve women's economic and political rights by offering women employment opportunities and a chance to develop small home businesses.

The story of Jasminka is not yet finished. She just keeps on getting better, improving personally and professionally. Her belief in the empowerment of women through coalitions, cooperative efforts, and making networks endures: "Overall, we are smaller than a grain of sand, I mean, as individuals. But we can be quite strong if we join forces."

Gardening My Own Soul

Jasminka has noted that her love of children has been her biggest inspiration, and that her lifelong motivation has been to make children happy. But to be able to do so and remain smiling and

---

Women in Public Life and Politics, Sarajevo: IMIC, Center for Interdisciplinary Postgraduate Studies & TPO Foundation Sarajevo, 244.
[27] Dubravka Zarkov, 2002, "Feminism and the Disintegration of Yugoslavia: On the Politics of Gender and Identity," *Social Development Issues*, 24.3.

positive she has had to find a way to relax and acquire a sense of inner peace. This was very important to the success of her work. She has tended to so many children during her work at the Los Rosales Center that it seems she must have been attracted to its name for a reason. For she saw the children there as beautiful roses, gifts for those who knew how to approach, love, and nurture them. Being with them and living for them enabled her to see how to help them blossom physically, psychologically, and spiritually, revealing the miracle of life. She believes that these children have been given to us for a reason—to test our humanity as we witness genuine beauty.

Jasminka did not explicitly mention her faith in God or the importance of that part of her identity, but one must conclude that her faith in God is very important to her. She mentioned God occasionally in the context of truth, justice, and love, believing that by his mercy all lives are created and interconnected. Thus she accepted the responsibility to care for children with special needs as a test from God. Faith is an intimate part of her life but she does not refer it easily, keeping that part of her inner life to herself; others can learn about it only from her actions. She does not preach, but loves and teaches what genuine believers should do.

Jasminka also planted, literally, a rose garden in her yard; she claims gardening replenishes her positive energy. Flowers, plants, and nature provide for her a compelling revelation that she feels brings her closer to others and to God:

> I like working in the garden, I like to plant and I like to weed, I like harvesting, I like to dig. I love flowers, but I love vegetables much more. It brings me such joy to see the tomatoes ripen; [I love] when I can pick the peppers, when I can smell them while I'm bringing them in from the garden.

Gardening is like her work with children and women, in which she enjoys the magical moments of planting the seeds of love, goodness, and care and is able to see the growth and fruit of her labor. The garden's solitude gives her energy and peace. Watering, weeding, and fertilizing plants renew the balance and patience needed for her work. The garden is also where she remembers her husband, with whom she built it. "Every time I walk in that garden I know that I am not alone. Again, the two of us are there. Not physically, but the two of us are together again in that garden." She misses her husband greatly.

Jasminka has also found that by reading she has been able to refresh and renew herself when she has been particularly stressed and exhausted. When faced with the betrayal of her friends at the beginning of the war, for instance, she took to books to search for answers:

> A book is really a person's best friend. In those moments when you think the world is in ruins and has come to an end, when you have experienced something that you could not have imagined, when someone who was your friend for forty years says that she can no longer be your friend ... and you haven't done anything wrong aside from having a particular first and last name.

For Jasminka, reading was the answer to everything. She managed to survive the war, the exile to Croatia, her battles for the Los Rosales Center, and her personal struggle to keep her family together and nurse her husband until his death: "I would spend all night reading and it was [then] easier for me to handle the illness within my home." While reading, one is not alone; one learns there are always others who have been through something similar.

Finally, Jasminka re-energizes herself through friends. She knows that good people, like good books, can empower one.

Conclusion

A persistent advocate for children and women, Jasminka Rebac has made a mark in her community and the region of Herzegovina. Committed to teaching as her lifework, she energetically accepted the greatest challenges in education, from years working in a village school to decades directing an institution for children with special needs. Her proactive care for the most vulnerable has impressed and impacted many but also changed her life immeasurably. She has been blessed by these children's beauty, as roses in the garden of life. Her natural perspective on people as humans rather than as carriers of ethnic or religious identities, led her to proceed during and after the war on an unusual path, returning to West Mostar and refusing to abide by the local nationalist educational agenda. Jasminka has also been an important player in the struggle for women's empowerment in Mostar during and after the war, from renewing a sense of personal care and femininity to organizing employment opportunities and professional development for women. She has been and still is exceptional in her capacity to work across ethnic divisions in Mostar, and in providing undivided care for children with special needs. She stands out in an environment where an incredible investment in cooperative efforts toward restored mutual life has failed. Her vibrant garden of children and women is a gift to both herself and her community.

BIBLIOGRAPHY

Abazović, Dino. *Za naciju i Boga.* Sarajevo: Magistrat, 2006.
Abrahamsdotter, Emina. "Preispitivanje modela religijskog obrazovanja u BiH." In *Religijsko i školovanje u otvorenom društvu. Preispitivanje modela religijskog obrazovanja u BiH*, 81-100. Sarajevo: Open Society Fund of Bosnia and Herzegovina, 2009.
Alibašić, Ahmet. "Vjersko obrazovanje u javnim školama u Bosni i Hercegovini: Ka modelu koji podržava suživot i uzajamno razumijevanje." In *Religija i školovanje u otvorenom društvu. Preispitivanje modela religijskog obrazovanja u Bosni i Hercegovini.* Sarajevo: Open Society Fund of Bosnia and Herzegovina, 2009.
Andjelic, Neven. *Bosnia and Herzegovina. The End of a Legacy.* London: Frank Cass, 2003.
Appleby, R. Scott. *The Ambivalence of the Sacred: Religion, Violence and Reconciliation.* Lanham, MD: Rowman and Littlefield, 2000.
Arendt, Hannah. *The Human Condition.* Chicago: University of Chicago Press, 1958.
Atanacković, Petar. "Religijsko obrazovanje u javnom školstvu. Prilog razmatranju problema ideološke ofanzive Crkve u društvima u tranziciji." *Divided God. Project of intercultural dialog.* 2007-2008. http://www.pozitiv.si/dividedgod/index.php?option=com_content&task =view&id=206& Itemid=68 (accessed April 25, 2013).
Babić, Mile. *Nasilje idola.* Sarajevo: Did, 2000.
Bakšić-Muftić, Jasna. *Ženska prava.* Sarajevo: Faculty of Law, University of Sarajevo, 2006.
Bakšić-Muftić, Jasna, and Maja Ljubović. *Socio-economic Status of Women in BiH: Analysis of the Results of the Star Pilot Research Done in 2002.* Sarajevo: Jež, 2003.
Barry, Kathleen. "Toward a Theory of Women's Biography." In *All Sides of the Subject. Women and Biography*, edited by Theresa Iles. New York: Teachers College Press, Columbia University, 1992.
Benhabib, Seyla. *Situating the Self. Gender, Community and Postmodernism in Contemporary Ethics.* Cambridge: Polity Press, 1992.
Berger, Peter L. *The Desecularization of the World. Resurgent Religion and World Politics.* Grand Rapids: Eerdmans, 1999.

Blagojević Hughson, Marina. "Gender barometar BiH 2002." *Gender Barometer.* 2002. http://www.gb.rs/wp-content/uploads/2013/03/Gender-Barometar-BIH-2002.pdf (accessed September 5, 2013).
—. *Rodni barometar u Srbiji: razvoj i svakodnevni život.* Belgrade: United Nations Development Program, 2012.
Blagojević, Jelisaveta, Katerina Kolozova, and Svetlana Slapšak. *Gender and Identity: Theories from and/or on Southeastern Europe.* Belgrade: Women's Studies and Gender Research Center, 2006.
Bland Mintoff, Jana, ed. *Nobody Can Imagine Our Longing. Refugees and Immigrants in the Mediterranean.* Austin: Plain View Press, 1996.
Bolkovac, Kathryn. *The Whistleblower: Sex Trafficking, Military Contractors, and One Woman's Fight for Justice.* New York: Palgrave Macmillan, 2011.
Borić, Besima. *Vlada KS-a trebala bi dati ostavku zbog problema u GRAS-u.* Sarajevo, April 10, 2013.
Boulding, Elise. *Cultures of Peace. The Hidden Side of History.* New York: Syracuse University Press, 2000.
Bringa, Tone. *Being Muslim the Bosnian Way: Identity and Community in a Central Bosnian Village.* New Haven: Princeton University Press, 1995.
Broz, Svetlana. *Good People in an Evil Time: Portraits of Complicity and Resistance in the Bosnian War.* Translated by Ellen Bursac. New York: Other Press, 2005.
Brunner, C. Cryss. *Sacred Dreams Women and Superintendency.* Albany: State University of New York Press, 1999.
Čaušević, Jasmina. *Rodno inkluzivne zajednice u BiH.* Sarajevo: TPO Foundation, 2012.
Čengić, Nejra Nuna. "Noise, Silence, Voice. Life Stories of Two Female Peace Activists in BiH." In *Women Narrating their Lives and Actions,* edited by Renata Jambrešić Kirin and Sandra Prlenda. Zagreb: Institute for Ethnology and Folklore & Center for Women's Studies, 2013.
Chaitin, Julia. "How do I ask them about the war? Collecting and understanding the stories of soldiers and victims of war." *Social Science Research Network Electronic Library,* 2002.
Chin, Jean Lau, Bernice Lott, Joy Rice, and Janis Sanchez-Hucles, ed. *Women and Leadership. Transforming Visions and Diverse Voices.* Hoboken: Wiley-Blackwell, 2007.
Cockburn, Cynthia. *The Line. Women Partition and Gender Order in Cyprus.* London: Zed Books, 2004.
—. *The Space Between Us. Negotiating Gender and National Identities in Conflict.* London: Zed Books, 1998.

—. "Against the Odds: Sustaining Feminist Momentum in Post-war Bosnia-Herzegovina." *Women's Studies International Forum*, March-April 2013: 26-35.

Cvitković, Ivan. *Sociološki pogledi na naciju i religiju*. Vol. II. Sarajevo: Center for Empirical Research of Religion, 2012.

Davie, Grace. *Religion in Britain since 1945: Believing Without Belonging*. Oxford: Blackwell, 1994.

Decosterd, Mary Lou. *How Women are Transforming Leadership. Four Key Traits Powering Success*. Santa Barbara, CA: Praeger, 2013.

Denzin, Norman. *Interpretive Biography*. Thousand Oaks, CA: Sage, 1989.

Deschaumes, Ghislaine Glasson and Svetlana Slapšak. "Žene Balkana za mir. Aktivistkinje prelaze granice." *Profemina*, 2003.

Diamond, Louise and John MacDonald. *Multi-track Diplomacy: A Systems Approach to Peace*. 3. West Harford, CT: Kumarian Press, 1996.

Done per la pace, Reti solidaritea femminile nella ex Jugoslavia. Venice/Mestre: cura delle Donne in Nero, 1996.

Duhaček, Daša. "Engendering Political Responsibility. Transitional Justice in Serbia." In *Civic and Uncivic Values, Serbia in the Post-Milošević Era*, edited by Ola Listhaug, Sabina Ramet and Dragana Dulić. Budapest: CEU Press, 2011.

Eliot, George. *Middlemarch: A Study of Provincial Life*. Edinburgh: William Blackwood and Sons, 1907.

Enloe, Cynthia. *Bananas, Beaches and Bases: Making Feminist Sense of International Politics*. Berkeley: University of California Press, 1990.

Etnički sastav stanovništva Bosne i Hercegovine, po općinama i naseljima, popis iz 1991. godine. Sarajevo: Bosnia and Herzegovina Department of Statistics, newsletter 234, 1991.

Fagan, Adam. "Civil Society in Bosnia Ten Years after Dayton." In *Peace Without Politics? Ten Years of International State-building in Bosnia*, edited by David Chandler. New York: Routledge, 2006.

Feministes contra la guerra. Barcelona: Dones x Dones, 2006.

Fletcher, Joyce K. *Disappearing Acts: Gender, Power, and Relational Practice at Work*. Cambridge, MA: The MIT Press, 2001.

Funk, Julianne. "Women and the Spirit of Suživot in Postwar Bosnia-Herzegovina." In *Spirituality of Balkan Women. Breaking boundaries: The Voices of Women of ex-Yugoslavia*, edited by Nadija Furlan Štante and Marjana Harcet. Koper, Slovenia: Univerzitetna Založba Annales, 2013.

Galtung, Johan. "Violence, Peace and Peace Research." *Journal of Peace Research*, 1969.

—.*Three Approaches to Peace. Peacekeeping, Peacemaking, and Peacebuilding*. Vol. II, in *Peace, War and Defense: Essays in Peace Research*, edited by Johan Galtung. Copenhagen: Christian Ejlers, 1976.

Gantz, Marshall. "Telling Your Public Story. Self, Us, Now." *Center for Whole Communities*. http://www.wholecommunities.org/pdf/Public%20Story%20Worksheet07Ganz.pdf (accessed November 14, 2013).

—. "Why Stories Matter." *Sojournes, Faith in Action for Social Justice*. 2009. www.sojo.net/magazine/2009/03/why-stories-matter (accessed September 3, 2013).

Gearon, Liam. *Citizenship through Secondary Religious Education*. London: Routledge, 2004.

Gilligan, Carol. *In a Different Voice. Psychological Theory and Women's Development*. Cambridge, MA: Harvard University Press, 1983.

Giten, Swami Dyhan. "On Intuition and Healing." In *Silent Whisperings of the Heart – An Introduction to Giten's Approach to Life*. www.selfgrowth.com/articles/GITEN2.html, 2012.

Guide for Civilian Victims of War: How to enjoy the right to protection as a civilian victim of war in the Federation of Bosnia and Herzegovina. Sarajevo: International Commission on Missing Persons, Missing Persons Institute of Bosnia and Herzegovina, the Center for Free Access to Information, 2007.

Hampton, David. "The Fog of Religious Conflict." *Harvard Divinity Bulletin*, 2012.

Hastings, Adrian. *The Construction of Nationhood – Ethnicity, Religion, Nationalism*. Cambridge: Cambridge University Press, 1997.

Helms, Elissa. "Women as Agents of Ethnic Reconciliation? Women's NGOs and International Intervention in Postwar Bosnia–Herzegovina." *Women's Studies International Forum*, 2003: 15–33.

—. *Innocence and Victimhood, Gender, Nation, and Women's Activism in Postwar Bosnia-Herzegovina*. Madison, WI: University of Wisconsin Press, 2013.

Hunt, Swanee. *This Was Not Our War, Bosnian Women Reclaiming Peace*. Durham: Duke University Press, 2004.

—. *Worlds Apart. Bosnian Lessons for Global Security*. Durham: Duke University Press, 2011.

Husremović, Dženana, Steve Powell, Ajla Šišić, and Dolić Aida. *Obrazovanje u BiH: Čemu učimo djecu? Analiza sadržaja udžbenika nacionalne grupe predmeta*. Sarajevo: Open Society Fund of Bosnia and Herzegovina, ProMENTE, 2007.

Iles, Theresa, ed. *All Sides of the Subject. Women and Biography.* New York: Teachers College Press, Columbia University, 1992.
Jones, Jonathan. "Defining 'Moral Imagination'." *Postmodern Conservative* Blog of *First Things.* July 1, 2009. http://www.firstthings.com/blogs/postmodernconservative/2009/07/01/defining-moral-imagination/ (accessed November 7, 2013).
Kapo, Midhat. *Nacionalizam i obrazovanje. Studija slučaja Bosna i Hercegovina.* Sarajevo: Open Society Fund of Bosnia and Herzegovina, 2012.
Karić, Enes. "Naše bošnjaštvo i naše muslimanstvo." *Ljiljan,* February 1998.
Kašić, Biljana. "The Aesthetic of the Victim within the Discourse of War." In *War Discourse, Women's Discourse. Essays and Case Studies from Yugoslavia to Russia,* edited by Svetlana Slapšak. Ljubljana: ISH – Faculty for Postgraduate Studies in Humanities, 2000.
Kristić, Alen. *Religija i moć.* Sarajevo: Rabic, 2009.
Lederach, John Paul. *Building Peace. Sustainable Reconciliation in Divided Societies.* Washington D.C.: United States Institute of Peace Press, 1997.
—. *The Moral Imagination. The Art and Soul of Building Peace.* Oxford: Oxford University Press, 2005.
Leydesdorf, Selma. *Surviving the Bosnian Genocide: The Women of Srebrenica Speak.* Translated by Kay Richardson. Bloomington: Indiana University Press, 2011.
Lieblich, Amia. *Looking at Change. Natasha, 21: New Immigrant from Russia to Israel.* Vol. 1, in *The Narrative Study of Lives,* edited by Ruthellen Josselson and Amia Lieblich. Thousand Oaks, CA: Sage, 1993.
Lieblich, Amia, Rivka Tuval-Mashiach, and Tamar Zilber, ed. *Narrative Research: Reading, Analysis and Interpretation.* Thousand Oaks, CA: Sage, 1998.
Lott, Bernice. "Discourses on Women, Feminism and Leadership." In *Women and Leadership: Transforming Visions and Diverse Voices,* edited by Jean Lau Chin, Bernice Lott, Joy Rice, and Janis Sanchez-Hucles. Hoboken: Wiley-Blackwell, 2007.
Madacki, Saša and Mia Karamehić, ed. *Dvije škole pod jednim krovom.* Sarajevo: Center for Human Rights, University of Sarajevo and the Alumni Association of CIPS, 2012.
Merdjanova, Ina and Patrice Brodeur. *Religion as a Conversation Starter. Interreligious Dialogue for Peacebuilding in the Balkans.* New York: Continuum, 2009.

Mesić, Stjepan. "Serbia Endangers Region by Rehabilitating Chetniks." *Balkan Transitional Justice, Balkan Insight*, March 2013: http://www.balkaninsight.com/en/article/rehabilitating-chetniks-dangerous-for-the-region.
Mojzes, Paul. *Balkan Genocides. Holocaust and Ethnic Cleansing in the Twentieth Century.* Lanham, MD: Rowman and Littlefield, 2011.
—. *Yugoslavian Inferno: Ethnoreligious Warfare in the Balkans.* New York: Continuum, 1994.
Mujkić, Asim. *We, the Citizens of Ethnopolis.* Sarajevo: Center for Human Rights, University of Sarajevo, 2008.
Muratta, Sachiko. *The Tao of Islam. A Source Book on Gender Relationships in Islamic Thought.* Albany: State University of New York Press, 1992.
Narayan, Uma. "Colonialism and Its Others: Considerations on Rights and Care Discourses." *Hypatia*, 1995: 133–140.
Noddings, Nel. *Starting At Home: Caring and Social Policy.* Berkeley: University of California Press, 2002.
Nussbaum, Martha. *Sex and Social Justice.* Oxford: Oxford University Press, 1999.
—. *Women and Human Development. The Capabilities Approach.* Cambridge: Cambridge University Press, 2000.
Nye, Joseph S. Jr. *Soft Power: The Means to Success in World Politics.* New York: PublicAffairs, 2005.
Pankhurst, Dona. *Gendered Peace Women's Struggles for Post-war Justice and Reconciliation.* London: Routledge, 2009.
Petrič, Natalija. "Nacionalne politike u suzbijanju rodno zasnovanog nasilja u Srbiji, Hrvatskoj i Bosna i Hercegovini – Položaj žrtava." Novi Sad: ACIMSI University, 2012.
Pickering, Paula M. *Peacebuilding in the Balkans: A View from the Ground Floor.* Ithaca: Cornell University Press, 2007.
Popov-Momčinović, Zlatiborka. "'Male' religijske manjine u sistemu verske nastave u BiH: Između nevidljivosti i negativnih stereotipa." In *Religijsko i školovanje u otvorenom društvu. Preispitivanje modela religijskog obrazovanja u BiH*, 51-68. Sarajevo: Open Society Fund of Bosnia and Herzegovina, 2009.
Porter, Elisabeth J. *Peacebuilding: Women in International Perspective.* London: Routledge, 2007.
Porter, Natalie, and Jessica Henderson Daniel. "Developing Transformational Leaders. Theory to Practice." In *Women and Leadership: Transforming Visions and Diverse Voices*, edited by Jean

Lau, Lott, Bernice Chin, Joy Rice and Janis Sanchez-Hucles. Hoboken: Wiley-Blackwell, 2007.
Ramet, Sabina. *The Three Yugoslavias. State Building and Legitimation, 1918-2005.* Bloomington: Indiana University Press, 2006.
Rees, Madeleine. "International Intervention in Bosnia and Herzegovina: The Cost of Ignoring Gender." In *The Postwar Moment: Militaries, Masculinities and Peacekeeping,* edited by Cynthia Cockborn and Dubravka Zarkov. London: Lawrence and Wishard, 2002.
Robinson, Fiona. *The Ethics of Care. A Feminist Approach to Human Security.* Philadelphia: Temple University Press, 2011.
Rosenthal, Gabriele. *Reconstruction of Life Stories. Principles of Selection in Generating Stories for Narrative Biographical Interviews.* Vol. 1, in *The Narrative Study of Lives,* edited by Ruthellen Josselson and Amia Leiblich. Thousand Oaks, CA: Sage, 1993.
Ruddick, Sara. *Maternal Thinking. Toward a Politics of Peace.* Boston: Beacon Press, 1989.
—. "The Rationality of Care." In *Women, Militarism, and War. Essays in History, Politics, and Social Theory,* edited by Jean Bethke Elshtain and Sheila Tobias, 229-254. Savage, MD: Rowman and Littlefield, 1990.
Saikia, Yasmin. "Overcoming the Silent Archive in Bangladesh: Women Bearing Witnesses to Violence in the 1971 'Liberation' War." In *Women and The Contested State. Religion Violence and Agency in South and Southeast Asia,* edited by Lawrence Skidmore. Notre Dame: University of Notre Dame Press, 2007.
Savić, Svenka. *Vojvođanke. 1917-1931. Životne priče.* Novi Sad: Futura publikacije, 2001.
—. *Životne priče žena. Ah šta ću ti ja jadna pričati.* Novi Sad: Futura publikacije, 2008.
Schaaf, Kathe, Kay Lindahl, Kathleen S. Hurty, and Guo Cheen. *Women, Spirituality and Transformative Leadership: Where Grace Meets Power.* Woodstock, VT: Skylight Paths Publishing, 2011.
Schirch, Lisa. "Strategic Peacebulding. State of the Field." *Peace Prints: South Asian Journal of Peacebuilding,* Spring 2008.
Sells, Michael A. *The Bridge Betrayed. Religion and Genocide in Bosnia.* Berkeley: University of California Press, 1996.
Simmons, Cynthia. *Women Engaged/Engaged Art in Post-War Bosnia: Reconciliation, Recovery, and Civil Society.* Pittsburgh: Center for Russian and East European Studies, University of Pittsburgh, 2010.

Sito-Sucic, Daria. "Mostar: one family, three armies, a divided city." *Reuters*, April 2012: http://www.reuters.com/article/2012/04/02/uk-bosnia-mostar-idUSLNE83102N20120402.

Slapšak, Svetlana. "Hunting, Ruling, Sacrificing. Traditional Male Practices in Contemporary Balkan Cultures." In *Male Roles, Masculinities and Violence. A Culture of Peace Perspective*, edited by Ingeborg Breines, Raewyn Connell, and Ingrid Eide. Paris: UNESCO, 2000.

—. "Identities Under Threat on the Eastern Borders." In *Thinking Differently, A Reader in European Women Studies*, edited by Gabriele Griffin and Rosi Braidotti. London: Zed Books, 2002.

—. "The Use of Women and the Role of Women in the Yugoslav War." In *Gender, Peace and Conflict*, edited by Inger Skjelsbaek and Dan Smith, 161-183. Thousand Oaks, CA: Sage, 2001.

Spahić Siljak, Zilka. "Women, Religion and Politics in Bosnia and Herzegovina." In *Religion, the Secular and the Politics of Sexual Difference*, edited by Linell E. Cady and Tracy Fessenden. New York: Columbia University Press, 2013.

—. *An Analysis on the Image of Woman in the School: Religious Textbooks in Bosnia and Herzegovina*. Vol. 2, in *Women and Religions*, edited by Michaela Moravčíková and Lucia Grešková. Bratislava: Institute for State-Church Relations, 2008.

—. *Contesting Female, Feminist and Muslim Identities. Post-socialist Contexts of Bosnia and Herzegovina and Kosovo*. Sarajevo: Center for Interdisciplinary Postgraduate Studies, University of Sarajevo, 2012.

—. "Images of Women in Bosnia, Herzegovina, and Neighboring Countries, 1992-1995." In *Muslim Women in War and Crisis: from Reality to Representation*, edited by Faegheh Shirazi. Austin: University of Texas Press, 2010.

—. "Do It and Name It: Feminist Theology and Peacebuilding in Bosnia and Herzegovina." *Journal for Feminist Studies in Religion*, 2013.

—. *Women, Religion and Politics: The Impact of Religious Interpretations of Judaism, Christianity, and Islam on the Status of Women in Public Life and Politics in Bosnia and Herzegovina*. Sarajevo: IMIC, the Center for Interdisciplinary Postgraduate Studies, TPO Foundation, 2010.

Spahić-Šiljak, Zilka, Aida Spahić, and Elmaja Bavčić. *Baseline Study: Women and Peacebuilding in BH*. Sarajevo: TPO Foundation, 2012.

Spivak, Gayatri Chakravorty, *Outside in the Teaching Machine*. New York: Routledge, 1993.

Steinem, Gloria. *Outrageous Acts and Everyday Rebellions.* New York: McMillan, 1995.
Stojaković, Gordana. *Neda jedna biografija.* Novi Sad: Futura publikacije, 2002.
Stuebner, Renata. *The Current Status of Coexistence and Religious Education in Bosnia and Herzegovina.* Washington D.C.: United States Institute of Peace Press, 2009.
Suyemoto, Karen L. and Mary B. Ballou. "Conducted Monotones to Coacted Harmonies. A Feminist (Re)conceptualization of Leadership Addressing Race, Class, and Gender." In *Women in Leadership. Transforming Visions and Diverse Voices*, edited by Jean Lau Chin, Bernice Lott, Joy Rice, and Janis Sanchez-Hucles. Hoboken: Wiley-Blackwell, 2007.
Swift, Jonathan. *The Works of Dean Swift comprising A Tale of a Tub, The Battle of the Books with Thoughts and Essays on Various Subjects, Together with The Dean's Advice to a Young Lady on her Marriage.* New York: Derby & Jackson, 1857.
The Right to Social Protection in Bosnia and Herzegovina: Concerns on Adequacy and Equality. Sarajevo: The Mission of the OSCE to Bosnia and Herzegovina, 2012.
Thomassen, Ristin. *To Make Room for Changes. Peace strategies from women organisations in Bosnia and Herzegovina.* Johanneshov, Sweden: The Kvinna Till Kvinna Foundation, 2006.
Topić, Tanja, Aleksandar Živanović, and Aleksandar Žolja. *Mirovni aktivizam u Bosni i Herzegovini.* Banja Luka: Helsinki Citizens' Assembly, 2008.
Turner, W. Victor. *The Ritual Process: Structure and Anti-structure.* Harmondsworth: Penguin, 1969.
Van Manen, Max. "Phenomenological Pedagogy and the Question of Meaning." In *Phenomenology and Educational Discourse*, edited by Donald Vandenberg, 41-65. Durban: Heinemann Higher and Further Education, 1997.
Vlaisavljević, Ugo. *Etnopolitika i građanstvo.* Mostar: Udruga građana Dijalog, 2006.
Vöckler, Kai. "Politics of Identity – The Example of Mostar, Bosnia and Herzegovina." Barcelona, June 24-26, 2010.
Wadud, Amina. *Qur'an and Woman – Rereading the Sacred Text from a Woman's Perspective.* Oxford: Oxford University Press, 1999.
Yuval-Davis, Nira. "Women, Ethnicity and Empowerment." In *Shifting Identities Shifting Racisms. A Feminism and Psychology Reader*, edited

by Kum-Kum Bhavnani and Ann Phoenix, 179-198. London: Sage, 1994.
Zaharijević, Adriana, ed. *Neko je rekao feminizam? Kako je feminizam uticao na žene XXI veka.* 4. Sarajevo: Sarajevo Open Center, Heinrich Böll Foundation, CURE Foundation, 2012.
Zajović, Staša. *Žene za mir.* Belgrade: Žene u crnom, 1996.
Žarkov, Dubravka. "Feminism and the Disintegration of Yugoslavia: On the Politics of Gender and Identity." *Social Development Issues*, 2002.

INDEX

A

absence of personal violence, xxxi
absence of structural violence, xxxi
Academy for Young Leaders, 128, 139
Adnan, 295, 297
Adnan Hasanbegović, 295
agnostic, xxi, xxiii, 172
agnosticism, 99
Alija Izetbegović, 92, 116, 190
Amra Pandžo, xxii, xxxii, 283
Ana and Otto Raffai, 308
anti-trafficking, 319, 323, 324, 333
Asian traditional fan, xxxv
assimilation, xxx, 25
atheist, 292, 343, 344
atheistic, 24

B

balija, 75
balinkuša, 190
Banja Luka, xxii, xxxii, 10, 48, 63, 96, 107, 109, 111, 112, 113, 114, 116, 117, 119, 120, 122, 128, 129, 130, 131, 132, 138, 141, 142, 144, 145, 146, 148, 155, 157, 158, 163, 165, 166, 167, 170, 174, 178, 197, 231, 293, 330, 390
Baseline Study, xxi, 5, 73, 142, 179, 234, 249, 318, 375, 389
Belgrade, 71, 72, 74, 75, 76, 78, 79, 81, 84, 87, 90, 92, 93, 104, 114, 141, 151, 188, 219, 237, 247, 287, 317, 319, 325, 335, 337, 383, 391
Besima Borić, xxii, 153, 170, 213, 214
Bible, 64, 99, 293, 343
BiH Woman, 171
Bijeljina, xxii, 170, 195, 290, 317, 318, 319, 322, 325, 327, 331
Biljana Plavšić, 117
biographical method, xxv
biographies, xx
Bosansko Grahovo, xxii, 39, 40, 42, 44, 45, 46, 47, 49, 59, 60, 63
Bosniac, xxi, 3, 77, 81, 101, 116, 131, 132, 144, 146, 147, 163, 177, 179, 181, 190, 200, 209, 219, 222, 231, 236, 238, 239, 240, 241, 259, 261, 283, 288, 289, 290, 291, 298, 307, 329, 352, 353, 357, 363, 365, 369
Bosniac/Muslim, 14, 16, 25, 26, 242, 287, 329, 349
Bosnian, xi, xii, xv, xvi, xvii, xviii, xix, xxvi, xxix, xxx, xxxv, 13, 14, 17, 19, 45, 54, 60, 64, 71, 73, 75, 78, 105, 136, 137, 158, 159, 161, 163, 172, 185, 189, 219, 260, 262, 276, 295, 310, 311, 317, 329, 352, 361, 366, 376, 383, 385, 386

Bosnian peacebuilding fan, xxxv
boundaries, xiii, xvi, xxxv, 85, 90, 112, 154, 155, 174, 231, 259, 384
Bratunac, xxii, 123, 177, 178, 179, 180, 181, 183, 188, 189, 190, 194, 195, 199, 200, 201, 203, 207, 209, 221, 222
brotherhood, 13, 185, 213, 238, 251, 283, 328, 363

C

care, xxiii, xxvi, xxvii, xxviii, 16, 17, 39, 40, 41, 42, 49, 50, 52, 55, 56, 62, 68, 69, 73, 78, 102, 119, 135, 150, 185, 187, 192, 193, 194, 206, 218, 219, 220, 234, 239, 243, 263, 278, 280, 313, 325, 337, 342, 350, 351, 353, 356, 357, 358, 359, 363, 365, 369, 371, 374, 379, 381, 387, 388
care ethics, xxiii, xxvii
CARE International, 72, 98
care-oriented, xxviii, 234
Catholic, 13, 23, 36, 39, 47, 64, 69, 141, 172, 174, 182, 302
Center for Civic Education in Calabasas, 254
Centre for Non-violent Action, 284, 295
Četnik, 20, 185, 186, 241
Christmas, 51, 188, 192, 334
citizen identity, 259, 263
civic education, 121, 248, 249, 250, 252, 253, 254, 255, 257, 258, 263, 266, 280

Civitas, 248, 249, 250, 252, 255, 256, 258, 259, 261, 262, 263, 264, 270, 355
collaborative, xxx, 60
communication, 3, 29, 30, 45, 59, 60, 64, 67, 77, 90, 108, 114, 116, 123, 147, 156, 162, 164, 215, 250, 256, 257, 283, 309, 314, 338, 370, 377
communism, 181, 268, 269, 271
Communist Party, 213, 328, 335, 337
compassion, xv, xxiii, xxvi, xxvii, xxviii, 50, 51, 53, 69, 164, 215, 218, 273, 295, 350, 353, 363, 369
concentration camp, 146
conciliator, 305
conflict, xvii, xix, xxii, xxiv, xxxi, xxxii, xxxiii, 4, 11, 12, 49, 69, 86, 147, 292, 297, 300, 306, 308, 309, 342, 345, 352, 363, 371, 383, 385, 389
confrontation, xxxiii
consistency, 266, 313
constructive chaos, 291
Criminal Code of the FBiH, 170
Croat, xxiii, 7, 16, 26, 43, 47, 50, 63, 69, 77, 86, 87, 88, 101, 123, 131, 144, 146, 147, 163, 181, 186, 209, 219, 231, 236, 238, 240, 241, 259, 261, 287, 290, 291, 298, 327, 352, 353, 363, 365, 369
Croat/Catholic, 26, 30, 63, 66, 303
Croatian, xxi, 43, 47, 49, 53, 63, 73, 136, 137, 141, 144, 147, 221, 237, 242, 291, 327, 357, 364, 366, 370
Croatian Defense Council, 3, 16

cura, 73, 94, 384
CURE Foundation Sarajevo, 72, 73
Cynthia Cockburn, xii, xvii, 9, 11, 18, 200, 321
Cyrillic name plate, 148
Cyrillic or Latin scripts, 156

D

Danka Zelić, xxii
David Hampton, xxxiii, 49
decision-making, xix, 13, 14, 27, 35, 36, 53, 56, 102, 125, 143, 149, 203, 210, 275, 334, 340, 345
democratization, 107, 108, 119, 127, 154, 161, 162, 266, 303, 319, 332
de-secularization, xxiii
directive force, xxx, 51, 324
displaced, 13, 19, 44, 73, 117, 144, 161, 165, 177, 195, 200, 202, 209, 214, 217, 219, 220, 369
divided city, 352, 389
divided schools, 26, 255, 256
divinity, xxxiii, 49, 209, 385
domestic violence, 3, 5, 11, 34, 142, 143, 148, 167, 168, 169, 170, 171, 174, 226, 319, 346
double moral standard, 151, 336
doyenne, 77, 109, 138, 142, 231, 335

E

Eid, 238
Elisabeth Porter, xii, xix, xxviii, 43, 123, 156, 205, 224, 267, 273, 293, 323, 353
Elise Boulding, xxvii, 278
Elissa Helms, xvii, xviii, xxix, 54, 199, 277, 313, 337, 375
empathy, 16, 68, 268, 272, 276
empowerment, xi, xvi, xxix, xxx, 35, 40, 62, 95, 97, 98, 121, 138, 149, 161, 200, 205, 258, 308, 311, 324, 351, 373, 374, 378, 381, 390
entity border, xxiii, 138, 156, 160, 332, 338
EPIL, 24, 100
epiphanies, xxv, 17
essentialize, xxix, 53, 149, 232
ethnic, xv, xviii, xxi, xxii, xxiii, xxxv, 6, 13, 17, 18, 25, 36, 43, 46, 49, 50, 53, 54, 64, 69, 71, 72, 73, 74, 75, 77, 111, 129, 130, 131, 132, 136, 137, 139, 155, 156, 162, 163, 174, 181, 182, 189, 199, 200, 209, 214, 220, 223, 231, 233, 236, 237, 238, 249, 260, 262, 267, 268, 283, 289, 291, 303, 307, 328, 339, 341, 344, 352, 353, 357, 358, 359, 361, 363, 366, 367, 369, 370, 378, 381
ethnic box, 14, 49, 238, 358, 370
ethnic identity, 18, 64, 137, 243, 268, 352, 357, 361
ethnically homogenized, xx, 45, 67, 237, 289
ethnocentric, xxx
ethno-national, xv, xxiv, xxxiii, xxxiv, 29, 74, 77, 99, 100, 101, 105, 112, 136, 138, 154, 155, 158, 165, 166, 167, 174, 181, 182, 187, 195, 198, 203, 221, 223, 233, 234, 236, 243, 251, 257, 259, 261, 263, 268, 291,

292, 297, 300, 301, 309, 327, 329, 341, 343, 346, 367, 378
Extraterritorial High School, 367

F

faith-based, xxiv, 18, 284, 285, 292, 293, 294, 298, 310, 314
fatwa, 19
FBiH, 7, 8, 11, 26, 227
FBiH Law on Social Protection, 8
Federation of BiH, xxiii, 7, 11, 108, 115, 121, 155, 156, 160, 171, 199, 217, 222, 227, 228, 240, 290, 357
feminine, xxix, xxx, 53, 69, 232
feminism, xviii, xxvi, xxviii, xxxi, 18, 19, 27, 57, 58, 94, 95, 96, 100, 103, 105, 133, 134, 139, 203, 230, 276, 280, 333, 335, 336, 337, 338, 374
feminist, xviii, xix, xxiii, xxvii, xxviii, xxix, xxx, 4, 9, 11, 19, 27, 36, 55, 57, 58, 60, 69, 82, 86, 87, 94, 95, 96, 97, 100, 103, 133, 134, 143, 152, 223, 258, 309, 312, 314, 318, 319, 322, 333, 334, 335, 337, 338
feminist identity, xviii, 57, 133, 139, 311, 312, 373
feminist theology, 19
Fiona Robinson, xxvii, 42, 102, 150, 187, 278, 313, 342, 353
forgiveness, 23, 66, 374, 375
forgiving, 23, 164
four mothers, 194
friends, xi, xiv, 45, 50, 71, 75, 76, 77, 79, 85, 89, 90, 91, 92, 97, 103, 104, 105, 110, 112, 114, 144, 145, 146, 147, 148, 149, 154, 155, 157, 160, 172, 178, 179, 180, 181, 182, 183, 184, 185, 194, 197, 207, 208, 209, 231, 249, 265, 302, 332, 363, 364, 365, 368, 369, 370, 372, 380

G

gender, xi, xvi, xix, xxi, xxvii, xxix, xxxv, 7, 9, 32, 36, 55, 57, 102, 108, 109, 118, 121, 122, 124, 129, 135, 138, 143, 149, 150, 168, 187, 203, 214, 215, 227, 228, 229, 230, 251, 269, 271, 275, 276, 277, 278, 309, 310, 311, 334, 335, 336, 337, 376
gender equality, xi, xxi, 57, 108, 109, 118, 121, 124, 135, 138, 143, 148, 149, 203, 214, 215, 227, 228, 229, 230, 251, 269, 271, 275, 276, 309, 311, 335, 337
Gender Equality Act, 121
Gender Equality Law, 33, 228, 229
gender hierarchy, 55, 57
George Eliot, xiv, 146
Gloria Steinem, 149
Grand Mufti, 101, 234, 307

H

HcA Banja Luka, 124, 126, 128, 132
HcA Tuzla, 126, 127, 129
healing, xiv, 18, 19, 20, 23, 36, 68, 163, 164, 209, 291
Helsinki Committee of the Republika Srpska, 290
hijab, 18, 27, 29, 30, 311

hijabi feminist, 27
honorary men, 276, 280
Human Rights Watch, 323
humanity, xi, xiii, xvi, xx, xxii, xxvi, xxxiii, xxxv, 5, 7, 12, 40, 67, 68, 74, 82, 101, 104, 105, 111, 119, 174, 180, 182, 184, 193, 209, 224, 288, 311, 350, 359, 379
HVO, 3, 5, 16, 17

I

ICTY, 7, 9
IDEA, xxx, 51, 203, 373
identity, xvi, xxi, xxii, xxxii, 13, 15, 17, 26, 30, 31, 39, 64, 67, 69, 71, 73, 89, 94, 96, 105, 112, 146, 148, 152, 174, 181, 186, 200, 236, 237, 238, 241, 242, 259, 260, 262, 272, 274, 284, 289, 291, 306, 328, 338, 379
Igman, 92
Igor and Mirjana Galo, 130
international, xxi, xxiii, 6, 7, 12, 15, 94, 102, 125, 126, 137, 218, 219, 227, 228, 232, 257, 311, 320, 321, 322, 332, 340, 346, 352
international organizations, 12, 94, 102, 218, 219, 228, 232, 322, 332
Interreligious Council, xxiv
IPTF, 322
Islamic feminist, 311, 312
Israel, 247, 248, 249, 252, 253, 289, 386
Ivo Marković, 101, 302

J

Jadranka Miličević, xxii, 71, 72, 104
Jasminka Rebac, viii, 380
Jean Lau Chin, xxix, xxxi, 60, 223, 386, 390
Jew, xxi, 101, 129, 247, 249, 258, 261, 268, 272, 273, 274, 311
Jewish, xxi, 101, 247, 249, 272, 273, 311
Johan Galtung, xxxi, 144, 180, 385
Jonathan Jones, xxxii, xxxiii
journalist, 92, 124, 132, 300, 306, 317, 318, 322, 324, 327, 330, 332, 333, 346
Journalist Association of Republika Srpska, 132
justice, xxi, xxiii, xxvii, xxviii, xxxii, 5, 7, 8, 9, 10, 27, 36, 40, 49, 53, 58, 61, 105, 179, 184, 193, 227, 267, 268, 273, 279, 295, 296, 301, 313, 324, 331, 353, 363, 379

K

Karadžić, 80, 287
Klelija Balta, 110

L

Law on domestic violence, 33, 226
Law on Gender Equality, 124, 171
leadership, xvi, xxii, xxvii, xxix, xxx, 19, 49, 51, 55, 60, 97, 115, 149, 151, 160, 203, 217, 221, 222, 223, 234, 235, 236, 251, 256, 258, 285, 292, 297, 300, 312, 318, 324, 327, 343, 345, 353, 354, 367, 370, 373

leadership styles, xxix
leadership traits, xxii, xxx, 373
Lederach, xiii, xxiv, xxxi, xxxii, xxxiii, 9, 46, 49, 56, 60, 118, 119, 156, 164, 196, 202, 218, 224, 259, 262, 292, 293, 297, 309, 313, 323, 345, 358, 359, 371, 377, 386
legacy, xxi, xxxiv, 273, 295, 296, 297, 300, 321
legal protection, 6, 96, 226
Lepa Mlađenović, 74, 77, 87, 133
Leszek Kołakowski, 266
Lidija Živanović, xxii, 107, 108, 130, 142, 156, 160, 231, 293
life story, xiv, xxv, xxxv, 73, 179, 250, 319, 351
light of humanity, xiii, xv, xxxiv
Lisa Shirch, xxxii
Li-Woman, 57, 62
ljudskost, xiii, 224, 288
Los Rosales, 350, 353, 354, 355, 356, 359, 373, 376, 379, 380
love, xii, xiii, xxxiii, 29, 39, 51, 52, 56, 65, 68, 72, 77, 104, 145, 157, 173, 192, 208, 210, 237, 247, 248, 273, 274, 279, 288, 296, 304, 332, 342, 349, 350, 353, 357, 359, 378, 379

M

Madeleine Rees, 321, 322
magazine, xv, 82, 113, 143, 171, 286, 317, 321, 322, 330, 331, 332, 346, 385
mahala, 238, 239, 287, 361, 365
Makarska, 354, 365
Manjača, 146
Marina Blagojević Hughson, 151

Marko Oršolić, 101, 285
Martha Nussbaum, 53, 111, 267, 353
Marxist, 24, 251, 337
Mary Lou Décosterd, xxx, 34, 51, 55, 88, 115, 160, 201, 221, 250, 292, 324, 373
Maybe Airport, 91
Medica Zenica, 4, 6, 8, 9, 10, 11, 12, 17, 18, 19, 21, 22, 23, 27, 30, 36, 89, 117, 156, 171, 285
memorial service, 299
meta term, xxxii
Ministry for Labor, 217
minorities, 131, 132
minority, 25, 72, 87, 98, 108, 129, 130, 131, 139, 214, 261, 262, 268, 269, 344
Monika Hauser, 19
monority, 129
moral dilemma, xi, xxxiii, 188, 191, 287, 346
moral imagination, xiii, xvi, xxxii, xxxiii, xxxv, 49, 119, 166
Mostar, xxii, 63, 77, 96, 110, 123, 178, 194, 218, 231, 237, 261, 291, 302, 349, 350, 351, 352, 354, 357, 358, 360, 361, 363, 365, 368, 369, 370, 371, 373, 381, 389, 390
mother, 21, 22, 39, 51, 57, 63, 71, 75, 84, 108, 145, 178, 182, 184, 188, 189, 192, 193, 194, 205, 236, 237, 283, 291, 296, 313, 327, 334, 335, 350, 360, 365, 368
motherhood, xxix, 192, 209, 311
motherly love, 192
multicultural, 18, 65, 71, 130, 220, 249, 268, 294, 339, 351, 363

multiculturalism, 241, 268
Muslim, xvii, 3, 13, 14, 15, 16, 18, 19, 20, 23, 27, 29, 31, 33, 36, 45, 50, 55, 57, 133, 147, 162, 182, 183, 187, 189, 190, 193, 213, 237, 238, 239, 240, 249, 274, 276, 283, 287, 295, 299, 302, 303, 305, 306, 307, 308, 309, 310, 311, 312, 314, 367, 368, 383, 389
Muslim feminist, 27, 311, 312

N

Nada Golubović, xxii, 115, 141, 142
naming ritual, 21, 22
NATO, 89
negative peace, xxxi
neighbor, xi, xiv, xx, 13, 14, 15, 26, 36, 40, 41, 42, 45, 50, 52, 54, 55, 58, 71, 84, 108, 130, 138, 144, 145, 147, 148, 154, 155, 160, 163, 178, 180, 182, 183, 185, 194, 197, 201, 209, 210, 231, 237, 238, 239, 240, 249, 303, 370, 372
neighborhood, 16, 50, 93, 178, 183, 195, 238, 287, 361, 365
neighborliness, 45
Nel Noddings, xxvii, xxviii, 42, 185, 342
Neretva, 13, 357, 369, 370, 376
network of peace, 164
network of support, 9, 85, 199
non-believer, 33, 236
non-Communist, 181

O

OHCHR, 321, 323

Old Bridge, 291, 351, 369
Oluja, 80, 88
Olympic Games, 272
Omarska, 146, 291
Oneness, 306
ordinary women, xxxiv, 148, 199
Orthodox Christian, 13, 15, 23, 36, 50, 64, 65, 137, 299, 317, 343
OSCE, 8, 116, 150, 153, 156, 160, 219

P

Pan Radio, 318, 333, 347
parliament, 93, 103, 121, 153, 171, 204, 214, 224, 227, 228, 339, 358
parliamentarian, 224, 228
Partisan family, 98, 213, 237
path, xxxiv, 35, 36, 54, 62, 67, 104, 167, 174, 207, 208, 240, 260, 301, 302, 306, 357, 381
patriarchal, xix, 19, 28, 32, 56, 58, 102, 107, 134, 135, 162, 168, 204, 275, 296, 297, 300, 312, 315, 334, 335, 337, 338, 375
patriarchal prejudice, 204
peace journey, xviii, 54, 354
peacebuilding, xi, xv, xvi, xviii, xix, xxi, xxiii, xxiv, xxvi, xxvii, xxviii, xxxi, xxxii, xxxv, 23, 27, 36, 40, 42, 45, 46, 51, 64, 82, 90, 99, 104, 105, 108, 109, 115, 123, 125, 129, 141, 142, 143, 144, 148, 150, 156, 163, 164, 172, 173, 180, 203, 205, 208, 217, 224, 232, 234, 235, 277, 279, 284, 290, 292, 293, 297, 300, 302, 306, 308, 313, 323, 338, 339, 340, 341, 343, 345, 372

Pitchwise festival, 97
politics, xviii, xix, xxviii, xxxiii, 14, 26, 75, 79, 125, 153, 171, 178, 195, 203, 204, 205, 215, 216, 218, 220, 224, 228, 230, 233, 234, 241, 243, 251, 264, 273, 274, 277, 292, 332, 337, 343, 351, 353, 368
positive peace, xxxi
Povratak, 349, 366, 367
pravi ljudi, 350
Prijedor, 10, 111, 163, 291, 325
prison camp, 111
public dialogue, xxxiv, 340, 341

Q

Qur'an, 22, 29, 32, 36, 100, 299, 306, 311, 312

R

Radio Free Europe, 113
Radmila Žigić, xxii, 317
Rahela Džidić, xxii, 355
Randall Puljek-Shank, 308
rationality of care, xxviii, 52, 360
re-building, xix, xxxii, 42, 46, 60, 64, 160, 219, 232
reconciliation, xi, xv, xvi, xviii, xx, xxi, xxxiv, 12, 23, 25, 39, 41, 42, 67, 69, 90, 101, 102, 107, 109, 114, 126, 137, 138, 143, 150, 156, 162, 164, 167, 171, 173, 178, 199, 201, 234, 235, 254, 256, 257, 279, 287, 291, 294, 299, 303, 305, 306, 309, 318, 333, 339, 343, 346, 347, 370, 374, 375

refugee, 3, 4, 5, 13, 15, 16, 17, 18, 36, 43, 44, 65, 72, 73, 78, 80, 81, 82, 83, 87, 117, 146, 165, 166, 174, 177, 179, 199, 200, 215, 217, 219, 220, 221, 222, 223, 234, 240, 248, 249, 349, 354, 366, 367, 368, 369
refugee camp, 4, 72, 80, 81, 82, 83, 369
refugee return, 61, 201, 202, 221
relational space, 9, 323
relationship, xi, xvii, xix, xx, xxxii, xxxiii, 31, 35, 45, 46, 48, 55, 59, 60, 63, 69, 86, 109, 156, 163, 164, 174, 178, 195, 197, 202, 205, 223, 224, 232, 254, 293, 296, 307, 323, 338, 353, 354, 369, 370, 374
religious divide, 301, 314
religious education, 26, 64, 101, 173, 303, 304, 307, 311, 314, 343, 344
religious identity, xxi, xxiv, 13, 17, 18, 27, 58, 67, 71, 74, 181, 209, 220, 233, 236, 247, 283, 289, 290, 301, 311, 354, 361, 378, 381
religious teaching, 235, 344
Republika Srpska, xxiii, 7, 10, 108, 111, 116, 117, 120, 121, 124, 129, 131, 132, 151, 153, 155, 156, 160, 171, 189, 190, 199, 205, 221, 222, 227, 228, 231, 287, 303, 329, 330, 332
returnee, 42, 47, 62, 65, 162, 166, 221
Roma, 98, 105, 129
RS Criminal Code, 170
Rumi, v, xiii, xxxiv

S

Sabiha Husić, xxii, 3, 100, 171
safe place, 12, 142, 183
Salafi, 310
Sara Ruddick, xxviii, 42, 52, 102, 150, 192, 232, 359, 360
Sarajevan, 247, 287
Sarajevan identity, 288
Sarajevo, xi, xvii, xxi, xxii, xxiv, 3, 4, 5, 7, 8, 14, 15, 25, 26, 28, 31, 55, 57, 64, 71, 72, 73, 74, 75, 77, 78, 84, 90, 91, 92, 93, 94, 95, 96, 99, 101, 105, 107, 110, 112, 114, 115, 116, 117, 119, 120, 130, 133, 142, 150, 151, 153, 156, 157, 158, 171, 178, 179, 205, 213, 216, 217, 219, 220, 226, 229, 230, 234, 237, 240, 241, 243, 247, 248, 249, 254, 262, 264, 268, 271, 272, 273, 276, 283, 284, 285, 287, 288, 289, 290, 293, 295, 302, 303, 304, 312, 318, 335, 336, 341, 344, 367, 375, 378, 382, 383, 384, 385, 386, 387, 389, 390, 391
self-empowerment, 4, 237
self-sacrificing micro-matriarchy, 151, 375
Serb, 15, 17, 42, 43, 47, 50, 62, 63, 65, 69, 78, 105, 123, 132, 147, 163, 177, 181, 185, 186, 200, 201, 205, 209, 221, 232, 236, 237, 238, 240, 241, 243, 259, 274, 283, 287, 288, 289, 291, 295, 303, 327, 329, 332, 346, 352
Serb/Orthodox, 40, 63, 66
Serbian, xxi, 7, 62, 73, 80, 83, 84, 87, 90, 91, 92, 105, 132, 136, 137, 146, 220, 222, 237, 242, 288, 295, 302, 317, 327, 328, 330, 331, 352, 366
Serbo-Croatian, 213
service, 14, 24, 279, 285, 358
siege, 72, 75, 77, 90, 92, 116, 220, 287, 288
Small Steps, 284, 293, 298, 301, 314
smart flexible, 118
Social Democratic Party, 214, 240, 327
socialist, xvii, xx, xxiii, 28, 57, 67, 71, 96, 133, 213, 238, 269, 273, 276, 283, 285, 292, 295, 300, 336, 337, 349, 360, 363, 389
solidarity, xxiii, 41, 46, 74, 75, 90, 122, 269, 270, 273, 280
Spaniards, 356
spark of humanity, xxxiv, 120, 184
Specijalna škola, 356
spirituality, 302, 310
Srđan Aleksić, 132, 329
Srebrenica, 89, 123, 222, 386
Stanojka Tešić, xxii, 190, 209
Staša Zajović, 76, 77, 84
State Agency for Gender Equality, 228
Stop modern slavery, 325
suffering, xxviii, 13, 15, 19, 43, 44, 65, 113, 159, 163, 164, 165, 179, 209, 221, 243, 256, 268, 288, 298, 299, 306, 307, 329, 357, 369
Šukrija Pandžo, 283, 296
survivors, xiv, 3, 4, 5, 8, 10, 11, 12, 17, 18, 20, 36, 89, 111
suživot, xvi, 304, 382
Svetlana Broz, xviii

Svetlana Slapšak, xvii, xix, 85, 89, 155, 337, 383, 384, 386
Swanee Hunt, xii, xvii, xviii, xix, 158, 159, 163, 361

T

The Whistleblower, 321, 383
Theresa Iles, xxv, 42, 147, 295, 319, 353, 382
trafficking, 318, 319, 320, 321, 322, 323, 324, 325, 346, 383
transformative, 203, 258
Tunnel of Hope, 92

U

umbrella term, xxxii
UN Security Council Resolution 1325, 35, 125, 339, 378
UN Women, xi, xxi, 102
United States, 12, 81, 215, 247, 249, 252, 253, 271, 345, 352, 386, 390
United Women, 10, 142, 144, 149, 153, 154, 167, 168, 170, 171, 174
unity, xxiii, 13, 185, 213, 238, 251, 283, 328, 363
universal, xxiii, 234, 243, 250, 251, 259, 263, 279
universe, xxxv, 20
UNSCR 1325 Action Plan, 229, 339
Ustaša, 186, 241

V

Vehid Šehić, 110, 293

Virginia Woolf, xvii

W

wartime rape, 3, 5, 8, 9, 10, 12, 17, 19, 22, 77, 78, 116, 285
Women in Black, 71, 74, 76, 77, 78, 79, 81, 82, 83, 84, 85, 86, 89, 91, 92, 93, 94, 95
wunderkind, 271

Y

Yugoslav identity, 14, 237, 238
Yugoslav National Army, 146, 327, 363
Yugoslavia, xvi, xvii, 7, 13, 46, 62, 67, 71, 77, 81, 89, 112, 114, 117, 141, 146, 162, 163, 174, 182, 186, 213, 227, 251, 269, 271, 273, 324, 327, 328, 335, 336, 349, 350, 360, 366, 378, 384, 386, 391

Z

Zagreb, xviii, 15, 39, 45, 91, 114, 141, 144, 145, 157, 335, 367, 383
Žarana Papić, 89
Zdravko Grebo, 110, 114, 285
Zejneba Sarajlić, 200
Žene ženama, 72, 94
Zenica, xxii, 3, 4, 5, 7, 8, 9, 10, 11, 12, 13, 16, 17, 18, 19, 21, 22, 23, 25, 29, 35, 36, 110, 115, 117, 120, 156
Zoran Levi, 114, 129